# *Introduction to Economics*

HARPERCOLLINS COLLEGE OUTLINE

# Introduction to Economics

**Stephen D. Casler, Ph.D.**
Allegheny College

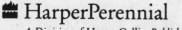 HarperPerennial
*A Division of HarperCollinsPublishers*

To my students, whose questions over the years have led to the explanations presented here.

*An American BookWorks Corporation Production*

**Project Manager:** Mary Mooney
**Editor:** Robert A. Weinstein

Library of Congress Cataloging-in-Publication Data

Casler, Stephen D.
   Introduction to economics  /  Stephen Casler.
      p.    cm.
   Includes bibliographical references and index.
   ISBN: 0-06-467113-5  (pbk.)  :  $15.00
   1. Economics.   I. Title.
HB171.5.C315   1992
330—dc20                                                                91-55388
                                                                              CIP

97 98 99  ABW/RRD  10  9  8  7  6

# *Contents*

# *Preface*

The typical text in introductory economics provides encyclopedic treatment of the range of problems considered important by economists. Students often find it difficult to determine which material is most essential for understanding economic questions, the presentation offered is not always accessible, but there are a few alternatives when problems are encountered except to read and reread the author's explanation.

This book attempts to provide a solution to these problems. It can be used for individual courses in micro- or macroeconomics for a one semester course in both micro and macro theory. Critical concepts are clearly identified through use of outline-like headings. The overriding objective is to provide straightforward and comprehensive explanations of the major models encountered in introductory classes. Special care has been taken in dealing with those areas that typically cause students difficulty. Essential assumptions are spelled out, and all the steps involved in difficult derivations are shown. Numerous examples and graphs show exactly how economic theory is applied to particular problems. The conditions leading to various equilibrium states are presented along with the common-sense reasons why these states represent equilibrium.

Following the traditional breakdown of subject matter in introductory classes and textbooks, this book is composed of three sections. The introduction consists of two chapters. The first deals with the fundamental problems of scarcity and choice. The second covers supply-and-demand analysis. The techniques used to transform real-world events into graphical representations and to interpret graphs for their real-world relevance are completely developed.

Chapters 3–12 cover introductory macroeconomics. The basics of finding equilibrium gross national product using graphs and equations and the range of techniques for deriving and using the spending multipliers are given prominent treatment. The relationship between the model of aggregate supply and demand and the simple expenditure model is considered explicitly. In this way, students are able to observe how the effects of outside shocks to the economy are transmitted from gross national product and the price level to each component of total spending. The role of government is explained, and the means by which it is able to alter the level of economic activity are investigated using the complete macro model. Macroeconomic treatment of international trade is considered in chapter 11. In chapter 12, as the analytical high point of the introductory course or the starting point at the intermediate level, the IS-LM model is introduced.

Chapters 13–25 present the subject matter of introductory microeconomics. The basics are contained in chapters 13–19, where the fundamental definitions and assumptions used by microeconomists are presented. Using these building blocks, the various types of market structure including perfect competition, monopolistic competition, oligopoly, and monopoly are discussed comprehensively. The logic underlying optimality conditions (utility maximization for consumers and profit maximization for firms) is fully explained. In chapters 20–25 specific applications include coverage of the labor market, public goods and externalities, input markets for capital and land, and international trade. Chapters 24 and 25 present the details involved in a more analytical treatment of microeconomic theory. The material in these chapters represents the highest level of difficulty encountered in introductory classes and provides an easy-to-follow introduction to microeconomic analysis at the intermediate level.

Chapter 26 provides a quick reference to many of the tools of economic analysis. The most important definitions, assumptions, analytical techniques, and optimizing conditions used by economists are explained. The material is grouped so that similarities in reasoning and differences in closely related concepts can easily be seen.

Thanks to Earl Adams, Ahmad Afrasiabi, Ken Ainsworth, Asuman Baskan, Tim Bushnell, John Golden, and Don Goldstein for reviewing specific chapters. Thanks to Robert Weinstein for his thoughtful comments on the entire manuscript, to Mary Mooney for keeping me on schedule, to Wayne Newland for his work on graphs, and to Fred Grayson for the opportunity to undertake this work.

Stephen D. Casler

# Part I

## *Introduction*

# 1

# *Fundamental Concepts: Scarcity, Choice, and Production Possibilities*

*Economics is primarily concerned with the efficient allocation of scarce resources among competing uses. In approaching this problem, economists take two distinct paths. Microeconomics examines actions taken by individuals and firms and is concerned with the conditions leading to efficient use of resources. Macroeconomics examines the overall performance of the economy; it seeks to determine the factors leading to full utilization of society's resources using economic aggregates, broad-based measures of economic activity.*

*To understand how economists conduct analysis, it is necessary to be familiar with the building blocks used to describe economic relationships and to formulate and present economic models. These building blocks consist of the definitions, assumptions, graphs, and equations required to develop and communicate ideas. When combined with the economist's methodological approach, models are developed to explain and predict real world economic phenomena.*

*Economics consists of more than theories regarding economic problems. An important part of economic analysis is testing theories against real-world data and applying models to real-world situations. Such empirical analysis and application involves familiarity with a wide range of economic data and the ability to transform raw data into meaningful summary measures.*

*In this chapter, the fundamental concepts underlying the study of economics are introduced, along with the basic building blocks used in economic analysis. Economic theory is then applied to the task of representing the problem of scarcity and choice. This is accomplished through use of a graphic device known as the production-possibilities curve.*

# SCARCITY AND CHOICE

All economic problems arise from the problem of scarcity. The resources and products that individuals and society wish to consume are finite or limited in their availability, while the desire and ability of individuals to consume products are virtually without bounds. Allocating scarce resources involves determining the value of the goods and services people consume. The sacrifices that must be made to achieve consumption of certain bundles of goods can then be evaluated.

## Price

To allocate scarce resources, *prices* are used. The vast number of prices in a free market economy reflects the interrelationship between the availability of products and the desire to possess them. The economy's price system allows individuals to determine what goods they can afford and in what quantities. Thus, given the incomes they have to work with, individuals are free to substitute between goods in accordance with their relative prices. For example, if the price of gasoline is $1 per gallon while the price of a candy bar is 50 cents, each time a consumer decides to purchase a gallon of gasoline he or she implicitly gives up the ability to purchase two candy bars.

Prices provide a measure of the relative scarcity of goods and services. A higher price for a good may imply high costs of production; large quantities of other resources must be used to obtain an additional unit of some desired good. High prices may also reflect absolute scarcity, implying that only a limited quantity of the good is available to satisfy consumer demand for it. In some cases, such as a particular work of art, it may even be impossible to obtain or produce additional units.

## The Production-Possibilities Curve and Opportunity Cost

From society's perspective, the sacrifices involved in choosing between alternate bundles of goods can be represented by the *production-possibilities curve*. As the name implies, this curve is a graphic representation of the maximum outputs that can be produced with available inputs. To portray the major issues involved, economists assume that all goods can be placed into two major categories whose levels are measured along each axis of a graph. The production-possibilities curve then shows the cost of acquiring more of one good in terms of the other, based upon the economy's ability to produce both of them, given the resources and technology available. The amount of one good that must be given up to acquire more of another is called *opportunity cost*. The production-possibilities curve and opportunity cost are considered more fully later in this chapter.

Aside from the production-possibility model, the problems of scarcity and choice are also present in the economist's model of supply and demand. The ability of producers to provide goods and services to individuals at various prices is broadly covered by the concept of *supply*. The desire by individuals to consume goods and services at various prices is broadly covered by the concept of *demand*. For each commodity produced in the economy, the inter-action between supply and demand leads to the determination of the price and the quantity of output that is produced and sold. Virtually all areas of study in economics can be classified into those under the heading of supply, those under the heading of demand, and those based on interrelationships between supply and demand. Because supply and demand analysis is so important, a separate chapter is devoted to it.

# MICROECONOMIC AND MACROECONOMIC THEORY

Modern treatment of economic problems has been split into *microeconomics* and *macroeconomics*. Microeconomics is concerned with individual products and decisions made by individual firms and consumers. Macroeconomics is concerned with the functioning of the overall economy.

## Micro-economics

Microeconomics is divided into several categories of decision making. With regard to the actions of consumers, microeconomics is first concerned with the choices individuals make in determining how to spend their income. Taking prices of goods as given, individuals must decide how to allocate their income over the goods and services they may wish to purchase in a way that provides them with the greatest level of satisfaction. Second, microeconomics deals with how individuals decide on the quantity of the labor or other resource endowments, such as capital or land, that they wish to sell to firms in exchange for income.

With regard to the actions taken by firms, microeconomics is first concerned with how inputs should be used in the production of output. The prices of inputs, such as the labor, fuel, and machinery used in production processes, determine what input combinations or proportions will lead to the greatest profit or least cost to the firm. Second, based on production costs and the prices at which their goods will sell in the market, firms must decide how much output to produce. Finally, combining the actions of individuals and firms, microeconomics is concerned with the determination of prices for both the inputs used in the production process and the outputs produced.

## Macroeconomics

Macroeconomics is concerned with the problems of *economic growth, unemployment,* and *inflation.* Each of these factors is an indicator of the overall state of the economy and how fully resources are utilized. Higher economic growth generally implies higher living standards. Lower unemployment suggests that society is making good use of its labor resource. Low rates of inflation reflect stable valuations of goods and services in terms of money. Such stability is important for both individuals and firms in planning for future economic activities. By law, government has a macroeconomic responsibility for ensuring that output growth rates are high and that unemployment and inflation rates are low. Through *monetary* and *fiscal policies,* government seeks to ensure that these goals are attained. Therefore, in addition to considering the actions of consumers and investors, macroeconomics is concerned with the implications of government activity for aggregate economic activity.

## Distinctions between Microeconomics and Macroeconomics

The major distinction between micro- and macroeconomic analysis is in the groups that are the focus of study in each branch. In microeconomics, individuals and firms are the main agents whose actions are analyzed. In macroeconomics, the actions of broad groupings or *aggregates* of agents—such as all consumers, government, and all investors—form the basis for analysis.

The use of aggregates is not confined to macroeconomics. For example, in microeconomics reference is often made to *market demand* when discussing the demand of all individuals in the market for a particular good. Similarly, *market supply* refers to the supply of a particular product by all firms producing it. In addition, although microeconomics deals primarily with the actions of individual consumers and individual firms, the consumer or the firm used in analysis is thought to represent the typical consumer or firm. Finally, for understanding the actions of fundamental economic units, the *household* (a group of individuals) and the *industry* (a group of firms) are often used as bases for microeconomic analysis. The specific topics considered in macroeconomics are presented in Chapters 3 to 12. Microeconomic topics are presented in Chapters 13 to 25.

# UNDERSTANDING ECONOMIC THEORY: DEFINITIONS, ASSUMPTIONS, GRAPHS, AND EQUATIONS

More than one student has noted that economics is nothing more than common sense applied to everyday decisions concerning work, investment, production, and consumption. Despite the truth of this statement, economics is also an academic disipline that requires organized thought if one is to understand it. In pursuing this discipline, economists use organized common sense, along with definitions, assumptions, graphs, and equations, to describe the underlying nature of economic activity. The combination of these factors is the foundation upon which economic thought is organized.

## Economic Models

In viewing the problems of the real world, economists combine definitions, assumptions, graphs, and equations to form *economic models*. These models are simple representations of complex real-world economic phenomena. A good economic model will identify the key variables of concern, appropriately reflect interrelationships between variables, and then offer insight into the basic nature and workings of the underlying problem. Aside from helping to understand the nature of economic relationships, economic models are often used to make predictions of future economic events, given present changes in the state of the economy.

## Definitions

To communicate effectively with others regarding the economy and to identify precisely the economic problem under consideration, it is essential to understand the definitions of the words in the economist's basic vocabulary. This is sometimes problematic because the economist's vocabulary includes words used in everyday life that often have very different meanings to economists. As an example, consider the word *investment*. For most individuals, this word implies the purchase of any asset upon which a monetary return is expected. For noneconomists, *investment* can refer to the purchase of a stock in the stock market or the purchase of a new machine by the owner of a factory. For economists, the term *investment* refers solely to the purchase of newly produced machinery or equipment used to facilitate the production of other goods and services. To make the distinction between investment in machinery and the purchase of assets earning a monetary return, economists use the term *financial investment*.

A good habit to acquire in studying economics is to be sure that any new terminology is understood at the time it is encountered. The index may have to be used to trace the meaning of difficult concepts back through the text. By reaching the point at which the basic term is understood, study can proceed upon a solid foundation.

## Assumptions

Economists make frequent use of simplifying assumptions. Because the activities taking place in the real-world economy are simultaneously affected by so many factors, considering all of them at once is impossible. Therefore, in conducting analysis, economists first isolate the most important features of a problem. By focusing attention on a particular industry, product, or individual, the complications of the real world are greatly reduced; key factors and relationships can be more readily identified. Some of the more important types of assumptions used by economists include the *ceteris paribus* assumption, assumptions regarding the behavior of individuals and firms, and assumptions regarding technology. Economists also make assumptions regarding the time frame of analysis. Finally, to manage effectively the many variables encountered in economic analysis, broad groupings or taxonomies are established that assign variables with similar characteristics to certain categories.

### THE *CETERIS PARIBUS* ASSUMPTION

The Latin expression *ceteris paribus* means "other things being equal." Once the boundaries of analysis for a given economic problem are determined, interrelationships between variables can be examined by considering changes in each of them, one at a time. For example, an economist might wish to analyze solely the effects of a rise in the wage of automobile workers on the supply of automobiles. Many other things may affect the supply of automobiles, but an economist might want to ask: "*Ceteris paribus*, what effect will a rise in the wage have on the supply of automobiles?" An economic model that relates the wage and other important variables to the supply of automobiles would then be used to observe the effects of the changing wage by itself, with all other variables held at some fixed level.

### BEHAVIORAL ASSUMPTIONS

*Behavioral assumptions* are also important in the study of economics. They represent assumptions concerning the motives of individuals and firms. For example, firms may be assumed to want to maximize profit or to minimize cost. In deciding on which market basket or collection of goods to purchase, individuals may be assumed to want to maximize the satisfaction or utility they obtain by consuming them.

### TECHNOLOGICAL ASSUMPTIONS

*Technological assumptions* are those made concerning how inputs are converted into output. For example, the *law of diminishing returns* states that as more and more units of some input such as labor are applied in the production of some output, with all other inputs, such as capital, held constant, the amount of additional output produced by successive units of labor will become smaller and smaller. Note in this example that the *ceteris paribus* assumption is used to suggest that all inputs other than labor are constant; only labor is allowed to vary.

## TIME FRAMES: THE SHORT AND LONG RUN

In conducting economic analysis, the time allowed to elapse in considering a problem can have a large impact. To simplify analysis, economists split time into two broad categories: the *long run* and the *short run*. These categories generally do not refer to time periods of specific length; they refer to the number of variables that are allowed to change within the period of analysis. In the long run, all variables are subject to change, and the effects of these changes are observed. However, in the short run, at least one variable is not allowed to change; assessing the impact of the one or several factors allowed to change is the subject of inquiry.

## CATEGORIZING INPUTS: FACTORS OF PRODUCTION

To develop an economic model, it is often important to assign items of a similar nature into a broader category representative of the entire class. In this way, the number of items to be considered is reduced without greatly detracting from the realism of the model. For example, in macroeconomics, broad aggregates are used. Individuals are classified as consumers; banks and other financial institutions are classified as financial intermediaries; and federal, state, and local governments are classified as government.

One of the most important and frequently used classifications places inputs used in the production process and the payments received by inputs into four groupings. These input categories are land, labor, capital, and entrepreneurial ability.

**Land.** *Land* represents both the physical setting upon which production takes place and natural resources used as an input. Thus the land upon which a farmer grows crops falls into this category, as does the iron ore used in a blast furnace to produce steel.

**Labor.** *Labor* refers to human effort hired to exert physical or mental power in the production of output. All types of laborers are contained within this broad category, including blue-collar and white-collar laborers, male and female laborers, and white and black laborers.

**Capital.** *Capital* refers to the machinery and buildings used in the production process to produce other goods. As seen in the durability of machines and buildings, capital goods tend to have long lifetimes and are said to *depreciate* or lose their value through wear and tear, over time. Unless preceded by the adjective *financial*, the term *capital* does not refer to money assets held by the firm.

**Entrepreneurial Ability.** *Entrepreneural ability* refers to the skill with which factors of production are organized and business opportunities are exploited by the owner or manager of a business (the entrepreneur).

**Factor Payments.** In return for services in producing output, the factors of production receive *factor payments*. The payment for land is *rent*; payments to labor are *wages*; the payment to capital is *interest*. Entrepreneurs receive *profits*

*Graphs and Equations*

A picture can be worth a thousand words, but to ensure that those words make sense, it is necessary to interpret the picture in a meaningful way. In economic analysis, graphic depiction of events is one of the most common methods of conveying ideas. Therefore, to understand economics, it is necessary to have a fundamental understanding of graphs. For the most part, economists limit their graphic analysis to graphs with only two axes (or dimensions). It is difficult to interpret graphs drawn with three axes and impossible to draw a meaningful graph with more than three dimensions. Because economic quantities and values are almost always positive, graphic analysis in economics is usually limited to the northeast, or upper-right, quadrant of a typical two-dimensional graph.

### FUNDAMENTALS OF GRAPHICAL ANALYSIS

The basis for any graph is the $x$ and $y$ axes, sometimes called the *ordinate* and *abscissa*. These are nothing more than number lines representing all the possible values that the variables $x$ and $y$ can take. These number lines meet at the *origin*,g of graphs. rigin where both $x$ and $y$ take the value zero. In conducting analysis using a graph, it is usually assumed that there is a relationship between $x$ and $y$ and that values of $y$ are dependent on values of $x$. Traditionally, the variable measured on the horizontal axis is $x$, and it is the *independent* wo-dindependentvariable. The variable measured on the vertical axis is $y$, the *dependent* teredependentvariable.

Figure 1.1 shows two important graphic relationships. The graph on the left shows an upward-sloping curve; the graph on the right shows a downward-sloping curve. A *direct relationship* is said to exist between $y$ and $x$ in the left diagram; increases in the value of $x$ are associated with increases in the value of $y$. In the graph on the right, $y$ and $x$ are *indirectly related*; a rise in the value of $x$ is associated with a decrease in the value of $y$. The curves provide a means of quickly determining values of $y$ given values of $x$. For example, according to the graph with the positive slope, when $x$ equals 5, $y$ equals 4. When $x$ equals 8, $y$ cquals 6. Based on the relationship shown in this graph, it would be easy to construct a table showing how each $x$ value is associated with a particular $y$ value. Values from a table that shows the relationship between two variables can also be used to plot a curve on a graph.

### GRAPHING TWO FUNCTIONS AT ONCE

In portraying economic relationships, economists often place two curves in the same graph. This sometimes causes problems for students because it is not clear how to use both curves together. The key to making sense out of graphs showing more than one curve is to treat each curve separately. In other words, to find the $y$ values associated with a given $x$ value when two curves are shown,

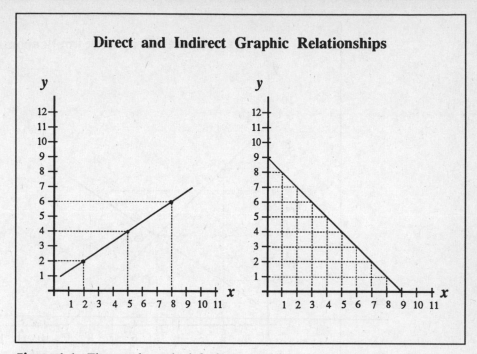

**Figure 1.1** *The graph on the left shows y as directly or positively related to x, while the graph on the right shows an inverse or indirect relationship between y and x.*

ignore one of the curves; then find the y value associated with x on the second. Next, ignore the second curve and find the y value associated with x on the first. Unless the curves intersect above a given x value, each x value will be associated with two y values.

Consider Figure 1.2. When x equals 2, y equals 7 on the downward-sloping curve but equals 2 on the upward-sloping curve. A value of x equal to 8 leads to a y value of 1 on the downward-sloping curve and a y value of 6 on the upward-sloping curve. When x equals 5, the value of y equals 4 for both the upward- sloping and downward-sloping curves. This is the point where the lines cross.

## THE SLOPE OF A LINE

The *slope* of a line provides important information about the responsiveness of one variable to changes in the value of another. With y graphed on the vertical axis and x graphed on the horizontal axis, the slope of a line at some point is defined as the change in y resulting from a one-unit change in x. Values of y move up or down along the vertical axis, a change that is often called the *rise*. Values of x move side to side along the horizontal axis, a change that is often called the *run*. The slope is defined as the rise, or the change in y, divided by the run, the change in x.

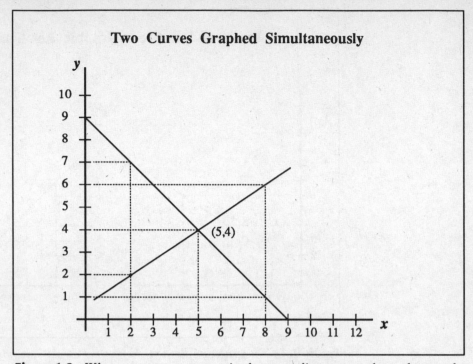

**Figure 1.2** *When two curves appear in the same diagram, each x value can be associated with either of two y values, depending on the curve considered. Given a value of x, find y values for each curve separately.*

Finding the slope of a straight line is easy because its slope is the same at all points. At any point, the ratio of the change in *y* to the change in *x* can be calculated by letting *x* increase by one unit and then measuring the change in *y*. From the graph of the upward sloping line shown in Figure 1.1 or 1.2, each 1 unit increase in *x* leads to a 2/3 unit increase in *y*. When *x* rises in value from 5 to 8, *y* rises in value from 4 to 6. The run is 3 units and the rise is 2 units. The slope of the line is 2/3, the ratio of the rise to the run. For a downward-sloping line, an increase in *x* is associated with a decrease in *y*; therefore, the rise, or change in *y*, is negative. From the graph of the downward sloping line shown in Figure 1.1 or 1.2, each 1 unit increase in *x* corresponds to a 1 unit decrease in *y*. The slope is −1.

Curved lines present a different problem because their slope is different at each point. To find the slope of a curved line at a particular point, a straight line is drawn that just touches (is *tangent* to) the curved line at the point of interest. Next, the slope of this straight tangent line is found. This slope will equal the slope of the curved line at the point of interest. (With a knowledge of calculus, the slopes of lines can easily be found by taking the derivative of the equation for the line and calculating its value at the point of interest.)

## SHAPES OF CURVES

The *shape* of a curve conveys important information about the nature of the relationship between the variables being graphed. With *y* dependent upon *x*, a straight line relationship between *x* and *y* implies that *y* changes by the same amount each time *x* is increased by one unit. Figure 1.3 shows other possible relations between *y* and *x*.

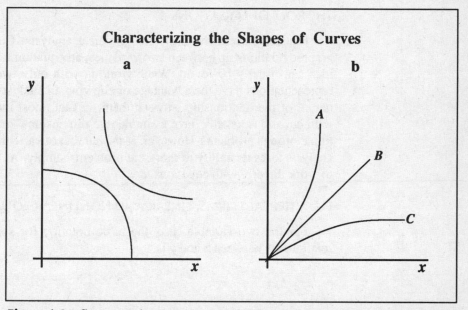

**Figure 1.3** *Convex and concave curves are shown in Figure 1.3a, with the higher curve being convex with respect to the origin. As shown in Figure 1.3b, from top to bottom curves A, B, and C are, respectively, increasing at increasing, constant, and decreasing rates.*

Both curves in Figure 1.3a have negative slopes. The bottom curve is said to be *concave* with respect to the origin. The concave curve shown is often used in economics to form a boundary containing points between the *x* and *y* axes and points on the curve. Along the concave curve, each unit increase in *x* leads to larger and larger declines in *y*. The top curve in Figure 1.3a is said to be *convex* with respect to the origin The convex curve is used to establish a boundary containing all points lying on or above the curve. Along the convex curve, each unit increase in *x* leads to smaller and smaller declines in *y*.

In Figure 1.3b, all three curves start from the origin. However, observe for the top curve, *A*, that as *x* increases unit by unit, the increase in *y* becomes larger and larger. Curve *A* in Figure 1.3b is said to be increasing at an *increasing rate*. The middle curve, *B*, is a straight line and shows that *y* increases by a constant amount as *x* increases. In the bottom curve, *C*, as *x* increases unit by unit the increase in $y$ becomes smaller and smaller. Curve C is said to be increasing at a *decreasing rate*.

Each of the curves shown in Figure 1.3b plays an important role in economic analysis. For example, curve $C$, which increases at a decreasing rate, is representative of the law of diminishing returns. If $x$ is assumed to represent some input and $y$ represents output, increases in the amount of input $x$ lead to smaller and smaller increases in the amount of output $y$ produced by $x$.

## THE ROLE OF EQUATIONS

Equations form the basis for graphical analysis. Corresponding to any graphic relationship between two variables, an equation representing the same idea can usually be found. When working with only two variables, graphic representations have the advantage of allowing an analyst to grasp quickly the nature of the relationship between them. In fact, most individuals who work with equations usually have a simple two-dimensional graph in mind as they think through problems. However, as the number of variables increases, graphic analysis loses its ability to represent problems simply. At this point it is easier to work directly with equations.

## FUNCTIONAL FORMS: LINEAR AND NONLINEAR EQUATIONS

For the two-variable case, the basic notation for specifying a funtional relationship between $x$ and $y$ is

$$y = f(x)$$

which is read "$y$ equals $f$ of $x$." This notation signifies that the variable $y$ is a *function* of $x$. The nature of the function is not specified.

In conducting analysis, economists spend a great deal of time trying to determine the exact nature of the relationship between $y$ and the various $x$'s upon which $y$ may depend. In other words, economists try to find an explicit equation or functional form to replace $f(x)$. If the variable $y$ is observed to increase at an increasing rate as $x$ increases, an economist might model the relationship as $y = x^2$. If this function does a good job of representing the behavior of the consumer, firm, or other economic entity whose actions are being investigated, it may be used in the economist's model.

At the introductory level, the equations used to model economic behavior tend to be very simple. Linear equations are frequently used because they often capture the essential features of economic relationships. For example, a linear equation can be used to describe accurately the relationship between household consumption expenditures and household income. In introductory classes, relationships that require use of nonlinear equations, such as the convex and concave curves shown in Figure 1.3, appear most often in graphical form.

**Linear Equations.** An example of a linear equation is the function

$$y = 4 + 2x$$

This function is graphed in Figure 1.4. Observe that when $x$ is zero, $y$ equals 4. This value corresponds to the y *intercept*. Also observe that as $x$ increases by one unit $y$ will increase by two units. This is the equation's *slope*: the change in $y$ given a one unit change in $x$.

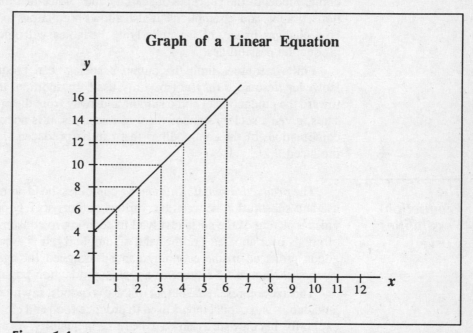

**Figure 1.4**   *A straight line based on the equation $y = 4 + 2x$ is shown. Here the slope of the line is 2 and its intercept is 4.*

For example, as $x$ increases from 3 to 4, $y$ rises from 10 to 12. The slope of the line is the change in $y$ (12 – 10) divided by the change in $x$ (4 – 3). This value is 2/1=2, the same as the coefficient in front of $x$ in the equation. The standard form for such a linear equation is

$$y = b + mx$$

If the variable $x$ was raised to a power other than 1 (recall $x^1 = x$) or if $x$ appeared in the denominator of a fraction, the equation would be *nonlinear*. Corresponding to the specific equation given above, $b$ is a value representing the intercept, the value of $y$ when $x$ is zero. The letter $m$, the coefficient in front of $x$, is a value representing the equation's slope.

# THE ECONOMY'S PRODUCTION POSSIBILITIES

The production-possibilities curve is the starting point for understanding the nature of the fundamental economic problem. It represents a simple economic model of the concepts of scarcity and choice that makes use of definitions, graphs, and assumptions. It also allows predictions to be made regarding how changes in any of the underlying variables will affect the economy's production possibilities.

Finite resources limit the output a society can produce and consume. However, resources may not be fully used. In addition, they can be shifted toward the production of some outputs and away from the production of others. Thus, given a society's endowment of resources, it is not clear exactly which combinations of the commodities that can be produced should be or will be produced.

## The Production-Possibilities Curve

The *production-possibilities curve* combines the ideas of efficient resource use and substitution between the various outputs society can produce. It provides a picture of the costs involved in deciding to consume one combination of goods over another. For the sake of simplicity, it is assumed that all of the goods produced in the economy can be assigned (or aggregated) into two categories. Figure 1.5 represents a typical production-possibilities curve.

The axes represent the output of the two goods, say food and clothing. The land, labor, and capital inputs used to produce food and clothing are not shown explicitly, but they are assumed to be finite in quantity. As more inputs are used in the production of food, the production of clothing declines, and vice versa. This is why the production possibilities curve slopes downward. Given resource endowments and the state of technology, if inputs are fully and efficiently used, the economy will operate at a point on its production-possibilities curve. These are points such as *A*, *B*, *C*, and *D* in Figure 1.5. If some resources are not used or resources are not used efficiently, the economy will operate under its production-possibilities curve.

### THE LOCATION OF THE PRODUCTION-POSSIBILITIES CURVE

The production-possibilities curve represents a boundary between those output combinations available to society and those not available. The location of the curve therefore reflects the problem of scarcity. The further the curve is from the origin, the more abundant is the output available to society. The problem of choice involves determining where on the curve society will consume. Society can choose, by some means, to have any single combination of goods on the curve.

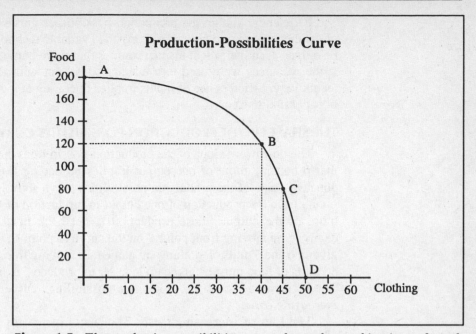

**Figure 1.5**  *The production-possibilities curve shows the combinations of goods society can consume while making full and efficient use of its resources. Goods given up in moving from one point on the curve to another represent opportunity cost. Thus, in moving from point B to point C, the opportunity cost of 5 extra units of clothing is 40 units of food.*

At the intercepts of the production-possibilities curve, society produces as much as possible of one output and none of the other. Other points on the curve represent specific combinations of both outputs. For example, at point *B* in Figure 1.5, society consumes 120 units of food and 40 units of clothing. It is not possible for society to consume any output combinations beyond the production-possibilities curve; given the state of technology and available resources, these combinations are not attainable. Society can consume at any point on or under the curve. However, points under the production-possibilites curve imply either the underemployment or inefficient use of inputs.

**Resource Endowments.** A key determinant of how much output society can produce is the amount of resources available. Because production involves the transformation of inputs into outputs, the available quantities of land, labor, and capital limit the amount of output that can be produced.

**The Role of Technology.** One of the most important factors in determining the quantity of the outputs that can be produced given available resources is the state of *technology*. The state of technology determines how efficiently inputs to production processes can be converted into output. Improvements in technology imply that fewer inputs are necessary to produce the same amount of output or that the same amount of inputs can be used to produce more output.

**Efficiency.** Within the production-possibilities curve model, the concept of efficiency refers to how effectively the available technology is used. Using resources in an inefficient manner implies that more output could be produced if the resources were used in a manner consistent with the existing state of technology. Efficient use of inputs implies operating at a point on the production-possibilities curve.

## THE SHAPE OF THE PRODUCTION-POSSIBILITIES CURVE

The downward slope of the production-possibilities curve reflects the fact that producing more of one output implies producing less of the other. The concave shape of the production possibilities curve shows that in transferring inputs from the production of one output to production of the other, more and more of the output whose production is cut back must be sacrificed. For example, in moving from point *B* on the curve to point *C*, 40 units of food are given up and 5 units of clothing are gained. In moving from point *C* to point *D*, 80 units of food must be given up in order to produce 5 extra units of clothing. The concave shape of the production-possibilities curve reflects the *law of increasing costs*.

**The Law of Increasing Costs.** The law of increasing costs, an important assumption regarding the nature of technology, states that inputs cannot be transferred perfectly from the production of one good to the production of another. For example, the transfer of inputs from the production of food to the production of clothing will lead to greater and greater reductions in food output for each unit increase in clothing output. Alternatively, each unit decrease in food output results in lesser and lesser increases in the clothing output. Beginning at any point on the production-possibilities curve, this assumption is based on the idea that the first resources transferred from production of one output to the production of another are those that can most readily be used in either type of productive activity. Those resources transferred later are less readily adaptable to use in alternate forms of productive activity; they therefore lead to greater decreases in output in the sector from which they are taken and smaller increases in output in the sector to which they are transferred.

**Opportunity Cost.** The *opportunity cost* of a good is defined as all the alternative economic goods and services that must be given up in order to acquire more of it. The production-possibilities curve allows the direct measurement of opportunity cost. In Figure 1.5, the opportunity cost of acquiring 5 more units of clothing in moving from point *B* to point *C* is 40 units of food (food is given up). In moving from point *C* to point *D*, the opportunity cost of acquiring 5 units of clothing is 80 units of food. At the intercept on the food axis (point *A*), the opportunity cost of consuming 200 units of food is the 50 units of clothing that must be given up to be at that point. The opportunity cost of acquiring more units of a particular good is always stated in terms of the amounts of other goods that must be given up.

Examples of opportunity cost go beyond the production possibilities model. For example, consider the decision to purchase one gallon of gasoline for a dollar when candy bars cost 50 cents. It can be stated that the opportunity cost of one gallon of gasoline is the two candy bars that must be given up to acquire the gallon of gasoline. Next, consider the opportunity cost of a college education. In addition to the alternative goods and services that could be purchased with tuition money, the measure of opportunity cost includes the potential four years of income lost by attending school instead of working.

## SHIFTING THE PRODUCTION-POSSIBILITIES CURVE

The location of the economy's production-possibilities curve depends upon society's endowment of resources and its ability to transform those resources into desired outputs via the existing technology. It follows that an increase in the endowment of resources or an improvement in technology will cause the production-possibilities curve to be located further from the origin. This is illustrated in Figure 1.6a. As can be seen, because of technological change or an increase in available resources, the outer curve enables consumption of greater quantities of both food and clothing.

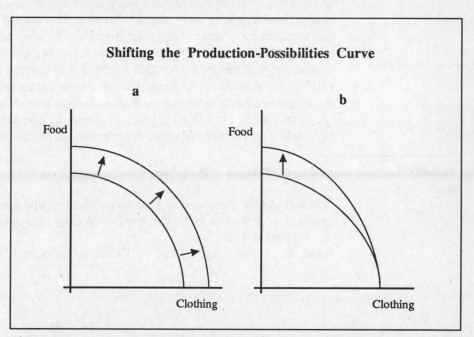

**Shifting the Production-Possibilities Curve**

**Figure 1.6** *As shown in Figure 1.6a, the production-possibilities curve will shift out at all points given an increase in society's endowment of resources or economy-wide technological change. In Figure 1.6b, technological change in the food sector causes the production-possibilities curve to shift out at all points except the clothing intercept.*

**Technological Change in One Sector.** Sometimes technological changes occur only in the production of one output. If this is the case, the intercept for the affected output will shift outward, while the other intercept remains stationary. Figure 1.6b illustrates this case. Given an improvement in the technology associated with production of food, the food intercept has shifted out.

It is important to note that more of both goods can be produced throughout the new range of production possibilities, except at the intercept where only clothing is produced. How can both food and clothing output be increased when technological change affects only the food sector? Technological change implies both that the same amount of output can be produced with less input and that more output can be produced with the same amount of input. Therefore, input use can be reduced to some extent in the food sector and can still result in higher food output. The resources freed from use in the food sector can be transferred to the clothing sector to increase output there as well.

*Throughout the text, and in other courses in economics, the basic building blocks of economic analysis described in this chapter are used. These building blocks enable development of other models that describe many of the most interesting and perplexing problems of our time. Here these building blocks have been used to analyze the problem of scarcity and choice in the context of the simple production-possibilities model. This model is developed assuming that society's endowment of resources is fixed, that the state of technology is given, and that inputs are not perfectly transferable in the production of output. In subsequent chapters, various aspects of the problem of scarcity and choice will be examined from both a microeconomic and a macroeconomic perspective.*

## Selected Readings

Heibroner, Robert L. *The Worldly Philosophers*. New York: Simon and Schuster. 1967.

Marshall, Alfred. *Principles of Economics*. Philadelphia: Porcupine Press. 1982.

Pearce, David W. *The MIT Dictionary of Modern Economics*. Cambridge, MA: MIT Press. 1986.

Smith, Adam. *The Wealth of Nations*. Chicago: University of Chicago Press. 1976.

# 2

## *Supply-and-Demand Analysis*

*In observing economic activity, the most obvious roles played by economic agents are those of buyers and sellers, also called consumers and producers. Depending upon the situation, these roles are interchangeable. Producers act as buyers when they hire inputs for the production process. They act as sellers when the goods produced are made available to consumers in the marketplace. Consumers act as buyers when they purchase these products. Income used to make purchases is earned through the sale of labor or other resources that are used as inputs by producers. In selling labor or other resources to producers, the consumer acts as a seller.*

*The factors underlying the sales and purchases of inputs and outputs are the subject of this chapter. The key elements in the decision by firms to provide goods for sale are considered, as are the factors underlying the decision by consumers to purchase goods and services. For individual products, a model is developed that examines the potential response of sellers and buyers to various product prices. The object of inquiry is to find the single price satisfying both producers and consumers and the exact amount of output that will be produced and sold.*

# THE SUPPLY CURVE FOR AN INDIVIDUAL PRODUCT

By definition, the *supply curve* for a product represents the quantity of the product that will be offered for sale by producers at each price that might exist. For simplicity, it is assumed that the product is homogeneous; regardless of who produces the product, its characteristics are always the same. An example might be wheat or gasoline of a certain quality. The factors involved in determining the shape and location of the product supply curve include the responsiveness of the amount supplied to the price of the product, the state of technology (how efficiently inputs can be transformed into the product), the number of firms producing the product, the price of the inputs used to produce the product, and the ability of firms to produce other products that might provide a greater reward.

## The Shape of the Supply Curve

A product supply curve is graphed with the price of the product on the vertical axis and the quantity of the product on the horizontal axis. In accordance with the *law of supply*, it is assumed that the product supply curve slopes upward. This shape reflects the idea that firms require higher prices to induce them to sell more units of a product. Figure 2.1 shows a typical supply curve.

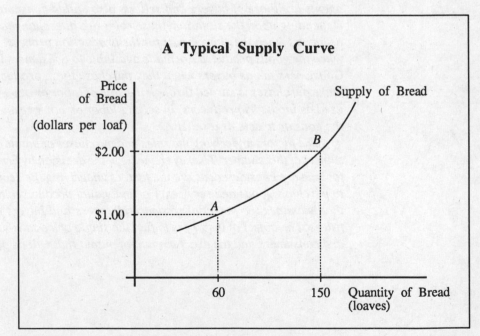

**A Typical Supply Curve**

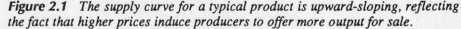

**Figure 2.1**   *The supply curve for a typical product is upward-sloping, reflecting the fact that higher prices induce producers to offer more output for sale.*

Here the product offered for sale is bread, perhaps made by a small-town bakery. At point *A*, the price of the product is $1 per loaf, and 60 loaves are offered for sale. If the price rises to $2 per loaf, 150 loaves are offered for sale, as shown at point *B*.

The assumption of an upward-sloping supply curve is in turn based upon the relationship between the costs of production and the price received when a product is sold. The difference between the selling price of a product and the cost of producing it represents the *profit per unit* received by the producer. As the price of the product rises, the profit from selling it will grow. However, in the short run, when not all inputs are free to vary, production costs will rise as more and more of the product is produced. Hence, a higher price is needed to cover costs. It is the combination of potentially higher profits and greater costs that induces or requires firms to offer more for sale at a higher price.

## The Location of the Supply Curve

Given its upward slope, the problem of determining exactly where a supply curve will be located remains. Will it be located far to the left side of the graph, signifying that lower levels of the product will be offered for sale over the range of relevant prices? Or will the curve be located further to the right, signifying that more will be offered for sale at those same prices? In Figure 2.2 two supply curves are presented. Suppose the initial supply curve is $S_1$ on the left. What factors would cause this supply curve to *shift* to the right into the position occupied by supply curve $S_2$? Similarly, if $S_2$ is the initial supply curve, what

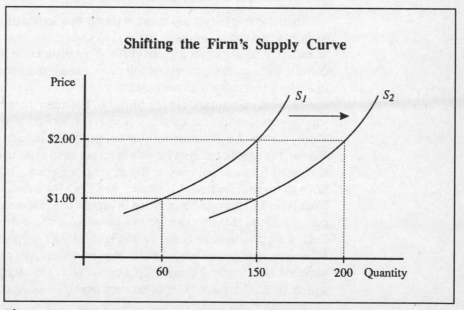

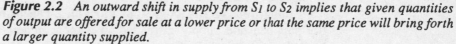

**Figure 2.2** *An outward shift in supply from $S_1$ to $S_2$ implies that given quantities of output are offered for sale at a lower price or that the same price will bring forth a larger quantity supplied.*

factors would cause it to shift left into the position occupied by $S_1$? Answers to these questions are discussed next.

## SUPPLY SHIFT FACTORS

The factors that will cause a supply curve to shift to the left or the right are those affecting the product's availability at the set of possible product prices. The supply curve will shift to the right when

1. More firms enter the market and produce additional units of output at each possible price.

2. Costs of production are lowered, causing a product's price to be associated with higher profits for firms in the market. Thus, *technological improvements* or *reductions in the price of any factor of production* will lower costs and induce firms to sell more at any given price.

3. Changes in the prices of related outputs can also cause supply to shift. Related outputs are products produced with similar inputs and similar technology. If the price of televisions with 19-inch screens goes up, the supply of televisions with 12-inch screens may go down as producers attempt to reap higher profits by selling the 19-inch sets.

## MOVEMENTS ALONG THE SUPPLY CURVE

In discussing the supply curve, it is important to distinguish between factors that cause the entire supply curve to shift and factors that lead to consideration of different points along a given curve. This distinction is conveyed under the definitions of *quantity supplied* and *supply* and more generally, the definitions of *endogenous* and *exogenous* variables.

**Quantity Supplied versus Supply.** The term *supply* refers to the entire supply curve, while the *quantity supplied* refers to a particular point on the supply curve. An increase in quantity supplied refers to an increase in the amount of a product offered for sale in response to a rise in its price. More output is offered for sale, but only at the new higher price. In Figure 2.1, when the price of bread rises from $1 per loaf to $2 per loaf, the quantity supplied rises from 60 to 150 loaves. An increase in supply refers to a shift right in the supply curve, perhaps due to a change in technology or to a decline in factor prices. Such a supply increase is shown in Figure 2.2 as supply shifts from $S_1$ to $S_2$. More output will be offered for sale at every price. At a price of $1, the amount supplied rises from 60 along supply curve $S_1$ to 150 along supply curve $S_2$. At a price of $2, the quantity supplied rises from 150 along supply curve $S_1$ to 200 along supply curve $S_2$.

**Endogenous versus Exogenous Variables.** The distinction between quantity supplied and supply is related to a more general distinction between variables in a model. *Endogenous* variables are variables, such as price in the supply diagram, that cause movements along the curve. *Exogenous* variables are variables, like technology, that are not on either of the axes of the supply curve's graph but nonetheless have an effect on the curve by causing it to shift. In the more general case, the values of endogenous variables (like price) are determined within an economic model; exogenous variables (like technology) are determined outside the model and are taken as given.

# THE DEMAND CURVE FOR AN INDIVIDUAL PRODUCT

By definition, the *demand curve* for a product represents the quantity of the product that consumers will be willing to purchase at each possible price. The responsiveness of the quantity demanded to the price of the product determines the shape of the demand curve. The factors involved in determining the location of the demand curve include consumer tastes (preferences consumers have for particular products), consumer incomes, the number of consumers available to purchase the product, the price of other goods that either complement or substitute consumption of the good, and expectations regarding the future price of the product.

## The Shape of the Demand Curve

A product demand curve is graphed with the price of the product on the vertical axis and the quantity of the product on the horizontal axis. In accordance with the *law of demand*, it is assumed that the product demand curve slopes downward. *Ceteris paribus*—with all else constant—this shape reflects the idea that consumers are willing to purchase more of a given good only if its price is lower. Figure 2.3 shows a typical demand curve. Again, the product offered for sale is bread. At point *A*, the price of the product is $1 per loaf; consumers are willing to purchase 150 loaves at that price. If the price rises to $2 per loaf, the amount consumers are willing to purchase falls to 30 loaves, as shown at point *B*.

### THE LAW OF DIMINISHING MARGINAL UTILITY

Consistent with the fact that most people love a bargain, the assumption of a downward-sloping demand curve is based upon the relationship between the price that must be paid to acquire a particular product and the satisfaction that comes from consuming it. According to the *law of diminishing marginal utility*, as more and more units of a particular good are consumed, the additional satisfaction that accompanies each unit of consumption is assumed to decline. To ensure that the satisfaction that comes from consumption of a good exceeds the satisfaction that comes from holding on to the money used to buy the good

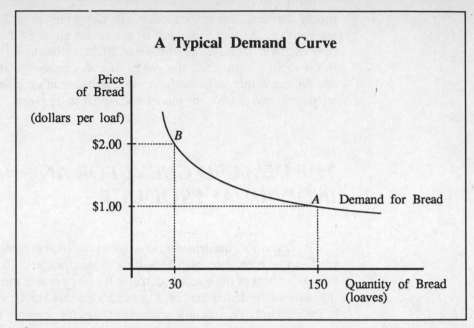

**Figure 2.3**  *The typical demand curve slopes downward, reflecting the assumption that lower prices are required to induce consumers to purchase more units of a product.*

(or perhaps buying another good), a lower price is required to induce additional purchases.

## The Location of the Demand Curve

Given its downward slope, the problem of determining exactly where the demand curve will be located remains. If located far to the left of the graph, it signifies that lower quantities of the product will be demanded at any of the possible prices than if the curve was located further to the right. In Figure 2.4 two demand curves are presented. Suppose the initial demand curve is $D_1$ on the left. What factors would cause this demand curve to shift to the right into the position occupied by demand curve $D_2$? Similarly, if $D_2$ is the initial demand curve, what factors would cause it to shift left into the position occupied by $D_1$? Demand shift factors are discussed next.

### DEMAND SHIFT FACTORS

The factors that will cause a demand curve to shift to the left or the right are those affecting the desire of consumers to purchase the product at the set of possible prices. The demand curve will shift to the right when

1.  Consumer tastes change in favor of the product.

2.  Consumer incomes rise, enabling consumers to purchase more of all goods, including the good under consideration.

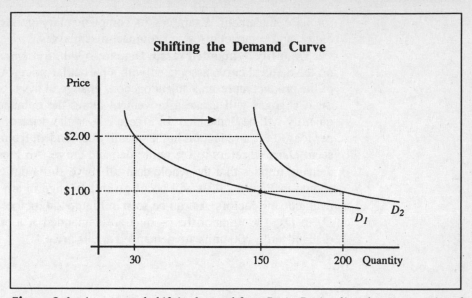

**Figure 2.4** *An outward shift in demand from $D_1$ to $D_2$ implies that more units of output are desired at any given price or that a higher price can be charged for the same quantity.*

3. The number of consumers in the market for the good increases, as might occur with an increase in population.

4. The price of another good (a complement or substitute) changes, making the product under consideration more desirable.

5. Expectations of a future price increase for the product induce consumers to purchase more of the product now. For example, increases in federal taxes on alcoholic beverages taking effect in January of 1991 led many consumers to make liquor purchases in December 1990.

**Complementary and Substitute Goods.** With regard to point 4 above, changes in the prices of another good, the relationship between the goods under consideration plays an important role. If two goods are substitutes, consumers can use one good in place of the other. Thus if the price of a good rises, there will be an increase in the demand for its substitute. Examples of substitute goods include butter and margarine, coffee and tea, and foreign and domestic automobiles.

If two goods are complements to each other, the enjoyment that comes with the use of one good is enhanced by consuming the other along with it. Thus a decline in the price of a complementary good will lead to a rise in the demand for its complement. Examples of complementary goods include bread and butter, and compact discs and compact-disc players.

**Quantity Demanded versus Demand.** *Quantity demanded* refers to a point on the demand curve associated with a particular price. A change in the price of the product represents an endogenous change in the supply- demand model. Such changes will cause a movement along the demand curve, and a new quantity will be demanded. In Figure 2.3, as the price of bread rises from $1 per loaf to $2, a reduction in the quantity demanded, from 150 to 30 loaves, is seen. *Demand* refers to the entire demand curve. An increase or decrease in demand implies that the whole demand curve shifts out or in. Such a shift is shown in Figure 2.4. It will occur given a change in any of the (exogenous) demand shift factors. As can be seen in Figure 2.4, before demand shifts from $D_1$ to $D_2$, 150 units of the product are demanded at a price of $1. After the demand shift, 200 units are demanded at this price.

# EQUILIBRIUM AND SUPPLY-AND-DEMAND ANALYSIS

By itself, a supply or demand curve represents an infinte number of price-quantity combinations. To be useful in analyzing real-world situations, it is necessary to find the one price at which products are offered for sale and the one quantity of the product that is both sold and purchased. To determine this single price and single quantity, the concept of *equilibrium* is used.

Supply-and-demand analysis involves locating the equilibrium price and quantity for particular goods and considering the effects of changes in the location of the supply or demand curve on equilibrium price and quantity. This analysis is discussed in the following sections.

## Equilibrium

*Equilibrium* is a frequently used concept in economic analysis. In its broadest sense, equilibrium refers to a situation in which there are no forces that will tend to change that situation. With regard to the supply and demand model, equilibrium is said to occur when the price at which producers will supply a certain quantity of a product equals the price at which consumers will demand the same quantity of the product.

## Locating Equilibrium in the Supply-Demand Model

To find the point of equilibrium, the supply and demand curves for the product are plotted together in a single graph. When this is done, as shown in Figure 2.5, an intersection of the two curves appears at point $E$. Here, the price of $1.35 per loaf is associated with a quantity demanded of 80 loaves of bread and a quantity supplied of 80 loaves. In other words, at a price of $1.35 per loaf,

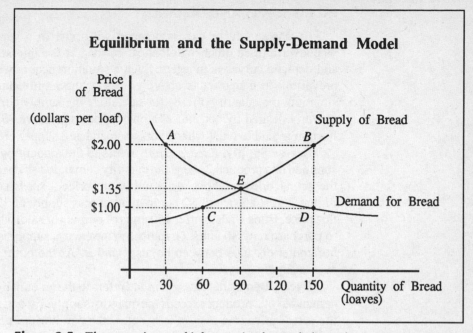

**Figure 2.5** *The one price at which quantity demanded equals quantity supplied is found at the intersection of the supply and demand curves. This represents the equilibrium price in the supply-demand model. At this price, excess supply and demand are zero.*

producers are willing to sell 90 loaves, and consumers are willing to purchase 90 loaves. Because one price equates the quantity supplied along the supply curve and the quantity demanded along the demand curve, this is the point of equilibrium.

In spite of the fact that they are graphed together, the supply and demand curves still represent the separate actions of buyers and sellers. Thus, as in the previous examples, at a price of $1 per loaf, 60 loaves are supplied for sale, while 150 loaves will be demanded. Similarly, at a price of $2 per loaf, 150 loaves are offered for sale, while the quantity consumers wish to purchase falls to 30 loaves. Only at a price of $1.35 per loaf will the quantity demanded exactly equal the quantity supplied.

Finding the equilibrium price and quantity by finding the point of intersection of the supply and demand curves is equivalent to the mathematical problem of solving a system of two simultaneous equations with two unknowns. The supply and demand curves can each be represented by a separate independent equation, with quantity as a function of price. The one price-quantity combination that holds true or satisfies both equations represents the equilibrium price and quantity.

## EXCESS SUPPLY AND DEMAND

Excess supply or excess demand will exist in a supply-demand model whenever a price other than that established at the intersection of the supply and demand curves is in effect. Such a situation occurs when the actual price prevailing in a market is above or below the equilibrium price. In such a situation, the quantity offered for sale along the supply curve cannot equal the quantity desired by consumers along the demand curve. Given this fact, equilibrium is said to exist when excess demand and supply are zero.

**Excess Supply.** *Excess supply* refers to the amount by which the quantity supplied of a product exceeds the quantity demanded at a particular price. When the actual price is above the equilibrium price, excess supply will exist. In Figure 2.5, at a price of $2 per loaf, an excess supply of 120 loaves exists. At this price, firms wish to offer 150 units of output for sale, while consumers wish to purchase only 30 units. Graphically, the excess supply is represented by the horizontal distance between points A and B. At the point of equilibrium (E), excess supply is zero.

**Excess Demand.** *Excess demand* refers to the amount by which the quantity demanded of a product exceeds the quantity supplied at a particular price. When the actual price in a market falls below the equilibrium price, excess demand will result. In Figure 2.5, at a price of $1 per loaf, an excess demand of 90 loaves exists. Firms are willing to produce only 60 loaves of bread, while consumers wish to purchase 150 units. Graphically, the excess demand is represented by the horizontal distance between points C and D. At the point of equilibrium, excess demand is zero.

## The Stability of Equilibrium in the Supply-Demand Model

Excess supply or excess demand means that equilibrium has not been achieved; one price is associated with a quantity supplied that does not equal the quantity demanded. Questions concering the stability of equilibrium pertain to whether excess supply and demand will last. Beginning from a point of disequilibrium (any point at which supply and demand do not cross), if there are forces that move a product's price and quantity to the equilibrium point, the equilibrium is said to be stable.

## EXCESS SUPPLY AND STABILITY

In a situation of excess supply, the actual price is greater than the equilibrium price. The quantity of output that producers wish to sell exceeds the quantity consumers wish to purchase. If prices are allowed to move down without restraint, those producers who are able to lower their price below the prevailing price and still make a profit will do so to be rid of their excess output. As the price of output falls, the quantity of output demanded increases along the demand curve; lower prices induce more consumers to purchase the product. Simultaneously, output offered for sale is reduced along the supply curve; lower prices make the productive activity of some producers unprofitable and lower the quantity supplied. The combination of a higher quantity demanded and a lower quantity supplied causes the excess supply to shrink. This process continues until excess supply is zero and equilibrium is established. Note that the equilibrium point is arrived at without shifting either the supply or demand curve.

## EXCESS DEMAND AND STABILITY

If excess demand exists, the actual price is less than the equilibrium price. Those consumers willing to purchase the product at a price higher than the prevailing price will attempt to do so. If the price is free to move upward, their actions will bid up the going market price, causing the quantity supplied to increase. As the price of output rises, some consumers will no longer be willing to purchase the product. The quantity of output demanded falls, and the excess demand shrinks. This process continues until excess demand is zero.

Therefore, when prices and quantities are free to vary, there are forces that will cause excess supply and demand to shrink toward zero and lead to the establishment of the equilibrium price and quantity. As the price of the product changes, there is a *movement* along both the supply curve and the demand curve. In neither the adjustment from excess demand nor from excess supply is there a shift in the supply curve or the demand curve.

## Interference with the Price Mechanism

Sometimes prices are not free to vary, as when the government imposes rent controls on housing or minimum wages for labor. In this case, excess demand or supply can persist. An equilibrium price that equates the quantity supplied with the quantity demanded will not be achieved. The supply-demand model can still be said to be in equilibrium, but only in the sense that as long as the government's law is in force, there are no forces that will cause change. Unless the government-maintained price happens to be the equilibrium price, quantity supplied will not equal quantity demanded.

### THE MINIMUM WAGE

The labor market is an input market in which the services of labor are bought and sold. In this market, firms purchase the services of labor to produce output; individuals sell their labor services in exchanges for wages. The basic forces underlying the shapes of the supply and demand curves in input markets are same as those found in output markets.

The effects of a minimum-wage law on the labor market are shown in Figure 2.6. At a wage of $3 per hour, the labor market would be in equilibrium. However, because the government has set a minimum wage of, say, $4 per hour, the quantity of labor supplied equals 150 million laborers; the quantity of labor demanded at the minimum wage equals 145 million. Quantity supplied therefore exceeds quantity demanded at the minimum wage. The excess supply of labor represents *unemployment* of 5 million workers. Note that the minimum wage is said to be a *price floor* because lower wages are not allowed by the government.

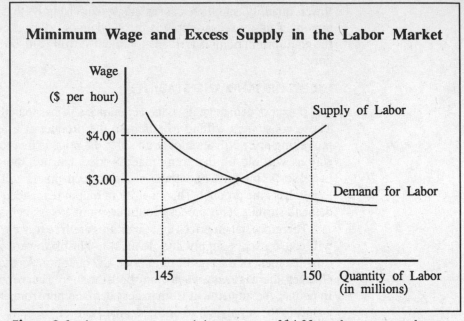

Figure 2.6 *A government-set minimum wage of $4.00 per hour causes the quantity supplied of labor to exceed the quantity demanded. Unemployment of 5 million workers results.*

## OTHER TYPES OF PRICE CONTROLS

Other examples of interference with the price mechanism include *price ceilings* and *usury laws*.

**Price Ceilings.** An example of a price control in the form of a price ceiling was the limit placed on the price of gasoline after the first Arab oil embargo in 1974. This control led to excess demand for gasoline, which manifested itself in long waiting lines at gasoline stations. Such price controls show no consideration for what people are willing to pay for products or the value of time lost to individuals while waiting. Doctors, dock workers, the unemployed, and those not in the labor force are all treated equally. All must wait in line.

**Usury Laws.** Usury laws are limits on the rate of interest paid by consumers. During periods when interest rates are high (usually during periods of high inflation), these laws benefit those consumers able to obtain loans. However, some individuals who are willing to pay the established rate of interest or even a higher rate are unable to obtain loans. This implies that there may be funds in the hands of potential lenders that are used for purposes less valuable than those the disappointed borrowers had in mind. Similarly, the fact that some businesses are willing to pay a higher rate of interest but cannot obtain loans means that some worthwhile investments may not be undertaken.

# CONDUCTING ANALYSIS WITH THE SUPPLY-DEMAND MODEL

Used in conjunction with the supply and demand shift factors, the combined supply-demand graph provides a powerful means of conducting analysis. It allows predictions to be made regarding the likely effects on price and quantity of various exogenous changes in real-world variables. Basically, if changes occurring in the real world cause change in any of the shift factors affecting either the supply curve or the demand curve, one of these curves will shift to a new location. A new equilibrium price and quantity will then be established.

In conducting supply-and-demand analysis, two important considerations must be kept in mind.

1. The product being analyzed must be clearly recognized. In other words, which product's supply-and-demand curves will be used in the analysis? For example, investigating the effects of a rise in the price of milk on soft-drink consumption involves use of the supply and demand graph for soft drinks. Since milk is a substitute for soft drinks, a rise in the price of milk will cause the soft drink demand curve to shift out.

2. The real-world changes that occur must be classified as either demand or supply shift factors; one change occurring in the real world does not cause *both* the supply and the demand curves to shift simultaneously. However, if two or more real-world changes occur, there is a good chance that both supply and demand will shift.

The key to making successful predictions concerning the price and quantity of a good in a particular market involves examining what kind of shift factor the real world change represents. The change is assigned to the appropriate supply or demand shift category (for example, changing technology or taste); then the implications of the change are observed using the supply-demand model.

## The Effects of a Supply Increase

Consider the market for gasoline and suppose a new means of refining oil is discovered. Of the possible supply and demand shift factors, this represents a change in technology that should make gasoline production less costly. Such technological changes affect the supply curve; more gasoline can now be offered for sale at every price. It follows that the gasoline supply curve will shift to the right. This is shown in Figure 2.7.

Initially the gasoline supply curve is $S_0$ and the gasoline demand curve is $D_0$. The equilibrium price is $1.05 per gallon, while the equilibrium quantity is 50,000 gallons. With the technological change affecting gasoline production, the supply curve shifts right to $S_1$. The result is a a new intersection between

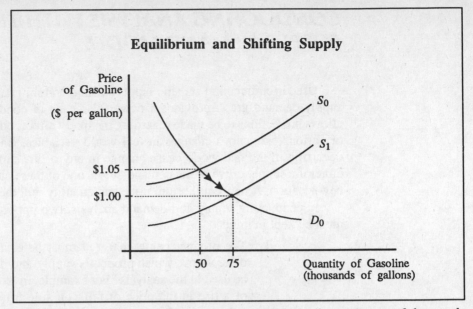

**Figure 2.7**   *A rightward shift in supply caused by a change in one of the supply shift factors results in a lower equilibrium price and a higher equilibrium quantity.*

supply curve $S_1$ and the original demand curve. At this new intersection, there is a decline in the equilibrium price of gasoline, from $1.05 per gallon to $1 per gallon; there is an increase in the equilibrium quantity demanded and supplied, from 50,000 gallons to 75,000 gallons.

## OTHER SUPPLY SHIFT FACTORS

Other factors that would cause such an outward shift in gasoline supply include a decline in input costs due to falling input prices or entry of new firms into the gasoline refining industry.

## THE PROCESS IN REVERSE

Suppose the gasoline market was in equilibrium at the intersection of supply curve $S_1$ and demand curve $D_0$. If oil became more expensive because of war in the Mideast, supply would shift left to $S_0$; the equilibrium price of gasoline would rise, and the equilibrium quantity would fall.

## THE SUPPLY SHIFT'S EFFECT ON DEMAND

Observe that the new means of refining oil affects only the supply curve. Even though the supply curve shifts out, it has no effect on the location of the demand curve. (Demand does not shift in response to a supply shift.) Instead, the outward shift in supply causes a *movement* downward along the existing demand curve to the new point of equilibrium.

## The Effects of a Demand Increase

Still considering the gasoline market, suppose that consumers' incomes rise. This implies that consumers will wish to purchase more of all goods, including gasoline. Sorting through the list of possible supply and demand shift factors, it is seen that a change in income is a demand shift factor. It follows that the demand curve for gasoline will shift, in this case to the right, as shown in Figure 2.8.

The initial supply curve and demand curves are $S_0$ and $D_0$. Equilibrium occurs at a price of $1.05 per gallon, at which 50,000 gallons are produced and sold. The rise in income causes demand to shift right to $D_1$. The new equilibrium is found at the intersection of demand curve $D_1$ and the original supply curve. The quantity of gasoline supplied increases upward *along* the supply curve (whose location is unaffected by the change in income) until the new equilibrium price and quantity for gasoline are established at $1.15 and 80,000. Thus, the shift right in demand causes equilibrium price and quantity to rise.

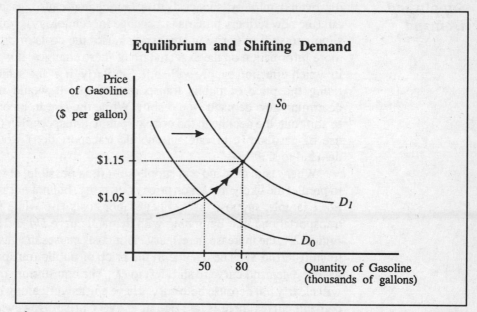

**Figure 2.8**  *A rightward shift in demand caused by a change in one of the demand shift factors results in a higher equilibrium price and quantity.*

### OTHER DEMAND SHIFT FACTORS

Other factors that would cause a rightward shift in the demand curve include changing tastes for certain modes of transportation using more gasoline (e.g., a desire for bigger cars), an increase in population, a rise in the price of substitute fuels, a fall in the price of complements like automobiles, or expectations that gasoline prices will rise in the future.

### THE PROCESS IN REVERSE

If the gasoline market was initially in equilibrium at the intersection of demand curve $D_1$ and supply curve $S_0$, a fall in income would cause the demand curve to shift left; reduced quantities of gasoline would be demanded at all possible prices. Equilibrium price would fall along with the equilibrium quantity.

### THE DEMAND SHIFT'S EFFECT ON SUPPLY

When the demand curve shifts out, it has no effect on the location of the supply curve. (Supply does not shift in response to a demand shift.) Instead, the outward shift in demand causes a *movement* upward along the existing supply curve to the new point of equilibrium.

## Simultaneous Shifts in Supply and Demand

Changes in real-world variables do not always come individually. Suppose that in the gasoline market at the same time a new process for refining oil was discovered, refinery labor costs rose. One change causes gasoline supply to shift out (the new refinery process is a change in technology), while the other causes supply to shift in (a rise in labor costs raises the costs of production). Without more information on the exact nature of these changes, it is not possible to say in which direction supply will shift. Similarly, if at the same time income was rising the price of public transportation fell, it would not be possible to determine how demand would shift. While the rise in income causes demand to shift out, the decline in the price of public transportation (a substitute for the use of gasoline in private-automobile transportation) would cause gasoline demand to shift in.

Where both demand and supply shift, it is possible, at least in some cases, to predict the likely impact on price or quantity, but not *both* price and quantity. For example, suppose that refinery labor costs rise while the price of public transportation falls. Beginning with demand curve $D_0$ and supply curve $S_0$ in Figure 2.9, the increase in refinery labor costs causes the gasoline supply curve to shift left to $S_1$. The decline in the price of public transportation causes the gasoline demand curve to shift left to $D_1$. The equilibrium quantity of gasoline will clearly fall because both curves have shifted left; along both the supply and demand curves there is less output at every price. However, the effect on the equilibrium price is ambiguous. The shift left in supply along the original demand curve ($D_0$) would normally cause the equilibrium price to rise. On the other hand, the shift left in demand along the original supply curve ($S_0$) would normally cause the equilibrium price to fall.

### INTERPRETING SIMULTANEOUS SHIFTS

One of the most common mistakes made by students using supply-demand analysis given simultaneous shifts in both the supply and demand curves is to assume that the situation shown in the supply-and-demand diagram they have drawn is an exact reflection of the situation in the real-world market. In cases where the demand and supply curves are both shifting, students will tend to draw shifts so that they offset each other exactly. The diagram will show that the net result is no change in equilibrium price or quantity.

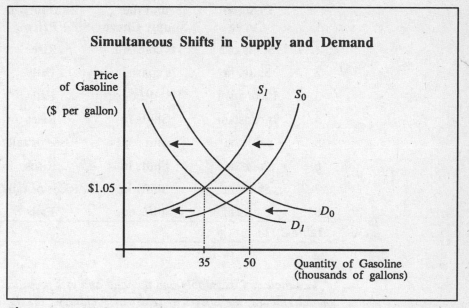

**Figure 2.9** *A leftward shift in supply occurring at the same time as a leftward shift in demand will definitely lower equilibrium quantity. However, the effects on equilibrium price are theoretically ambiguous despite appearances in the graph.*

For example, as shown in Figure 2.9, because the inward shift in supply and the inward shift in demand offset each other, students will conclude that price remains the same. However, we do not really know whether the shifts of the supply and demand curve will offset each other exactly. All we really know is the direction the curves are shifting. Perhaps the demand curve is shifting far to the left, and the supply curve is shifting a little to the left. In this case, equilibrium price will probably fall. In order really to determine whether equilibrium price will rise or fall, it is necessary to know the exact magnitude of the shifts in both supply and demand. Unless this information is given, it is not possible to make any prediction concerning the effect of these changes on price, even if the supply-demand diagram that we drew for analysis happens to suggest that prices have gone up, down, or remained the same.

## SUPPLY AND DEMAND SHIFTS: THE RANGE OF POSSIBILITIES

Table 2.1 presents the complete list of possible outcomes, given both simple and simultaneous shifts in supply and demand. These outcomes can easily be verified by drawing some supply and demand diagrams for yourself.

### Effects on Equilibrium Price and Quantity, Given Demand and Supply Shifts

| | If the Demand Curve | and the Supply Curve | Equilibrium Price | Equilibrium Quantity |
|---|---|---|---|---|
| 1. | Shifts out | Is constant | Rises | Rises |
| 2. | Shifts in | Is constant | Falls | Falls |
| 3. | Is constant | Shifts out | Falls | Rises |
| 4. | Is constant | Shifts in | Rises | Falls |
| 5. | Shifts out | Shifts out | Rises or falls | Rises |
| 6. | Shifts out | Shifts in | Rises | Rises or falls |
| 7. | Shifts in | Shifts in | Rises or falls | Falls |
| 8. | Shifts in | Shifts out | Falls | Rises or falls |

*Table 2.1*

*As simple as it is, supply-and-demand analysis provides an important means of determining the effects of real-world changes on the two most important economic variables in any market: price and quantity. The shapes of the supply and demand curves are seen to depict certain assumptions concerning the behavior of producers and consumers. The exact quantities supplied and demanded at various prices are determined by the shift factors affecting both supply and demand. Much of the theoretical and empirical work done by economists relates to estimating the shapes of supply and demand curves: determining how responsive quantities supplied and demanded are to price changes and to changes in various shift factors. This will be seen often in future chapters, especially in the study of microeconomics.*

# Part II

*Macroeconomic Theory*

# 3

## *An Overview of Macroeconomic Measures and Theory*

*T*his chapter introduces the major aggregates used as the basis for macroeconomic analysis. It sets the stage for development of a complete model of the economy as a whole, discussed in later chapters. This model describes the interrelationships among macroeconomic aggregates. It allows analysis of the effects of changes in aggregates on other aggregates and enables predictions to be made concerning the future state of the economy, given changes occurring in the present. The concepts and definitions presented here are important in understanding what the aggregates in economic models are, how they are related to one another, and how they can affect the economy as a whole.

Changes in the output of tangible goods and services are fundamentally important in determining a society's standard of living. Therefore, further definitions deal with the relationship between real and nominal measures of economic activity, a distinction useful for separating the effects of price changes from the effects of changes in the output of actual goods and services. Finally, attention is focused on inflation and unemployment—the problems they cause, and their importance within the study of macroeconomics.

Macroeconomic theory is concerned with the performance of the economy as reflected in aggregate measures of economic activity. While the actions of individuals and firms are important, only broad measures of their economic activities form the basis of analysis. The ultimate goal of macroeconomics is to understand those factors that will lead to high levels of *economic growth and low unemployment and inflation. Toward this end, macroeconomics also deals with how government spending, taxes, and changes in the money supply affect the economy and how macroeconomic policy can be used to improve the economy's performance.*

*Modern macroeconomic analysis originated with the publication of* The General Theory of Employment, Interest, and Money, *by John Maynard Keynes in 1936. Keynes was troubled by the fact that the theories used by economists at that time could not explain the persistence of mass unemployment during the Great Depression. Using the major aggregates of economic activity, including consumption, investment, and government spending, Keynes developed a model that serves as the foundation for virtually all forms of macroeconomic analysis today. Even those economists who do not consider themselves to be Keynesians generally make use of the components of the basic Keynesian model. Since Keynes's time, many economists have sought ways of linking microeconomics and macroeconomics by developing the micro foundations of macroeconomics. Treatment of this foundation usually lies beyond the scope of an introductory economics course. However, a number of important microeconomic concepts are present in macroeconomic analysis.*

# ACCOUNTING CONVENTIONS AT THE MACROECONOMIC LEVEL

Because macroeconomic theory is based upon aggregate measures of economic activity, it is important to have a solid understanding of these measures and their relationship to one another. These relationships are officially documented in the *National Income and Product Accounts* which show the connection between *gross national product*, the main indicator used to measure the economy's performance, and its components. In addition to gross national product, other important aggregates are the quantity of money, price level, rate of interest, unemployment rate, rate of inflation, and the components of aggregate expenditure, which include consumption, investment, government spending, and net exports.

## Calculating the Economy's Gross National Product

Gross national product (GNP) is a measure of the value of the total final output produced in the economy in a given time period, usually one year. Except for a few minor adjustments, there are several equivalent ways to calculate GNP. First, GNP is equal to the sum of *values added* by firms as they produce output. Second, GNP is equal to the value of *expenditure* on the final goods and services produced. Third, GNP is equal to the sum of *factor payments*, the wages, interest, profit, and rent paid to *factors of production*. All methods of calculating GNP yield the same value; together, they provide important information on how expenditure and income are related.

## THE VALUE ADDED APPROACH

*Value added* can be thought of as the difference between the value of a product at the time of its entry into a manufacturing process and its value at the end of that process. For example, in a simple economy in which land is free and there is no capital, if a farmer plants corn in the spring and harvests corn in the fall, there will be a difference between the value of the seeds planted and the value of the harvested corn sold. This difference represents value added. In this simple economy, value added is attributable to wages paid to the farmer for his or her labor. Although the productivity of the sun and soil play a role, because they are not compensated, only the farmer's wages will count toward value added.

Similar situations occur throughout the economy as industries transform raw inputs into final outputs. One industry's finished ouput often represents an input for another industry at the next stage of the production process. For example, the tire and battery industries produce finished goods that are used as inputs to the automobile industry. Value is added as these and other inputs to the auto industry are assembled into automobiles by the land, labor, capital, and entrepreneurial skills employed by automakers.

According to the value-added approach to calculating GNP, the sum of values added by each of the industries in the economy is equal to GNP. Thus, only the values *added* by the tire, battery, automobile, and other industries are counted toward GNP. If the final value of output for all industries was also counted, there would be double counting. For example, if the value of the tires produced by the tire company was added to the final value of automobile output, the value of tire output would be counted twice.

## THE FINAL EXPENDITURES APPROACH

After passing through the entire production process, individual goods reaching the market have a certain final value. This value is equal to the total value added in producing them. According to the final expenditures approach, the value of all final goods and services produced in the economy in a given year equals GNP. These goods may be placed into certain categories, depending upon the type of good or who purchases them. For macroeconomic analysis, these categories include *consumption goods*, *investment goods*, *government goods*, and *net exports*.

It is extremely important to note that GNP for any year is composed only of final goods and services produced *in that year*. For example, sales of items such as used automobiles do not count in current GNP because they were already counted in a past GNP. Similarly, purchases of stock in the stock market will not increase GNP; such purchases represent a transfer of ownership in a pre-existing corporation from the old stockholder to the new. Finally, note that only *final* sales are counted. As in the value-added approach, if the sale of the battery that goes into an automobile were counted as part of GNP along with the entire automobile, GNP would be too high because of double counting: the sale of the battery would be counted for both the battery itself *and* as part of the sale price of the car.

## THE FACTOR PAYMENTS APPROACH

Ignoring taxes and depreciation, using the *factor payments approach*, GNP is equal to the sum of the payments to the factors of production responsible for producing the goods and services sold in the economy. This approach to measuring GNP is closely related to the value-added approach. Specifically, the value added to any product includes the wages, interest, profit, and rent paid, respectively, to the laborers, owners of capital, entrepreneurs, and owners of land who take part in the production process and thereby add value to raw inputs.

## APPROACHES TO MEASURING GNP: AN EXAMPLE

The relationships among the value added, final-expenditure, and factor payment approach is seen in Table 3.1. A simple hypothetical economy is shown in which there are three sectors. As shown in the factor payments, the agricultural sector uses land and labor to create an output worth $10. This output is sold to the transportation sector. Using the inputs capital and labor, the trans-

### Alternative Methods of Calculating GNP

|  | Agricultural Sector | Transportation Sector | Retail Sector | Final Sale (GNP) |
|---|---|---|---|---|
| Initial Value | 0 | 10 | 14 | |
| | | | | **Total** |
| Value Added | +10 | +4 | +9 | 23 |
| **Factor Payments** | | | | **Total** |
| Wages | 3 | 3 | 6 | 12 |
| Interest | 0 | 1 | 0 | 1 |
| Profit | 0 | 0 | 3 | 3 |
| Rent | 7 | 0 | 0 | 7 |
| Total | 10 | 4 | 9 | 23 |

*Table 3.1*

portation sector transports the output of the agricultural sector to the retail trade sector, adding a value of $4. The product, now worth $14, is made available for final consumption using labor and entrepreneurial skills that add $9 worth of value. The sum of the values added is $23, which equals GNP in this simple economy.

At each stage of the process, value added equals the sum of the factor payments for each sector. For example, agriculture adds $10 of value. This value added is composed of the $3 wage payment and $7 rent payment to the laborers and landowners responsible for agricultural output. The transportation sector adds $4 of value because of the wages and interest it pays to laborers and capital owners. In the retail-trade sector, the $9 worth of factor payments are comprised of $6 of wages and $3 of profit. The sum of the factor payments equals $23, which equals GNP.

The final product is sold to consumers for a price of $23. Its final sale price, equivalent to GNP using the final-expenditure approach, is equal to the sum of the values added or the sum of the factor payments. If GNP was calculated as the sum of the sale price over all sectors of the economy—that is, the sum of the initial value and the final sale— there would be double counting, and a number far in excess of GNP would result.

## Gross National Product and Disposable Income

GNP is the most important measure used to determine overall economic performance; it is the primary variable in most macroeconomic models. In turn, one of the most important determinants of GNP is personal consumption expenditure. For most individuals, *disposable income*, individual income left after taxes, is the most important determinant of personal consumption expenditure. Given the dependencies among macroeconomic variables, it is important to be familiar with the other measures that are added to and subtracted from GNP in determining disposable income.

### NET NATIONAL PRODUCT AND THE CAPITAL CONSUMPTION ALLOWANCE

The *capital consumption allowance* is a measure of the degree to which the nation's capital stock has depreciated during a year. Because a part of the expenditure for capital goods (equipment and structures) is used to replace worn-out capital equipment, the economy is no better off in new productive capacity with this expenditure. To measure that part of production that actually augments wealth in the economy and adds to its productive capability, the capital consumption allowance is subtracted from GNP. The resulting measure is known as *net national product*.

As seen in Table 3.2, GNP equals $5,514.6 billion in the third quarter of 1990. The capital consumption allowance is $579.3 billion. Therefore, net national product equals $4,935.3 billion.

## Relation of GNP and Disposable Income 1990[a]

| | |
|---|---:|
| GNP: | $5,514.6 |
| Minus: | |
| capital consumption allowance: | 579.3 |
| Equals *Net National Product*: | $4,935.3 |
| Minus: | |
| indirect business taxes and business transfer payments: | 482.9 |
| Equals *National Income*: | $4,452.4 |
| Minus: | |
| undistributed corporate profits and corporate profits taxes: | 175.8 |
| contributions for social security: | 511.3 |
| Plus: | |
| interest to individuals: | 217.0 |
| transfer payments: | 696.4 |
| Equals *Personal Income*: | $4,678.7 |
| Minus: | |
| personal tax payments: | 709.5 |
| Equals *Disposable Personal Income*: | $3,969.2 |

[a]Measured in 1990 dollars. Data are from the *Economic Report of the President* 1991 for the third quarter of 1990.

**Table 3.2**

## NATIONAL INCOME

*Indirect business taxes* are sales taxes, excise taxes, and property taxes paid by businesses. These taxes increase the price of products over and above the value imparted through payments to factors of production. *Business transfer payments* represent business liability payments for personal injury, corporate gifts to nonprofit organizations, and bad debts. Subtraction of indirect business taxes and business transfer payments from net national product yields *National Income*.

As seen in Table 3.2, in 1990, indirect business taxes and business transfer payments equal $482.9 billion. Subtracting this amount from 1990's $4,935.3 net national product yields national income, equal to $4,452.4 billion.

According to definitions used in formulating the National Income and Product Accounts, national income represents the "income that originates in the production of the goods and services attributable to labor and property supplied by residents of the United States." It therefore equals the value of wage, interest, profit, and rent payments to the factors of production for their productive activities.

## PERSONAL INCOME

In estimating the income that individuals are free to spend or save, account must be taken of corporate income taxes levied on the profits of corporations. Also, some of these profits, known as *undistributed corporate profits* are not paid to corporate shareholders and therefore do not add to the spendable income of individuals; they are used by corporations for purchases of capital or other expenses. In addition, businesses (and homeowners) pay interest on debts and individuals earn income through ownership of interest-bearing assets. Only the difference between these two adds to personal income. Aside from these considerations, Social Security taxes are paid by workers to the government and the government augments, through *transfer payments*. the incomes of veterans, retirees, welfare recipients, and other individuals. When corporate income taxes, undistributed corporate profits, and Social Security taxes are subtracted from national income, and when transfer payments and interest earnings are added, *personal income* is calculated.

In Table 3.2, undistributed corporate profits and corporate profits taxes amount to $175.8 billion, and Social Security taxes equal $511.3 billion. Subtracting these amounts and adding $217 billion in interest to individuals and $696.4 billion in transfer payments yields personal income equal to $4,678.7 billion.

## DISPOSABLE INCOME

Personal income less *personal income taxes* equals *disposable personal income*. In 1990, personal tax payments amounted to $709.5 billion. Therefore, since personal income equals $4,678.7 billion, disposable income equals $3,969.2 billion.

# REAL GNP, NOMINAL GNP, AND THE PRICE INDEX

In 1990 GNP of the U.S. economy was $5,518.9 billion. In 1970 GNP was $1,015.5 billion. On the surface it appears that GNP increased by a factor of 5 between 1970 and 1990. However, aside from rising production of goods and services, the prices at which those goods and services are valued have also gone up. The measures of GNP shown for 1970 and 1990 represent *nominal GNP* values, GNP values calculated using the prices of those time periods. To separate the increase in GNP due to changes in output from the increase due to changes in prices, *real GNP* must be calculated. Knowing how real output is changing reveals how the available quantity of actual goods and services has increased and is extremely important in gauging the performance of the economy.

Calculating real values from nominal values is one of the most important skills an economist can possess. Aside from the time spent by economists in developing sound theoretical measures for this purpose, each year much time and money are spent by the government gathering the data and estimating the *price indices* necessary to transform nominal into real values. Such indices include the consumer price index, the implicit price deflator for GNP, and the producer price index. The formula for calculating real values, given nominal values, is simple, and familiarity with the appropriate price measures required for their calculation is easily acquired.

## Nominal versus Real GNP

*Nominal GNP* refers to GNP calculated at the prices prevailing in the time period when the output is produced. It is also known as *current dollar GNP*. Current or nominal GNP for 1990 can be thought of as the sum of values of final goods and services produced in 1990, where values are determined by the prices shoppers would actually see in the stores that year.

*Real GNP* is GNP calculated at the prices that prevailed in some *base year*. A base year is an arbitrarily chosen benchmark year; prices from the base year are used to value the quantities produced in other years before, during, or after the base year. By weighting the output produced in different years with the prices of the chosen base year, the effects of price changes between years are removed. This makes comparison of real output levels between different time periods possible.

## Calculating Real GNP

To understand the conversion process from nominal to real values, consider a simple economy in which only one good is produced. Suppose in 1980 10 units of the good were produced at a price of $2 each. Nominal GNP in 1980 therefore equals $20. In 1990, 15 units of the good are produced at a price of $4 each, so nominal GNP is $60. On the surface it appears that GNP has risen by a factor of 3. However, if the 1990 price is replaced with the 1980 price and GNP for 1990 is recalculated, the value of real GNP equals $30.

Because its prices were used, 1980 is the base year. Because they are valued using the same prices, the output actually produced in these two years can be compared. Using the ratio of real GNP in 1990 to real GNP in 1980, output is seen to be 1.5 times as great in 1990 as it was in 1980 ($30/$20 = 1.5). This ratio is the same as the ratio of actual output produced in 1990 to that produced in 1980 (15/10 = 1.5).

It is important to note that the base year price chosen does not have to be a price that prevailed in either 1980 or 1990. For example, if 1985 was chosen as the base year and the product's price in 1985 was $3.00 per unit, real GNP in 1980 would equal $30 and real GNP in 1990 would equal $45. Once again, by rebasing the price used to form values in the years under consideration, comparisons of actual output changes can be made. The ratio of real GNP values for 1980 and 1990 with 1985 as a base year is $45/$30 or 1.5.

## THE PRICE INDEX

To calculate real GNP given nominal GNP, a *price index* is used. A price index is a ratio of the *price level* in the current year to the price level in the base year. The economy's price level in any year is a single summary measure of all prices in the economy. The price index is calculated using weights based upon a *market basket* of goods representative of a typical variety of product purchases at the time.

The price index as published by the government always appears as a single number. For example, in 1970, the price index used to calculate real GNP equals 42 with 1982 used as a base year. This number means that a typical product costing 42 cents in 1970 cost $1 in 1982. The price index in 1990 is 131.5 with 1982 as a base year. This means that it takes about $1.32 in 1990 to purchase an equivalent market basket of goods costing $1 in 1982. How much would $1 in 1990 purchase in 1982? Because $1 in 1982 is equivalent to $1.32 in 1990, it follows that $1 in 1990 is equivalent to about 76 cents in 1982 ($1.00/$1.32 = .76). Price indices are stated in percentage terms and always equal 100 in the base year. In a base year there is no difference between nominal and real values.

## CONVERTING NOMINAL TO REAL VALUES

To transform nominal values into real values, divide the nominal value by an appropriate price index. To understand why this technique works, let $Q_{90}$ represent the real output produced in the economy in 1990 and let $P_{90}$ represent the price level for that year. Consistent with the definition of a price index, the ratio of prices in some current year to some base year, $P_{90}/P_{82}$ is the price index between 1990 and 1982 (note that 1982 is the base year). Nominal GNP in 1990 is real output for 1990 multiplied by the price level for 1990. Notationally,

$$Nominal\, \text{GNP}\ (1990) = P_{90}\, Q_{90}$$

To transform or *deflate* nominal GNP into real GNP, divide the nominal GNP value by the price index. This calculation appears as

$$\frac{Nominal\,\text{GNP}}{Price\,Index} = \frac{P_{90}\,Q_{90}}{\dfrac{P_{90}}{P_{82}}} = \frac{P_{82}}{P_{90}}\,P_{90}\,Q_{90} = P_{82}\,Q_{90} = Real\,\text{GNP}$$

After this calculation, the output of actual goods in 1990 is valued at the prices prevailing in 1982; the effects of price changes over the 1982–1990 time period are removed.

**Calculating Real GNP: An Example.** To transform nominal values into real values, divide by the price index. Nominal GNP in 1990 was $5518.9 billion; the price index stated as a percentage with 1982 as a base was 131.5 It follows that real GNP stated in terms of 1982 dollars equals

$$\frac{5,518.9}{131.5} = 41.696 \times 100 = \$4,196.9\,billion$$

Multiplication by 100 is necessary because, by convention, the price index is stated as a percentage (if the denominator increases 100-fold, the numerator must also).

If nominal GNP from various years is deflated using 1982 as a base year, it is possible to compare the actual or real output produced in these years without the effects of different prices. Thus, nominal GNP in 1970 equals $1,015.5 billion and the price index for 1970 with 1982 as a base year equals 42. Real GNP for 1970 expressed in 1982 dollars therefore equals $2,417.9 billion. Given the values for real GNP in 1970 and 1990, real output is seen to rise by a factor of 1.74, far less than the five-fold increase suggested by the nominal GNP values.

## BASE YEARS

The government regularly changes base years to avoid distortions in what constitutes a typical market basket of goods. Depending on the data set used, you are likely to find different base years. Before 1982, the last base year in use was 1972. Following 1982, the next base year is 1987.

**Published Price Indices**

The government estimates a number of price indices that are used to deflate GNP and other nominal measures of economic activity. A partial list of such indices includes the implicit price deflator, the consumer price index, and the producer price index. The *implicit price deflator* is estimated by the U.S. Department of Commerce, Bureau of Economic Analysis. Both the *consumer price index* and the *producer price index* are calculated by the U.S. Department of Labor, Bureau of Labor Statistics. These indices, along with data on the

National Income and Product Accounts, can be found in the *Economic Report of the President*, an annual publication of the U.S. Government Printing Office. The choice of which price index to use depends upon the types of goods involved in the deflation process.

### THE IMPLICIT PRICE DEFLATOR

The implicit price deflator is the price index used to calculate real GNP, given nominal GNP. It is a broad-based price index, estimated using a market basket consisting of the entire range of goods and services actually produced in the economy. It therefore does not account for changes in the prices of imports.

### THE CONSUMER PRICE INDEX

The consumer price index (CPI) is the price index used to calculate real spending by typical urban consumers. The CPI is calculated using weights based on the fraction of expenditures on each of the goods and services consumed in a typical consumer's market basket. For example, typical households spend about 15 percent of their income on food and 30 percent on housing. Therefore, in calculating the consumer price index, food prices account for 15 percent of the index's value and housing prices account for 30 percent. Because it is the most representative price index for the goods purchased by consumers, it is appropriate to deflate consumer income using the CPI; a measure of real consumer income is thereby determined.

### THE PRODUCER PRICE INDEX

The producer price index is the price index used to calculate the real value of goods and materials purchased by producers as inputs to production processes.

## WHAT GNP DOES NOT MEASURE

Because gross national product is a summary measure of economic performance, it is tempting to believe that higher levels of GNP are associated with a higher standard of living for everyone. However, GNP does not account for all aspects of personal well-being. In addition, GNP is not a comprehensive measure of all economic activity. Before blindly accepting or using GNP as a measure of well-being and economic activity, the following factors should be considered.

## Income Distribution and Population

The magnitude of a country's GNP does not say anything about the income of individual citizens and does not reflect how income is distributed among individuals. If a country with a large GNP also has a large population, individual incomes might be very low compared with those in countries with smaller GNPs and smaller populations. By dividing GNP by population to form *per capita* GNP, this confusion can be resolved. In 1989, GNP in the United States equaled $5,200.8 billion. With a population of 248.762 million, per capita GNP equaled $20,906.73.

In terms of income distribution, the output of a country with a very high GNP might be shared among a few very rich individuals. In this situation, measures of *median income* provide much more information on the distribution of wealth. By definition, 50 percent of all individuals in a country have an income above the median level, and 50 percent have an income below the median. For U.S. families in 1989, median income was equal to $35,975.00.

## Environmental Costs, Wars, and Natural Disasters

GNP does not account for the costs incurred in natural or man-made disasters. An oil spill having negative environmental repercussions will not lower GNP. However, the cleanup activities will cause GNP to rise. Similarly, a flood might cause death and wipe out housing and businesses. While the output lost because businesses are destroyed does reduce GNP, GNP does not account for the value of the structures destroyed or lives lost. As with the cleanup after an oil spill, reconstruction activities will tend to raise GNP.

## Non Market Activities

GNP measures only market activities. Housework and do-it-yourself work counts toward GNP if performed by a housekeeper or worker paid for the service, but work done by individuals for themselves does not. Unless reported to the government, barter transactions are not included. This failure to include nonmarket transactions can lead to serious underestimation of productive activities in less-developed economies where barter is common. Similarly, GNP does not account for economic activity that is against the law. The proceeds from illegal gambling, prostitution, and drug sales are not included.

## Leisure

One very important good for most individuals is leisure time. However, if more time is spent pursuing leisure activities, less time is available for market activities. Even though GNP might be lower as a result, it is not necessarily true that society's welfare is reduced.

# INFLATION AND UNEMPLOYMENT

Inflation and unemployment are the two most obvious signs of trouble for the macro economy. Both problems have a direct effect on the well-being of individuals. Each tends to undermine faith in the ability of our economic system to provide a stable standard of living. As a means of highlighting the ineptitude of their rival's economic policies, some politicians have gone so far as to form a *misery index*, defined as the sum of the inflation and unemployment rates.

Measuring inflation and unemployment and their effects on individuals is discussed below. Later chapters tend to treat the rates of unemployment and inflation like any other variable in the macro model. The personal pain and suffering of individuals due to their presence can easily be overlooked. Therefore, to understand the real-world relevance of macroeconomics for individuals, the various costs associated with inflation and unemployment should constantly be kept in mind. Finding solutions to these problems constitutes one of the most important reasons for studying economics.

## Measuring Inflation and Its Costs

*Inflation* refers to a sustained increase in the economy's price level. The *inflation rate* is the rate of change in the price index between any two *adjacent* years. If $P_0$ is last year's price index and $P_1$ is this year's,

$$Inflation\, Rate = \frac{P_1 - P_0}{P_0} \times 100$$

The inflation rate expresses the difference between the price level in two adjacent years as a percentage of the price level in the earlier year.

As a concrete example of the inflation rate calculation, the consumer price index in 1989 was 124.0 with 1982 as a base year. The consumer price index in 1990 was 130.7. The rate of inflation over these years is calculated as

$$\frac{130.7 - 124.0}{124.0} \times 100 = 5.4\%$$

### CATEGORIES OF INFLATION

Inflation is often categorized according to its severity. At one extreme are the low 2 to 4 percent rates of inflation experienced by the U.S. economy from the end of World War II until the mid 1960s. Inflation in this range raised little concern; it did not cause sudden declines in the purchasing power of money, and it could be anticipated and accounted for in loan and wage contracts. At the other extreme is the *hyperinflation* experienced by Germany in the 1920s, during which the price level rose by 42 billion percent. Such inflation destroys all faith in a nation's currency and can lead an economy to ruin.

The high-single-digit and low-double-digit rates of inflation experienced in the U.S. during the 1970s and early 1980s were a source of great concern regarding the stability of the economy. The recessions of 1974–1975 and 1982 were due at least in part to the government's efforts to control inflation. Other countries often experience rates of inflation in the high- double-digit or even triple-digit range. Many countries are able to tolerate such *galloping* rates for years without economic collapse.

## THE COSTS OF INFLATION

During periods of inflation, individuals will tend to keep more of their cash in banks, where interest earnings offset losses in the value of money. The extra trips taken to the bank involve time and travel costs, classified by economists as *shoe-leather costs*. It is sometimes argued that if inflation is fully anticipated and prices and incomes rise uniformly, there are no real costs to inflation except shoe-leather costs.

However, certainty and uniformity regarding the rate of inflation seldom exist. Inflation tends to affect all individuals in society in one way or another, and more than shoe-leather costs are involved. Individuals with higher levels of income may be better able to protect themselves against inflation by purchasing assets less likely to lose value during times of inflation. Examples include art objects, precious metals, and real estate. The costs of inflation are categorized below.

**Wealth Transfers.** When the rate of inflation is high, wealth is transferred from lenders to borrowers because the dollars in which a loan is paid back buy less than they could at the time of the loan. Money held as cash or placed into savings accounts with a rate of interest lower than the rate of inflation loses some of its purchasing power. In such circumstances, individuals with fixed incomes, such as retirees, tend to lose wealth. In extreme circumstances, money saved over an entire lifetime can become almost worthless.

**Uncertainty.** The presence of inflation makes planning for the future more difficult. This in turn can affect economic growth because investment priorities are altered. If inflation creates uncertainty concerning the future, short-term investments become more common; worthwhile long term investments may not be made.

**Transactions Costs.** During times of inflation, money is no longer a safe store of value. It can purchase fewer real goods and services as the price level rises. To offset the effects of inflation, households will keep their cash in interest-bearing assets. Aside from the time costs associated with more trips to the bank to obtain money for purchases, lack of faith in money's ability to hold its value can lead to substitution of barter transactions for money-based transactions. Hence, the efficiency gained through the use of money is lost.

**Anti-Inflation Policy.** In response to high rates of inflation, governments engage in policies designed to bring about recessions, which cause unemployment to rise. While such actions can cause prices to stabilize, there is a cost to those who lose their jobs.

## Measuring Unemployment and its Costs

From the economist's perspective, when individuals are willing to work for the prevailing market wage but are unable to find work at that wage, unemployment is said to exist. Officially, the *unemployment rate* is defined as the percentage of the total *labor force* (those individuals with jobs or seeking employment) who do not have jobs. It does not include *discouraged workers*, those individuals who have searched for work but have given up because of a lack of opportunities.

In 1990, the unemployment rate was 5.5 percent for all civilian workers. This rate is composed of unemployment rates for various groups. While the overall unemployment rate was 5.5 percent, the unemployment rate was 5.4 percent for females, 11.3 percent for blacks, and 15.5 percent for teenagers.

### CATEGORIES OF UNEMPLOYMENT

As with the inflation rate, it is possible to categorize types of unemployment and to consider the costs of unemployment. Categories include *frictional*, *structural*, and *cyclical* unemployment. Unlike the categories of inflation, which are based on severity, categories of unemployment reflect the underlying causes of unemployment.

**Frictional Unemployment.** The frictional unemployment rate refers to the fraction of the total unemployment rate attributable to workers between jobs as they seek a better match between their skills and salary expectations and the requirements and salary offers of employers. For example, a steel-worker might quit work in Pennsylvania and move to Ohio, drawn by the prospect of better pay for the same or similar work.

**Structural Unemployment.** Structural unemployment refers to individuals out of work because technological change has made their skills obsolete. For example, assembly-line workers may have few opportunities to find new jobs using their skills if they are replaced by robots.

**Cyclical Unemployment.** The cyclically unemployed are individuals out of work because the economy is in a state of recession. Individuals who are cyclically unemployed generally return to work in the same or a similar position when the recession is over.

Of the three categories of unemployment, only frictional unemployment is desirable; a better match of skills between workers and employers should lead to higher overall productivity. Structural unemployment implies that labor resources are not fully utilized; it can be cured through education, retraining, or acceptance by workers of lower quality jobs and lower pay. Cyclical unemployment also wastes resources because individuals with useful skills are inactive; for this reason, the government seeks to insure that the economy operates as close to the full-employment level as possible.

## THE COSTS OF UNEMPLOYMENT

The costs of unemployment are naturally felt most directly by those who are unemployed. Aside from reductions in family income, high rates of unemployment have been associated with increased crime rates, increased suicide rates, and other signs of increased social and personal stress. However, the reduced levels of overall expenditure that occur when the unemployment rate is high have an effect on all members of society; because unemployed workers face reduced consumption possibilities, income levels for everyone are likely to grow more slowly during times of high unemployment. The precise relationship between deviations in the level of GNP from the full-employment level and changes in the rate of unemployment is known as *Okun's Law*. Each 1 percent rise in the unemployment rate above the full employment level is associated with a 2 to 3 percent decline in GNP below its potential level.

Because GNP can affect investment, future economic growth can be reduced by high rates of unemployment in the present. Along with these effects, the federal budget is more likely to be in deficit during periods of high unemployment; welfare benefits increase, and tax revenues fall. With a recession-induced budget deficit, funding for important public projects such as health programs, highways, and education may be reduced or postponed.

# INTEREST RATES

Aside from GNP, unemployment, the price level, and the inflation rate, the economy's rate of interest provides important information to individuals about borrowing costs and financial investment opportunities. It also plays an important role in determining the state and level of economic activity. The interest rate represents the price of money. This is true in the sense that when money is borrowed the interest rate determines how much in addition to the original loan must be repaid.

Because it represents a rate of return on money that is readily available to anyone who places funds in interest bearing assets, (e.g., savings accounts, government bonds) the interest rate has an important function in determining the level of investment. Investors will compare the potential return from their investment to the interest rate. Investments that yield a rate of return less than the interest rate will not be undertaken; earning the interest rate on the funds to be used for investment is more profitable than undertaking the investment. This fact and others regarding the decision to invest are discussed more fully in Chapter 4.

## Real versus Nominal Interest Rates

The *real interest rate* is the amount by which the nominal or prevailing interest rate exceeds the rate of inflation. For those who lend money, it represents the return after the effects of inflation are removed.

To estimate the real rate of interest, substract the inflation rate from the nominal rate of interest. For example, if the nominal rate of interest is 12 percent and the rate of inflation is 5 percent, the real rate of interest is 7 percent. Thus, an individual who loans someone $1 at the beginning of the year would be repaid about $1.12 at the end of the year. However, because of inflation, in real terms the individual who loaned the money could not purchase as many goods with the $1.12 as he or she could at the beginning of the year. In fact, the $1.12 would purchase the equivalent of about $1.07 of goods at the beginning of the year, implying that the real rate of interest earned is 7 percent.

It is important to distinguish between calculating the real rate of interest (subtract the inflation rate from the nominal rate of interest) and calculating the real level of GNP (divide the nominal level of GNP by the price index).

*The definitions and concepts presented in this chapter serve as the basis of the macroeconomic model to be developed in the following chapters. The next two chapters make use of many of these relationships—especially the connection between GNP, consumption, and disposable income—in setting forth the simple Keynesian model. In subsequent chapters, more details are presented concerning the components of aggregate expenditure and their influence on the level of output, unemployment, and inflation. In addition, a more complete picture of interconnections within the macro economy will emerge as the relationships between money, the interest rate, prices, and real output are developed. The importance of government activity in affecting the performance of the economy and in controlling inflation and unemployment is then considered. Finally, the effects of international trade are discussed to complete the basic model of the macro economy.*

## Selected Readings

Council of Economic Advisers. *Economic Report of the President*. Washington, D.C.: U.S. Government Printing Office. 1991.

Keynes, John M. *The General Theory of Employment Interest and Money*.

U.S. Department of Commerce, Bureau of Economic Analysis. *The National Income and Product Accounts, 1929–82*. Washington, D.C.: U.S. Government Printing Office. 1986.

# 4

## The Components of Aggregate Demand

---

*The macroeconomic relationships considered in the next two chapters serve as the foundation for all further developments of macroeconomic theory. This chapter begins with a discussion of the macroeconomic circular flow. For the U.S. economy, this flow shows the connection between the income generated in the productive activities of firms and the demand for the goods and services by consumers, investors, government, and foreign trade.*

*Each component of aggregate demand is then examined for the underlying economic factors that determine its value. Individual demand components are seen to be causally related to other, more fundamental variables. Finally, the economy's aggregate expenditure function is derived. This function serves as the basis for determining the equilibrium level of GNP. Understanding how this equilibrium level is established and the forces that cause it to change represent the main focus of the study of macroeconomics.*

## THE MACROECONOMY AND THE CIRCULAR FLOW

The connection between the aggregates used in analyzing macroeconomic activity can be seen in the *circular-flow diagram.* As shown in Figure 4.1, the economic agents are consumers, financial intermediaries, government, and

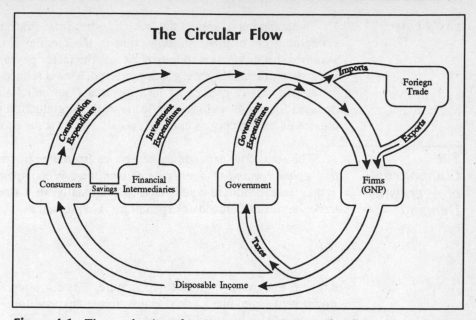

## The Circular Flow

**Figure 4.1** *The production of output generates income that flows to government in the form of taxes and to consumers in the form of disposable income. This income is transformed into consumption, investment, and government expenditure. Imports represent expenditure on foreign goods by Americans and leave the expenditure stream. Exports are purchases of American goods by foreigners and are therefore part of total expenditure on U.S. goods.*

firms. The major expenditure categories include consumption, investment, government spending, and foreign trade.

To produce output, firms pay the factors of production an income equal to the value of output produced, that is, GNP (see the value added approach and factor payment approach to calculating GNP in Chapter 3). Part of this income is paid to government in the form of *taxes*, while the remainder goes to consumers in the form of *disposable income*. Consumers spend part of their disposable income and save the rest. The portion spent becomes *consumption expenditure*, while *savings* are used by financial institutions to finance *investment expenditure*. Taxes collected by the government are used to finance *government expenditure*. Part of consumption, investment, and government expenditure flows out of our economic system and is used to purchase *imports*. On the other hand, foreign demand for American products—*exports*—add to total expenditure on U.S. goods. With everything in balance, the value of expenditure on U.S. goods equals the value of GNP. The equivalence of GNP and the value of expenditure is consistent with the final expenditures approach to calculating GNP presented in Chapter 3.

**Say's Law**

In attempting to answer the "which comes first, chicken or egg?" question concerning the ultimate starting point in the circular flow, it is sometimes assumed that production of output creates the factor payments that lead to the expenditure demand for the goods produced. This is related to *Say's law* which states that *supply creates its own demand.* The belief that the expenditure demand for goods and services leads to their production or supply (demand creates its own supply) is called *Keynes's law* by some economists.

**The Components of Aggregate Demand**

The sum of all expenditure categories from the circular flow is known as *aggregate demand* or *aggregate expenditure.* When spending is in balance, aggregate expenditure equals GNP. Notationally, in a world without foreign trade, aggregate demand or expenditure is expressed as

$$E = C + I + G \tag{4.1}$$

where $E$ represents aggregate expenditure, $C$ is consumption expenditure, $I$ is investment expenditure, and $G$ is government expenditure. With foreign trade, the expenditure function is written

$$E = C + I + G + (Ex - \text{Im}) \tag{4.2}$$

where $Ex$ represents exports (American goods purchased by foreigners) and *Im* represents imports (foreign goods purchased by Americans). Each component of aggregate demand has special characteristics important in developing the basic macro model. Each may be functionally related to variables such as GNP, the interest rate, expectations or confidence, or other factors that determine their values.

# THE CONSUMPTION FUNCTION

The largest component of aggregate demand is consumption expenditure, accounting for about 65 percent of GNP. The *consumption function* explains the determinants of aggregate consumption expenditure and serves as the most important building block in the basic macroeconomic model. Developed by Keynes in his *General Theory*, the consumption function is based upon the observed direct relationship between consumption expenditure and income. Consumption tends to increase as income increases.

Development of an economic model of consumption behavior involves finding an equation that represents this relationship as realistically as possible. The Keynesian consumption function, in the absense of any taxes, is written as a very simple linear equation:

$$C = a + mpc \text{ (GNP)} \qquad (4.3)$$

where $C$ denotes consumption expenditure, $a$ denotes *autonomous consumption*—the level of consumption when GNP is zero, and $mpc$ is the *marginal propensity to consume*. When the values of autonomous consumption and the marginal propensity to consume are estimated using real-world data, this function presents a very close approximation to the actual relationship between consumption and GNP.

## Graphical Portrayal of the Consumption Function

The consumption function is a linear (or straight-line) function. Graphically, consumption is measured on the vertical axis because it is dependent on GNP, measured on the horizontal axis. Autonomous consumption, $a$, is the intercept of the consumption function. Given the equation for the consumption function, this is true because when GNP is zero, consumption must be equal to $a$. The marginal propensity to consume, $mpc$, (described more fully below)

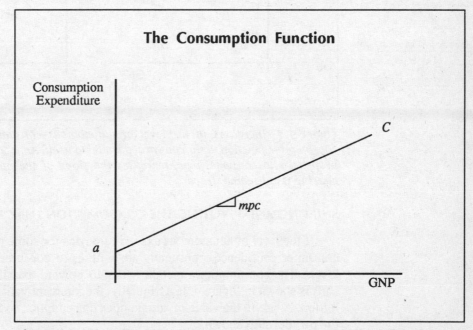

**Figure 4.2** *The relationship between consumption expenditure and GNP is known as the consumption function. It is a linear relationship based on the equation $C = a + mpc$ (GNP).*

represents the slope of the consumption function. As shown in Figure 4.2, the consumption function is an upward-sloping straight line.

## THE CONSUMPTION FUNCTION AS A STRAIGHT LINE

Observe that the form of the consumption function shown in Equation 4.3 corresponds exactly to the form of a straight line given by the standard equation $y = mx + b$. In Equation 4.3, $C$ takes the place of the dependent variable $y$, GNP corresponds to the independent variable $x$, $a$ corresponds to the intercept $b$, and the multiplicative factor $mpc$ in front of GNP corresponds to the slope coefficient $m$.

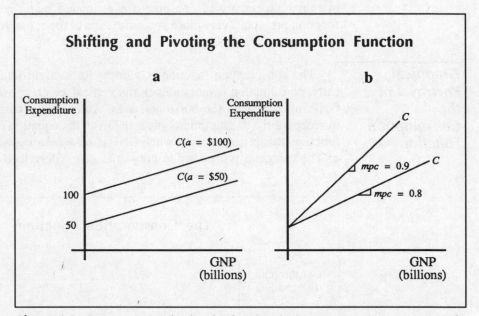

**Figure 4.3** *Increases in the level of autonomous consumption, a, cause the consumption function to shift upward, parallel to itself. An increase in the marginal propensity to consume, mpc, increases the slope of the consumption function, causing it to become steeper.*

## SHIFTING AND PIVOTING THE CONSUMPTION FUNCTION

If the level of autonomous expenditure rises for some reason, say a rise in consumer confidence, consumers are willing to consume more at all GNP levels. The consumption function will shift upward, parallel to itself. Such a shift is shown in Figure 4.3a. Originally, the intercept value, $a$, is equal to $50 billion. A rise in the value of autonomous consumption to $100 billion causes the parallel shift shown.

If the marginal propensity to consume increases for some reason, the consumption function becomes steeper and pivots upward from its intercept. In Figure 4.3b, the marginal propensity to consume is seen to increase from 0.8 to

0.9. A $1 change in GNP is associated with a 90-cent change in consumption along the steeper consumption function compared with an 80-cent change along the more horizontal consumption function.

## The Marginal Propensity to Consume

The marginal propensity to consume is the change in consumption expenditure that occurs with a change in GNP. Symbolically, the marginal propensity to consume (*mpc*) appears as

$$mpc = \frac{\Delta C}{\Delta GNP}$$

Changes in the denominator are assumed to induce changes in the numerator; thus, a change in GNP causes a change in consumption.

The marginal propensity to consume is a fraction between zero and 1. Empirically, it is based upon changes in observed aggregate consumption, given changes in income. Thus, given an increase or change in GNP of $1, consumption might increase or change by 60 cents, in accordance with a marginal propensity to consume of 0.6. Because changes in consumption and GNP are measured in dollars, the marginal propensity to consume is unit free (the dollar units cancel). Because the consumption function is a straight line, its slope, the marginal propensity to consume is constant regardless of the level of income. Whether GNP is $1 billion or $1 trillion, the marginal propensity to consume will be the same.

### CALCULATING THE MARGINAL PROPENSITY TO CONSUME

If GNP rises from $4 trillion to $5 trillion and consumption rises from $3 trillion to $3.6 trillion, the marginal propensity to consume is

$$\frac{\Delta C}{\Delta GNP} = \frac{\$3.6 - \$3.0}{\$5.0 - \$4.0} = \frac{0.6}{1} = 0.6$$

Therefore, to determine the value of the marginal propensity to consume, form the ratio of the change in consumption to the change in GNP that brings about the change in consumption.

## The Average Propensity to Consume

The average propensity to consume (*apc*) is defined as the fraction of income composed of consumption. Notationally, the average propensity to consume is the ratio of consumption expenditure to income:

$$apc = \frac{C}{GNP}$$

The formula for the average propensity to consume is concerned with the ratio of the *level* of consumption to the *level* of GNP along the consumption function. This differs from the marginal propensity to consume which is concerned with the *change* in consumption that occurs with a *change* in GNP.

If income equals $4 trillion and consumption equals $3 trillion, the average propensity to consume equals

$$\frac{C}{GNP} = \frac{\$3.0}{\$4.0} = 0.75$$

If consumption rises to $3.6 trillion and GNP rises to $5 trillion, the average propensity to consume will equal

$$\frac{C}{GNP} = \frac{\$3.6}{\$5.0} = 0.72$$

In this example, the average propensity to consume declines with the increase in income. This result holds true for any consumption function of the form

$$C = a + mpc(GNP)$$

To see this, divide both sides of the consumption function by GNP to obtain the average propensity to consume:

$$apc = \frac{C}{GNP} = \frac{a}{GNP} + mpc$$

Because autonomous consumption and the marginal propensity to consume (*a* and *mpc*) are assumed to be constants, the ratio of autonomous consumption to GNP on the right hand side of the equation will become smaller as GNP increases. Therefore, the average propensity to consume decreases as GNP increases.

## Autonomous Consumption

Besides representing the level of consumption when income is zero, autonomous consumption, *a*, incorporates a number of factors related to the consumption of goods and services by households. These factors include consumer confidence, wealth, and the interest rate. Together, these factors help determine the magnitude of autonomous consumption; therefore, they are important in establishing the precise location of the consumption function.

## CONSUMER CONFIDENCE OR EXPECTATIONS

In the macro model, it is assumed that autonomous consumption becomes larger when consumers are more optimistic. Consistent with an increase in the value of the intercept of a straight-line equation, the consumption function will shift up parallel to itself. Consumers increase consumption by a uniform amount at all income levels.

## THE VALUE OF ASSETS AND WEALTH EFFECTS

Autonomous consumption is also related to the value of assets (such as stocks, bonds, and savings accounts) held by individuals. The value of assets does not represent income, but it is expected that households with higher asset holdings will consume more at all levels of income.

Assets with values tied to the value of money change in value when the economy's price level changes. For example, a family with money in a savings account will find the value of this asset diminished when the price level rises. The family will no longer be able to purchase the same quantity of goods and services. Thus, increases in the price level working through assets tied to the value of money can reduce autonomous consumption and shift the consumption function down. If the price level falls, autonomous consumption will rise because the purchasing power of assets rises. Changes in asset values that affect autonomous consumption (brought on by price level or other effects) are classified, more or less synonymously, as *wealth*, *real balance*, and *Pigou* effects.

Increases in the value of assets held by households will cause autonomous consumption to increase, in turn causing the consumption function to shift up. For example, increases in stock prices or the value of houses (the most important asset held by most families) will cause autonomous consumption to rise. Such increases in asset values were observed in the late 1970s and 1980s as stock and housing prices soared in value. Consumption expenditure also rose across income levels, reflecting an upward shift in the economy's consumption function.

## INTEREST RATE EFFECTS

Aside from depending on income, some of the goods consumers purchase are sensitive to the interest rate. Examples include such *consumer durables* as automobiles and washing machines. When the rate of interest rises, it is expected that purchases of those durables sensitive to the interest rate will decline.

If the interest rate to purchase a new car rises by 1 percent, the ability of a family to purchase the car will decline, even though the price of the car and family income are steady. The change in the interest rate has caused the change in consumption. This change is reflected in a smaller $a$ value and a downward parallel shift of the consumption function.

## The Consumption Function and the Savings Function

Consumers have two choices regarding the income they receive. They can spend it or save it. The savings function is often derived in simple models under the assumption of no government. In this case, all taxes equal zero, and disposable income and GNP are the same. Therefore, savings plus consumption equal GNP. Using $S$ to denote savings, it follows that

$$S = GNP - C$$

From Equation 4.3, the consumption function is written

$$C = a + mpc \text{ (GNP)}$$

Therefore,

$$S = GNP - a - mpc \text{ (GNP)}$$

Collecting and rearranging terms,

$$S = -a + (1 - mpc)GNP \tag{4.4}$$

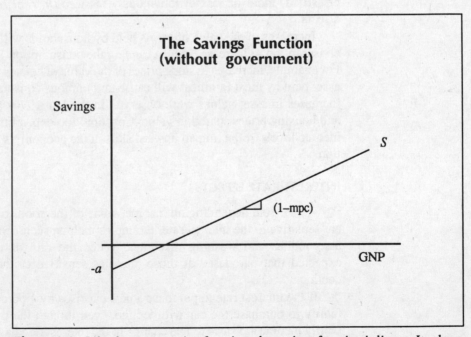

**The Savings Function
(without government)**

Savings

$S$

$(1-mpc)$

GNP

$-a$

**Figure 4.4**  *Like the consumption function, the savings function is linear. Its slope, $(1-mpc)$, is the marginal propensity to save. Its intercept, $-a$, is the negative of autonomous consumption.*

The coefficient $(1 - mpc)$ represents the *marginal propensity to save*. Given a $1 rise in GNP, savings will rise by this amount. As seen in Figure 4.4, when graphed, this savings function has an intercept equal to minus the level of autonomous consumption and a slope equal to the marginal propensity to save. From the consumption function, autonomous consumption represents the amount of consumption that takes place when income is zero. From the savings function, minus autonomous consumption can be thought to represent the *dissavings* that takes place to pay for this consumption.

## THE MARGINAL PROPENSITY TO SAVE

The marginal propensity to save is defined as the change in savings that takes place given a one dollar change in GNP. For example, if the marginal propensity to consume is 0.8 and GNP rises by $1, consumption will rise by 80 cents. Therefore, because consumers spend or save the entire amount of any change in income, savings will rise by 20 cents. This is equivalent to the marginal propensity to save $(1 - 0.8)$ multiplied by the $1 change in income. The sum of the marginal propensity to save and the marginal propensity to consume is 1. This reflects the fact that all disposable income goes either to consumption expenditure or savings.

## The Consumption Function and Taxes

With taxes, consumption becomes a function of *disposable income* rather than GNP. To account for the presence of taxes, the basic consumption function shown in Equation 4.3 has to be modified slightly. The consumption function with taxes appears as

$$C = a + mpc \ (DI)$$

The letters DI denote disposable income. By definition, disposable income is GNP after taxes. It is therefore possible to write

$$DI = GNP - \text{Tax Revenues}$$

## PROPORTIONAL, PROGRESSIVE, AND LUMP-SUM TAXES

Taxes are either related to income or not related to income. Taxes unrelated to the level of income include those imposed on cigarettes and liquor, and property taxes. *Lump-sum taxes* are also independent of income. An example of a lump-sum tax would be a tax of the same amount placed on each individual in a country. For example, with a U.S. population of 250 million people, if the government imposed a head tax of $10 per person, it would collect $2.5 billion in revenues.

Taxes based on a fixed percentage of income are said to be *proportional*. Thus, a simple proportional tax, $t$, on income would collect $t$(GNP) dollars in revenue. For example, if the proportional tax rate is 28 percent, 28 cents in tax revenue will be collected for every dollar of GNP. With a GNP level of $5,000 billion and a proportional tax rate of 28 percent, $1,400 billion in taxes will be collected.

In reality, income taxes are *progressive*. That is, tax rates rise with income. For example, under 1990 U.S. tax law, as income increases, the income tax rate rises from 15 to 28 to 33 percent. Calculating these different tax rates at different income levels greatly complicates development of the basic model without adding greatly to the explanation of how equilibrium GNP is determined. Therefore, only lump-sum and proportional taxes are usually considered in introductory discussions.

## INCORPORATING TAXES INTO THE CONSUMPTION FUNCTION

Denoting the revenues collected from lump-sum taxes as $T$ and those collected from proportional taxes as $t(\text{GNP})$, total tax revenues equal $T + t\,(\text{GNP})$. Disposable income is then calculated as

$$\text{DI} = \text{GNP} - \text{Tax Revenues}$$

$$\text{DI} = \text{GNP} - T - t(\text{GNP})$$

$$\text{DI} = (1 - t)\text{GNP} - T$$

The consumption function takes the form

$$C = a + mpc\,(\text{DI})$$

or

$$C = a + mpc[(1 - t)\text{GNP} - T]$$

and finally, after rearranging terms,

$$C = a - mpc(T) + mpc\,(1 - t)\text{GNP} \qquad\qquad (4.5)$$

Note that terms related and unrelated to the level of GNP have been gathered together. Graphically, this consumption function appears as the lowest line shown in Figure 4.5.

The consumption function with taxes is still a straight line; GNP is not raised to any power and does not appear in the denominator of a fraction. With consumption graphed on the vertical axis and GNP on the horizontal, the multiplicative factor $[mpc(1 - t)]$ represents the slope of the consumption function. The remaining terms, $a - mpc\,(T)$, represent the intercept.

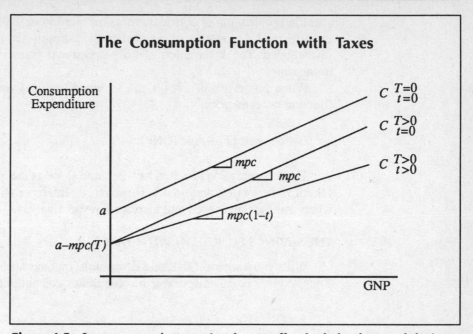

**Figure 4.5** *Lump-sum and proportional taxes affect both the slope and the intercept of the consumption function. Higher lump-sum taxes, T, cause the consumption function to shift down, while a higher proportional tax rate, t, causes it to become more horizontal.*

In Figure 4.5, the top line represents the consumption function without taxes. With government, because lump-sum taxes are subtracted from autonomous consumption, the intercept $a - mpcT$ will be lower than the intercept $a$. The consumption function therefore shifts downward, parallel to itself, when lump-sum taxes are present.

Because the marginal propensity to consume, $mpc$, and 1 minus the proportional tax rate $t$ are both between zero and 1, their product will result in a smaller fraction than the $mpc$ alone. Therefore, when proportional taxes are present, the consumption function will be more horizontal. This is seen in the lowest curve shown in Figure 4.5.

Increases in lump-sum tax rates will cause the consumption function to shift further down. Increases in the proportional tax rate will cause the function to become even more horizontal.

**Consumption with Zero Proportional Taxes.** Because lump-sum taxes do not affect the slope of the consumption function, they are often used instead of proportional taxes to analyze the general effects of tax changes on consumption behavior and other components of aggregate expenditure. It is easier to consider the effects of shifts in a curve rather than both shifts and slope changes. As with other assumptions used in economics, this assumption is justified to the extent that it does not detract from the power of the model to explain the specific problem under consideration. One would not make this assumption if the effects of a proportional tax change on consumption behavior were being investigated. The assumption of no proportional taxes makes such analysis impossible.

When proportional taxes, $t$, are assumed to equal zero, the consumption function takes the form

$$C = a - mpc\,(T) + mpc\,(\text{GNP}) \qquad\qquad (4.6)$$

This consumption function has the same slope as the original consumption function shown in Equation 4.3. However, its intercpet will shift up and down when taxes are decreased and increased, respectively.

## THE SAVINGS FUNCTION WITH TAXES

With government, GNP and disposable income are no longer the same. Thus, savings equals disposable income minus consumption expenditure:

$$S = \text{DI} - C$$

With proportional taxes equal to zero, disposable income equals GNP minus lump sum taxes:

$$\text{DI} = \text{GNP} - T$$

The consumption function is as shown in Equation 4.6. The savings function then appears as

$$S = (\text{GNP} - T) - (a - mpc(T) + mpc\,(\text{GNP}))$$

$$S = -a + mpc(T) - T + \text{GNP} - mpc\,(\text{GNP})$$

or

$$S = -a - (1 - mpc)T + (1 - mpc)\text{GNP} \qquad\qquad (4.7)$$

Like the consumption function, the savings function shown here is linear. The intercept of this function is

$$-a - (1 - mpc)T$$

Because the proportional tax rate is zero, the slope of the savings function is $(1 - mpc)$, the marginal propensity to save.

# THE INVESTMENT FUNCTION

The second major component of private domestic expenditure is *investment*. Investment expenditure represents new purchases of capital goods, the machinery and structures necessary to produce other goods and services. It generally composes about 15 percent of GNP. Categories of investment include *residential* and *nonresidential* investment. Nonresidential investment can be broken down into *structures* and *durable equipment*. Of all the components of aggregate expenditure, investment is the least stable because it is subject to large increases and decreases over relatively short time periods.

As defined here, *investment* does not refer to purchases of financial assets like stocks. Such purchases represent a transfer of ownership of existing capital goods and other assets produced in previous years. Goods produced in previous years are not included in calculating this year's GNP.

## Investment and Inventories

Aside from being defined as goods used in the production of other goods, investment goods have a lifetime extending beyond the year in which they are produced. Thus, in addition to machinery and buildings, *inventories*, goods produced in one year for use in another, are included as a part of investment expenditure. As with the other components of GNP, inventories and other forms of investment are counted as part of GNP in the year they are *produced*.

Firms desire to hold some of their output as inventory to smooth out their production of output rather than gear up or shut down production with each surge or lapse in demand. Unfinished goods working their way through a firm's production process are counted as inventories. Inventories are also held for speculative purposes; this involves purchasing goods now for sale later in anticipation of future price increases.

## Investment Flows and the Capital Stock

Investment represents new purchases of capital goods such as machinery and buildings. Such goods do not wear out or depreciate immediately. Each year purchases of investment goods are added to purchases of investment goods from previous years to form the economy's total *capital stock*. Investment is said to be a *flow* because it represents an addition to the capital stock already in existence. *Depreciation*, the wearing-out of capital, also represents a flow because it represents decreases in the capital stock. By way of analogy, investment can be thought of as a stream flowing to a lake and increasing the lake's size. The lake represents the capital stock. Depreciation can be thought of as a stream flowing *away* from a lake. So long as the flow into the lake (investment) exceeds the flow from the lake (depreciation), the size of the lake (the capital stock) will increase. By definition, *net investment* equals total or gross investment minus depreciation. It represents the actual increase or decrease in the capital stock that occurs each year.

## The Determinants of Investment Expenditure

Investment goods are mainly used in the production of other goods and services. As a result, their purchase is dependent upon confidence or the expectation that they can be used profitably by producers. This is likely to be the case when sales are high. Investment activity therefore depends upon the level of output produced by firms; this level is affected in turn by the economy's overall level of output, GNP.

Using expected sales as a basis for calculation, firms compare the costs of capital goods with the revenues expected from future sales of output to form a *rate of return* on investment, the percentage by which the revenues earned from an investment exceed the cost of the investment. As long as the rate of return on an investment exceeds the market rate of interest, it is to the firm's benefit to undertake the investment.

Suppose the purchase of a capital good costs the firm $100 but at the end of the year yields revenue equal to $115. The percentage by which revenue exceeds cost is

$$Rate\ of\ return = \frac{\$115 - \$100}{\$100} \times 100 = 15\%$$

If the market rate of interest is 12 percent, the firm earns three percent more by purchasing the investment good than it would earn if it placed its funds in a financial asset earning the rate of interest. This is true whether the firm has money available to spend on the investment good or has to borrow it. If the money is borrowed at the prevailing 12 percent rate of interest, with a 15 percent rate of return, the firm will earn 3 percent above its cost of borrowing by undertaking the investment.

## Investment Demand

*Investment demand* refers to the relationship between the economy's rate of interest and the level of investment that firms across the economy will desire to undertake. To derive the investment demand curve, the actions of a typical firm are examined. The results are then generalized for all firms.

### THE INVESTMENT DEMAND SCHEDULE FOR A FIRM

Firms usually have more than one investment project to consider and must decide which investment projects to undertake. For example, a construction company might consider the purchase of a new bulldozer or a new dump truck. Depending on the relationship between the rate of return on these investments and the prevailing market rate of interest, the firm will purchase one, both, or neither of these goods.

By ranking investment opportunities by their expected rates of return, the situation faced by a typical firm might be as depicted in Figure 4.6. The firm has five projects to consider. The first yields a return of 20 percent, the second 15 percent, the third 10 percent, the fourth 5 percent, and the fifth 3 percent. If

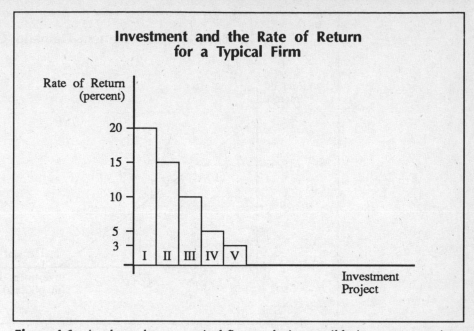

**Figure 4.6** *As shown here, a typical firm ranks its possible investment projects by their expected rates of return. As long as the rate of return exceeds the market rate of interest, an investment should be made. At a rate of interest of less than or equal to ten percent, projects I, II, and III will be undertaken.*

the market rate of interest is 12 percent, the first and second projects should be undertaken because they yield a rate of return higher than the interest rate. If the market rate of interest falls to 9 percent, the first, second, and third projects should be undertaken.

## THE INVESTMENT DEMAND SCHEDULE FOR THE ECONOMY

Conceptually, by aggregating the investment-demand schedules for all firms in the economy, the economy's investment-demand schedule can be found. At the economy-wide level, as each additional project is considered, large differences between rates of return for projects are assumed to vanish. A smooth investment demand curve results, as shown in Figure 4.7. Investment should rationally be made when the rate of return exceeds the rate of interest, no matter how small the difference between the two. Therefore, for practical purposes, the market rate of interest determines the cutoff point between investments that should and should not be undertaken. As shown in Figure 4.7, if the market rate of interest is 12 percent, $400 billion of investment will be undertaken. If the interest rate drops to 9 percent, $500 billion of investment will be undertaken.

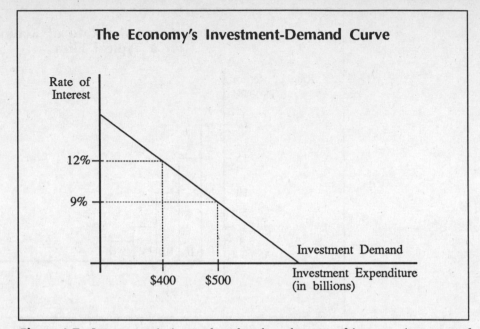

**Figure 4.7** *Investment is inversely related to the rate of interest. At a rate of interest of 9 percent, $500 billion of investment will be undertaken. If the interest rate rises to 12 percent, investment falls to $400 billion.*

**Investment-Demand Shift Factors.** If investors lose confidence or expected sales decline, expected rates of return will fall, and the investment-demand curve will shift in. Investors will now wish to reduce investment levels at all interest rates. Thus, the level of expected sales (usually captured by GNP) and the level of confidence determine the location of the investment-demand curve. This is shown in Figure 4.8a. At a 7 percent rate of interest, before the investment-demand shift, $400 billion of investment takes place. Because of an increase in investor confidence, the investment-demand curve shifts out. The the level of investment rises to $450 billion at an interest rate of 7 percent.

**The Slope of the Investment-Demand Curve.** The sensitivity of investment demand to the interest rate is reflected in its slope. Compared with a more vertical investment-demand curve, a more horizontal investment demand signifies that a greater increase in investment will occur when interest rates fall. In Figure 4.8b, when the investment-demand function becomes more horizontal, a 1 percent decrease in the interest rate leads to a greater increase in investment. As the interest rate drops from 7 percent to 6 percent, investment increases by $25 billion along the steeper curve. Along the more horizontal curve, this 1 percent decline leads to a $40 billion increase.

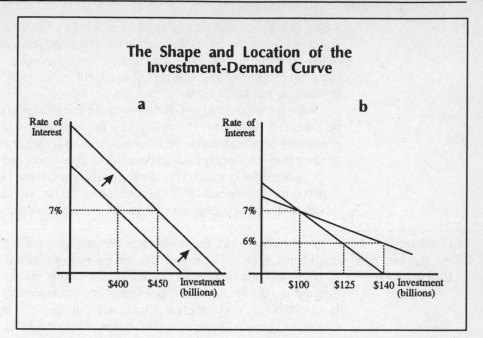

**Figure 4.8** *As seen in Figure 4.8a, a rise in confidence or expected sales causes the investment demand curve to shift out. More investment is undertaken at each rate of interest. In Figure 4.8b, investment is more sensitive to the interest rate when the investment-demand curve is more horizontal. A 1 percent decline in the interest rate leads to a $40-billion increase along the more horizontal curve and $25 billion along the more vertical curve.*

## Investment as a Function of Output

In the simple macro model, it is almost always assumed that investment is autonomous with respect to the level of GNP. However, in deciding upon the amount of capital equipment necessary to meet the demand for their products, firms surely take expected sales into consideration. They do so to bring their actual capital stock to a level that is capable of producing expected output at the least cost. At the macro level, expected or actual GNP serves as a measure of expected sales. In more advanced forms of the macro model, these relationships are made much more explicit. For example, the *accelerator model* of investment is based on the assumption that investment is positively related to changes in expected sales.

### THE MARGINAL PROPENSITY TO INVEST

One simple means of incorporating output effects into the investment function is to assume that investment, $I$, takes the form

$$I = I_0 + mpi(\text{GNP})$$

where $I_0$ captures that part of investment that is a function of the interest rate and confidence; the coefficient *mpi* is the *marginal propensity to invest*. Each dollar increase in GNP will lead investment to increase by the *mpi*. If the marginal propensity to invest is 0.12 and GNP increases by $1, the increase in investment will be 12 cents.

Relating investment to GNP through the marginal propensity to invest can be especially important in applications of the model where investment has previously been assumed to be autonomous with respect to output. This is true because predictions of the model concerning investment can be erroneous when output effects are ignored. Therefore, to understand more fully the relationship between investment and GNP, this version of the investment function is useful whenever the effects of some change in GNP are considered.

## Investment Demand in the Macro Model

In the real world, the investment-demand curve is a function of investor confidence, expected sales or GNP, and the rate of interest. It is also a function of taxes and investment tax credits. In the simple macro model, investment demand is assumed to be independent of, or *autonomous*, with respect to the level of GNP. This assumption is valid when the focus of analysis is not on the effects of changing output on investment. Thus, the level of confidence will

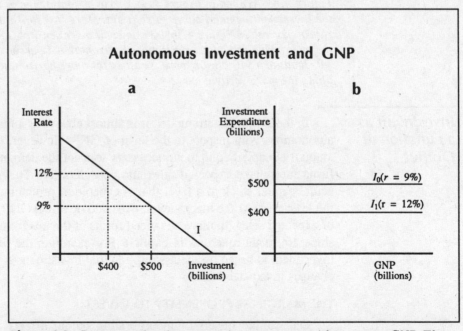

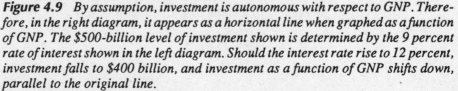

**Figure 4.9**  *By assumption, investment is autonomous with respect to GNP. Therefore, in the right diagram, it appears as a horizontal line when graphed as a function of GNP. The $500-billion level of investment shown is determined by the 9 percent rate of interest shown in the left diagram. Should the interest rate rise to 12 percent, investment falls to $400 billion, and investment as a function of GNP shifts down, parallel to the original line.*

determine the location of the investment-demand curve, and the interest rate will determine the exact level of investment expenditure.

### GRAPHING INVESTMENT AS A FUNCTION OF GNP

When graphed as a function of GNP, investment expenditure will appear as shown in the right-hand side of Figure 4.9. Here the assumption that investment is autonomous with respect to GNP is made explicit. Along the top line, regardless of the level of GNP, investment remains fixed at $500-billion. This $500-billion level of investment is consistent with the 9 percent rate of interest shown on the the left side of Figure 4.9. Should the market rate of interest rise from 9 percent to 12 percent, investment declines, in the left diagram *along* the investment demand curve, from $500-billion to $400-billion. The rising interest rate and causes the horizontal invesment-demand curve to *shift* down in the right diagram to the $400-billion level.

# THE GOVERNMENT EXPENDITURE FUNCTION

Government activities are extremely important in the modern macroeconomy. Government expenditures and transfer payments comprise about 20 percent of GNP. It is usually assumed that government expenditure is autonomous, or independent of GNP. The fact that Congress and the president do not systematically alter government spending levels during recessions and booms suggests that this hypothesis is reasonable in the short run. Thus, Figure 4.10, which graphs government expenduture as a function of GNP, looks exactly like the autonomous investment-expenditure function graphed in Figure 4.9. This curve will shift up when government spending rises and down when government spending falls.

# IMPORTS AND EXPORTS

Few if any countries are totally self-sufficient in the goods they require as inputs for production or final consumption. Trade with other countries is essential to acquire these goods and provides important markets for goods made in the U.S. In today's world, such trade is becoming increasingly important. Exports (sales of American goods to foreigners) presently amount to about 12 percent of GNP and therefore provide jobs for many Americans. Exports depend upon foreign tastes for American goods, relative prices between countries, and

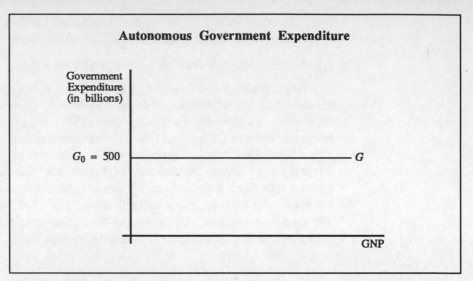

**Figure 4.10**  *Actions of Congress and the president determine the level of government spending. It is assumed to be autonomous with respect to GNP. When government increases or decreases spending, the government-expenditure function shifts up or down parallel to itself.*

foreign income levels. Aside from relative prices, these factors generally lie beyond the control of individuals in the U.S. Hence, export demand is assumed to lie outside the factors considered in the basic macro model. In addition to American tastes for foreign goods and relative prices, imports depend on American income levels. Thus as GNP in the U.S. rises, Americans are assumed to purchase more of all goods, including foreign goods.

## Net Exports in the Expenditure Function

In a model that considers foreign trade, *aggregate expenditure* is defined as the sum of consumption, investment, government spending, and net exports. *Net exports* are defined as exports minus imports, $(Ex - Im)$. Exports, $Ex$, are added and imports, $Im$, are subtracted because aggregate expenditure measures spending on American-produced goods only. Within consumption, investment, and government expenditure are the foreign goods purchased by American consumers, investors, and the U.S. government. Subtracting imports avoids counting them as a part of expenditure on U.S. goods. Adding exports assures that foreign expenditure on Amercian-made goods is included in total expenditure.

### A NET EXPORT FUNCTION

A typical net export function is represented by the equation

$$Net\ Exports = (Ex - Im) = X - m(GNP)$$

where $X$ represents the level of net exports that is independent of U.S. income. Factors such as tastes and foreign income will determine the value of $X$. The coefficient $m$ represents the *marginal propensity to import* foreign goods. As GNP rises in the U.S., Americans desire to purchase more of all goods, including goods produced by foreigners. Thus if $m$ equals .08, for each dollar increase in GNP, imports will rise by 8 cents. In reality, net exports will also be a function of the relationship between U.S. interest rates and interest rates in the rest of the world. These relationships are fully discussed in Chapter 11.

### NET EXPORTS IN THE SIMPLE MACRO MODEL

Inclusion of the net-export function complicates the economy's overall expenditure function. Therefore, net exports are assumed to equal zero throughout most of the development of the simple macro model. Because of the important role they play in the modern macro economy, Chapter 11 is devoted entirely to treatment of trade effects within the macro economy.

## THE SHAPE OF THE AGGREGATE EXPENDITURE CURVE

*Aggregate expenditure* is defined as the sum of the individual components of aggregate demand. Thus, with net exports assumed to equal zero, aggregate expenditure is the sum of consumption, investment, and government expenditure. Because the consumption function is a function of GNP, aggregate expenditure is also a function of GNP. In graphing aggregate expenditure, expenditure is measured on the vertical axis, and GNP is measured on the horizontal.

*Graphing the Aggregate Expenditure Function*

There are two ways to develop the graph of the aggregate-expenditure function. First, when the horizontal investment-expenditure function in Figure 4.9 and the horizontal government-expenditure function from Figure 4.10 are added together a new horizontal $I + G$ curve will result. This horizontal curve can then be added to the upward-sloping consumption function. At each point along the upward-sloping consumption function, the same amount of investment plus government expenditure is added. Therefore, the aggregate-expenditure function will have the same slope as the consumption function, but it will be located above it at each point by an amount equal to the sum of autonomous investment and autonomous government expenditure.

Figure 4.11 shows the consumption function ($C$) as the upward sloping dotted line at the bottom of the graph. Addition of investment expenditure (which is constant at every level of GNP) to consumption ($C + I$) leads to the middle dotted line. Finally, addition of government expenditure (also constant at every GNP level) to the sum of consumption and investment expenditure $(C + I + G)$ leads to the solid aggregate expenditure line on top.

## The Equation for the Expenditure Function

A second and more precise way to derive the aggregate-expenditure function is through use of the simple equations that underlie the consumption, autonomous-investment, and autonomous-government expenditure functions. From Equation 4.6, without proportional taxes, the consumption function has the form

$$C = a - mpc(T) + mpc(\text{GNP})$$

When investment and government expenditure are autonomous with respect to GNP, their values are taken as given. In terms of equations, this means that $I = I_0$ and $G = G_0$, where $I_0$ represents the level of investment determined by the interest rate and $G_0$ represents the level of government spending determined by Congress and the president. As the sum of consumption, investment, and government spending, aggregate expenditure $(E)$ may be written

$$E = C + I + G$$

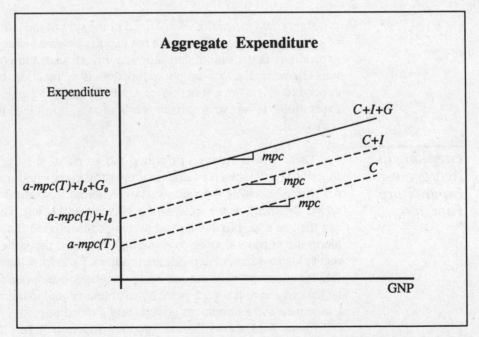

**Aggregate Expenditure**

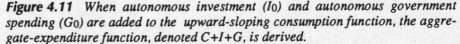

**Figure 4.11** *When autonomous investment ($I_0$) and autonomous government spending ($G_0$) are added to the upward-sloping consumption function, the aggregate-expenditure function, denoted C+I+G, is derived.*

Incorporating the consumption function and the specific values of investment and government spending, it follows that

$$E = a - mpc\ (T) + mpc\ (\text{GNP}) + I_0 + G_0$$

Gathering together those parts of the function that are independent of GNP leads to the following linear aggregate-expenditure function:

$$E = (a - mpc\ (T) + I_0 + G_0) + mpc\ (\text{GNP}) \qquad (4.8)$$

As seen in the top line of Figure 4.11, the intercept of the equation is

$$(a - mpc\ (T) + I_0 + G_0)$$

because none of these components varies with GNP. The slope of the equation is the coefficient appearing in front of the variable GNP, the marginal propensity to consume. Observe that because GNP is graphed on the $x$ axis, *mpc* corresponds to the slope coefficient in the standard form of a straight-line equation: $y = mx + b$. The sum of other components correspond to the intercept $b$.

The fact that Equation 4.8 represents a linear equation can be seen clearly when values replace the letters used to represent the marginal propensity to consume and the components of autonomous expenditure. For example, suppose the marginal propensity to consume is 0.8; autonomous consumption, $a$, equals $50 billion; investment, $I$, equals $300 billion; government spending, $G$, equals $500 billion; and tax revenues, $T$, equal $450 billion. With these values inserted into Equation 4.8, the expenditure function appears as

$$E = 490 + .8(\text{GNP})$$

## SHIFTING AND PIVOTING THE AGGREGATE EXPENDITURE FUNCTION

With its slope and intercept clearly marked, understanding how the expenditure function shifts and pivots is straightforward. First, as seen in Figure 4.12a, the curve will shift given changes in any of the autonomous variables on the intercept. Thus, a rise in autonomous consumption expenditure, a rise in investment, a rise in government expenditure, or a decline in taxes will all cause the aggregate-expenditure function to shift upward, parallel to its original location.

Without proportional taxes and net exports, only a change in the marginal propensity to consume will cause the slope of the aggregate-expenditure function to change. A rise in the marginal propensity to consume causes the expenditure function to become steeper. Because it also appears as a multiplicative factor for lump-sum taxes ($-mpc(T)$), a rise in the marginal propensity

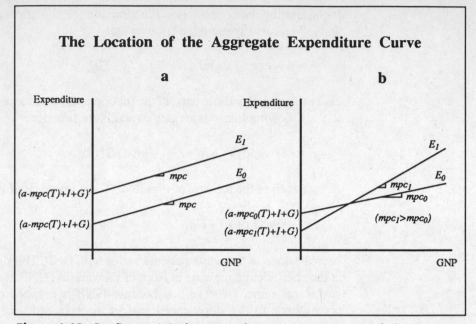

**Figure 4.12** *In figure (a), because they appear as part of the intercept* $(a - mpc(T) + I + G)$, *the aggregate-expenditure curve will shift up parallel to itself given a rise in autonomous consumption, investment, government spending or a decline in taxes. In figure (b), a rise in the marginal propensity to consume increases the slope (mpc) and decreases the intercept of the expenditure function.*

to consume also causes the expenditure function to shift down. These effects are shown in Figure 4.12b.

*In this chapter, an in-depth look at the components of GNP has led to development of the economy's aggregate expenditure function. Each of the components of aggregate expenditure is seen to play a special role in adding to the overall level of economic activity. Each is seen to be functionally dependent upon other variables inside and outside the economic system. In the next chapter, the notion of equilibrium in the macro economy is given meaning, and the role of aggregate expenditure is explored more fully.*

# 5

# *The Basic Macro Model*

*In this chapter a simple macroeconomic model is developed and examined with respect to the establishment of equilibrium, the stability of equilibrium, and changes in the point of equilibrium. This is especially important because the equilibrium level of GNP directly affects the level of unemployment and the rate of inflation. The concept of the multiplier, which explains how changes in autonomous spending affect GNP, is also discussed. The basis for this model is the economy's expenditure function, defined as the sum of consumption, investment, and government expenditure, derived in the previous chapter. The model connects the major aggregates into a coherent picture of how the economy operates. Subsequent chapters add details to the model to make it more realistic and to consider the full implications of macroeconomic shocks.*

## EQUILIBRIUM IN THE MACRO ECONOMY

*Equilibrium* refers to a situation in which there are no forces that will cause change. In the supply-demand model, equilibrium was seen to occur at the point where the supply curve crossed the demand curve. In the macroeconomic sense—in terms of the aggregate measures considered so far—supply corresponds to the final value of all products produced, GNP. Assuming no foreign trade, demand corresponds to aggregate expenditure ($E$), the sum of consumption, investment, and government expenditure. To achieve equilibrium in the macroeconomy, supply equals demand in the sense that the value of goods produced must equal the value of the goods purchased. This equilibrium condition is written

$$GNP = E \qquad\qquad (5.1)$$

or

$$\text{Macro Equilibrium:} \, GNP = C + I + G \qquad\qquad (5.2)$$

## The Expenditure Function and Equilibrium

Macroeconomic analysis at the introductory level makes use of several graphic relationships. Using such relationships, the notion of equilibrium can be clearly represented. With aggregate expenditure measured on the vertical axis and GNP measured on the horizontal, all points of equilibrium are located along a 45-degree line emanating from the origin. The 45-degree line cuts the 90-degree angle between the expenditure and GNP axis in half. It corresponds to the equation $E = GNP$; this is exactly the condition required for equilibrium seen in equation (5.1). The slope of the 45-degree line is 1. Along the line, each $1 rise in GNP corresponds to a $1 rise in expenditure.

### USING THE 45-DEGREE LINE

The 45-degree line makes it possible to convert horizontal GNP values into equivalent vertical expenditure values. As shown in Figure 5.1, a value of GNP equal to $3,000 billion corresponds along the 45-degree line to a value of aggregate expenditure exactly equal to $3,000 billion. When GNP rises to $5,000 billion, expenditure is also $5,000 billion along the 45-degree line. For any point lying below the 45-degree line, the level of GNP (the horizontal distance) is greater than the level of expenditure (the vertical distance). For any point above the 45-degree line, the level of expenditure is greater than the level of GNP.

### FINDING EQUILIBRIUM USING THE 45-DEGREE-LINE DIAGRAM

When the aggregate expenditure function is graphed along with the 45-degree line, their intersection represents the point of equilibrium. Only at the point of intersection does the level of GNP, working through the expenditure function, lead to a level of expenditure that exactly equals GNP. In Figure 5.1, this amount is seen to equal $4,000 billion.

For GNP levels above $4,000 billion, the expenditure line is below the 45-degree line. Therefore, GNP is greater than expenditure. Conversely, when GNP is less than $4,000 billion, the expenditure line lies above the 45-degree line. Therefore, expenditure is greater than GNP.

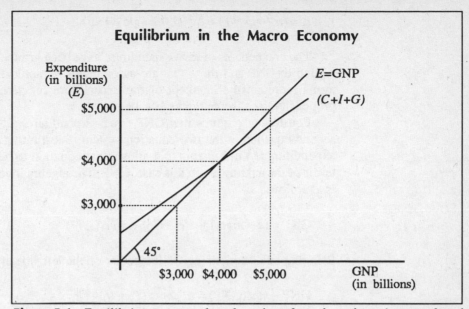

**Equilibrium in the Macro Economy**

*Figure 5.1 Equilibrium occurs when the value of goods and services produced (GNP) exactly equals the values of goods and services purchased (E). Along the expenditure function (C + I + G), this can occur only at the point of intersection with the 45-degree line.*

## SOLVING FOR EQUILIBRIUM GNP USING EQUATIONS

Finding the equilibrium level of GNP graphically corresponds to the mathematical problem of solving for two unknowns, given two independent equations. The unknowns are GNP and aggregate expenditure. The equations are the equilibrium condition and the general form of the expenditure function. Of all the algebraic derivations used in macroeconomics, finding the equilibrium level of GNP is the most basic and the most important.

The expenditure function is derived as follows. In Chapter 4 it was shown that the consumption function in an economy with lump-sum taxes ($T$) takes the form

$$C = a - mpc\,(T) + mpc\,(\text{GNP}) \tag{5.3}$$

Because investment and government spending are autonomous with respect to GNP, their equations are $I = I_0$ and $G = G_0$. The aggregate-expenditure function is written as

$$E = C + I + G$$

or

$$E = (a - mpc\ (T) + I_0 + G_0) + mpc\ (\text{GNP}) \qquad (5.4)$$

The components of total expenditure have been grouped into those that are related to GNP and those that are autonomous. Graphically, the autonomous terms represent the intercept of the expenditure function, and the marginal propensity to consume represents the slope.

Equilbrium requires that GNP equal expenditure, GNP = $E$. This is the second equation in the two-equation system. Substituting GNP for aggregate expenditure ($E$) in Equation 5.4 allows that equation to be written entirely in terms of the unknown—in this case, GNP. The algebra involved in the solution is as follows:

$$\text{GNP} = (a - mpc(T) + I_0 + G_0) + mpc(\text{GNP})$$

Bringing terms containing GNP together on the left side of the equation yields

$$\text{GNP} - mpc(\text{GNP}) = a - mpc\ (T) + I_0 + G_0$$

Factoring out the level of GNP on the left side, we find

$$(1 - mpc)\text{GNP} = a - mpc\ (T) + I_0 + G_0$$

Finally, solving for the equilibrium level of GNP, it is observed that

$$\textit{Equilibrium } \text{GNP} = \frac{1}{1 - mpc}\ (a - mpc\ (T) + I_0 + G_0) \qquad (5.5)$$

All of the terms on the right side of this equation are independent of GNP and are assumed to be known when conducting analysis. Thus, once consumers decide on autonomous consumption and the marginal propensity to consume, investors decide on the level of investment, and the government decides on the the level of taxes and government spending, a single value for equilibrium GNP can be found.

**Solving for Equilibrium GNP: An Example.** Suppose the marginal propensity to consume is 0.8, autonomous consumption expenditure is $100 billion, lump-sum taxes are $500 billion, investment is $500 billion, and government spending is $600 billion. From Equation 5.5, equilibrium GNP is calculated as

$$\text{GNP} = \frac{1}{1 - 0.8}\ (100 - 0.8(500) + 500 + 600) = 5\ (800) = \$4{,}000 \text{ billion}$$

The graphical version of the equilibrium GNP level is seen in Figure 5.1. The two equations in the macro economy are represented by the 45-degree line (showing all possible equilibrium points) and the expenditure function. The point at which these lines cross represents the unique level of expenditure and GNP that satisfies both equations. Only at a GNP level of $4,000 billion will expenditure and GNP be exactly equal.

## The Stability of Equilibrium

Although it is possible to define, locate, and calculate the economy's equilibrium level of GNP, it is important to consider the question whether this equilibrium is *stable*. As with the simple supply-demand model, the *stability of equilibrium* relates to whether departures from equilibrium set into motion forces that cause equilibrium to be restored. The nature of the forces present when GNP is not at its equilibrium value provide insight into the relationship between the production of output and the decisions to purchase that output.

### DISEQUILIBRIUM: EXPENDITURE IN EXCESS OF GNP

In addition to showing the equilibrium level of GNP, Figure 5.2 shows two other GNP levels, $GNP_1$ above the equilibrium value and $GNP_2$ below it. Neither of these GNP levels is associated with the intersection of the 45-degree line and the expenditure function. So neither GNP level can be an equilibrium level.

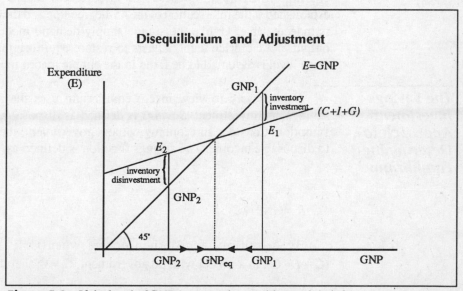

**Figure 5.2** *If the level of GNP is not at the equilibrium level, forces exist to restore equilibrium. When actual GNP is above equilibrium GNP, production exceeds expenditure, and inventories rise above desired levels. Production will be cut back, and GNP will fall. When actual GNP is below equilibrium GNP, production falls short of expenditure. Inventories fall below desired levels. Production will increase, and GNP will rise.*

Suppose that the economy is producing $GNP_1$. Along the expenditure function, the level of expenditure is $E_1$. $GNP_1$ has a greater value than $E_1$. Therefore, at $GNP_1$, the value of final goods and services produced is greater than aggregate expenditure on these goods; the quantity of goods supplied exceeds the quantity purchased. The excess of goods produced over goods purchased represents a surplus that will be placed in inventories. Because inventories are a part of investment, the value of these surplus goods represents an *unplanned* or *unintended inventory investment* ($GNP_1 - E_1$). The presence of this undesired inventory signals firms to cut back on production of goods and services. In doing so, GNP will be reduced, and the economy will move toward equilibrium.

### DISEQUILIBRIUM: GNP IN EXCESS OF EXPENDITURE

If the economy is producing at $GNP_2$, expenditure level $E_2$ exceeds production. To provide the goods being purchased, firms will draw upon their inventories and find them falling below desired levels. The presence of *unplanned* or *unintended inventory disinvestment* ($E_2 - GNP_2$) signals firms to increase production, thereby increasing GNP and moving the economy toward equilibrium.

Inventory excesses or shortages arise whenever the economy deviates from the equilibrium level of GNP. Because they both push the economy toward equilibrium GNP, the presence of these forces means that the equilibrium established at the intersection of the 45-degree line and the expenditure function is indeed stable. Unlike the simple supply-demand model, it is assumed that output, not the price level, adjusts to restore equilibrium. This is because the price level is assumed to be fixed in the simple macro model.

## The Savings-Investment Approach to Determining Equilibrium

Another way to view macro equilibrium uses the relationship between savings and investment. *Savings* is defined as disposable income minus consumption. Consider an economy without government; then GNP is equivalent to disposable income. The savings function is defined as

$$S = GNP - C \qquad (5.6)$$

By definition, equilibrium occurs when GNP equals expenditure ($C + I + G$). In a model with no government, $G = 0$; therefore,

$$GNP = C + I$$

and

$$GNP - C = I$$

Since we already defined GNP – C as savings, we see that in equilibrium savings equals investment: $S = I$.

## SAVINGS, INVESTMENT, AND EQUILIBRIUM: GRAPHIC PORTRAYAL

With no government, taxes are zero, and the consumption function shown in Equation 5.3 can be written

$$C = a + mpc \, (\text{GNP})$$

Using the definition of savings in Equation 5.6

$$S = \text{GNP} - [a + mpc \, (\text{GNP})]$$

or

$$S = -a + (1 - mpc)\text{GNP}$$

This is the equation for a straight line with an intercept equal to minus the level of autonomous consumption spending and a slope equal to the marginal propensity to save, $(1 - mpc)$. Because both savings and investment are measured in dollars, their functions can be shown together in the same graph. As with the simple supply-demand model, each function is considered separately.

Figure 5.3 shows the economy's autonomous investment function along with the economy's savings function. Because investment is assumed to be independent of GNP, it appears as a horizontal line. Equilibrium GNP is determined at the point where the savings and investment lines cross. This point of intersection occurs at a level of GNP equal to $3,500 billion. Below $3,500 billion, investment exceeds savings. In this situation, consumption and investment are high relative to the quantity of goods produced, causing GNP to increase. Because savings is a function of GNP, ultimately the level of savings will increase enough to just equal investment. Above $3,500 billion, savings exceeds investment. Consumption and investment are low relative to the output being produced, causing GNP to decrease. Only when savings exactly equals investment is there no upward or downward pressure on GNP.

## THE PARADOX OF THRIFT

An example of how a lack of aggregate demand can lead to lower levels of income and consumption is the *paradox of thrift*. In Figure 5.4, consider the effect of a decision by consumers to save more at all levels of income. Initially, savings equals investment when GNP equals $3,500 billion. Because all consumer income goes either to consumption or savings, if consumption decreases at all income levels, savings will increase at all income levels. Consumers increase savings by reducing their level of autonomous expenditure, *a*. It falls

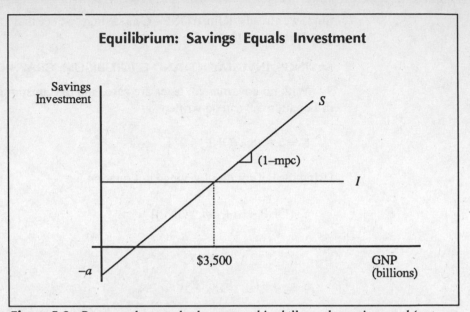

**Figure 5.3** *Because they are both measured in dollars, the savings and (autonomous) investment functions can be shown together in one graph. In a simple economy without government, the equilibrium condition that GNP equals expenditure implies that savings will equal investment. Here, equilibrium GNP is found to equal $3,500 billion.*

from 100 to 80. This will cause the savings function to shift up, parallel to itself. As a result, the savings function will now intersect the investment function at a lower level of GNP. Equilibrium GNP falls to $3,000 billion.

Because the level of investment is fixed, the upward shift in the savings function leads to no change in the equilibrium level of savings. Therefore, the goal of increased savings, which led to this adjustment, will not be achieved. However, because autonomous consumption, *a*, and GNP have fallen, the level of consumption will also fall. Consumers are therefore worse off because of their decision to save more. Consumption has fallen, but savings has not risen.

The decline in autonomous consumption and the upward shift in the savings function that occur in the savings-investment diagram corresponds to a simultaneous and corresponding downward shift in the expenditure function $(C + I)$. This leads to a lower intersection of the expenditure line with the 45-degree line. Hence, consistent with the events shown in Figure 5.4, GNP will decline.

**The Fallacy of Composition.** The paradox of thrift is an example of a *fallacy of composition*. Such a fallacy occurs when the result of an action taken by an individual is assumed to hold for society if the action is taken simultaneously by all individuals. Typically, it is assumed that savings is a good thing for an individual. Therefore, it may also be a good thing for society as a whole. However, a decision by one individual to save more is unlikely to have any

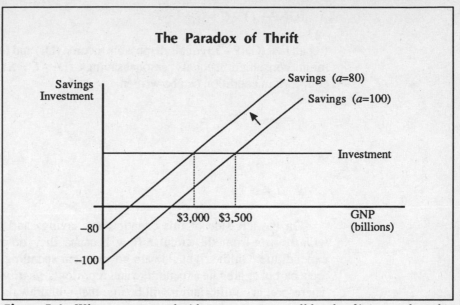

**Figure 5.4** *When consumers decide to save more at all levels of income, the value of autonomous consumption, a, is decreased. This leads to a lower equilibrium level of GNP and lower consumption; savings do not rise.*

perceptible impact on GNP because one individual's decision to consume less cannot significantly affect the economy. Therefore, savings will increase for that individual, and his or her income will not be affected.

This is not true for society as a whole. When all individuals decide to save more, the economy's savings function shifts upward, but savings does not change. Because of the decision to be more thrifty, autonomous consumption falls, income is reduced, and then consumption falls again because of the decline in income. Instead of making people better off, everyone suffers because of their collective decision to increase savings.

## SAVINGS-INVESTMENT EQUILIBRIUM WITH GOVERNMENT

The presence of government in the model adds only a slight complication to the savings-investment approach to determining equilibrium. With government, the equilibrium condition that GNP equals expenditure can be seen in two ways: (1) the equivalence of injections and withdrawals and (2) the equivalence of savings and investment.

**The Equivalence of Injections and Withdrawals.** In the model with government, equilibrium occurs when expenditure equals GNP

$$GNP = C + I + G$$

Subtracting consumption and taxes from both sides of this equation yields

$$(GNP - T) - C = G + I - T$$

Recall that $(GNP - T)$ equals disposable income (DI) and that disposable income minus consumption equals personal savings, $(DI - C = S)$. Thus the economy's equilibrium condition can be written

$$S = G + I - T$$

or

$$S + T = G + I \qquad\qquad (5.7)$$

On the left side of this equation are savings and taxes; they represent *withdrawals* from the circular flow because they do not add to aggregate expenditure. On the right side are government spending and investment; they are a part of aggregate expenditure and represent *injections* to the circular flow. Therefore, in equilibrium it will be true that withdrawals equal injections.

**Total Savings Equals Investment.** Government savings can be defined as the excess of tax receipts over government spending $(T - G)$. With $G$ moved to the left side of Equation 5.7, we observe that

$$S + (T - G) = I$$

In other words, when the economy is in equilibrium, the sum of personal savings and government savings is equal to investment. Note that a government budget deficit occurs when $(T - G)$ is negative. *Ceteris paribus*, all else equal, this implies that investment will be lower when a government deficit exists than when the government's budget is balanced or in surplus.

# THE MULTIPLIER

Macroeconomic analysis is concerned with how changes in various components of expenditure affect the level of GNP. Such analysis makes use of the *multiplier*. The multiplier represents the change in GNP that occurs given a change in some component of autonomous expenditure: autonomous consumption $(a)$, autonomous investment $(I)$, government spending $(G)$, or lump sum taxes $(T)$. Knowledge of the size of the multiplier is essential to macroeconomic analysis. For example, the government sometimes targets a desired level of GNP and uses changes in government spending or taxes to achieve this target. Missing the target can lead to unemployment or inflation.

Intuitively, the multiplier reflects the effects of the chain of numerous transactions that take place in the economy, given an increase in spending. Basically, the amount one person spends to purchase a product becomes income for the next person in the chain, the person selling the product. In turn, that person saves some of the amount received and spends the rest on another product. As subsequent individuals in the chain receive income, a certain amount is spent, and the rest is saved.

For example, suppose there is $1 of new government spending and the marginal propensity to consume across individuals is 0.8. The seller from whom the government purchases its good receives $1. Of that dollar, 80 cents ($0.8 \times $1) is spent on another good, and 20 cents ($0.2 \times $1) is saved. The seller who received 80 cents spends 64 cents ($0.8 \times 80$) and saves 16 cents ($0.2 \times 80$). The person who receives 64 cents spends 51 cents ($0.8 \times 64$) and saves 13 cents ($0.2 \times 64$). As the chain continues, the total amount of expenditure increases. However, even after three links in the chain, we can see that the value of expenditure well exceeds the initial dollar.

## The Multiplier and Equilibrium GNP

Consideration of the multiplier involves examining the effects of shifting the aggregate-expenditure function given changes in one of the autonomous variables. It therefore corresponds analytically to considering the effects of the various shift factors discussed in the simple model of supply and demand. Shifts in the expenditure function occur given changes in consumer confidence or wealth that affect autonomous consumption ($a$), changes in investor confidence or the interest rate that affect investment expenditure ($I$), and changes in government spending ($G$) or lump sum taxes ($T$) brought about by the actions of Congress and the president.

From Equation 5.5, the formula for the equilibrium level of GNP is

$$\text{GNP} = \frac{1}{1-mpc}\,(a - mpc\,(T) + I_0 + G_0)$$

Change in any one of the autonomous variables ($a$, $I$, $T$, or $G$) will cause GNP to change. This change in GNP will be a constant multiple of the change in the autonomous variable. Because the marginal propensity to consume ($mpc$) is less than 1, $\frac{1}{1-mpc}$ will be greater than 1. Therefore, the change in GNP will exceed the change in the autonomous variable that causes the change in GNP. This is the essense of the multiplier.

## Deriving the Multiplier

Suppose the level of GNP rises from $4,000 billion to $4,500 billion. This change in GNP can be denoted $\Delta\text{GNP} = $500 billion. Similarly, a change in investment from $500 billion to $600 billion can be expressed as $\Delta I = $100 billion. This change notation is extremely useful for analyzing multiplier effects. For the simple macro model, and depending on the component of autonomous expenditure that is allowed to change, the multipliers of concern include the autonomous consumption multiplier $\frac{\Delta \text{GNP}}{\Delta a}$, the investment multiplier $\frac{\Delta \text{GNP}}{\Delta I}$, the government expenditures multiplier $\frac{\Delta \text{GNP}}{\Delta G}$, and the tax multiplier, $\frac{\Delta \text{GNP}}{\Delta T}$.

Multiplier analysis begins with finding algebraic expressions for each of these multipliers. For example, given that a change in investment causes a change in GNP—with autonomous consumption, government spending, and taxes held constant—Equation 5.5 leads to the relationship

$$\Delta \text{GNP} = \frac{1}{1 - mpc} \Delta I$$

Dividing both sides of this equation by $\Delta I$ yields the investment multiplier:

$$\frac{\Delta \text{GNP}}{\Delta I} = \frac{1}{1 - mpc}$$

Because the marginal propensity to consume is less than 1, $\frac{1}{1 - mpc}$ will be greater than 1. Therefore, the change in investment is less than the change in GNP that it brings about, $\Delta I < \Delta \text{GNP}$. The term $\frac{1}{1 - mpc}$ is known as the multiplier because it multiplies the change in autonomous expenditure and transforms it into the change in GNP.

## THE MULTIPLIER: A GRAPHICAL PERSPECTIVE

The economic meaning of the multiplier can be visualized in the expenditure–45-degree-line diagram. Assume that the component of autonomous expenditure that changes is investment. Figure 5.5 shows that an increase in investment (perhaps brought about by a decline in the rate of interest) will cause the expenditure function to shift up, resulting in a new, higher equilibrium level of GNP. Graphically, multiplier analysis is concerned with the question of how the upward shift in the expenditure function affects the equilibrium level of GNP. Equilibrium points are found on the 45-degree line.

Point $E_0$ represents the original intersection between the 45-degree line and the expenditure function $(C + I_0 + G)$. A new expenditure function results from the increase in investment from $I_0$ to $I_1$. It is shown by the expenditure line labeled $(C + I_1 + G)$. Equilibrium occurs at point $E_1$ for this expenditure line.

In equilibrium, expenditure equals GNP; therefore, in moving from one equilibrium point along the 45-degree line to another, the change in GNP equals the change in expenditure. The distance representing the change in GNP ($\Delta$GNP), from $E_0$ to point $A$, must equal the change from $A$ to $E_1$. The change in investment ($\Delta I$) is contained within the distance from $A$ to $E_1$. We can see that the change in GNP is larger than the change in investment.

Because it is a function of GNP, consumption will also rise, given the increase in GNP caused by the increase in investment. This increase in consumption is said to be *induced consumption*, consumption induced by the increase in GNP. We assumed government spending to be autonomous and fixed. Therefore, the change in consumption ($\Delta C = mpc\ \Delta$GNP) represents the remaining component of the expenditure change shown in moving from point $A$ to $E_1$ in Figure 5.5.

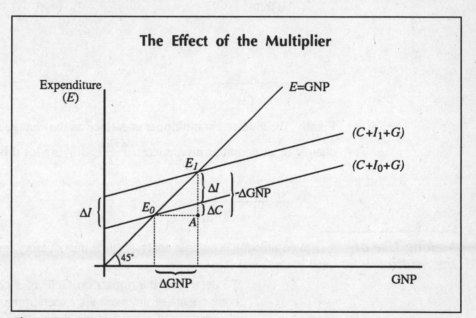

**Figure 5.5** *A rise in investment, $\Delta I$, causes the expenditure function to shift up. Because of the multiplier, the change in GNP exceeds the change in investment that brings it about: $\Delta GNP > \Delta I$. This is because the change in GNP causes consumption to rise.*

**The Multiplier Formula.** The shift in the expenditure function shown in Figure 5.5 is entirely consistent with the previously derived formula for the investment multiplier. From Figure 5.5, the total change in GNP ($\Delta$GNP) brought about by the change in investment ($\Delta I$) is the sum of the initial change in investment and the induced consumption:

$$\Delta GNP = \Delta I + \Delta C \qquad (5.8)$$

or

$$\frac{\Delta GNP}{\Delta GNP} = \frac{\Delta I}{\Delta GNP} + \frac{\Delta C}{\Delta GNP} \qquad (5.9)$$

By definition, the change in consumption caused by a change in GNP is the marginal propensity to consume. Symbolically, it appears in equation 5.9 as $\frac{\Delta C}{\Delta GNP}$. Thus, simplifying the terms on the left and right sides of the equality,

$$1 = \frac{\Delta I}{\Delta GNP} + mpc$$

and

$$1 - mpc = \frac{\Delta I}{\Delta GNP}$$

Finally, the investment multiplier is defined as the change in GNP caused by a change in autonomous investment: $\frac{\Delta GNP}{\Delta I}$. Solving for this multiplier yields

$$\frac{\Delta GNP}{\Delta I} = \frac{1}{1 - mpc} \qquad (5.10)$$

## Making Use of the Multiplier

In conducting economic analysis at the introductory level, the multiplier is used in three ways:

1. To determine the impact on GNP of a change in any of the components of autonomous expenditure. Estimation of such changes involves calculating the *multiplier effect*.

2. To determine how much a given component of aggregate expenditure must be changed to achieve a desired change in GNP.

3. Given knowledge of the change in GNP and the change in autonomous expenditure that brought it about, to estimate the size of the multiplier and the marginal propensity to consume.

## THE MULTIPLIER AND THE MULTIPLIER EFFECT

By definition, the multiplier represents the change in GNP that occurs given a $1 change in one of the components of aggregate expenditure. When multiplied by the total change in autonomous expenditure that occurs, the *multiplier effect* is found. Determining the multipler effect follows directly from the formula for the multiplier shown in Equation 5.10. Solving for the change in GNP brought about by the change in investment, it is seen that

$$\Delta \text{GNP} = \frac{1}{1 - mpc} \Delta I$$

Suppose the marginal propensity to consume is 0.8 and there is a $150-billion increase in investment. The value of the multiplier is

$$\frac{1}{1 - 0.8} = 5$$

and the multiplier effect is (5 x 150) = $750 billion. The multiplier value of 5 therefore represents the $5 increase in GNP that will occur given $1 worth of additional autonomous expenditure. The multiplier effect is $750 billion, the total amount GNP will rise, given the $150-billion increase in autonomous expenditure.

## THE MULTIPLIER: ACHIEVING A GNP TARGET

Rather than estimate the change in GNP that will occur given a change in autonomous expenditure, it is sometimes of interest to calculate the change in autonomous expenditure necessary to bring about some desired change in GNP. For example, with a 0.8 marginal propensity to consume, suppose that equilibrium GNP equals $4,000 billion and the level of GNP that would lead to full employment is $4,500 billion. The problem is to find out how much investment would have to change to bring about this desired change in GNP.

From the multiplier formula (5.10), multiplying both sides by $\Delta I$ results in

$$\Delta \text{GNP} = \frac{1}{1 - mpc} \Delta I$$

The unknown to be solved for is the change in investment. Multiplying both sides of this equation by $(1 - mpc)$ yields the desired solution:

$$\Delta I = (1 - mpc) \Delta \text{GNP}$$

Given a marginal propensity to consume of 0.8 and a change in GNP of $500 billion,

$$\Delta I = (1 - 0.8)500 = \$100 \text{ billion}$$

## THE MULTIPLIER AND THE MARGINAL PROPENSITY TO CONSUME

With knowledge of the change in GNP and the change in autonomous expenditure that brings it about, the multiplier and the marginal propensity to consume can be determined. For example, suppose that a change in investment of $100 billion is observed to cause a $1000 billion change in GNP. The multiplier is seen to equal 10, a fact that can be verified by making use of the multiplier equation:

$$\frac{\Delta \text{GNP}}{\Delta I} = \frac{1}{1 - mpc}$$

Inserting the values for the change in GNP and the change in investment yields

$$\frac{1000}{100} = \frac{1}{1 - mpc} = 10$$

Because the marginal propensity to consume is the only unknown, it can easily be found. Multiplying both sides of this equation by $(1 - mpc)$ we have

$$1 = (1 - mpc) \times 10$$

or

$$(1 - mpc) = \frac{1}{10}$$

Finally,

$$mpc = 1 - \frac{1}{10} = 0.9$$

*Other Expenditure Multipliers*

So far, the multiplier has been derived from an initial change in the level of investment. Other components of autonomous expenditure include autonomous consumption spending ($a$), government spending ($G$), and lump sum taxes ($T$). Had the change been in autonomous consumption expenditure or government expenditure, the resulting multiplier would have the same form as the investment multiplier. By replacing $\Delta I$ with $\Delta a$ or $\Delta G$ in the derivations shown, the multiplier is seen to equal $\frac{1}{1 - mpc}$. The one exception is the tax multiplier. Because taxes are preceded by the coefficient $-mpc$, the shift in the expenditure function resulting from a change in taxes will equal $-mpc\Delta T$, and the formula for the tax multiplier will equal $\dfrac{-mpc}{1-mpc}$. The formulas for each of the economy's multipliers are shown in Table 5.1.

## The Economy's Expenditure Multipliers[a]

| Multiplier | Formula |
|---|---|
| Investment Expenditure | $\dfrac{\Delta GNP}{\Delta I} = \dfrac{1}{1-mpc}$ |
| Autonomous Consumption | $\dfrac{\Delta GNP}{\Delta a} = \dfrac{1}{1-mpc}$ |
| Government Expenditure | $\dfrac{\Delta GNP}{\Delta G} = \dfrac{1}{1-mpc}$ |
| Autonomous Taxes | $\dfrac{\Delta GNP}{\Delta T} = \dfrac{-mpc}{1-mpc}$ |

[a]Each multiplier represents the change in GNP that will occur given a $1 change in the autonomous variable considered.

*Table 5.1*

## The Tax Multiplier

Although it has the same denominator, unlike the multipliers for the other components of autonomous expenditure, the tax multiplier is multiplied by minus 1. Instead of 1, in its numerator it has the marginal propensity to consume. The minus sign is explained by the fact that an increase in taxes represents a reduction rather than an increase in autonomous expenditure. The marginal propensity to consume in the numerator reflects the fact that tax cuts or increases pass through the hands of consumers before affecting expenditure.

### THE TAX MULTIPLIER AND THE MARGINAL PROPENSITY TO CONSUME

According to the consumption function, each dollar increase in consumer income leads to an increase in consumer spending equal to the marginal propensity to consume multiplied by the dollar. It follows that filtering tax cuts through consumers reduces the magnitude of the multiplier. For example, if the marginal propensity to consume is 0.8 and consumers are granted a $1 tax decrease, the $1 of extra income results in only 80 cents of additional expenditure. The remainder goes to savings. If the government had spent the dollar directly, one full dollar of expenditure would take place. In other words, a $1 tax cut will shift the expenditure function up by 80 cents ($mpc\Delta T$), whereas a change in government spending will shift it by by a full dollar ($\Delta G$).

## The Balanced-Budget Multiplier

Multiplier analysis is often used to determine the effect on GNP of changes in government spending and taxes. One very important application of the multiplier occurs where increases in government spending are exactly offset by increases in taxes. This equal change in spending and taxation will leave the government's overall budget unchanged. The question is, What effect on GNP will such changes have?

The *balanced budget multiplier* combines the tax multiplier with the government expenditures multiplier to analyze the effects on GNP of tax and government expenditure changes of equal magnitude. It provides an important example of the relationship, in magnitude, between the tax multiplier and the other expenditure multipliers. Finally, it challenges conventional common sense regarding the outcome of a simultaneous increase in taxes and government spending by the same dollar amount. Most people incorrectly predict that such a simultaneous change will have no effect on GNP.

### CALCULATING THE BALANCED-BUDGET MULTIPLIER

The balanced-budget multiplier works by considering a change in government expenditure and an equal change in taxes. If the budget is balanced initially, such a change in taxes and expenditure will keep the government's budget in balance. Also, the equal changes in taxes and government spending will not cause the budget to become more unbalanced if it is initially unbalanced.

Equal changes in government spending and taxes imply that $\Delta G = \Delta T$. Given these changes, the ultimate effect on GNP will be the sum of the government-expenditures multiplier effect and the tax-multiplier effect. From Table 5.1 and the definition of the multiplier effect, the change in GNP that occurs with a simultaneous rise in government spending and taxes is

$$\Delta \text{GNP} = \frac{1}{1 - mpc} \Delta G + \frac{-mpc}{1 - mpc} \Delta T$$

Because $\Delta G = \Delta T$ it is possible to substitute $\Delta G$ for $\Delta T$:

$$\Delta \text{GNP} = \left( \frac{1}{1 - mpc} + \frac{-mpc}{1 - mpc} \right) \Delta G$$

Because the government and tax multipliers within the parentheses have a common denominator,

$$\Delta \text{GNP} = \left( \frac{1 - mpc}{1 - mpc} \right) \Delta G = \Delta G$$

or,

$$\Delta \text{GNP} = \Delta G$$

In other words, a simultaneous and equal increase in government spending and taxes leads to an increase in GNP equal to the amount of the tax increase *or* the government-expenditure increase.

On the surface, before estimating the actual change in GNP, it seems that a change in government expenditures matched by an equal change in taxes should have no effect on the level of GNP. But the effect of the rise in government spending is not exactly offset by the effect of the equal rise in taxes: The tax multiplier is smaller than the government-expenditures multiplier, implying that the government-expenditure-multiplier effect will exceed the tax-multiplier effect on GNP.

As seen above, the exact amount by which the government-expenditure-multiplier effect exceeds the tax-multiplier effect is equal to the change in government expenditures. By assumption, this is exactly equal to the change in taxes. The balanced-budget multiplier is said to equal 1 because GNP will increase by 1 times the change in government spending or 1 times the change in taxes when *both* are changed simultaneously by the same magnitude.

### THE BALANCED-BUDGET MULTIPLIER: AN EXAMPLE

Suppose the government decides to increase both government spending and taxes by $50 billion. Assume that the marginal propensity to consume is 0.8. The government-expenditures multiplier, $\frac{1}{1 - mpc}$, will equal 5. The tax multiplier, $\frac{-mpc}{1 - mpc}$, will equal minus –4. A $50-billion increase in government spending by itself would cause GNP to rise by $250 billion. A $50-billion tax increase working alone causes GNP to fall by $200 billion. Therefore, the tax and government expenditure effects do not cancel; the net increase in GNP, given the $50 billion increase in both taxes and government spending, equals $50 billion.

## The Importance of the Multiplier

The multiplier takes changes in autonomous expenditure and magnifies their ultimate effect on GNP. This means that relatively small changes in autonomous consumption, investment, government expenditure, or taxes can have large impacts on the overall level of economic activity. A seemingly minor decline in investment can lead to a large decrease in GNP and cause unemployment rates to rise severely. For government stabilization policy, the presence of the multiplier means that small changes in the federal budget can have large impacts on GNP. For example, if actual GNP is below desired GNP, the government need only increase its expenditures by a fraction of the *GNP gap* to attain the desired GNP level.

## THE ACTUAL SIZE OF THE MULTIPLIER

Empirically, the marginal propensity to consume out of disposable income is about 0.9, implying that the economy's most simple expenditure multiplier is about 10. However, estimates of the actual size of the multiplier suggest that its value is far less, somewhere near 2 in value. The difference between the value of the simple multiplier, derived from the formula $\frac{1}{1 - mpc}$, and its real world counterpart is due to several factors.

**Income Taxes.** The simple multiplier does not take income taxes into account. As shown in the Appendix to this chapter, income taxes reduce the multiplier's value: As income goes up, part of the income flows to the government in the form of taxes, preventing consumers from spending it.

**International Trade.** The simple multiplier does not account for the effects of international trade. Rises in American GNP lead U.S. consumers to purchase more of all goods, including foreign goods. To the extent that consumers purchase foreign goods over American goods, American GNP will not rise, and the value of the multiplier will be reduced.

**Inflation.** The simple multiplier does not account for the fact that increases in GNP are often associated with increases in the interest rate and price level. These rises can reduce the level of investment and consumption, partially and perhaps totally offsetting the initial increase in autonomous expenditure that leads to the simple multiplier effect. The role of interest rates, prices, and net exports, and their effects on the multiplier, are considered more fully in later chapters.

*This chapter has introduced the simplest form of the macro model used for analyzing macroeconomic problems. In its present state, the model is far from complete. For example, although the interest rate is seen to be an important determinant of investment, which in turn is an important determinant of GNP, no discussion of how the interest rate is determined has been presented. In addition, the link between GNP and unemployment has not been developed, and the role of prices and inflation in the macro economy has not been covered. Finally, the implications of international trade have not been fully explored. In subsequent chapters, the determination of interest rates and the role of prices are both incorporated into the model. A step in this direction is taken in the next chapter by considering the importance of money and its effects on interest rates.*

# APPENDIX: MORE ON THE MULTIPLIER

This appendix presents a number of details regarding the calculation of multipliers. First, we derive the autonomous tax multiplier discussed in this chapter and shown in Table 5.1. Second, we show how the multiplier formula can be derived when proportional taxes are included in the simple model. Finally, we present two alternative methods of deriving the multiplier formula that some students may find useful.

## The Tax Multiplier

From Equation 5.5, the equation for the economy's equilbrium level of GNP appears as

$$GNP = \frac{1}{1 - mpc}\,(a - mpc\,(T) + I_0 + G_0)$$

Given a change in taxes, $\Delta T$, and the change in GNP it will cause, this equation implies that

$$\Delta GNP = \frac{-mpc}{1 - mpc}\,\Delta T$$

Solving for the change in GNP brought about by a change in taxes,

$$\frac{\Delta GNP}{\Delta T} = \frac{-mpc}{1 - mpc}$$

This is the formula for the tax multiplier shown in Table 5.1.

## The Multiplier with Proportional Taxes

In the more realistic case when proportional taxes are included in the macro model, it was shown in Chapter 4 that the consumption function takes the form

$$C = a - mpc\,(T) + mpc(1 - t)GNP$$

In equilibrium, GNP equals aggregate expenditure:

$$GNP = C + I + G$$

or

$$GNP = a - mpc\,(T) + mpc\,(1 - t)GNP + I + G$$

Solving for GNP yields

$$GNP = \frac{1}{1 - mpc\,(1 - t)}\,(a - mpc(T) + I + G)$$

Using the derivations shown in this chapter to consider the effects of a change in autonomous consumption expenditure, investment expenditure, or government expenditure, the multiplier can be seen to equal $\dfrac{1}{1 - mpc\,(1 - t)}$. Given a change in the level of lump sum taxes, $T$, the multiplier will equal $\dfrac{-mpc}{1 - mpc\,(1 - t)}$.

### THE EFFECT OF PROPORTIONAL TAXES ON THE MULTIPLIER

Comparing these multipliers with the expenditure multipliers shown in Table 5.1 without proportional taxes, it is observed that the only difference is in the denominator, where the marginal propensity to consume is multiplied by 1 minus the proportional tax rate. Because the range of values for the proportional tax rate and the marginal propensity to consume is between zero and 1, this product will be smaller than the marginal propensity to consume alone; 1 minus this product will therefore be larger than one minus the marginal propensity to consume alone. The presence of a larger denominator in the multiplier formula means that the overall ratio will be smaller. The reduction in the size of the multiplier due to the presence of proportional taxes is attributable to the fact that part of any increase in GNP flows to the government by way of the income tax and is not used to increase aggregate expenditure.

## Deriving the Multiplier Using Algebra

As an alternate means of deriving the multiplier, recall that in equilibrium,

$$GNP_0 = \frac{1}{1 - mpc}\,(a - mpc\,(T) + I_0 + G_0)$$

Given a change in investment from $I_0$ to $I_1$, GNP will increase from its initial value of $GNP_0$ to $GNP_1$. Forming the difference between the original level of GNP and the new level with all other autonomous expenditure components held constant, it follows that

$$\text{GNP}_1 - \text{GNP}_0 = \frac{1}{1 - mpc} (I_1 - I_0)$$

Using *delta* notation,

$$\Delta\text{GNP} = \frac{1}{1 - mpc} \Delta I$$

and, consistent with the definition of the multiplier,

$$\frac{\Delta\text{GNP}}{\Delta I} = \frac{1}{1 - mpc}$$

Depending on the change in autonomous expenditure, this approach to calculating the multiplier results in the same formulas as those shown in Table 5.1.

## Deriving the Multiplier Using Calculus

A knowledge of calculus provides for a straightforward derivation of the multiplier formula. Beginning with the equation for equilibrium GNP,

$$\text{GNP} = \frac{1}{1 - mpc} (a - mpc\,(T) + I + G)$$

From a mathematical perspective, finding the derivative of the equilibrium GNP equation with respect to $a$, $I$, $G$, or $T$ corresponds to finding the derivative of the expression

$$y = b(x + c)$$

with respect to $x$, where $b$ and $c$ are constants. The expression can be rewritten as

$$y = bx + bc$$

and because $b$ and $c$ do not vary with $x$, its derivative is

$$\frac{dy}{dx} = \frac{d(bx + bc)}{dx} = \frac{d(bx)}{dx} + \frac{d(bc)}{dx} = b\frac{dx}{dx} + 0 = b$$

By definition, the investment multiplier represents the change in GNP given a $1 change in investment—a definition that exactly corresponds to the derivative of GNP with respect to investment, holding constant all other components of aggregate expenditure. In other words,

$$\frac{d(\text{GNP})}{dI} = \frac{1}{1 - mpc} \frac{d(a - mpc\,(T) + I + G)}{dI}$$

$$= \frac{1}{1 - mpc}\left(\frac{dI}{dI}\right) + \frac{1}{1 - mpc} \frac{d(a - mpc\,(t) + G)}{dI}$$

Note that $\dfrac{1}{1 - mpc}$ has been factored out as a multiplicative constant. Because only investment is assumed to change, the term on the far right is the derivative of a constant and equals zero. Therefore, this expression reduces to

$$\frac{d(\text{GNP})}{dI} = \frac{1}{1 - mpc}$$

This again is the standard formula for the investment multiplier.

# 6

## *Money in the Macro Economy*

*B*ecause it avoids the need for barter, money facilitates the exchange of the commodities produced in the economy. In addition, money is itself a commodity, with an opportunity cost equal to the rate of interest. These and other factors concerning the importance of money are investigated in this chapter. By looking at the money market, it is shown how the quantity of money and the prevailing rate of interest are determined. The rate of interest helps determine the level of investment, which helps determine the equilibrium level of GNP. Therefore, consideration of money's relation to the interest rate makes the macro model developed in the previous chapters more complete.

Before continuing with further development of the model, the definition of money is explored more fully. Next, the role of both private and public banks in creating the economy's money supply is considered, along with the factors behind the demand for money. The function of the Federal Reserve Bank in controlling the money supply is of special concern with regard to establishing and implementing monetary policy. Attention is focused on the economic goals of this agency and the means at its disposal to achieve them.

# THE DEFINITION OF MONEY

Money can be thought of as a commodity that plays several important roles in the economy. It is a *store of value*, a *medium of exchange*, and a *unit of account*. Money is a store of value in the sense that it preserves its nominal, or face value. Thus, unlike perishable commodities, a unit of currency such as a dollar is always worth a dollar, and a dime is worth a dime, as long as the government issuing it remains in existence. As a medium of exchange, money serves as a substitute for virtually all other commodities; money can be traded directly for commodities. Sellers are willing to take money in exchange for their product with the knowledge that as buyers, they can freely transform money into other commodities. Money is a unit of account because virtually every commodity offered for sale has a price denominated in terms of money. The prices that prevail for the various products offered for sale are in units of dollars per unit of the product being sold; for example, $10,000 per automobile or 69 cents per pen. The unit of account varies from country to country. In the United States, the dollar is the unit of account; in Great Britain, the pound; in Japan, the yen.

## Money Exchange versus Barter

Before money came into existence, *barter* was the basis for exchange. Under a barter system, one good is traded for one or more other goods. A distinct disadvantage of barter is that the parties engaging in a transaction must be willing to exchange their products for the other's products. The requirement of this *double coincidence of wants* as a prerequisite for exchange makes engaging in trade costly; the time it takes to match willing buyers and sellers under barter is far greater than under a money system. With the development of money, goods could be traded for money rather than goods traded for goods. As long as money is seen as a perfect substitute for the goods and services sold in various markets, buyers and sellers can match their desire for money and the goods purchased.

## Commodity Money and the Modern Money Supply

In the past, objects serving as money also had intrinsic value; they could be used for purposes besides exchange. Salt, which can be used as a seasoning or to preserve food, and gold coins, which can be melted down and recast for use in ornamentation, are examples. In the modern economy, printed paper serves as money in most countries. Such currency has little or no use outside of its function as money. It derives its value from a government decree or *fiat* that states that the paper has value. Money's value also comes from the faith people have that if the currency is accepted as payment for some good, the currency will have value in purchasing a commodity in a subsequent transaction.

## MONETARY CLASSIFICATION: M1 AND M2

In the U.S. economy, currency is printed at the mint under the supervision of the Federal Reserve System. However, in defining the overall money supply, various aggregates are used to differentiate monetary assets. These aggregates are based upon the degree of *liquidity* of the asset—how easily a particular monetary asset can be used to purchase commodities.

The most liquid form of money is M1, which is composed of coins and paper money as well as checking-account deposits. M2 represents everything categorized under M1 along with savings accounts, money-market funds, and time deposits of less than $100,000. For example, a 60-day $1,000 certificate of deposit is classified under M2. Note that M2 is less liquid than M1 because in order for a commodity to be purchased, the M2 asset must first be converted into M1 funds. Although higher-order money aggregates exist, attention is usually focused on M1 in discussing the economy's money supply. In terms of the functions that money serves, M1 corresponds to the medium of exchange function of money and M2 to the store-of-value function.

# THE BANKING SYSTEM AND THE CREATION OF MONEY

The money supply is determined through the relationship between the private banking system and the nation's central bank. In the United States, the central bank is organized as the Federal Reserve System (Fed). Private banks, which are composed mostly of commercial banks, savings and loan associations, and savings banks, are in business for a profit. The Fed acts to coordinate private banking activity and to conduct *monetary policy* in the public interest. Although the Fed has ultimate control over the nation's money supply, the actions of the private banking system are also extremely important in creating money. The process by which private banks create money is discussed in the following section. Next, the means by which the Fed exercises control over the money supply are discussed.

**How Private Banks Create Money**

In the United States and elsewhere around the world, money creation by private banks is based on the system of *fractional reserve banking*. Under this system, banks are allowed to lend a fraction of their total deposits. To understand how this system enables banks to create money, it is important to understand the distinction between a bank's assets, liabilities, and reserves.

*Assets* represent something *owned* by the bank such as loans to customers or the money used by the bank's owners to start the bank.

*Liabilities* are debts *owed* by the bank to individuals or institutions. A bank's most important liabilitites are the demand deposits (checking accounts) of its customers.

*Reserves* are the difference between the money the bank possesses in the form of deposits and what it lends to borrowers. Under the fractional reserve banking system, banks are required to hold up to 12 percent of the deposits they receive in the form of reserves. The rest of the deposits received by the bank can be lent out. Most reserves are kept in an account held by the private bank at the Federal Reserve. If banks choose to keep more in reserves than required by law, they are said to hold *excess reserves*.

## THE PROCESS OF MONEY CREATION: AN EXAMPLE

To understand the process of money creation, consider the simple case of an economy with only one private bank. It is assumed that any funds in the bank's possession not required as reserves will be lent out. Suppose that the required reserve ratio is 20 percent and that an individual deposits $100 in the bank. The bank will have to keep $20 on hand as required reserves, but it can immediately lend $80. The bank's *balance sheet*, which shows the relationship between the bank's assets, liabilities, and reserves appears in Table 6.1.

### The Bank's Balance Sheet (Round 1)

| ASSETS | | LIABILITIES | |
|---|---|---|---|
| Reserves: | $20.00 | Deposits: | $100.00 |
| Loans: | $80.00 | | |
| Total: | $100.00 | Total: | $100.00 |

*Table 6.1*

Observe that the bank's total assets, seen as the sum of its loans and reserves, equal its total liabilities.

Assume that all loans made by the bank are ultimately used for the purchase of some commodity. The person or firm that receives the funds in exchange for the commodity deposits the money in the bank. The bank's deposits will rise by $80. The amount the bank must keep in reserve will rise by $16 (20 percent of $80). The remaining amount, $64, can be lent by the bank. After this second round of deposits and loans, the bank's new balance sheet appears as in Table 6.2.

## The Bank's Balance Sheet (Round Two)

| ASSETS | | LIABILITIES | |
|---|---|---|---|
| Reserves: | $36.00 | Deposits: | $180.00 |
| Loans: | $144.00 | | |
| Total: | $180.00 | Total: | $180.00 |

*Table 6.2*

After a third round of transactions, the $64 in new loans finds its way back to the bank as a deposit. Eighty percent of this deposit, or about $51, will be lent, and 20 percent, about $13, will be placed in reserves. Making these adjustments to the bank's assets and liabilities, at the end of this third transaction the bank's balance sheet appears as in Table 6.3.

## The Bank's Balance Sheet (Round Three)

| ASSETS | | LIABILITIES | |
|---|---|---|---|
| Reserves: | $49.00 | Deposits: | $244.00 |
| Loans: | $195.00 | | |
| Total: | $244.00 | Total: | $244.00 |

*Table 6.3*

After the third transaction, there are $244.00 of new deposits based on an initial deposit of $100. Individuals borrowing from the bank have made use of $195 for the purchase of commodities, $95 more than the initial $100 deposit.

This example is not realistic because there is only one bank and it is assumed that all loans are redeposited. However, even if more banks were included, the results would be the same. It would only be necessary to consider the balance sheets of the other banks involved in the string of transactions along with the original bank's. It is probably true that almost all of the cash lent to individuals by banks finds its way back to banks before long. There is an *opportunity cost* of holding cash—the interest that could be earned by placing it in an interest-bearing account. A decision by individuals to hold more cash rather than keep it in interest-bearing deposits will reduce the amount of new deposits created and the amount by which new loans can increase.

## THE BANK-EXPANSION MULTIPLIER

As the process of making deposits and loans continues, how much money will ultimately be created? The answer lies in recognizing that the additions to the amount of money in the economy represent a *geometric series*:

$$\$100 + 0.8(\$100) + 0.8^2(\$100) + 0.8^3(\$100) + \ldots$$

As can be confirmed by calculating the products shown, the first term in this sum represents the initial $100 deposit. The second term represents the $80 loan the bank was able to make after accounting for the 20 percent reserve requirment. When this loan finds its way back to the bank, the third term represents the $64 the bank can again lend after accounting for its reserve requirment (80 percent of the $80 deposit). Subsequent terms are interpreted in the same way. At each stage in the process, the amount the bank is able to lend decreases. Ultimately, after many transactions, the amount the bank can lend will reach zero, and the process will be complete.

**The Bank-Expansion Multiplier Formula.** The multiple by which deposits expand over some initial new deposit is known as the *bank expansion multiplier*. It equals 1 divided by the required reserve ratio. Therefore, given some original deposit, the total deposits generated in the banking system can be calculated as

$$Total\ Deposits = \frac{Original\ Deposit}{Required\ Reserve\ Ratio}$$

From the numerical example, given a required reserve ratio of 20 percent, the total amount of deposits created, including the $100 initial deposit which started the process, will equal

$$\frac{\$100}{0.2} = \$500$$

The value of new loans banks are able to create given some initial deposit is calculated using the following relationship:

$$Total\ Loans = \frac{Original\ Deposit}{Required\ Reserve\ Ratio} - Original\ Deposit$$

From the example, the total loans generated from an initial $100 deposit will equal

$$\$400 = \frac{\$100}{0.2} - \$100$$

The total reserves that will arise from some initial deposit is calculated as the product of the required reserve ratio and the total deposits generated by the bank-expansion multiplier:

*Total Reserves = Required Reserve Ratio × Total Deposits*

In the example, to cover the reserve requirement of the $500 in total deposits held by the bank, $100 = 0.2 × $500 must be held in reserve.

**Excess Reserves.** In the bank expansion multiplier formula, the total amount of money created is dependent upon the assumption that banks hold no *excess reserves*, reserves over those required by the fractional-reserve banking system. Should banks do so, the bank-expansion multiplier will be reduced accordingly. That is, rather than the required reserve ratio, the actual reserve ratio would be used in the above definitions.

Suppose that banks decide to hold 25 percent of deposits on reserve for some reason, even though the required reserve ratio is 20 percent. The total amount of new deposits arising from $100 of new deposits will equal $400 ($100/.25) rather than $500 ($100/.2) if the banks held no excess reserves. As long as there is a net gain to banks from making loans, it is not in their interest to hold excess reserves. Excess reserves may be held when economic conditions make lending extremely risky, when banks expect unusually high levels of withdrawals, or when potential borrowers postpone their borrowing.

**Monetary Contraction.** The process of money creation also works in reverse. Given a reduction in deposits, banks must adjust the amount of their outstanding loans downward so that required reserves are maintained. When a customer makes a withdrawal from a bank account, the money comes from the bank's reserves. Thus a decline in deposits of $100 would set into motion a contraction in the money banks are able to lend out. Using the bank-expansion multiplier in reverse, with a required reserve ratio of 20 percent, a withdrawal of $100 would cause total deposits in the banking system to fall by $500.

# THE ROLE OF THE FEDERAL RESERVE

Private banks are able to expand the existing money supply through the bank-expansion multiplier, but determination of the economy's intial money supply is a decision made by the Fed. In addition to determining the size of the nation's money supply, the Fed is responsible for international monetary transactions, such as buying and selling dollars or other currencies to change the nation's foreign *exchange rate*. The Fed is also responsible for establishing *margin requirements*, the percentage of a stock's price that a customer must pay if funds borrowed from a stock broker are to be used to purchase the stock.

Finally, the Fed is sometimes empowered to impose *credit restrictions* that alter the ease with which consumers are able to obtain credit.

The Federal Reserve System is composed of 12 regional banks. These regional banks act as banks for private banks in their respective regions; they accept deposits from and make loans to the private banks. They also act as clearinghouses for transactions among banks. Each regional bank is headed by a president. The Federal Reserve System as a whole is headed by a chairman and a seven-member board of governors; they are recommended for their positions by the president of the U.S. and confirmed by the Senate.

In formulating policy, the Fed is an independent government agency that acts on behalf of the public interest. Because Fed officials are appointed for 14-year terms and are not elected by the public, Fed policy does not have to take into consideration short-term political repercussions and public pressure. This fact is often the cause of debate whether the Fed should be responsible to elected public officials, especially during periods when the effects of Fed policy are unpopular and lead to potentially unfavorable election conditions.

## How the Fed Controls the Money Supply

Actions taken by the Fed to control the nation's money supply are called *monetary policy*. In formulating this policy, the Fed's goals are consistent with the overall macroeconomic objectives of ensuring high rates of economic growth and low rates of inflation. The Fed exercises control over the money supply through use of *open-market operations*, *changes in the reserve ratio*, *changes in the discount rate*, and *moral suasion*. Expansionary monetary policy involves increasing the money supply. Contractionary or restrictive monetary policy involves decreasing the money supply.

### OPEN-MARKET OPERATIONS

Open-market operations are purchases and sales of U.S. government securities, at the direction of the Federal Reserve Open Market Committee. U.S. government securities are a type of *bond*, or contract, that guarantees to pay its purchaser a fixed rate of interest over a fixed period of years. At the end of this period, the government bond is said to have matured and is cashed in for its original (face) value. Before its maturity date, the security can be sold in the economy's *bond market*.

Conceptually, except for the fact that a bond cannot be redeemed for its face value until the date of its maturity, the purchase of a bond is similar to putting money into a savings account. In return for making a deposit, the saver receives a passbook and the right to an interest payment each year the deposit is maintained. The original deposit still belongs to the saver and is received when the account is closed.

**Bond Sales and the Money Supply.** When the Fed purchases securities or bonds from individuals on the open market, it receives the bond and pays for it with cash. The public's holding of cash is thereby increased. This cash ultimately finds its way to the private banking system. It is used to increase bank reserves, thereby enabling banks to expand their lending. The economy's money supply is further increased through the bank-expansion multiplier. If securities are purchased directly from banks rather than from individuals, bank reserves are increased immediately.

When the Fed sells securities, individuals purchasing them must pay in cash. The public's holding of cash is thereby reduced. Thus deposits at banks are reduced; bank reserves fall; new lending must be curtailed; and the economy's money supply falls.

## CHANGING THE RESERVE RATIO

The required reserve ratio appears in the denominator of the bank-expansion multiplier formula. If the Fed lowers the reserve ratio, the value of the bank-expansion multiplier will increase. With the decline in the reserve ratio, banks find themselves with excess reserves and can therefore increase lending until their actual reserves are consistent with required reserves.

For example, suppose the reserve ratio is initially 20 percent, but is then cut to 10 percent. Banks were initially required to keep 20 cents of each dollar deposited on reserve; now they have 10 cents in excess reserves for each dollar of deposit. The bank-expansion multiplier rises from 5 (1/0.2) to ten (1/0.1). Initial deposits of $100 will now lead to $1,000 of total deposits, rather than the $500 of deposits that would arise if the reserve ratio remained at 20 percent.

## CHANGING THE DISCOUNT RATE

In its role as a bank's bank, the Fed makes loans to private banks at a rate of interest known as the *discount rate*. When private banks borrow money from the Fed, their reserves at the Fed are increased. Private banks are then able to make additional loans until their reserves again reach the required level. By lowering the discount rate, the Fed widens the gap between the interest rate earned by private banks for the loans they make and the rate they must pay the Fed to acquire the reserves necessary to cover those loans. Hence, when the discount rate is lowered, private banks have a greater incentive to borrow from the Fed, increase their loans, and increase the economy's money supply. Conversely, an increase in the discount rate reduces the gap between the rate of interest received from customers and the interest rate banks must pay the Fed. A bank's incentive to borrow from the Fed is reduced, and the money supply will fall.

## MORAL SUASION

*Moral suasion* refers to the Fed's ability to control the nation's money supply without implementing any specific policy. It does so by making suggestions to decisionmakers in the private banking sector. The ability of the Fed to control the nation's money supply gives it enormous power to affect the overall state of the economy, especially the state of the banking business. Since private banks are in business for profit, it is in the private banking system's general interest to act in a manner consistent with the Fed's objectives. For example, if the Fed announces that a more restrictive monetary policy may be required to ensure economic stability, private banks may voluntarily increase their reserves above required levels. They do so to avoid enactment of more stringent actions by the Fed to achieve its policy.

# THE MONEY MARKET

The equilibrium interest rate and quantity of money that prevail in the economy are determined in the money market. Therefore, the demand for money as well as its supply must be considered. The market for money is like the market for any other commodity. In a diagram, the price of the commodity appears on the vertical axis, and the quantity of the commodity appears on the horizontal. In the money market, because the opportunity cost of holding money is the interest that could be earned by placing it in an interest-bearing account, the interest rate assumes the role of the price of money. As seen in Chapters 4 and 5, the interest rate plays an important part in determining the economy's level of investment, which through the multiplier has an important impact on the overall level of GNP. Through the introduction of a supply-demand model for the money market, the stage is set for development of a more complete model of the macro economy. Through consideration of factors underlying the demand for money, the price level will also be incorporated into the basic model.

## The Demand for Money

The demand for money is based upon the desire by individuals to hold coins, currency, and demand deposits (M1). People desire money for making daily purchases; they also use money as a store of value. These uses underlie the major categories of money demand: the *transactions demand* and the *asset demand*.

### THE TRANSACTIONS DEMAND FOR MONEY

The *transactions demand* for money refers to money that individuals keep on hand to make daily purchases. Rather than taking a trip to the bank each time cash is needed, individuals usually carry a sufficient amount of cash to cover the ordinary expenses of the day or week. This transactions demand is affected by *income*, *interest rates*, and the *price level*.

**Income.** Individuals with higher levels of income tend to engage in more transactions or transactions requiring more money. They therefore carry more cash or have larger balances in checking accounts. As the nation's income increases, to the degree that personal income also rises, the average amount of money used for transactions is assumed to increase. Thus, the transactions demand for money rises with GNP.

**Interest Rates.** Higher interest rates imply that holding cash is more "expensive." The opportunity cost of holding cash is the interest that could be earned by keeping the money in an interest-bearing account. Thus, when the economy's interest rate rises, the amount of cash held for transactions purposes will decrease (trips to the bank to acquire cash are now relatively less expensive).

**The Price Level.** Higher prices for goods and services imply that more cash is necessary for daily transactions because goods and services cost more. Therefore, higer prices imply a higher transactions demand for money. For the macro economy, this effect results in greater money demand when there is a rise in the overall price level.

## THE ASSET DEMAND FOR MONEY

Aside from transactions purposes, money is also held as an *asset*. This occurs when other assets, such as bonds, are expected to fall in *price*. By definition, a *capital loss* occurs when the value of an asset owned by an individual declines. When bond prices are expected to fall because interest rates are expected to rise, individuals can avoid capital losses by selling bonds and holding cash (which maintains its face value) instead of bonds. Similarly, having cash available when bond prices are expected to rise enables individuals to purchase bonds at relatively low prices; individuals thereby reap *capital gains* when bond prices go up. As with the transactions demand for money, the amount of money held as an asset decreases when the interest rate rises.

## The Money-Demand Curve

The money-demand curve incorporates the factors underlying the transactions and asset demands for money into a graphic form. As in the development of the demand curve for an ordinary commodity, attention focuses first on the shapc of the money-demand curve in relation to the interest rate, or opportunity cost of money. Next, factors that lead to shifts in the location of the demand curve are considered.

### THE SHAPE OF THE MONEY-DEMAND CURVE

When the interest rate goes up, both the transactions and asset demands for money go down, reflecting the fact that the opportunity cost of holding money is the interest forgone by not placing it in an interest-bearing asset. With the interest rate graphed on the vertical axis and the quantity of money on the horizontal axis, the money-demand curve slopes downward. A typical money-demand cuve is shown in Figure 6.1a. At an interest rate of 7 percent, $500 billion of M1 is demanded. Should the interest rate drop to 5 percent, the quantity of money demanded will rise to $525 billion.

When money demand is more sensitive to the interest rate, a given change in the interest rate will lead to a larger change in the quantity of money demanded. This occurs when the money-demand curve is more horizontal. In Figure 6.1b, a one-percent drop in the interest rate from seven to six percent leads to a $5-billion increase in money demand along the more vertical curve but a $10-billion increase along the more horizontal curve.

## MONEY-DEMAND SHIFT FACTORS

Through the transactions demand for money, in addition to the interest rate, money demand is also a positive function of GNP and the price level. Neither

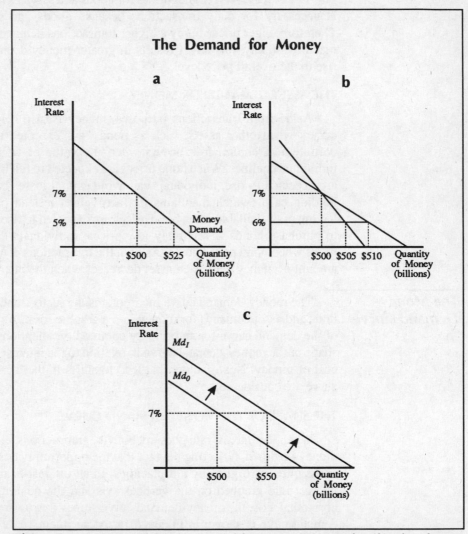

**Figure 6.1**   *In Figure 6.1a, the demand for money is inversely related to the rate of interest because at higher interest rates the opportunity cost of holding money is increased. In Figure 6.1b, a drop in the rate of interest causes a larger increase in the quantity of money demanded when the money-demand curve is more horizontal. As shown in Figure 6.1c, the money-demand curve will shift out, given a rise in the price level or GNP.*

of these variables appears explicitly on the axes of the money market diagram. They are therefore (exogenous) money-demand shift factors. Increases in either the price level or the level of income will cause more money to be demanded at every interest rate, implying that the money-demand curve has shifted out. In Figure 6.1c, the initial money-demand curve is labeled $Md_0$. A rise in the price level or an increase in GNP causes the shift out to curve $Md_1$. At a 7-percent interest rate, the quantity of money demanded rises from $500 billion to $550 billion.

## The Money-Supply Curve

The money-supply curve shows the relationship between the interest rate and the quantity of money supplied in the economy. As with the development of the money-demand curve, attention is focused on the shape of the curve and those factors that cause it to shift.

### THE SHAPE OF THE MONEY-SUPPLY CURVE

The fact that the Fed has power to control the money supply suggests that the money supply is independent of the rate of interest. If this is the case, the money-supply curve will appear as the vertical line shown in Figure 6.2a. Regardless of the rate of interest, the money supply is fixed at the $500-billion level established by the Fed. However, a vertical money-supply curve is not entirely realistic. At a very low interest rate, banks have a greater incentive to exercise caution in making loans. This might lead banks to hold excess reserves, thereby reducing the value of the bank-expansion multiplier. If this is the case, a higher interest rate will lead to lower excess reserves and a higher quantity of money supplied. Hence the money supply curve would have the upward slope shown in Figure 6.2b.

### SHIFTING THE MONEY-SUPPLY CURVE

Monetary policy will affect the location of the money-supply curve. Expansionary monetary policy will cause the money-supply curve to shift out. Contractionary policies cause it to shift in. Expansionary monetary policies include open market operations involving the purchase of bonds, reduction of the reserve ratio, reduction of the discount rate, and engaging in moral suasion to cause banks to make loans more freely. As seen in Figure 6.2c, such an outward shift implies that a greater quantity of money is supplied at each rate of interest.

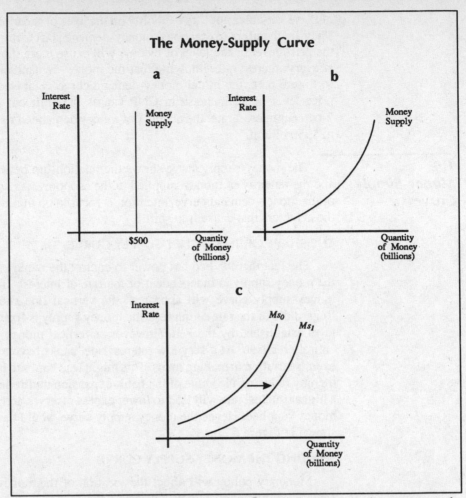

**Figure 6.2**  *If the Fed is assumed to have complete control over the money supply, the money-supply curve appears as a vertical line above the amount set by the Fed. When private banks are assumed to have some control as well, the money-supply curve is upsloping. Higher rates of interest induce banks to maintain lower excess reserves, increasing the value of the bank-expansion multiplier. In Figure 6.2c, the money-supply curve is seen to shift out when the Fed engages in expansionary monetary policy.*

# EQUILIBRIUM IN THE MONEY MARKET

Equilibrium in the money market occurs at the intersection of the money-demand and money-supply curves. Figure 6.3 shows an example in which the intersection leads to an equilibrium rate of interest of 9 percent and an equilibrium quantity of money equal to $600 billion.

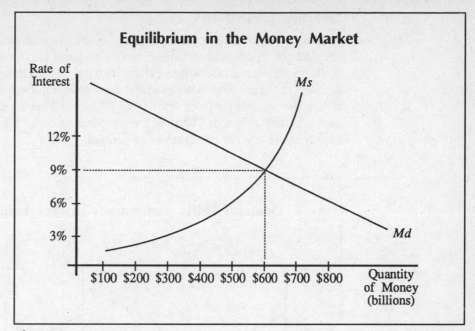

**Equilibrium in the Money Market**

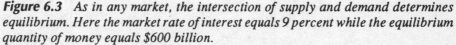

***Figure 6.3*** *As in any market, the intersection of supply and demand determines equilibrium. Here the market rate of interest equals 9 percent while the equilibrium quantity of money equals $600 billion.*

## Interest Rates in the Macro Economy

More than one interest rate actually exists in the economy. This is seen in the previous discussion of the interest rate people pay for loans, the discount rate banks pay to the Fed, and the interest rate individuals receive on their savings accounts. In addition, there is the *prime rate* of interest paid for loans by choice customers of private banks, *mortgage rates* paid by individuals for home loans, and the interest rate earned on certificates of deposit. These interest rates differ depending upon the *risk* associated with the loan, and the time length of the loan. Generally, more risky loans carry a higher interest rate, as do those for longer time periods. The interest rate that emerges from the intersection of the money-supply and money-demand curves should be thought of as an aggregate representation of the other rates. All interest rates are expected to move in relation to the interest rate established in the simple supply-demand model of the money market.

## The Effects of Shifting Money Demand and Supply

The money supply-demand diagram allows analysis of the effects of shifts of the money-demand and money-supply curves on the economy's interest rate and quantity of money.

## THE PRICE LEVEL EFFECT

An increase in the economy's price level causes an increased transactions demand for money and shifts the money-demand curve out. As a result, the equilibrium interest rate will rise along with the equilibrium quantity of money. As seen in Figure 6.4a, with an initial equilibrium interest rate of 9 percent, a rise in the economy's price level from 100 to 110 causes the money-demand curve to shift outward. The new money-demand curve intersects the money-supply curve at an interest rate of 11 percent.

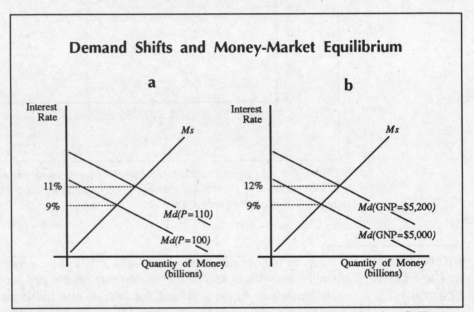

**Figure 6.4**   *As seen in Figures 6.4a and 6.4b, rises in the price level or GNP cause the money-demand curve to shift out and lead to a higher equilibrium rate of interest.*

## GNP EFFECTS

A rise in the level of GNP will also cause the money-demand curve to shift out, raising both the rate of interest and the equilibrium quantity of money. This shift is conceptually the same as the shift due to an increase in the price level. Figure 6.4b shows an outward shift in money demand due to a rise in GNP. The initial equilibrium rate of interest is 9 percent. A rise in GNP from $5,000 billion to $5,200 billion causes the outward shift in money demand. The equilibrium rate of interest rises to 12 percent.

## THE EFFECTS OF MONETARY POLICY

Expansionary monetary policy will cause the money-supply curve to shift out, leading to a lower equilibrium interest rate and a higher equilibrium quantity of money. Note that the Fed cannot control the money-demand curve; it has control only over the economy's money-supply curve. Therefore, if the Fed desires to achieve a certain rate of interest, it must adjust the money-supply curve so that it intersects money demand at the desired interest rate. Similarly, if the Fed wants to set the money supply at a particular level, it must accept the rate of interest associated with the money-supply curve's intersection with the money-demand curve at that quantity of money. In other words, the Fed cannot control both the money supply and the rate of interest simultaneously. If it wishes to set one at a particular level, the value of the other is automatically determined.

**Expansionary Monetary Policy: An Example.** In Figure 6.5, suppose the initial interest rate is 9 percent and the Fed desires to reduce it to 7 percent. By using open-market operations (buying bonds in this case), lowering the discount rate, or lowering the reserve ratio, the money-supply curve shifts right from curve $Ms_0$ to curve $Ms_1$ and the desired reduction in the interest rate occurs. However, note that the equilibrium money supply has risen from $500 billion to $535 billion. Because the Fed does not control the money demand curve, it must accept this increase in the equilibrium money supply if it wishes to control

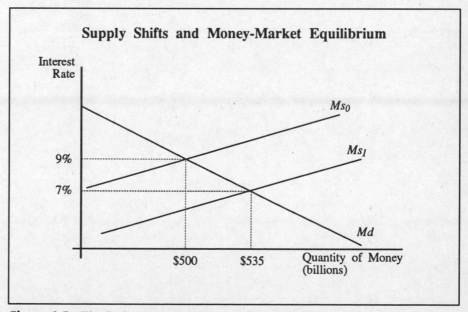

**Figure 6.5** *The Fed can control the rate of interest or the equilibrium quantity of money by shifting the money-supply curve. Increasing the money supply to lower the interest rate from 9 percent to 7 percent requires an increase in the equilibrium quantity of money from $500 billion to $535 billion.*

the rate of interest. If the Fed wishes to maintain the equilibrium money supply at $500 billion, it must live with the 9-percent interest rate that comes with it along the money-demand curve.

*Actions in the commodity market, where goods and services are produced and sold, reveal only part of the overall nature of macroeconomic activity. In this chapter the money market has been introduced. This market constitutes the second major component of the macro economy and the basic macro model. In discussing the factors underlying this market, the actions of private individuals in affecting money demand and the role played by private banks and the Federal Reserve System in creating the nation's money supply have been considered.*

*In the next chapter, events taking place in the money market are seen to have an effect on the economy's commodity market, while actions in the commodity market affect equilibrium in the money market. Understanding how these effects interrelate leads to development of a complete macroeconomic model. This model is capable of explaining movements in all major macro-economic variables. Variables include the level of GNP, the price level, the rate of interest, and levels of consumption, investment, and government spending that make up aggregate expenditure. Incorporating the role of government, with its obligation to promote economic stability, adds another dimension and allows consideration of policy responses to achieve and maintain stability.*

# 7

## Aggregate Demand, Potential GNP, and Long-Run Aggregate Supply

*Previous chapters have introduced the definitions required for the study of macroeconomics and simple models for determining the level of GNP and the interest rate. Left out thus far has been any mention of how the economy's overall price level is established. By developing and integrating the models found in previous chapters into a single model of aggregate demand and supply, this chapter shows how the price level is determined and how inflation originates. As in the demand and supply model for a single product, analysis begins with those factors affecting the shape and location of the aggregate demand and supply curves. When combined into one graph, these curves determine the economy's price level and equilibrium level of GNP.*

### INTEREST RATES, INVESTMENT, AND AGGREGATE DEMAND

As discussed in Chapter 6, the interest rate is determined in the money market. In the simple commodity-market model of Chapters 4 and 5, the interest rate plays an important role in determining the level of investment that, through the expenditure multiplier, helps determine the equilibrium level of GNP. On the other hand, as part of the transactions demand for money, the level of GNP (determined in the commodity market) is a shift factor for the money-demand curve. Knowledge of the level of GNP is therefore important for determining the location of the money-demand curve; in turn, this is important in determining the equilibrium rate of interest. Given these interconnections, there is a simultaneous relationship between equilibrium in the money market, where the interest rate is determined, and equilibrium in the commodity market, where GNP is determined.

In other words, in order to find the economy's equilibrium interest rate and level of GNP, it is necessary to consider the money market and the commodity market at the same time. Connections between the price level, the interest rate, investment, and GNP can then be fully developed. By showing the relationship between the economy's price level and levels of GNP consistent with equilibrium in both the commodity market and the money market, the economy's aggregate-demand curve incorporates these connections.

## Deriving the Aggregate-Demand Curve

By definition, the aggregate-demand curve shows the price levels and levels of GNP that are consistent with equilibrium in both the money and commodity markets. Figure 7.1 shows the economy's money market in diagram a, the investment demand schedule in diagram b, and the aggregate-expenditure function in diagram c. The aggregate-demand schedule shown in diagram d is derived by considering the effects of changes in the price level on the equilibrium level of GNP.

Suppose the initial price level is $P_0$. This price level establishes the location of the money-demand curve labeled $Md(P_0)$ in Figure 7.1a. The intersection of this money-demand curve and the money-supply curve determines the equilibrium interest rate, $r_0$. With this rate of interest, the level of investment will be $I_0$, as shown in Figure 7.1b. The equilibrium level of GNP in Figure 7.1c will be based upon expenditure level $E_0$ (which uses $I_0$ for the level of investment). Along expenditure curve $E_0$, the equilibrium GNP level is $GNP_0$. Because they are consistent with equilibrium in both the money and commodity markets, price level $P_0$ and GNP level $GNP_0$ shown in Figure 7.1d represent one point on the aggregate-demand curve.

To derive the rest of the aggregate-demand curve, it is necessary to see how the equilibrium level of GNP will change when the price level changes. A fall in the price level from $P_0$ to $P_1$ causes the money demand curve to shift inward in Figure 7.1a (less money is needed for transactions). This leads to a new lower interest rate, $r_1$. As seen in Figure 7.1b, the lower interest rate causes the level of investment to rise to $I_1$. The rise in investment causes the expenditure function in Figure 7.1c to shift up to $E_1$. A new level of equilibrium GNP is established at $GNP_1$. Therefore, another point on the aggregate-demand curve is found when the price level equals $P_1$ and GNP equals $GNP_1$. The derivation of all such price level–GNP combinations represents the aggregate demand

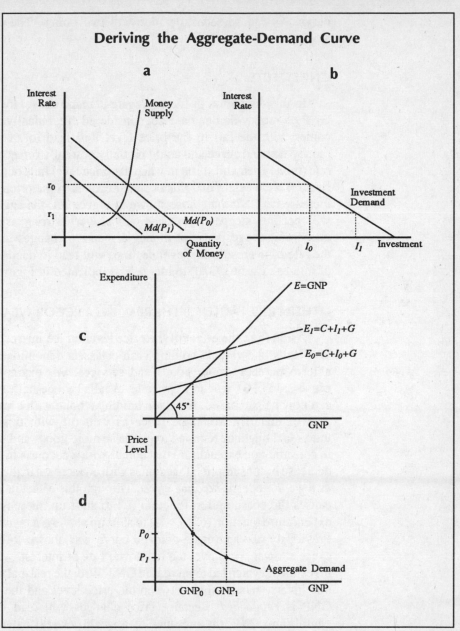

**Figure 7.1**   *In the money market (Fig. 7.1a), when the price level is $P_0$, the interest rate is $r_0$. At $r_0$ investment is $I_0$ (Fig. 7.1b). The expenditure function is then $C + I_0 + G$, and equilibrium GNP equals $GNP_0$ (Fig. 7.1c). A decrease in the price level to $P_1$ decreases money demand, which lowers the equilibrium interest rate to $r_1$. Declines in the rate of interest raise investment to $I_1$. This increases aggregate expenditure to $C + I_1 + G$, and equilibrium GNP equals $GNP_1$. The resulting inverse relationship between the price level and GNP is the aggregate-demand curve: As the price level falls, GNP increases.*

curve. As can be seen after deriving two points, The curve is downward–sloping.

## GNP EFFECTS

In this derivation of the aggregate-demand curve, the effects of increased GNP on money-demand are not considered. Technically, the rise in GNP that comes with the fall in the price level will lead to an outward shift in the money-demand curve and could partially or totally offset the fall in the interest rate (money demand shifts in when the price level falls but shifts out when GNP rises). To the extent that this occurs, declines in the price level lead to smaller increases in GNP than those shown in Figure 7.1; the aggregate demand curve will become steeper. However, unless very strong assumptions are made concerning the response of money demand to changes in the level of GNP or the rate of interest, price level declines will lead to declines in the market rate of interest, causing GNP to increase as indicated in Figure 7.1.

## OTHER PRICE FACTORS: THE REAL-BALANCE OR WEALTH EFFECT

Aside from the effect of the price level on the interest rate, when the price level falls, individuals holding cash or assets denominated in money will be able to purchase more goods and services. For example, if someone is in possession of $1 when the price level falls by one-half, twice as many goods can now be purchased. A person holding a bond with a value of $10,000 at its date of maturity would be twice as well off with this price decline. This individual might be tempted to purchase more goods and services. The increase in consumption expenditure that comes with a decrease in the price level, or the decrease in consumption that comes with an increase in the price level, is known as a *wealth* or *real-balance effect*. Through this effect, a fall in the price level causes the consumption function (*C*) to shift up, thereby causing the overall expenditure function (*C + I + G*) to shift up also. As a result, GNP will increase. Previously, the aggregate-demand curve was shown to be down-sloping because a lower price level led to a lower rate of interest, which led to increased investment, which led to increased GNP. With the real-balance, or wealth, effect this inverse relationship between the price level and the equilibrium level of GNP is *reinforced*. Because price changes will lead to larger changes in equilibrium GNP, the presence of a wealth or real balance effect makes the aggregate-demand curve flatter; a given decline in the price level will lead to a larger increase in GNP.

## Shifting the Aggregate-Demand Curve

The original locations of the economy's aggregate-expenditure curve, money-demand, and money-supply curves are all extremely important in determining the location of the aggregate-demand curve. Changes in the location of any one of these curves will cause the aggregate-demand curve to shift.

Depending on the ultimate sources of change, shift factors can be classified into commodity-market and money-market effects. From the commodity market, the factors leading to *outward* shifts in the aggregate-demand curve include increases in government expenditure, decreased taxes, increased consumer confidence, and increased investor confidence. From the money market, an increased money supply and a desire by individuals to hold less money will cause aggregate demand to shift out. If these variables change in the opposite direction, aggregate demand will shift in.

## DEMAND SHIFT FACTORS: THE COMMODITY MARKET

Factors that cause the aggregate-expenditure curve to shift up also cause the aggregate-demand curve to shift out. In Figure 7.1, if the expenditure curve shown in diagram c had initially been at a higher level when the price level was $P_0$, a higher equilibrium level of GNP would result. For example, suppose the price level $P_0$ was initially associated with expenditure function $E_1$, rather than $E_0$. Equilibrium GNP would then equal $GNP_1$. Price level $P_0$ and GNP level $GNP_1$ would represent a point on a *new* aggregate-demand curve. This point lies to the right of the aggregate-demand curve derived using the original expenditure function, $E_0$. This implies that the aggregate-demand curve had shifted to the right of the curve shown.

**Shifting Aggregate Demand: Commodity Market Factors.** The aggregate-expenditure curve would shift up and the aggregate-demand curve would shift out if the level of autonomous consumption expenditure ($a$), government spending ($G$), or investment expenditure ($I$) increased. Similarly, the expenditure function would shift up and the aggregate demand-curve would shift out if taxes ($T$) were decreased. Aggregate demand shifts in when autonomous consumption, investment, and government expenditure decline or when taxes are increased.

The use of either government-expenditure increases or tax decreases to shift the aggregate demand curve is known as *expansionary fiscal policy*. Recall that rises in autonomous consumption expenditure ($a$) occur with improvements in consumer confidence. For investment, a rise in investor confidence causes the investment-demand curve shown in Figure 7.1b to shift out, thereby increasing the level of investment at all rates of interest. A shift out in the investment-demand curve implies a shift up in the aggregate-expenditure curve and a shift out in the aggregate-demand curve. If international trade is included in the model, a rise in net exports will also cause the expenditure function to shift up and thereby cause the demand curve to shift out.

## DEMAND SHIFT FACTORS: MONEY-MARKET EFFECTS

A rise in the money supply due to expansionary monetary policy will cause the money-supply curve to shift to the right. This causes the aggregate-demand curve to shift right also. In Figure 7.1a, given the money-demand curve associated with price level $P_0$, if the money-supply curve shifted to the right of the supply curve shown, a lower equilibrium interest rate would result. A lower interest rate would cause a higher level of investment, an upward shift in the aggregate-expenditure line, and a higher level of equilibrium GNP. The association of a higher equilibrium GNP level with price level $P_0$ implies that the aggregate-demand curve has shifted out in response to the increase in the money supply.

An inward shift in the money demand curve would lead to a lower interest rate. Once again, this leads to a higher level of GNP at price level $P_0$. Hence, aggregate demand would shift out. This would occur if individuals decide to hold less money at all rates of interest. The actual distance aggregate demand will shift depends on how much the interest rate declines and the sensitivity of investment to changes in the interest rate.

**Price-Level Effects.** An inward shift in the money-demand curve caused by a decline in the price level will *not* cause the aggregate-demand curve to shift. Similarly, an increase in aggregate expenditure caused by a decrease in the price level through the real-balance or wealth effect will not lead to a demand shift. The price level appears on the axis of the aggregate-demand curve; therefore, price-level changes are associated with movements along (versus shifts in) the demand curve.

## Aggregate Demand Shifts and the Multiplier

The distance aggregate demand will shift is related to the expenditure multiplier discussed in Chapter 5. All of the commodity-market and money-market shift factors directly or indirectly cause changes in autonomous expenditure, the same type of change that underlies the economy's multiplier. However, because the multiplier transforms changes in autonomous expenditure into changes in GNP and changes in GNP affect the demand for money, the interest rate will also be affected.

At any given price level, the amount by which aggregate demand will shift with a change in autonomous expenditure can be broken into two separate effects. First there is the change in GNP brought on by the simple multiplier effect. Second, because rising GNP raises the transactions demand for money, there is the change in GNP caused by the change in the interest rate. Because the interest rate rises when GNP increases and vice versa, these effects will work in opposite directions.

### A SIMPLE MULTIPLIER EFFECT

Suppose the aggregate-expenditure line shifts up for some reason—say, a rise in consumer confidence. If money demand is not affected by the changes in GNP, the aggregate-demand curve will shift to the right by the full multiplier effect. As shown in Figure 7.2a, the original expenditure function is $E_0$. Without proportional taxes in the model, it has a slope equal to a marginal propensity to consume of 0.8. The corresponding level of equilibrium GNP is $5,000 billion shown in Figure 7.2b along demand curve $D_0$. The price level is assumed to equal 100. Given the marginal propensity to consume, the expenditure multiplier will be

$$\frac{1}{1-mpc} = \frac{1}{1-0.8} = 5$$

*Ceteris paribus*, with all else constant, a $100-billion rise in autonomous

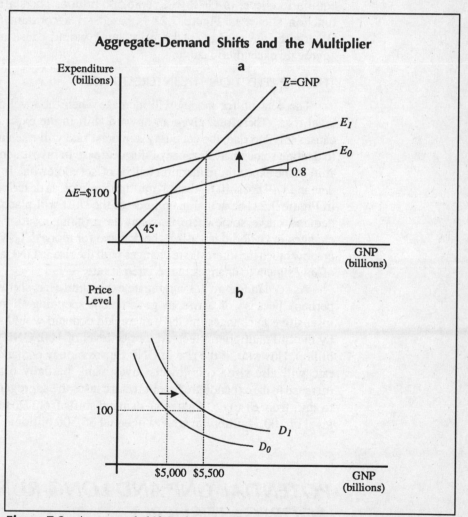

**Figure 7.2** *An upward shift in the expenditure function from $E_0$ to $E_1$ will lead to an outward shift in the aggregate-demand curve. When money demand is not sensitive to changes in GNP, this outward shift corresponds to the simple multiplier effect. Here, a rise in autonomous expenditure of $100 billion leads to a horizontal shift in demand of $500 billion.*

consumption expenditure will lead to a $500-billion increase in equilibrium GNP. Such an increase in GNP would also occur if any other component of autonomous expenditure, such as government spending or investment, rises by $100 billion.

The effects of the $100 billion increase in autonomous expenditure are shown as the upward shift in the expenditure function from $E_0$ to $E_1$. The rise in autonomous consumption causes the demand curve to shift out to from $D_0$ $D_1$ because, given the simple-multiplier effect, at a price level of 100 the equilibrium level of GNP will be $5,500 billion. The shift in the expenditure function shown in Figure 7.2a is based on a constant price level of 100. Otherwise, the change in the price level would cause another shift in the aggregate expenditure curve.

### THE GNP EFFECT ON THE INTEREST RATE

The demand for money will increase when the level of GNP or the price level rises. Therefore, given an upward shift in the expenditure function that causes GNP to rise, the economy's interest rate will rise and cause investment to decline somewhat. Because of this decrease in investment, the initial upward shift in the expenditure function will be offset somewhat. In this case, aggregate demand will not shift by the full multiplier effect, as described above and shown in Figure 7.2. The actual magnitude of the shift will place the new aggregate-demand curve somewhere between its original location and its location if changes in GNP did not affect the demand for money. This magnitude depends on how much the interest rate changes with the rise in GNP and on the sensitivity of investment to changes in the interest rate.

As seen in Figure 7.3, aggregate expenditure has shifted up from $E_0$ to $E_1$, perhaps because of a rise in government spending. If money demand was insensitive to changes in GNP, aggregate demand would shift outward to $D_1$, by the full multiplier effect. At a price level of 100, GNP would equal $5,500 billion. However, if the rise in GNP causes money demand to rise, the interest rate will also rise. This lowers investment, partially offsetting the original increase in the expenditure function and causes the aggregate-expenditure curve to shift from $E_1$ to $E_2$. Aggregate demand shifts from $D_0$ to only $D_2$. At a price level of 100, equilibrium GNP will equal $5,300 billion.

## POTENTIAL GNP AND LONG-RUN AGGREGATE SUPPLY

A demand curve for the economy has been derived, and its shape has been explained, along with the factors that cause it to shift. However, analysis of the ultimate equilibrium that will prevail in the economy is not complete. The

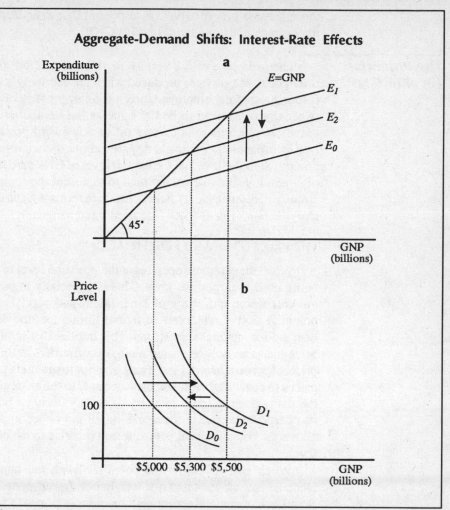

**Figure 7.3** *The upward shift in expenditure from $E_0$ to $E_1$ and shift in aggregate demand from $D_0$ to $D_1$ results from increased autonomous consumption, investment, government spending, or decreased taxes. These shifts do not account for the rise in the interest rate that accompanies increased GNP because of the increased transactions demand for money. When interest rate effects are incorporated, the resulting decline in investment partially offsets the initial shifts shown. Expenditure shifts down from $E_1$ to $E_2$, and demand shifts left, from $D_1$ to $D_2$. With the price level fixed at 100, equilibrium GNP is $5,300 billion.*

problem is that the aggregate-demand curve represents infinitely many GNP–price level combinations. Somehow the one price-GNP level that will prevail in the economy must be found. This is accomplished by combining the aggregate-demand curve with the economy's *aggregate-supply curve*. To develop the aggregate-supply curve it is important first to understand the definition and importance of the *potential* level of GNP.

## The Potential Level of GNP

The *potential*, or *full employment*, level of GNP represents the value of final goods and services produced when the economy's land, labor, and capital resources are fully employed, given the current state of technology. This level is usually considered to be the same as the *natural level* of GNP, a level of output at which there is no upward or downward pressure on the economy's rate of inflation. Economists disagree about the appropriateness of this terminology. Some believe that the natural level of GNP can be associated with levels of unemployment that are too high to represent the economy's potential or full employment level. Nevertheless, the three terms—*natural level*, *potential level*, and *full employment level*—are used interchangeably.

### THE PRICE LEVEL AND POTENTIAL GNP

When the economy operates at the potential level of GNP, its resources are being used at an optimal level. This is especially important in *input markets*, markets where the prices of land, labor, and capital are determined. Above potential GNP, high levels of output throughout the economy mean that the demand for inputs is very strong. This implies that input prices will rise. Input price increases will be passed along to consumers in the form of higher output prices, for two reasons. First, firms attempt to maintain profits by raising output prices to cover higher input costs. Second, to ration or allocate products among the many potential customers trying to buy during a boom, higher prices will be charged. The rise in input and output prices accompanying a level of GNP above the potential level is manifested in a rise in the economy's overall price level.

When GNP is below the potential level, the opposite situation occurs. Demand is weak in output markets; hence, fewer inputs are needed for production. Lack of demand for inputs causes input prices to fall. For example, in the labor market, high rates of unemployment might ultimately cause wages to decline in some industries. The decline in input costs will be passed along to consumers in the form of lower prices. Prices will also fall as firms compete to sell their products in weak markets. In turn, the economy's price level will fall.

**The Price Level and the Capacity Utilization Rate.** The *capacity-utilization rate* also plays a role in affecting the economy's price level. Capacity utilization refers to the fraction of the nation's available capital stock actually in use. There is a direct relationship between the capacity-utilization rate and GNP. For example, during the recession of 1982, the capacity-utilization rate stood at 75 percent. During the later stages of the expansion following this recession, in 1988 and 1989, capacity utilization rose to 84 percent. When capacity utilization is high, firms have less choice over which machines and processes to use. Therefore, machinery may be used more intensively. In addition, less efficient older machines may be called into service. The decrease in efficiency and increase in intensity raise the firm's costs; therefore, output prices rise. During recessions, capacity utilization falls. Firms can then make use of their most efficient machines; this reduces costs and puts downward pressure on prices. Thus, high rates of capacity utilization are associated with rises in the price level, and low capacity utilization rates are associated with price-level decreases.

## UNEMPLOYMENT AND POTENTIAL GNP

Because labor is one of the most important factors of production, to produce higher levels of GNP requires higher levels of employment. At the potential level of GNP, there is said to be "full employment." This does not mean, however, that there is zero unemployment. At the potential level, only *frictional unemployment* should occur, the unemployment that exists when individuals are between jobs, attempting to match their skills and salary expectations with the requirements and pay offers of employers.

At the full-employment or potential level of GNP, the unemployment that exists is called the *full employment* level of unemployment or the *natural* rate of unemployment. Like the natural level of GNP, this is the rate of unemployment at which there is no upward or downward pressure on wage growth and therefore no upward or downward pressure on the rate of inflation. The natural rate of unemployment is currently thought to be about 6 percent.

**Okun's Law.** It has been found that there is a rather stable indirect relationship between changes in unemployment and changes in GNP from the potential level. According to the original statement of Okun's law, each 3 percent decline in GNP below its potential level is associated with a 1 percent rise in the rate of unemployment. Recent estimates suggest that this percentage change in GNP is closer to 2. To see how Okun's law works, suppose GNP falls from its potential level of $5,000 billion to $4,500 billion. This represents a 10 percent drop in GNP from the potential level [(5,000 − 4,500)/5,000]. If each 2.5 percent decline in GNP from the potential level leads to a 1 percent rise in unemployment, unemployment will rise by 4 percent (10/2.5).

One reason that unemployment shows a lower percentage response than the change in GNP relates to the fact that firms are reluctant to lay off trained workers with every decrease in output. Payrolls can be significantly reduced through layoffs during periods of low output demand. However, training costs can easily exceed these short-term savings if unemployed workers choose to find jobs with other employers when conditions improve.

## Inflationary and Recessionary Gaps

Levels of GNP above or below the potential level will affect the economy's price level. *Inflationary gaps* occur when the economy is in equilibrium at a level of GNP above the potential level. The price level will tend to rise. Firms charge higher prices because of strong demand for their output, upward pressure on input prices (caused by the increased input demand required to produce the high level of output), and high capacity-utilization rates.

When equilibrium occurs below potential GNP, there is a *recessionary gap*. There is downward pressure on the price level because of slack demand in input markets, competition among firms to sell their output, and low capacity utilization. These effects can be seen in terms of adjustments in the equilibrium level of GNP using the aggregate-expenditure model and the aggregate-demand curve.

## AN INFLATIONARY GAP

In Figure 7.4, suppose the price level is equal to 80 and the initial aggregate expenditure curve is $E_0(P = 80)$. In Figure 7.4a, the intersection of this expenditure function with the 45-degree line leads to an equilibrium GNP of $6,000 billion. This is $1,000 billion above the potential level of GNP, which is assumed to equal $5,000 billion. In Figure 7.4b, the point of equilibrium corresponds to point A on the aggregate-demand curve; it is located above $6,000 billion at a price level of 80.

Because GNP is above the potential level, product demand, capacity utilization, and input demand are high; this places upward pressure on the price level. As the price level rises, the economy moves upward along the demand curve from point A toward point B. The rise in the price level causes money demand to rise. This leads to a higher interest rate, which reduces the level of investment. The decline in investment causes the aggregate expenditure curve to begin shifting downward from $E_0$ to $E_1$. Through the multiplier, the change in investment that causes the aggregate-expenditure function to shift from $E_0$ to $E_1$ will cause GNP to decline. The downward shift in aggregate expenditure corresponds to the upward movement along the aggregate-demand curve from point A to point B.

Upward pressure on the price level is relieved when the economy arrives at the potential level of GNP and the price level equals 100. This occurs along expenditure function $E_1(P = 100)$ when the level of GNP equals potential at $5,000 billion. Because the price-level change is responsible for the GNP reduction, there is no shift of the aggregate-demand curve. Changes in the price level cause movements along the aggregate-demand curve.

**Measuring the Inflationary Gap.** The *vertical* distance between expenditure function $E_0$ and expenditure function $E_1$ is defined as the inflationary gap. This is the amount components of aggregate expenditure must be lowered to return the economy to potential GNP. When the actual level of GNP is greater than the potential level, the *horizontal* distance between the potential level of GNP and the actual level of GNP is referred to as the (inflationary) *GNP gap*. In Figure 7.4, the GNP gap is $1,000 billion.

## A RECESSIONARY GAP

When the expenditure function crosses the 45-degree line at a GNP level below the potential level, a *recessionary gap* is said to exist. This situation is shown in Figure 7.5. In Figure 7.5a, expenditure function $E_0(P = 150)$ intersects

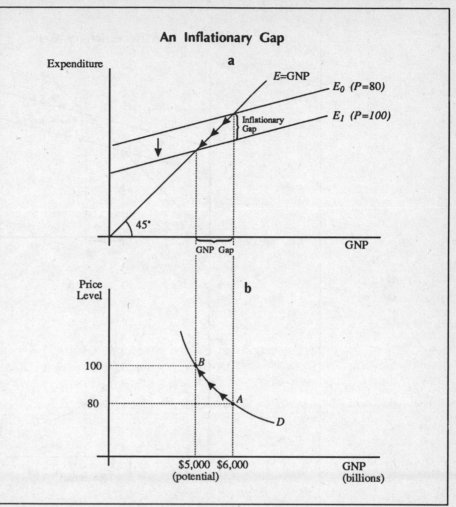

**Figure 7.4** *An inflationary gap occurs when the expenditure function crosses the 45-degree line at a level of GNP above the potential level. Upward pressure on the price level leads to increased money demand, a higher interest rate, and lower investment. The decrease in investment causes the expenditure function to shift down. These changes correspond to the movement along the aggregate demand curve, from P=80 to P=100.*

the 45-degree line at a GNP level of \$4,000 billion. In Figure 7.5b, along the aggregate-demand curve, this corresponds to point *A* above \$4,000 billion at a price level of 150. Because equilibrium GNP is below potential, there is low demand for inputs, low demand for output, and low capacity utilization. These factors place downward pressure on the price level. As the price level declines, money demand is decreased. In turn, the equilibrium interest rate falls, the level of investment increases, and the expenditure function shifts up, from $E_0$ to $E_1$.

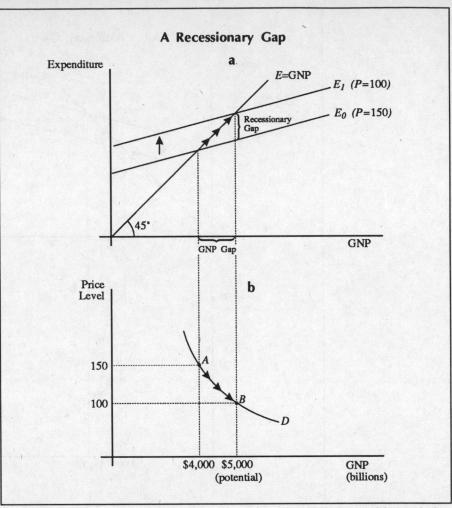

**Figure 7.5**  *A recessionary gap exists when the economy is in equilibrium below potential GNP. Downward pressure on the price level leads to lower money demand and a lower interest rate. This stimulates investment and causes aggregate expenditure to shift up. Downward pressure on the price level and upward pressure on expenditure is alleviated when potential GNP is restored.*

Through the multiplier, this increases the level of GNP. The fall in the price level and rise in GNP are seen as a movement along the economy's aggregate demand curve from point *A* toward point *B*. Downward pressure on prices stops when the potential level of GNP, $5,000 billion, is restored. This corresponds to the intersection of expenditure function $E_1(P = 100)$ and the 45-degree line.

**Measuring the Recessionary Gap.** As with the inflationary gap, a distinction is drawn between the amount GNP must change to restore potential GNP and the amount expenditure must change to shift the aggregate-expenditure curve through the 45-degree line above potential GNP. The recessionary gap is measured as the *vertical* distance between expenditure functions $E_0$ and $E_1$. For the recessionary gap, this represents the amount the components of autonomous expenditure have to be increased to shift the expenditure function upward to restore potential GNP. The (recessionary) GNP gap is \$1,000 billion, the difference between actual GNP and potential GNP.

## GNP GAPS AND THE FLEXIBILITY OF PRICES

It has been shown that price level changes can close inflationary and recessionary gaps. Therefore, when the economy deviates from the potential level of GNP, forces are present that *naturally* push the economy back to potential. In closing these gaps, government interference is not necessary.

However, if prices do not respond to deviations of GNP from the potential level, this self-adjustment will not occur. *Price rigidities* are then said to exist. Based on price-level changes since the end of World War II, there is little question that prices can move readily, though not immediately, in the upward direction. Therefore, inflationary gaps do tend to close themselves. However, prices may not be as free to move downward. The presence of price rigidities in the downward direction means that recessionary gaps may persist unless some sort of outside force, such as increases in government expenditure or tax cuts, is used.

**Price Rigidities and Unemployment Benefits.** Price rigidities in the downward direction stem from the fact that workers are strongly opposed to wage decreases and might be willing to endure long periods of unemployment rather than accept decreases. This problem may be exacerbated by the presence of unemployment benefits. In addition to cushioning the effects of unemployment for workers, unemployment benefits give workers some discretion over the job and pay characteristics they must accept. Workers will not actively seek new jobs when the wage or job characteristics are below their expected level. Because labor costs constitute about 70 percent of all input costs for firms, the inability to cut wages during recessions makes it difficult to decrease prices. The failure of the price level to fall in such circumstances implies that the interest rate will remain stable. Therefore, investment will not be stimulated, and GNP will not rise to the potential level. Recessionary GNP gaps will tend to persist.

**Price Rigidities and Long Term Contracts.** According to the *new Keynesian model*, wage flexibility in the upward and downward direction is not immediate because of long-term labor contracts, normally lasting about three years. Although workers covered under such contracts might like to have wage increases during inflationary gaps, the presence of a contract delays the rate at which wages rise. The presence of long-term contracts implies that recessionary and inflationary GNP gaps will not close until contracts are renegotiated. Such contracts add to price rigidities. On the other hand, *cost-of-living adjustments* (COLAs) written into labor contracts protect workers' real wages from falling;

they raise wages automatically to keep pace, either partially or totally, with increases in the price level.

## RECESSIONARY GAPS, INFLATIONARY GAPS, AND EQUILIBRIUM

There is an important difference between the inflationary and recessionary gaps shown in Figures 7.4 and 7.5 and the stability of equilibrium presented in Chapter 5. It is true that GNP above equilibrium signals producers to reduce output which in turn leads to a decline in GNP, just as the presence of an inflationary gap will lead to a decline in GNP. Similarly, GNP below equilibrium leads to a rise in GNP, as does the presence of a recessionary gap.

However, for both inflationary and recessionary gaps, the economy begins in a state of equilibrium; the expenditure function crosses the 45-degree line. The object of analysis is to determine what happens when the economy is for some reason at an *equilibrium* level of GNP above or below the *potential* level. Price level changes are responsible for the adjustment that takes place. When considering the question of stability, the object of analysis is to consider what happens when the economy is *not* in an initial state of equilibrium, when the economy is for some reason at a level of GNP above or below the equilibrium level. This equilibrium level may or may not be the potential level. Unplanned inventory investment and disinvestment are responsible for the adjustment that takes place.

## The Long-Run Aggregate-Supply Curve

Inflationary and recessionary gaps set into motion forces that cause the economy to return to the potential level of GNP, regardless of the economy's price level. It follows that in the long run, after all adjustments have been made, the economy always operates at the potential level of GNP and that the price level plays no real role. This implies that the economy's long-run aggregate-supply curve is a vertical line at the potential level of GNP, as shown in Figure 7.6. In the long run, the intersection of the long run supply curve and the aggregate-demand curve determine the economy's price level.

## VERTICAL AGGREGATE SUPPLY AND CLASSICAL ECONOMICS

A vertical supply curve is consistent with the notion held by classical economists that in the long run, only real factors—such as the available supplies of land, labor, and capital, and the efficiency with which inputs are transformed into output—determine how much an economy can produce. Money, and prices denominated in money, are important in exchange, but neither prices nor money ultimately affect how much output is produced. The vertical long-run supply curve is also known as a *classical aggregate-supply curve*.

**Vertical Supply and Potential GNP Growth.** In the real world, GNP does not fluctuate around a single potential value; it increases over the long run. In fact, since the end of World War II, GNP has grown at a rate of about 3.2 percent per year. This 3.2 percent rate can be thought of as potential GNP growth.

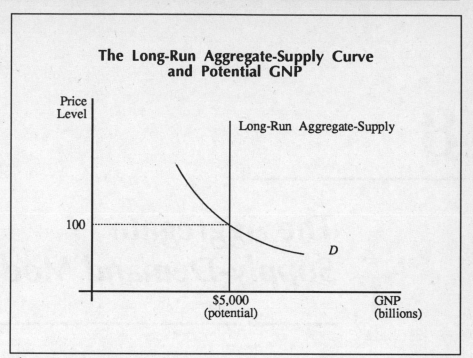

**Figure 7.6** *Because forces exist that restore the economy to potential GNP regardless of the price level, in the long run the aggregate-supply curve appears as a vertical line above potential GNP. Its intersection with the aggregate-demand curve determines the price level.*

The vertical long-run supply curve and the fixed level of potential GNP are assumptions that enable economists to examine macroeconomic forces within a simple context. For practical purposes, the level of GNP specified by the vertical aggregate-supply curve is assumed to represent potential GNP over the period of analysis.

*In this chapter, the aggregate-demand curve has been derived, and the factors which cause it to shift have been discussed. By considering the definition of potential GNP, inflationary and deflationary gaps lead to development of the long run supply curve. Combined with the aggregate-demand curve, this allows determination of the price level and level of GNP in the long run.*

*To model the economy's performance in short-run situations requires development of a short-run aggregate-supply curve. This curve and the complete model of aggregate demand and supply are considered in the next chapter.*

# 8

## The Aggregate Supply-Demand Model

*This chapter continues development of the aggregate supply-demand model. Attention is first focused on deriving the short-run aggregate-supply curve. Next, the aggregate-demand and aggregate-supply curves are combined, and a complete model of how the price level and equilibrium level of GNP are determined is achieved. This model allows analysis of virtually any factor that may affect the variables of the macro economy. It serves as the basis for understanding and finding solutions to the major macroeconomic problems of unemployment, inflation, budget deficits, and international trade imbalances considered in later chapters.*

## THE SHORT-RUN AGGREGATE SUPPLY CURVE

While the aggregate-supply curve is vertical above the potential level of GNP in the long run, in the short run the economy operates at levels below and sometimes above potential GNP. Completing the macro model requires developing a short-run aggregate-supply curve. This curve shows the relationship between the level of aggregate output and the price level necessary to produce that level of aggregate output in short-run situations. Combined with the aggregate-demand curve and the potential level of GNP, its use allows us to see the precise way the economy adjusts in the face of shocks to the system.

**The Shape of the Short-Run Supply Curve**

The relationship between the actual and potential level of GNP plays an important role in determining the shape of the aggregate-supply curve. When the economy operates above the potential level, higher prices are required if more output is to be produced. The higher prices cover the increased input costs that arise from intensive input use. Below the potential level of GNP, all resources are not fully used. Hence, lower input costs will lead to lower prices as firms compete to sell their output. These considerations suggest that the aggregate-supply curve is upward sloping in the short run. Such a supply curve is shown in Figure 8.1 along with the economy's long-run aggregate-supply curve.

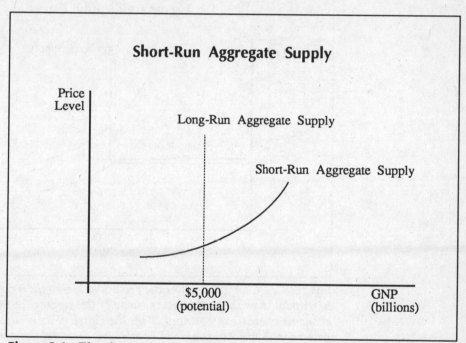

**Figure 8.1** *The short-run relationship between the price level and GNP is seen in the upward-sloping short-run aggregate-supply curve. In the long run, because potential GNP can be restored at any price level, aggregate supply is vertical.*

## THE COMBINED KEYNESIAN-CLASSICAL AGGREGATE SUPPLY CURVE

Assumptions regarding the flexibility of the price level have important implications for the shape of the aggregate-supply curve. For example, if wages and prices are inflexible in both downward and upward directions, the economy's aggregate-supply curve will be horizontal. Increases or decreases in GNP will not lead to changes in the economy's price level. Many economists believe that such price rigidities are more likely to occur when the economy is operating below the potential level of GNP.

On the other hand, when GNP rises above the potential level, it does not take long for the price level to increase. A horizontal aggregate-supply curve is known as a *Keynesian supply curve*. When joined with the vertical long-run or classical supply curve at the potential level of GNP, a supply curve shaped like a sideways *L* with a right angle at potential GNP emerges. Such an aggregate-supply curve incorporates the fact that prices do not readily move downward when GNP falls below potential and tend to rise quickly when GNP increases above potential. This curve is shown in Figure 8.2.

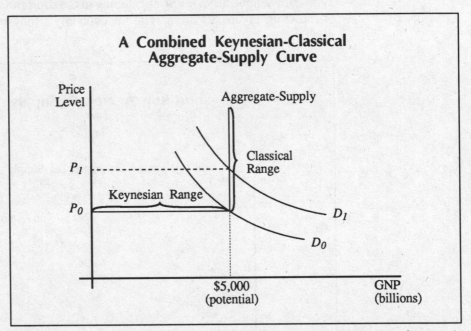

**Figure 8.2**  *Completely inflexible prices imply that the aggregate-supply curve is horizontal, seen in the Keynesian range of this aggregate-supply curve. When the economy operates at potential GNP, the classical or vertical range of the aggregate-supply curve is assumed to be effective. Demand shifts in the Keynesian range will affect only output. The shift in demand from $D_0$ to $D_1$ in the classical range will affect only the price level.*

**Shifts in the Keynesian Range.** In the aggregate supply-demand model, the price level and equilibrium GNP are determined at the point where the supply and demand curves cross. In Figure 8.2, demand curve $D_0$ intersects the supply curve at potential GNP between the Keynesian and classical ranges. Should aggregate demand shift left to intersect aggregate supply below the potential level of GNP, GNP would fall, but the price level would not. Should aggregate demand shift right to intersect aggregate supply in the vertical or classical range, the price level will increase, but GNP will not. This is shown in the shift in demand $D_0$ to $D_1$; GNP remains fixed, and the price level rises from $P_0$ to $P_1$.

The assumptions inherent in the sideways $L$-shaped aggregate-supply curve imply that its shape will change with such an outward demand shift. Because prices are downwardly inflexible, after the price level rises to $P_1$, it will not fall. Therefore, the horizontal or Keynesian range of the aggregate-supply curve will shift up to the price level established by the intersection of demand curve $D_1$ and the vertical portion of the supply curve. The economy's new supply curve is the sideways $L$ composed of the dotted horizontal line at price level $P_1$ and the vertical line above $P_1$ over the potential level of GNP.

## THE LUCAS, OR NEW CLASSICAL, SUPPLY CURVE

The *Lucas supply curve,* named after Robert Lucas of the University of Chicago, has a shape similar to the short-run supply curve portrayed in Figure 8.1. However, the reasons for its upward slope are not the same. According to Lucas, a general rise in the economy's price level should not lead to an increase in output; the relative increase in all revenues and costs does not increase real profits for individual firms. Hence, while there is an incentive to raise prices, there is no reason to offer more output for sale.

According to microeconomic theory, the typical supply curve for an individual firm is upward-sloping; a rise in the price of an individual producer's product will lead that producer to increase output. This is because higher prices can lead to greater profits. According to Lucas, when producers misperceive economy-wide price increases and interpret them as price increases affecting the relative price of their product, they will produce more, and the level of GNP will rise above potential. This explains the upward slope of the short-run aggregate-supply curve. However, once individual producers realize that their relative position has not improved (the price level has risen along with the price of their product), they will reduce production (but not prices), so that the potential level of output is once again attained. It follows that the Lucas supply curve will shift to the left with increases in the expected price level.

*Shifting Aggregate Supply*

Both the long-run and short-run supply curves are subject to shifts. However, the factors causing these shifts are very different. As might be expected, the distinction between long-run and short-run supply shift factors rests with the determinants of aggregate supply in the short run and the long run.

### SHIFTING LONG-RUN SUPPLY

The economy's long-run supply curve is a vertical line located above the potential level of GNP. Therefore, the long-run supply curve will shift outward or inward, given changes in those factors affecting the level of potential GNP. These factors include the size of the labor force, the size of the capital stock, the availability of natural resources, the way resources are used through entrepreneureal activity, and the state of technology prevailing in the economy.

## SHIFTING SHORT-RUN SUPPLY

In any time period, it is short-run aggregate supply that reveals how the economy's price level will change with changes in the level of output supplied. Because output prices are based primarily on input costs, economy-wide increases in the level of wages, rents, interest, or profit (paid, respectively, to labor, resource suppliers, owners of capital, and entrepreneurs) will lead to a higher price level at every level of output supplied. That is, as shown in Figure 8.3, with input price increases, short-run aggregate supply will shift in, or to the left. Such leftward shifts in supply are defined as *supply shocks*. Input price decreases cause the short-run aggregate supply curve to shift out to the right. When supply shifts out a lower price level is associated with each level of GNP.

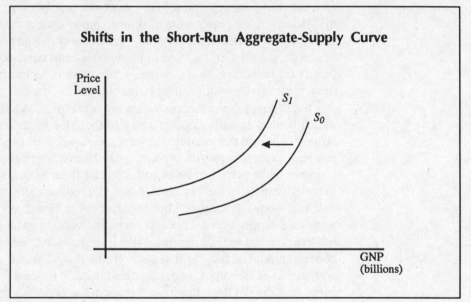

**Figure 8.3**  *A supply shock occurs when the short-run aggregate-supply curve shifts to the left. A higher price level is required for the production of all levels of GNP. Such shifts occur when input costs such as wages rise.*

**Taxes, Subsidies, and Regulation.** Another factor that can affect the relationship between the supply of output and the price level at which it is offered for sale is the rate at which businesses are taxed. Higher taxes on businesses will cause an inward shift in the short-run aggregate supply curve. On the other hand, government *subsidies*—payments to businesses for producing certain products or using certain inputs—reduce costs and cause the short-run aggregate supply curve to shift out. Finally, government regulation can force businesses to adopt more expensive technologies. For example, forcing electric utilities to use scrubbers to reduce the pollution that comes with burning coal adds to the cost of producing electricity, which in turn affects its price. The use of electricity by virtually every industry implies that all product prices will rise and that the price level at each possible level of GNP will rise. Hence, short-run supply will shift up. Because such technological changes can affect the potential level of GNP, long-run supply may also shift.

# THE AGGREGATE SUPPLY-DEMAND MODEL

When graphed together, the intersection of the aggregate demand- and supply-curves determines the economy's equilibrium level of GNP and its price level. As seen in Figure 8.4, aggregate demand crosses aggregate supply directly above the economy's potential level of GNP, $5,000 billion. The price level established by their intersection is 100. The short-run aggregate-supply curve shown has characteristics of both the Keynesian and the long-run supply curve. At levels of GNP below the potential level it is not steeply sloped. However, as the potential level is reached and surpassed, the slope of the aggregate-supply curve steepens and ultimately becomes vertical.

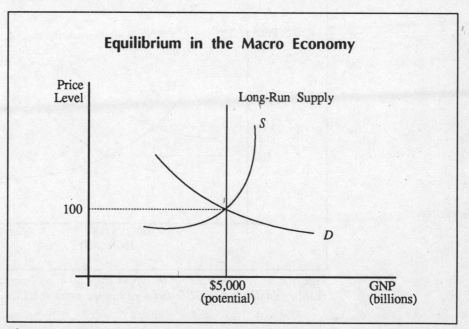

**Figure 8.4**  *When combined, the intersection of aggregate demand and aggregate supply determines both the equilibrium level of GNP and the price level. In the long run, this occurs at potential GNP.*

As with the simple model of supply and demand, it is possible to consider the effects shift factors on the location of the aggregate demand and supply curves. It is then possible to predict the changes in the price level and equilibrium level of GNP that will occur. The complete aggregate demand-supply model is a powerful tool for translating changes in real-world variables into changes in the price level and GNP. Given knowledge of how the unemployment rate and the individual components of aggregate demand respond to changes in the price level and GNP, predictions of changes in these variables can also be made.

## Supply Shifts and Equilibrium

Starting with an economy in equilibrium at the potential level of GNP and a price level of 100, Figure 8.5 shows the effects of a supply shock, an inward shift in the supply curve. Such a shift would occur with an economy-wide rise in factor payments—wages, rents, profits, or interest. It might also occur because of some sort of technological setback that causes production costs to rise. Finally, it might result from increased government taxes or regulations on businesses that cause production costs to rise. Examples of leftward shifts in supply include the supply shocks of the 1970s. These shocks occurred when oil prices quadrupled in 1973 and doubled in 1979.

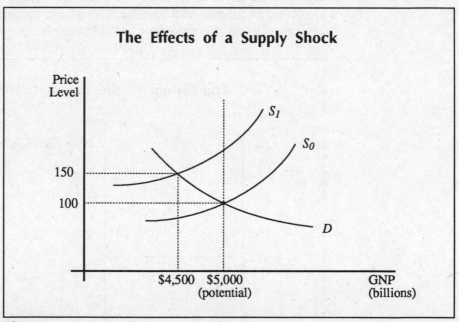

**Figure 8.5**  *A leftward shift in supply from $S_0$ to $S_1$ caused by higher input costs results in a decline in GNP and a rise in the price level.*

## ADJUSTMENT AFTER A SUPPLY SHOCK

The shift in the supply curve from $S_0$ to $S_1$ results in a rise in the price level from 100 to 150. Equilibrium GNP falls from $5,000 billion to $4,500 billion. As a result of the decline in GNP, under Okun's law, unemployment will rise. The simultaneous rise in the price level and the rate of unemployment is known as *stagflation*.

**The Effect on Consumption.** After the supply shock, GNP decreases and the price level increases. Because GNP is an important determinant of consumption, consumption will fall. The price-level rise will further affect the level of consumption if there is a *wealth or real-balance effect*. Such an effect is present when the value of assets tied to the value of money decreases because the price level has increased. For example, if a family has $100 in a savings account and the price level doubles, the purchasing power of the $100 asset is cut in half. After a supply shock, a real-balance effect will cause consumption expenditure to decline.

The effects of a leftward supply shift on consumption can be seen more readily by actually drawing the curves for the affected variables. Figure 8.6a shows consumption as a function of GNP. The fall in GNP from $5,000 billion to $4,500 billion due to the supply shift causes consumption to decline from $3,000 billion to $2,700 billion. Because the rise in the price level would reduce

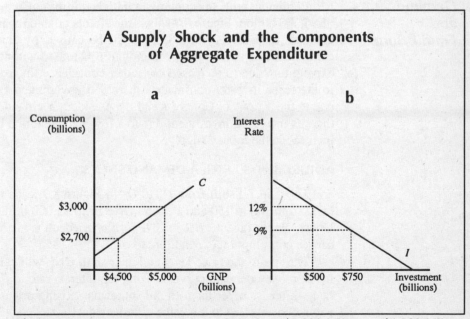

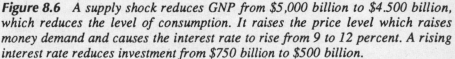

**Figure 8.6** *A supply shock reduces GNP from $5,000 billion to $4.500 billion, which reduces the level of consumption. It raises the price level which raises money demand and causes the interest rate to rise from 9 to 12 percent. A rising interest rate reduces investment from $750 billion to $500 billion.*

the value of assets tied to the value of money, the presence of a real-balance or wealth effect would cause the consumption function's intercept to decline and further reduce consumption (the consumption function would shift down because asset values, not income, are affected).

**The Effect on Investment.** The rise in the price level also implies that money demand will increase; there is an increased transactions demand for money. This will cause a rise in the interest rate (however, this effect could be partially offset by the decline in GNP). The rise in the rate of interest causes investment to fall. Suppose that the rise in the price level raises the interest rate from 9 percent to 12 percent. As seen in Figure 8.6b, this causes investment to decline from $750 billion to $500 billion.

**The Effect on Government Spending and Taxes.** Because government spending and taxes are assumed to be autonomous, they are not affected by price-level changes, changes in GNP, or changes in the other variables that have changed. There will be no change in their magnitude.

**A Positive Supply Shock.** Changes associated with a rightward shift in aggregate supply would be just the opposite of those described above; the price level would fall and GNP would rise. The implications of these changes for the rate of interest, level of unemployment, and the components of aggregate demand would also work in the opposite direction.

## Demand Shifts and Equilibrium

Beginning with an economy in initial equilibrium at a potential GNP level of $5,000 billion, Figure 8.7 shows the effects of an outward shift in aggregate demand. Such an outward shift might be caused by changes in one of the components of autonomous expenditure: increased autonomous consumption expenditure due to increased consumer confidence, increased investment due to increased investor confidence, increased government spending or a tax cut due to the actions of Congress and the president. Demand will also shift out if there is increased investment due to a lower interest rate brought about by an increase in the money supply.

### ADJUSTMENTS AFTER A DEMAND SHOCK

The demand shift from $D_0$ to $D_1$ in Figure 8.7 leads to a rise in the price level from 100 to 150 and a rise in GNP from $5,000 billion to $5,500 billion. Under Okun's law, the rise in GNP results in a decline in unemployment. It also causes consumption expenditure to rise.

The rise in the price level and the rise in GNP will cause an outward shift in the money-demand curve, causing the interest rate to rise. A rising interest rate will cause investment to fall somewhat. Rising prices also imply that the value of assets tied to the value of money declines. This will cause the level of consumption to decline if the real-balance or wealth effect is present. Thus, the real-balance effect could partially offset the rise in consumption due to the rise in GNP. As in the case of a supply shift, government expenditure and taxes are not affected (unless a change in one of these variables caused the demand shift

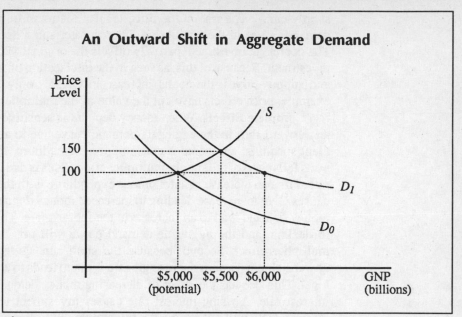

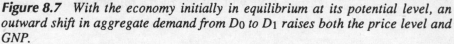

**Figure 8.7** *With the economy initially in equilibrium at its potential level, an outward shift in aggregate demand from $D_0$ to $D_1$ raises both the price level and GNP.*

in the first place). Compared with the aggregate demand increase, a decrease in aggregate demand will lead to an opposite series of effects.

## DEMAND SHIFTS: THE PRICE LEVEL AND THE SIMPLE MULTIPLIER

As discussed in Chapter 5, the simple multiplier overstates the amount by which GNP will increase given a change in autonomous expenditure. The effects of income taxes, international trade, the interest rate, and the price level are not accounted for. Under the assumption that money demand is not sensitive to changes in GNP, the complete aggregate demand-supply model allows explicit analysis of the amount by which the actual increase in GNP will fall short of the simple multiplier effect due to rising prices.

When money demand is not sensitive to GNP, an increase in some component of autonomous expenditure will cause the aggregate-demand curve to shift horizontally by an amount equal to the simple-multiplier effect. Suppose the marginal propensity to consume is 0.8 and investment rises by $200 billion. In Figure 8.7, if the price level did not rise, the rightward shift in aggregate demand would lead to a GNP level of $6,000 billion. The simple multiplier is seen to equal 5 and the multiplier effect is $1,000 billion.

Because the short-run aggregate-supply curve is upward-sloping, the price level will not remain at 100 but rises to 150, the level consistent with the intersection of the new aggregate-demand curve and the original aggregate-supply curve. The rise in the price level leads to an outward shift in money demand, a rise in the equilibrium interest rate, and a decrease in investment. The decline in investment partially offsets the original $200-billion increase in investment. Because of this, as seen in the intersection of the aggregate demand and supply curves, the actual increase in GNP is only $500 billion. In this example, price effects have cut the value of the multiplier effect by one-half.

**Complete Effects.** When money demand is sensitive to the level of GNP, an outward shift in the aggregate-demand curve due to an increase in government spending, autonomous consumption expenditure, investment or net exports falls short of the simple-multiplier effect. This is due to a rise in the interest rate. First, an increase in autonomous expenditure with the price level constant causes GNP to increase, leading to increased money demand. Outward shifts in money demand lead to an increase in the interest rate. This causes investment to decline, and the aggregate-demand curve will not shift right by the full multiplier effect. Second, because the short run aggregate-supply curve is upward-sloping, a shift out in aggregate demand leads to an increase in the price level. This also has the effect of increasing money demand, further raising the interest rate. A rising interest rate causes investment to fall. For these two reasons, GNP will not rise by the full simple multiplier effect.

## LONG-RUN EQUILIBRIUM AND POTENTIAL GNP

In the examples of shifting supply and demand described so far, levels of GNP differing from the potential level are achieved in the short run. However, levels of GNP below the potential level are associated with recessionary gaps and slack demand in input markets; this places downward pressure on input costs. Declines in input costs cause the short-run aggregate-supply curve to shift out. Thus, in the long run, forces exist that will shift the short-run supply curve to the right until potential GNP is restored. When GNP is above the potential level, an inflationary GNP gap exists. Upward pressure on input costs implies that the short-run supply curve will ultimately shift left, causing each level of output to be associated with higher price levels.

These facts are illustrated in Figure 8.8. In Figure 8.8a the economy is initially in equilibrium at a GNP level of $4,500 billion. Supply curve $S_0$ crosses the demand curve $500 billion below the potential GNP level of $5,000 billion. When input prices begin to fall, supply will begin to shift right. Eventually it coincides with supply curve $S_1$, which intersects the demand curve above the potential level of GNP.

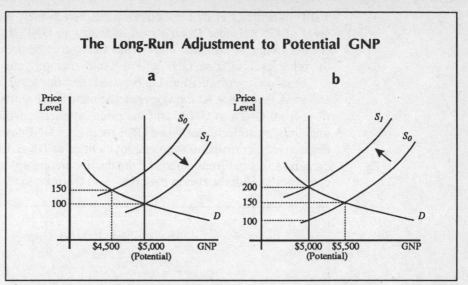

**The Long-Run Adjustment to Potential GNP**

**Figure 8.8** *In the long run, supply shifts ensure that the economy operates at potential GNP. In figure 8.8a, equilibrium GNP is below potential when supply curve $S_0$ crosses the demand at $4,500 billion. Downward pressure on input costs ultimately causes aggregate supply to shift from $S_0$ to $S_1$, restoring potential GNP. In figure 8.8b, GNP is above potential at the intersection of supply curve $S_0$ and the demand curve. Rising input costs eventually cause a leftward shift in supply from $S_0$ to $S_1$. Long-run equilibrium occurs at the potential level of $5,000 billion.*

In Figure 8.8b, in the long run, supply curve $S_0$ will shift upward toward curve $S_1$ until potential GNP is restored. Given the demand curve, this occurs at a price level of 200.

## The Phillips Curve

The *Phillips curve* is a statistical relationship that exists between the inflation rate and the rate of unemployment. It was originally estimated by economist A. W. Phillips in 1958 as a relationship between wage growth and unemployment. The Phillips curve shows that as unemployment declines, the rate of inflation tends to rise. At one time, this inverse relationship was believed to be stable and therefore useful in making predictions about rates of inflation expected at various levels of unemployment. The economy's performance in the 1970s upset this belief; several episodes of inflation and unemployment rising simultaneously were experienced.

### THE PHILLIPS RELATIONSHIP

The Phillips curve deals with the relationship between the rate of unemployment and the rate of inflation. However, the factors that lead to this relationship can be seen in terms of the price level and GNP through use of the aggregate demand-supply diagram. With a fixed aggregate supply curve, outward shifts in aggregate demand cause the price level to increase along with the level of GNP. Under Okun's law, increases in GNP are associated with decreases in unemployment. Thus, when the aggregate demand curve shifts out, the price level will rise, GNP will rise, and unemployment will fall.

Such an inverse relationship between the price level and unemployment is shown in Figure 8.9. As the aggregate-demand curve shifts from $D_0$ to $D_1$, GNP rises from $GNP_0$ to $GNP_1$ and the price level rises from $P_0$ to $P_1$. Because unemployment decreases when GNP increases, GNP levels $GNP_0$ and $GNP_1$, respectively, correspond to unemployment rates $U_0$ and $U_1$. Therefore, when demand shifts out from $D_0$ to $D_1$, the decline in unemployment from $U_0$ to $U_1$ corresponds with the rise in the price level from $P_0$ to $P_1$.

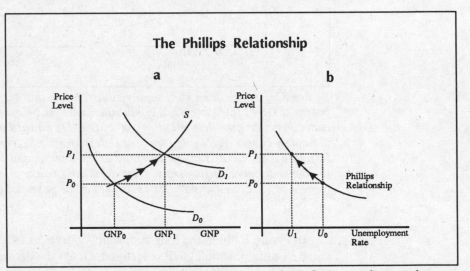

**Figure 8.9**  *The inverse relationship between the inflation and unemployment rates is known as the Phillips curve. Here this relationship is illustrated using the price level. Outward demand shifts along a fixed aggregate-supply curve lead to a higher price level, a higher level of GNP, and lower level of unemployment.*

### THE LONG-RUN PHILLIPS CURVE

The Phillips relationship between the price level and the unemployment rate stems from shifts in aggregate demand along a fixed aggregate-supply curve. Supply shocks in the 1970s were the reason for a breakdown in the stable Phillips relationship. A supply shock is a leftward shift in the aggregate-supply curve caused by higher factor prices such as oil prices. The reasons for the breakdown can be seen by reconsidering the derivation of the Phillips relationship.

In Figure 8.10, assume that the Phillips curve labeled $PC(S_0)$ is derived using supply curve $S_0$ given shifts in demand. One point on this Phillips curve is $P_0$, $U_0$. Here unemployment rate $U_0$ corresponds to GNP level $GNP_0$. After a supply shock, the aggregate supply curve shifts left to $S_1$. Price level $P_1$ is now associated with $GNP_0$ and with unemployment rate $U_0$. With this supply shift, the Phillips curve has shifted up to $PC(S_1)$. Therefore, no stable set of prices is associated with specific rates of unemployment.

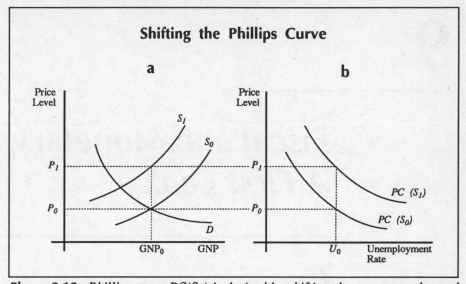

**Figure 8.10** *Phillips curve $PC(S_0)$ is derived by shifting the aggregate-demand curve along aggregate-supply curve $S_0$. When GNP equals $GNP_0$, the price level equals $P_0$, and the unemployment rate is $U_0$. If supply shifts to $S_1$, the price level equals $P_1$ when GNP equals $GNP_0$. Because unemployment rate $U_0$ now corresponds to price level $P_1$, the Phillips curve has shifted up to $PC(S_1)$.*

Because GNP always returns to potential in the long run regardless of the price level, unemployment equals the natural rate in the long run. Therefore, the *long-run* Phillips curve, like the long-run aggregate-supply curve, is vertical.

*The aggregate supply-demand model developed in this chapter incorporates the definitions and models of previous chapters into one simple diagram. By keeping in mind the various subcomponents that lead to the development of the supply-demand model, a complete understanding of the interrelationships between major macroeconomic variables is achieved. In subsequent chapters, this complete model is used to analyze the most important macroeconomic problems of our time. Attention will be focused on how government policy can be used to stabilize the economy after aggregate demand and supply shocks. In addition, the effects of budget deficits and international trade will be considered.*

# 9

## Fiscal and Monetary Policy: A First Look

*In the past several chapters, consideration of the interrelationship between various macroeconomic aggregates has culminated in the aggregate supply-demand model. The stage is now set for analysis of the government's ability to alter economic conditions to achieve its policy objectives. These objectives include achieving potential GNP growth and maintaining low rates of inflation, both of which reflect increased economic stability.*

*The variables government controls directly include the money supply, government spending, and taxes. Changes in government spending and taxes are classified as fiscal policy. As a component of aggregate expenditure, changes in government spending have a direct effect on the level of economic activity. Tax changes, on the other hand, must wait for the actions of consumers before any ultimate effect on expenditure occurs. Monetary policy involves increasing or decreasing the nation's money supply. This alters the interest rate and affects private investment decisions.*

*Important questions regarding fiscal and monetary policies relate to the relative effectiveness of each in achieving a desired objective. The speed with which a policy can be put into action, the size of the stimulus needed to achieve a desired effect, the effects of the policy on consumption, investment, the interest rate, and the price level are all important. In addition, trade-offs between policy goals, such as maintaining low unemployment and low inflation, must be taken into account. For example, an expansionary fiscal policy may cure the problem of high unemployment but simultaneously leads to inflation and a higher interest rate. A higher interest rate will reduce private investment. In designing appro-*

*priate responses to the problems that arise in the macro economy, the potential implications of all possible outcomes must be considered.*

# GOVERNMENT EXPENDITURE, DEBT, AND THE DEFICIT

Budget outlays by the federal government account for over 20 percent of total GNP. These outlays take the form of government purchases of specific goods and services. They also include transfer payments to individuals receiving social security, veterans benefits, and welfare payments. For the government's budget to be balanced, its outlays must be matched by budget receipts, which are predominantly composed of tax revenues. When the government's outlays exceed its receipts, a *budget deficit* occurs. Budget deficits are financed by the sale of bonds by the government to the government itself and to individuals. The cumulation of budget deficits from previous years that have not been paid off represents the *national debt.* In 1990, the federal budget deficit was about $220 billion. The total debt equaled $3,206 billion. As a basis for comparison, the debt and the deficit are often expressed as percentages of GNP. With a 1990 GNP level of $5518.9 billion, the deficit amounts to about 4 percent of GNP, and the debt amounts to about 58 percent of GNP.

In recent years, the government's deficits have become quite large and have added substantially to the national debt. This fact has caused some concern about the government's ability to pay its debt and the burden that will be experienced by future generations as the debt is repaid.

## Cyclical and Structural Deficits

To understand the nature of the federal deficit better, a distinction is made between the *cyclical deficit*—that part of the deficit arising from the state of the economy—and the *structural deficit*—that part due to government spending in excess of tax revenues when the economy is operating at potential GNP.

### THE CYCLICAL DEFICIT

A deficit caused by the automatic increase in welfare expenditures and decrease in tax revenues occurring during a recession is *cyclical* deficit. During recessions, it is desirable that the government run a cyclical deficit. An attempt to balance the budget and cover expenditures with additional taxes will lead to lower levels of disposable income for consumers, lower consumption, and therefore a lower level of GNP and a worse recession. Similarly, to stem inflationary pressures that arise when GNP rises above the potential level, it is desirable for the government to operate with a budget surplus. By doing so, the amount of money not spent will not add to aggregate expenditure during booms.

## THE STRUCTURAL DEFICIT

A deficit due to government spending and tax imbalance at the potential level of GNP is a structual deficit. Thus, if the economy is in equilibrium at the potential level of GNP and the government runs a deficit, a structural deficit exists. Because the economy is operating at the potential level, the cyclical deficit must be zero. The structural deficit found at the potential level of GNP serves as a reference point for gauging the size of the cyclical deficit. When the economy deviates from the potential level, the cyclical deficit equals the total deficit minus the structural deficit.

Suppose when the economy operates at the potential level of GNP the total deficit is $180 billion. By definition, this is the structural deficit. If the economy goes into recession and the total deficit rises to $250 billion, the cyclical deficit is the difference between the total deficit and the structural deficit, $70 billion. During a boom the economy moves from potential GNP to a level of GNP above potential. The rise in tax revenues and decline in welfare expenditures might reduce the total deficit to $150 billion. The structural deficit still equals $180 billion, but there is a *cyclical surplus* of $30 billion.

## PROBLEMS WITH THE STRUCTURAL DEFICIT

The presence of a structural deficit implies that the government spends more than it receives when GNP is at potential. Because it adds to aggregate expenditure, the presence of a structural deficit has an inflationary effect on the economy when GNP rises above the potential level. Without a structural deficit, aggregate demand would intersect the aggregate-supply curve at a lower GNP level; lower GNP levels are associated with lower price levels along the upward-sloping short run aggregate-supply curve. The presence of a structural deficit also causes rearrangement in the mix of overall expenditure. Specifically, government expenditure not financed through tax receipts leads to higher levels of consumption expenditure than would prevail if taxes were raised to match government spending levels. The expansionary nature of the deficit also leads to a higher interest rate, thereby reducing or *crowding out* private investment.

## *The National Debt*

Each year, as part of its outlay, the government pays off a fraction of the accumulated deficits incurred in previous years. That part of these accumulated deficits not paid off represents the national debt. Many individuals feel that the United States would be better off without this debt, and some have proposed a *balanced budget amendment* to the Constitution. This would ultimately reduce the national debt to zero.

## THE PROBLEM OF THE DEBT

On the surface, it is not obvious why the public debt is a greater problem to the economy than private debt. For example, homewoners in the U.S. readily accept 20- and 30-year mortgages in amounts that are equivalent to several or more years' income. Mortgage debt owed by individuals amounts to about $4,000 billion, an amount that exceeds the total national debt.

Arguments against budget deficits and government debt usually point to the repayment problems likely to be faced by future generations. To the extent that the bonds sold to finance the debt are held by foreigners, future generations of Americans will be burdened; income is transferred from the U.S. to foreign countries. However, if Americans own the bonds, payments on the debt go from one group of Americans to another. One group of Americans benefits at the expense of another, but there is no net loss to the U.S. economy.

Concerns that the national debt will ultimately bankrupt the economy are unfounded. The debt is denominated in U.S. dollars. The federal government has the power to print dollars to retire any debt. However, this could cause inflation.

If the budget deficits leading to the debt cause decreased investment expenditure, the decline in the rate of increase of the nation's capital stock could reduce the level of economic growth. Whether this decline in growth occurs depends greatly on how the government spends its money. Nonproductive government expenditures, such as military buildups far in excess of actual defense requirements or expenditure on social-welfare programs that do nothing to deal with the root causes of poverty and inequality, add nothing to future economic growth. On the other hand, debt brought on by higher educational expenditures; infrastructure improvements such as highway or airport construction; or inventions that result from defense, space, or other types of government expenditures can enhance the level of economic growth.

Finally, the debt and the deficit may tie the hands of policy-makers. The presence of a large debt or structural deficit may preclude engaging in expansionary fiscal policy (such as tax cuts or government spending increases) during a recession. The government's inability to act will prolong the recession.

**When Debt Is Accumulated.** Much of the government's debt has been contracted during times of war and recession. For example, during World War II, U.S. debt soared from 46 percent of GNP in 1941 to 122 percent of GNP in 1945. The deficit and debt also showed significant increases during the 1974–1975, 1982, and other recessions. The latter 1980s were an exception to this situation; peacetime economic growth coincided with continued large increases in the debt.

## FISCAL POLICY

*Fiscal policy* refers to changes in government expenditure and taxes designed to affect the level of GNP or the economy's price level. Deciding on appropriate fiscal policies is the job of the president and the Congress. This responsibility stems from the period just after World War II when the Employment Act of 1946 was passed. This act, a response to the devastating effects of unemployment during the Great Depression, made the federal government responsible for promoting "maximum employment, production, and purchasing power" in the economy. In 1978, Congress involved the federal government more deeply with the economy's performance by passing the Full Employment and Balanced Growth Act of 1978. This act set particular targets for macroeconomic performance, including a 4 percent level of unemployment and low rates of inflation.

## Lags in Fiscal Policy

In implementing fiscal policy to address a particular economic problem, account must be taken of the lag that occurs from the time the economic problem necessitating a policy response is recognized to the time the policy has an effect on the problem. Failure to consider lags can have important implications for the economy. For example, if a policy is enacted to fight unemployment, long lags could see the policy taking effect at a time when the unemployment rate had already fallen to the potential level. The additional stimulus caused by the expansionary fiscal policy might then lead to rates of unemployment below the full employment level, and higher rates of inflation could result. Lags in fiscal policy fall into three categories: the *recognition lag*, the *policy lag*, and the *implementation lag*.

### THE RECOGNITION LAG

The *recognition lag* refers to the time it takes to determine that an economic problem actually exists. Such lags occur because economic data regarding the present state of the economy are not readily available and changes in economic variables are not necessarily indicative of a macroeconomic problem. For example, a rise in the price level last month might be due to a rise in the level of economic activity above the potential level, or it could be due to temporary price adjustments for commodities in particular markets such as food and gasoline. The former change might benefit from an offsetting fiscal response that slows economic growth; a fiscal response to treat the latter price rise would be inappropriate.

**Economic Forecasting.** Sorting out the nature of changes in economic data to identify those reflective of potentially inflationary or recessionary conditions is an important objective of economic forecasting. The most important forecasting tool in use by government today is the *Index of Leading Indicators*, composed of several measures of economic activity, such as stock market prices and the number of new building permits issued. These measures are likely to move up or down before the overall level of economic activity increases or decreases.

Economic forecasts are based on past experiences and past relationships between variables. They are likely to be inaccurate when the economy faces events not previously experienced. For example, most economic models in use in the early 1970s were constructed under the hypothesis that aggregate-demand shifts were the most important source of economic fluctuations. When supply shocks occurred, predictions concerning inflation, unemployment, and GNP growth tended to be off the mark because methods of accounting for such shocks had not been incorporated into economic models.

### THE POLICY LAG

Once a problem has been recognized, policy must be formulated and enacted to deal with it. For fiscal policy, this implies that the president and the Congress must decide upon appropriate legislation. Unless there is a dire economic emergency, the speed with which this can be accomplished is not great. Decisions concerning how much should be spent, where funds will be spent, and on what social programs must be made. If taxes are to be raised or cut, consideration of who will bear the burden or receive the benefit is required. When constituents may not be pleased with the fiscal authority's policy choice, decisions tend to be slow in coming.

### THE IMPLEMENTATION LAG

Once the president and Congress have agreed to pursue a particular fiscal policy, the economy can respond very quickly. Changes in government spending, an important component of aggregate expenditure, cause an almost immediate change in GNP through the multiplier. As aggregate demand shifts inward or outward, the shape of the aggregate-supply curve determines the actual change in GNP and the corresponding price response.

With tax changes, the effects are not as direct. They depend on how consumers react to the change in their disposable income. For example, if a tax increase is seen as *temporary*, consumers may attempt to maintain their previous level of spending until pre-existing tax rates are restored. They can do so by making use of their savings. In this case, the tax increase may have no effect on the level of economic activity. However, if the tax change is seen as *permanent*, consumers are more likely to adjust their expenditure levels downward, and the tax change will have an effect on GNP. Historically, these considerations are verified in the Kennedy-Johnson permanent tax cuts of 1964, which led to increased GNP. The 1968 temporary tax surcharge, passed to reduce aggregate expenditure during the Vietnam War buildup, was ineffective. The tax cuts that took place in the early 1980s were also considered permanent.

## Automatic Stabilizers

Some components of fiscal policy require no direct action by the president and Congress. These components respond automatically to changes in the level of economic activity. For example, when unemployment is high, unemployment and welfare benefits rise as soon as those eligible for such payments apply for them. In addition, increases and decreases in income move individuals into higher and lower tax brackets because of the progressive tax system. During an economic boom, many families in the 15 percent tax bracket experience sufficient income gains to push them into the 28 percent bracket; others in the 28 percent bracket are pushed into the 31 percent bracket. A higher tax bracket means that less of the additional income can be used for consumption. This has the effect of dampening the boom and reducing the inflationary pressures present. During recessions, the process works in reverse: Falling income automatically places individuals in lower tax brackets; this partially offsets the reduction in disposable income caused by the recession and induces greater consumption.

# MONETARY POLICY

Changes in the economy's money supply designed to affect the interest rate, level of GNP, or rate of inflation are classified as *monetary policy*. Monetary policy is formulated and implemented by the Federal Reserve bank (Fed) under the leadership of the chairman of the Fed's *Board of Governors*. To control the money supply, the Fed relies on open-market operations, changes in the reserve ratio, changes in the discount rate, and moral suasion. Of these methods of control, open market operations—the buying and selling of government securities on the open market—has historically been most important. Open market operations are decided upon by the Federal Open Market Committee led by the Fed chairman. The Board of Governors is responsible for setting the reserve ratio and the discount rate.

## Lags in Monetary Policy

As with fiscal policy, monetary policy is subject to a recognition lag, a policy lag, and an implementation lag. Though similar in some respects, especially with regard to the recognition lag, there are also fundamental differences in how monetary policy is formulated and implemented.

### THE RECOGNITION LAG

Policymakers at the Fed face the same problems in determining the state of the economy as those faced by the fiscal authorities. To determine if intervention in the economy is called for, data must be analyzed and forecasts must be made. The time it takes to ascertain that a problem exists is classified under the recognition lag.

### THE POLICY LAG

The Fed's main concern is with the state of the economy in relation to the money supply. Since Fed officials are not elected, they do not have to be concerned with the short-run political implications of their actions. In addition, gauging and reacting to the performance of the economy is the Fed's main responsibility. Therefore, the Fed can react quickly to formulate a policy response to an economic situation. For example, the Federal Open Market Committee meets eight times a year to decide whether the money supply should be increased or decreased, given the current and predicted states of the economy.

### THE IMPLEMENTATION LAG

Once the money supply has been increased or decreased, the economy's interest rate will respond quite quickly. However, a change in the rate of interest does not imply that investment, the next variable in the chain, will respond as fast. Investment decisions are made by privately owned firms, not the government. Aside from the rate of interest, investment decisions are based on expectations concerning future sales, which in turn depend on the state of the economy. Thus, before firms will be willing to undertake new investment in response to a drop in the interest rate or to cancel investment plans in response to a rise in the interest rate, they may look for other signs about the state of the economy.

In addition, the time it takes to produce investment goods has an impact on how quickly monetary policy will affect the economy. Building large structures and complicated machines can take months or years. Because of these *building lags*, the effects of increased orders for new capital goods in response to a drop in the interest rate are not felt immediately after the decision to purchase them has been made. Given a rise in the rate of interest, filling pre-existing orders for new capital goods could keep the economy operating above the potential level long after the Fed's decision to decrease the money supply.

# KEYNESIANS, MONETARISTS, AND ACTIVIST INTERVENTION

In deciding whether monetary or fiscal policy should be used to stabilize the economy, economists have traditionally fallen into the *monetarist* or *Keynesian* categories. Because they see the economy as relatively stable and efficient without government, monetarists prefer limited government intervention. Keynesians believe that the economy is inherently unstable since it too often lingers in equilibrium at a GNP level below potential. They also see the economy's tendency to deviate from its potential level on a regular basis as proof that it requires government intervention to improve stability.

**The Keynesian Perspective**

Keynesians tend to believe that the government can play an important role in stabilizing the economy through the use of *discretionary policies*, policies decided upon in response to particular economic circumstances. Both monetary and fiscal policies are considered useful to achieve economic objectives for

Keynesians, although historically Keynesians have been prone to favor fiscal policy. They point to the economic record since the end of World War II as proof that discretionary fiscal and monetary policies can be used to achieve high levels of economic growth and low rates of unemployment. In this period, government has been actively involved in stabilization activities; business cycle downturns have been shorter and less severe than those in previous periods.

## The Monetarist Perspective

Monetarists tend to believe that activist government intervention in the economy causes more harm than good. They point to the *crowding-out* that occurs when increases in government expenditure lead to a higher interest rate and reduced investment. The high rates of inflation experienced since the end of World War II are also offered as proof of their contention. Aside from these factors, monetarists see the lags in fiscal and monetary policy as potential causes of instabilitity. For example, during a recession, the fiscal authorities might decide to increase government spending to fight high unemployment. If the economy is already making its way out of recession, the extra stimulus of government spending pushes the economy beyond potential GNP and leads to inflation. During the ensuing boom, lags in contractionary policy amplify existing recessionary forces, leading to a deeper recession than would have occurred without government intervention.

Instead of discretionary policies, monetarists would prefer to see the use of fixed rules to ensure the stability of the economy. Examples of fixed rules include the *full employment budget* and a constant money-supply growth rate. Being a monetarist does not imply that one believes in using only monetary policy, although monetary shocks are considered to be the major cause of instability. Instead, monetarism reflects a philosophy that government intervention, whether through monetary or fiscal policy, needs to be carefully controlled and limited to ensure the greatest degree of stability in prices and output. The rules suggested by monetarists are outlined in the following sections.

### THE FULL EMPLOYMENT BUDGET

The full employment budget is the budget the government would have at existing tax rates if the economy was operating at the potential level of GNP. Government expenditures are then adjusted to equal tax revenues at potential GNP. This amount is spent regardless of the actual level of GNP. In other words, given the level of tax revenues it receives when GNP is at potential, this is the amount of government spending that would make the structural deficit zero.

When the economy enters a boom period, the rise in GNP above the potential level leads to increased tax revenues through the progressive tax system. Because expenditure is fixed at a level that would lead to a balanced budget if actual GNP equaled potential GNP, a surplus accrues to the government. The additional aggregate expenditure that would occur if these funds were spent does not take place. Hence, government expenditure does not add fuel to the boom.

During a recession, tax revenues will automatically fall as the level of GNP falls below the potential level. With government expenditure fixed at the level that would balance the budget if potential GNP was maintained, a deficit occurs. The government does not make the recession worse by raising taxes or cutting spending to balance its budget.

## CONSTANT MONEY GROWTH AND THE QUANTITY THEORY OF MONEY

Monetarists believe that increases in the money supply in excess of output growth are ultimately responsible for inflation. The reasons for this belief can be observed through use of the *quantity theory of money*. This theory is based on the relationship between four variables: money supply, price level, real GNP, and velocity of circulation.

**The Velocity of Circulation.** By definition, the *velocity of circulation* represents the average number of times a dollar in the money supply is used for transactions (i.e., purchases of goods and services). The value of final goods and services purchased in any year is nominal GNP. To find the velocity of circulation, nominal GNP is divided by the money supply. Notationally, with $V$ representing velocity, $Q$ representing real GNP, $P$ representing the price level, and $M$ the money supply, velocity is defined as

$$V = \frac{PQ}{M}$$

To transform nominal GNP into real GNP, the nominal level of GNP is divided by the price level. It follows that multiplication of real GNP ($Q$) by the price level ($P$) equals nominal GNP.

When the ratio of nominal GNP to the money supply is a number greater than 1, the money supply is less than nominal GNP. Therefore some dollars must be used in *more than one purchase* of final goods and services. For example, suppose nominal GNP is $5,000 billion and the money supply (M1) is $1,000 billion. Because nominal GNP is greater than the quantity of money, the quantity of money available could not have been used to purchase all the goods and services produced unless some money was used more than once. The velocity of circulation equals 5 ($5,000/$1,000). A typical dollar in circulation is used in five transactions.

**The Quantity Theory of Money.** Rearranging the velocity equation leads to the following expression, known as the *equation of exchange*:

$$MV = PQ$$

Monetarists contend that the velocity of circulation is relatively stable and that real output equals potential GNP in the long run. Under the assumptions that the velocity of circulation is constant and that real output is at the potential level, the identity upon which the equation of exchange is based becomes the simple quantity theory of money. With $V$ and $Q$ fixed, this theory predicts that increases in the money supply ($M$) on the left side of the equation must lead to increases in the price level ($P$) on the right side.

The simple quantity theory of money had its origins in the historical period after the discovery of the North and South American continents. The influx of gold (then used as money) to Europe, the inability of output to increase in response to the monetary stimulus, and the apparent constancy of the velocity of circulation at the time led to a period of major inflation.

**The Constant Money Growth Rule.** Although too simple to capture the modern relationship between the money supply and the price level, the simple quantity theory underlies the thinking of most policymakers who state that any increases in the money supply must ultimately lead to inflation, regardless of the level of GNP. Keynesians counter this argument by noting that rises in the price level are less likely to occur when GNP is less than potential. Instead, the outward shifts in aggregate demand that occur when the money supply is increased will have a greater effect on GNP than on the price level. This is true because aggregate supply is relatively horizontal below potential GNP. However, if the assumptions of the simple quantity theory are true, the only way to ensure a stable rate of inflation is to have a stable rate of money growth. This explains the basic rationale behind monetarist thinking concerning the constant growth rate rule.

*Although they do not guarantee a perfectly smooth-running economy, fiscal and monetary policies used appropriately provide an important means of ensuring that economic events do not spin out of control, leading to large-scale depressions or extreme rates of inflation. The improved stability of the U.S. economy since the end of World War II supports this perspective.*

*Aside from its obligation to stabilize the level of economic activity, government also represents an important source of expenditure affecting the overall level of output and the mix of goods produced. If expenditure decisions are made without regard for the state of the economy, government spending can lead to greater overall instability. Expenditure not funded with sufficient tax revenues causes budget deficits and an increased national debt. Crowding out private investment may adversely affect the future level of economic growth*

*When faced with circumstances not experienced in the past, fiscal and monetary policies cannot always be used with precision to achieve desired objectives. For example, the supply shocks of the 1970s led to high rates of unemployment and inflation, a combination of effects not predicted by most economic models at that time. Yet with each new real world experience, the availability of more precise and timely data, and advances in economic theory, models of the economy become more sophisticated. This provides economists and government officials with the information needed to recommend and implement appropriate policy responses.*

**Selected Readings**

Baily, Martin N. and Arthur M. Okun. *The Battle Against Unemployment and Inflation.* New York: W. W. Norton. 1982.

Friedman, Milton. *Capitalism and Freedom.* Chicago: The University of Chicago Press. 1962.

Friedman, Milton. *Dollars and Deficits.* Englewood Cliffs, NJ: Prentice Hall, Inc. 1968.

Heilbroner, Robert and Peter Bernstein. *The Debt and the Deficit: False Alarms/Real Possibilities.* New York: W. W. Norton. 1989.

Rock, James M. *Debt and the Twin Deficits Debate.* Mountain View CA: Mayfield Publishing Co. 1991.

Sorkin, Alan L. *Monetary and Fiscal Policy in the Modern Era.* Lexington MA: Lexington Books. 1988.

Weintraub, Sidney. *Capitalism's Inflation and Unemployment Crisis.,* Reading, MA: Addison-Wesley Publishing Co. 1978.

# 10

## Fiscal and Monetary Policy: Aggregate Supply-Demand Analysis

*Both fiscal and monetary policy affect the economy's aggregate-demand curve. However, they do so by directly or indirectly affecting different components of aggregate expenditure. Changes in government spending affect aggregate expenditure directly. Tax changes must work through consumer expenditure to have their ultimate effect on GNP. By changing the interest rate through increases or decreases in the money supply, actions by the Fed affect the level of investment expenditure. The effects of the actions taken by the monetary and fiscal authorities are considered in detail in this chapter.*

### AGGREGATE DEMAND AND FISCAL POLICY

Fiscal policy works on either the government expenditure or the tax component of aggregate expenditure. It shifts the aggregate-demand curve to bring about changes in GNP and the price level. As shown in Figure 10.1, a $100-billion rise in government spending, perhaps in response to a high level of unemployment, causes the expenditure function to shift up. Through the multiplier, this leads to a $500 billion increase in GNP; it rises from $5,000 billion to $5,500 billion. The upward shift in the expenditure function corresponds to the rightward shift in the aggregate demand curve from $D_0$ to $D_1$ in the lower portion of Figure 10.1. Here it is assumed that money demand is not affected by changes in GNP. Therefore, the horizontal distance between $D_0$ and $D_1$ is the full multiplier effect.

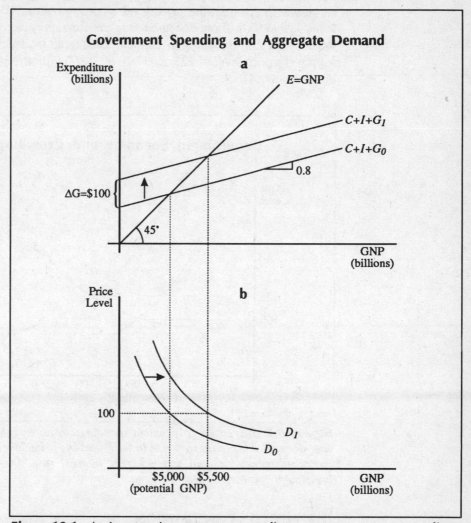

**Figure 10.1** *An increase in government spending causes aggregate expenditure to shift up and aggregate demand to shift out. Because aggregate demand is shown to shift by the full-multiplier effect, it is assumed that money demand is not affected by changes in GNP.*

*Government
Spending and
Crowding-Out*

When the aggregate supply curve is combined with the aggregate-demand curve, the effects of the price level changes that accompany aggregate demand shifts can be observed. Figure 10.2 shows the rightward shift in the aggregate-demand curve caused by a rise in government spending. If the aggregate-supply curve was horizontal, the price level would remain at 100, and GNP would increase by $500 billion. Because the aggregate-supply curve is upward sloping, the outward shift in aggregate demand leads to an intersection with aggregate supply at a price level of 125 and GNP of $5300 billion, $300 billion above the initial level of GNP.

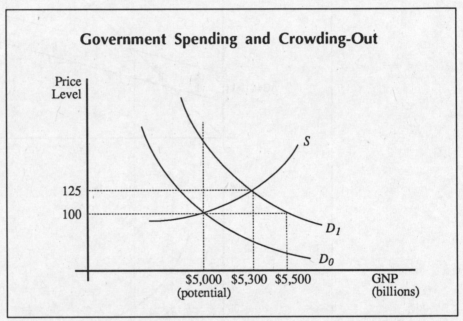

**Figure 10.2** *Increased government spending causes a rightward shift in aggregate demand. This leads to a rise in GNP and the price level. Both effects lead to increased money demand and a higher interest rate. The resulting decline in investment is known as crowding-out.*

## THE EFFECT ON CONSUMPTION

The change in GNP and the change in the price level will both have an effect on consumption. Consumption goes down when the price level goes up if there is a real balance or wealth effect. With this effect, the decline in the value of assets tied to the value of money (now worth less because of the higher price level) will cause consumption expenditure to fall. On the other hand, consumption is a positive function of GNP. Because GNP is higher after the demand shift, consumption should be higher. This will be the case if the positive change in consumption due to the increase in GNP is not offset by the decrease in consumption brought about by the real balance effect.

## THE EFFECT ON INVESTMENT: CROWDING-OUT

The rise in the price level and GNP shown in Figure 10.2 lead to increased money demand. With a higher price level and GNP, more money is needed for transactions. An outward shift in money demand will cause the interest rate to rise. Because the interest rate has increased, investment will fall.

Declines in investment and consumption expenditure brought on by increased government spending are called *crowding-out*. Crowding-out helps explain why GNP does not increase by the full multiplier effect, given the initial increase in government spending.

**Complete Crowding-Out.** The steepness of the aggregate-supply curve has an important effect on the degree of crowding out that takes place. In the extreme case of a vertical or classical aggregate-supply curve, the outward shift in aggregate demand raises the price level but fails to increase GNP. This is seen in Figure 10.3 where aggregate supply is vertical above $5,000 billion, the potential level of GNP. The outward shift in the aggregate-demand curve causes the price level to rise to 150. There is no change in GNP.

The rise in the price level will cause the interest rate to rise. This causes investment to fall. Through the real-balance or wealth effect, assets tied to the

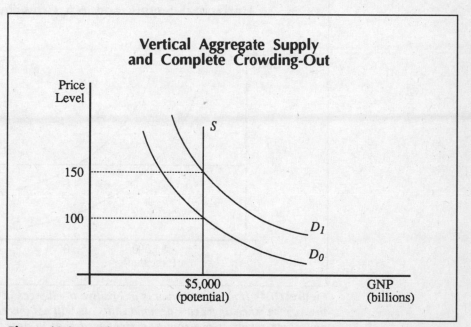

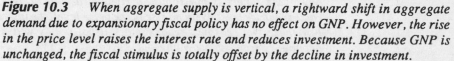

**Figure 10.3**   *When aggregate supply is vertical, a rightward shift in aggregate demand due to expansionary fiscal policy has no effect on GNP. However, the rise in the price level raises the interest rate and reduces investment. Because GNP is unchanged, the fiscal stimulus is totally offset by the decline in investment.*

value of money will decrease in value, causing consumption to fall. However, because GNP remains the same and equals the sum of consumption, investment, and government expenditure, it must be true that the rise in government expenditure is *totally* offset by the decline in private investment and consumption expenditure. A rise in government spending that is completely offset by declines in private expenditure is known as *complete crowding-out*. Because aggregate supply is likely to be steeper there, crowding-out due to expansionary fiscal policy is likely to be more complete when the economy operates near the potential level of GNP.

### NO CROWDING-OUT

At the other extreme from complete crowding-out is no crowding-out. Such a situation can arise with a Keynesian or horizontal aggregate supply when it is also assumed that money demand is not affected by GNP. As shown in Figure 10.4, an outward shift in aggregate demand from $D_0$ to $D_1$ leads to no increase in the price level. Therefore, there is no rise in the interest rate and no decline in investment. Because consumption is a positive function of GNP, it will rise.

While it is unlikely that the economy's aggregate-supply curve is horizontal over its full range, it may very well become nearly horizontal as the level of

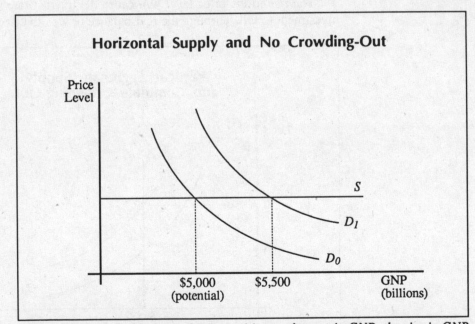

**Figure 10.4**  *If money demand is insensitive to changes in GNP, the rise in GNP that occurs when aggregate demand shifts out will not increase the interest rate. If aggregate supply is horizontal, a rightward shift in aggregate demand will not raise the price level. With no rise in the price level, the interest rate will not change. For these two reasons, expansionary fiscal policy will not cause investment to decline. There is no crowding-out.*

GNP falls below the potential level. Thus, while expansionary fiscal policy will likely lead to crowding out at levels of GNP around the potential level, an expansionary fiscal policy during recessions may have little impact on the price level or investment.

**GNP and Investment.** Expansionary fiscal policy causes the aggregate demand curve to shift right, raising GNP. If the assumption that investment is autonomous with respect to GNP is relaxed, investment will also increase. This is especially true during a recession. After demand shifts out, the price level response along the more horizontal, or Keynesian, range of the aggregate supply curve is likely to be small. Therefore, the increase in investment due to the increase in GNP will not be offset by a rising interest rate. Investment will not be crowded out. Instead it may be "crowded in." The *accelerator model* is used for analysis of investment as a function of changes in GNP.

**Crowding-Out and the Interest Rate.** Crowding-out occurs because outward shifts in the aggregate-demand curve raise the price level, which in turn raises the equilibrium rate of interest. If investment is insensitive to the rate of interest, investment will not decline with a rise in the rate of interest. In this situation, investment will not be crowded out.

## Tax Cuts and Crowding-Out

A cut in taxes will cause an upward shift in the expenditure function and a rightward shift in the aggregate-demand curve. This is the same effect as a rise in government spending. However, recall from chapter 5 that because tax cuts are filtered through consumers, the tax multiplier is smaller than the government-expenditures multipler. Therefore, a larger tax cut is necessary to shift aggregate demand out by the same distance as a shift caused by an increase in government spending.

The rise in the price level that results whenever aggregate demand shifts out along an upward-sloping supply curve implies that the interest rate will rise. Therefore, the tax cut will reduce or crowd out investment. The rise in GNP will increase consumption, althouth the rise in the price level could offset this increase somewhat if a real balance or wealth effect is present.

# AGGREGATE DEMAND AND MONETARY POLICY

A rise in the money supply causes the money supply curve to shift right along the money-demand curve leading to a fall in the interest rate. At this point, the effects of monetary policy pass from the money market to the commodity market. A falling interest rate causes the level of investment to increase. The increase in the level of investment causes the aggregate-expenditure curve to

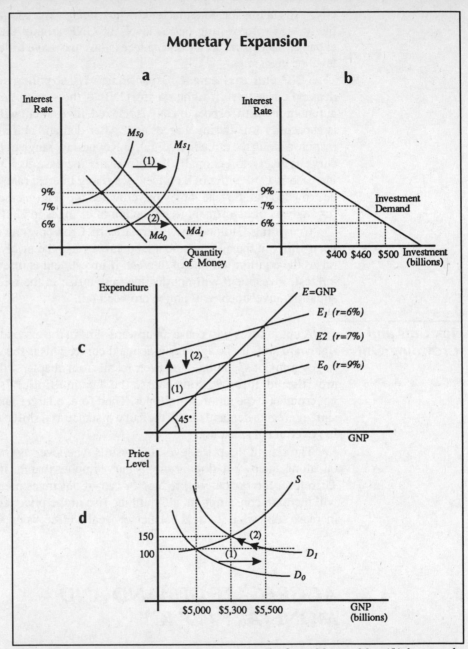

**Figure 10.5**  *An increase in the money supply from Ms0 to Ms1 (1) lowers the interest rate from 9 to 6 percent and raises investment. Aggregate expenditure shifts from E0 to E1, and demand shifts from D0 to D1. The resulting rise in the price level from 100 to 150 (2) causes money demand to shift out to Md1 and the interest rate to rise to 7 percent. This partially offsets the rise in investment; aggregate expenditure shifts from E1 to E2; and final equilibrium GNP is seen to equal $5,300 billion.*

shift up and the aggregate demand curve to shift out. At the economy's initial price level, GNP will be higher along the new aggregate-demand curve.

## Expansionary Monetary Policy: An Example

The nature of the adjustment resulting from the increase in the money supply is shown in Figure 10.5. Figures 10.5a and 10.5b represent the money market and the investment demand equation. The aggregate-expenditure function appears in Figure 10.5c and the aggregate demand-supply curves are shown in Figure 10.5d. Initially the money market is in equilibrium with money-supply curve $Ms_0$, money demand curve $Md_0$ and an interest rate of 9 percent. Given this rate of interest, in Figure 10.5b, the level of investment is $400 billion. In Figure 10.5c, this leads to expenditure function $E_0$ and an equilibrium level of GNP at potential of $5,000 billion. The $5,000 billion-equilibrium level of GNP is found in the aggregate supply-demand graph at the intersection of the supply curve and demand curve $D_0$. The equilibrium price level is equal to 100. For simplicity, it is assumed that money demand is not sensitive to changes in GNP.

### EXPANSIONARY MONETARY POLICY: INITIAL EFFECTS

The purchase of federal securities on the open market, a decrease in the discount rate, a decrease in the required reserve ratio, or moral suasion causes a shift out in the money-supply curve from $Ms_0$ to $Ms_1$. Along money-demand curve $Md_0$, this lowers the interest rate from 9 percent to 6 percent. In the investment-demand diagram, the reduction in the interest rate raises investment from $400 billion to $500 billion. The expenditure function shifts up from $E_0$ to $E_1$, by an amount equal to the rise in investment ($100 billion). Through the simple multiplier, GNP increases from $5,000 billion to $5500 billion (the marginal propensity to consume is 0.8). Given the shift in the expenditure function and the assumed insensitivity of money demand to changes in GNP, the aggregate-demand curve shifts right from $D_0$ to $D_1$, by the amount of the full multiplier effect. At a price level of 100, GNP equals $5,500 billion along demand curve $D_1$. This completes the first round of changes that occur in response to the increase in the money supply.

### EXPANSIONARY MONETARY POLICY: SECOND ROUND EFFECTS

Second-round effects must account for the fact that the price level will rise above 100. As seen in the aggregate supply-demand diagram, at the intersection of the aggregate-supply curve and demand curve $D_1$, equilibrium GNP will equal $5,300 billion. The price level rises to 150. While the aggregate supply-demand diagram is able to incorporate the effects of the rising price level to determine the ultimate level of GNP, the other curves in Figure 10.5 have not yet accounted for the price-level effects.

**The Price Level's Effect on the Money Market.** With the rise in the price level, the money-demand curve shifts out from $Md_0$ to $Md_1$; the interest rate rises from 6 to 7 percent. Rising prices have partially offset the interest-rate reduction brought about by the initial increase in the money supply.

**The Effect on Investment.** In the investment-demand diagram, the level of investment associated with a 7 percent rate of interest is $460 billion, not the $500 billion level that would occur in the absence of price effects.

**The Effect on Aggregate Expenditure.** With the rise in the price level, the partially offsetting rise in the interest rate, and the partially offsetting fall in the level of investment, the expenditure function shifts down from $E_1$ to $E_2$. The equilibrium level of GNP then equals $5,300 billion, an amount that appropriately corresponds to the equilibrium level established by the intersection of the aggregate-supply curve and demand curve $D_1$.

### EXPANSIONARY MONETARY POLICY: THE EFFECT ON CONSUMPTION

As in the case of expansionary fiscal policy, expansionary monetary policy causes the price level and the equilibrium level of GNP to rise. The rise in GNP will cause consumption to rise. The rise in the price level may partially offset this increased consumption if the wealth or real-balance effect is present. Consumers will not consume as much if the value of their assets is reduced by the price-level increase.

# SIMULTANEOUS USE OF FISCAL AND MONETARY POLICIES

An expansionary fiscal policy leads to a higher interest rate and less investment. Expansionary monetary policy lowers the interest rate and leads to higher investment. Attaining a GNP target without affecting the amount of investment requires that the interest rate remain unchanged after the policy has been implemented.

For example, suppose the fiscal and monetary authorities wish to increase the level of GNP but do not wish to see a decline in investment. One means to accomplish this goal is to increase the money supply and government spending simultaneously. Both policies shift the aggregate-demand curve out, raising GNP and the price level. This raises money demand and causes the interest rate to rise. However, the effects of the outward shift in the money-demand curve can be offset by the increase in the money supply. In other words, if the rightward shift in the money-demand curve is matched by a rightward shift in the money-supply curve, the interest rate remains unchanged.

Such a simultaneous change requires the coordination of both monetary and fiscal policies and perhaps an unlikely degree of cooperation between the Fed, the president, and the Congress. More realistically, the Fed adjusts its monetary policy after the fiscal authorities have decided upon their spending and taxation plans. Thus, throughout the 1980s, expansionary and potentially inflationary fiscal policy, as reflected in extremely large budget deficits, was counteracted by the Fed's policy of maintaining the interest rate at a level high enough to avoid inflation.

## Fiscal and Monetary Policy and the Phillips Curve

The Phillips curve shows the inverse relationship between the rate of inflation and the rate of unemployment. Under Okun's law, decreases in unemployment correspond to increases in GNP. Thus, the Phillips relationship is consistent with the rise in GNP and the price level that occurs when the aggregate-demand curve shifts out or the fall in GNP and the price level when the aggregate-demand curve shifts in. Because both fiscal and monetary policy affect the location of the aggregate demand curve, the direct relationship between price level and output changes that comes about through their use are consistent with the Phillips relationship. In the short run, policymakers can shift the aggregate-demand curve to achieve price-level and GNP targets.

# LONG-RUN MONETARY AND FISCAL EFFECTS

Whenever the economy's equilibrium GNP level differs from the potential or full-employment level, forces are set into motion that shift the aggregate-supply curve until potential GNP is restored. These forces are declining input costs during recessions and rising input costs during booms. Therefore, if monetary or fiscal policy leads to an intersection of aggregate supply and demand at a level of GNP other than the potential level, after the supply adjustments have occurred, the economy will find its way back to potential GNP. Thus, in the long run, monetary and fiscal policy have no effect on the level of GNP at which the economy operates. However, in spite of the fact that GNP ultimately returns to the potential level, the choice of fiscal or monetary policy does have an effect on the components of aggregate demand.

## The Long-Run Supply Adjustment

Figure 10.6 shows the economy's aggregate supply-demand diagram. Initially the economy is in equilibrium at the potential level of $5,000 billion. A rise in government spending, a cut in taxes, or a rise in the money supply causes demand to shift right from $D_0$ to $D_1$. The price level rises from 100 to 150, and equilibrium GNP rises to $5,300 billion. Because the economy is now operating above the potential level, there is an inflationary GNP gap. Higher demand for factors of production in input markets ultimately leads to factor price increases. This causes the aggregate-supply curve to shift left, raising the price level. Upward pressure on input prices continues until potential GNP is restored at the intersection of aggregate demand curve $D_1$ and aggregate supply curve $S_1$. As the price level rises, upward pressure is exerted on the interest rate.

## THE LONG RUN: FISCAL POLICY, GOVERNMENT SPENDING

If aggregate demand shifts out because of an increase in government spending, the ultimate restoration of potential GNP implies that private spending has been totally crowded out. To see this, recall that equilibrium GNP equals the sum of consumption, investment, and government spending. In the long run (after the supply adjustment and restoration of potential GNP), government spending is higher while the level of GNP is the same. The price level and interest rate are higher. It follows that some combination of consumption and investment must have fallen by an equal amount. This occurs as the aggregate-supply curve shifts left to restore potential GNP. The higher price level leads to a higher interest rate and a lower level of investment.

**Effects on Consumption.** Consumption may be affected in the long run if it is assumed that a real-balance or wealth effect is present. Through this effect, the rise in the price level reduces the value of money and assets with values tied to the value of money, leading consumers to consume less.

Aside from this effect, a rising interest rate might reduce purchases of *consumer durables*, such as automobiles and personal computers, that might be sensitive to the rate of interest. The occurrence of these consumption effects depends on whether consumption is assumed to be a function of the price level (through the real balance or wealth effect) or the rate of interest. Often, for simplicity, it is assumed that the price level changes affect only the interest rate and that only investment is a function of the interest rate.

## THE LONG RUN: FISCAL POLICY, TAXES

A cut in taxes provides consumers with more purchasing power. Consistent with Figure 10.6, this causes aggregate demand to shift out and GNP to rise above the potential level. In the long run, as the aggregate supply curve shifts left to restore potential GNP, the rising price level leads to a higher interest rate and reduced investment. When the potential level of GNP is restored, consumption has increased (because taxes were cut), government spending is the same (because it was not affected by the tax cut), and investment has decreased (because of a higher interest rate). In fact, investment has fallen by the same amount consumption has increased (GNP equals the sum of consumption, investment, and government spending). Because tax revenues have fallen, the federal government will run a larger deficit.

**The Real-Balance Effect.** A cut in taxes will raise consumption. However, the long run rise in the price level that comes with a tax decrease could reduce consumption somewhat if a real-balance or wealth effect is present; the value of assets tied to the value of money will be reduced. According to the real-balance effect, the reduction in asset values causes consumption to fall.

## THE LONG RUN: MONETARY POLICY

As with increases in government spending and tax cuts, expansionary monetary policy will lead to an outward shift in aggregate demand and a rise in the level of GNP above the potential level. Because expansionary monetary policy leads to a lower interest rate, the rise in GNP is fueled by a rise in the level of investment. However, in Figure 10.6, as aggregate supply begins to shift back to restore potential GNP, the rising price level raises the interest rate because money demand is increased. This chokes off the rise in investment. When potential GNP is finally restored, investment must be back at its original level because GNP equals the sum of consumption, investment, and government spending. It is assumed that neither consumption nor government spending has been affected by the change in the interest rate.

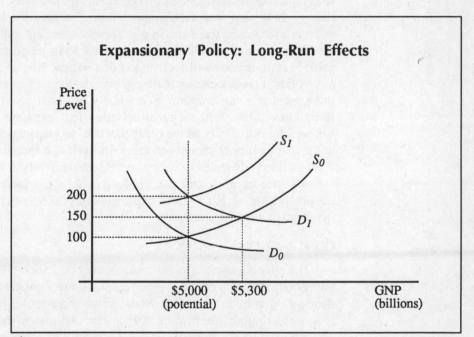

**Figure 10.6** *Expansionary fiscal or monetary policy causes aggregate demand to shift from $D_0$ to $D_1$. Because this leads to a GNP level above potential, input price increases will ultimately cause aggregate supply to shift left from $S_0$ to $S_1$. In the long run, potential GNP is restored, but at the higher price level of 200.*

**Possible Effects on Consumption.** When it is assumed that consumption is a function of the interest rate, both consumption and investment will increase with the initial fall in the rate of interest. They then decrease to their previous levels as the price level and the interest rate rise.

If, through a wealth or real-balance effect, consumption is a function of the price level, the final level of consumption may be lower than the initial level; the outward demand shift and inward supply shift raise the price level. In this case, because GNP equals the sum of consumption, investment, and government expenditures, and taxes and government spending are not affected by monetary policy, investment must be somewhat higher in the long run. Hence, the final interest rate will be somewhat lower than the initial interest rate.

### MONETARY AND FISCAL POLICY: LONG RUN DIFFERENCES

In terms of long-run effects, the use of fiscal or monetary policy is seen to have no effect on GNP. It always returns to the potential level. The price level will also increase after an expansionary monetary or fiscal policy. However, with regard to the components of aggregate demand, very different results can emerge. In the long run, GNP returns to the potential level. Therefore after all shifts are accounted for, a rise in government spending will lead to a decline in the components of private expenditure equal to its magnitude. Investment and perhaps consumption will decline. In other words, there is complete crowding-out. A cut in taxes causes a rearrangement in the mix of expenditure between investment and consumption. Specifically, investment will decline and consumption will rise. Without a real-balance effect, expanding the money supply has no long-run effects on the components of aggregate demand. With the rise in the money supply the interest rate falls at first, it then increases as the price level increases. Investment is first increased, then falls to its original level.

All three expansionary policies lead to short run increases in GNP above the potential level, but all three expansionary policies are inflationary because they lead to a higher price level.

### CONTRACTIONARY POLICIES

The effects associated with expansionary policies are the opposite of those under contractionary policies. When contractionary policies are used, aggregate demand shifts in, or to the left. Because the short-run aggregate-supply curve is upward sloping, the inward shift in demand means that GNP falls below potential and a recessionary GNP gap results. The economy's price level will begin to fall as aggregate supply shifts to the right. In the long run, potential GNP is restored.

# POLICY RESPONSES TO SUPPLY SHOCKS

In both 1973 and 1979 the world economy suffered from major increases in oil prices. These price increases led to historically high rates of inflation for the U.S. economy, along with high rates of unemployment. The reason for these effects can be readily seen in the aggregate supply-demand diagram. In Figure 10.7, assume that the economy is initially in equilibrium at the potential GNP level of $5,000 billion and a price level of 100. This equilibrium is established at the intersection of supply curve $S_0$ and demand curve $D_0$. The shock of suddenly higher oil prices causes aggregate supply to shift left from $S_0$ to $S_1$, equilibrium GNP falls to $4,500 billion, and the price level rises to 125.

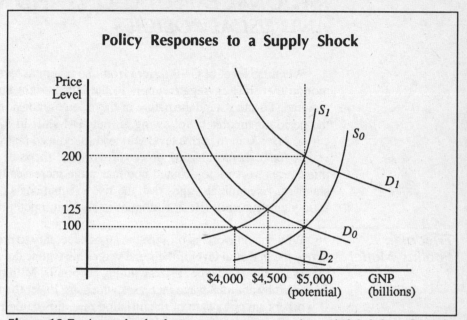

**Policy Responses to a Supply Shock**

**Figure 10.7** *A supply shock causes aggregate supply to shift left from $S_0$ to $S_1$, leading to an increased price level and decreased GNP. Should the fiscal or monetary authorities shift demand from $D_0$ to $D_2$ to restore the original price level, GNP will fall to $4,000 billion. Should demand be shifted out from $D_0$ to $D_1$ to restore potential GNP, the price level will rise to 200.*

Under Okun's law, the decline in GNP below the potential level will lead to an increase in unemployment. Unlike the Phillips relationship where the price level and GNP move in the same direction, supply shifts cause GNP and the price level to move in opposite directions. Because of the reduction in GNP below the potential level and the rise in the price level that comes with it, the economy is said to suffer from *stagflation*.

**Supply Shock: The Policy Dilemma**

For policymakers, a leftward supply shift, with its corresponding higher unemployment and higher price level, poses a dilemma of which problem to attempt to solve. Dealing with unemployment by shifting aggregate demand from $D_0$ to $D_1$ will lead to an even higher price level, 200. Fighting the rise in the price level by shifting demand from $D_0$ to $D_2$ will cause a further decrease in GNP to $4,000 billion and make unemployment even worse. A third option of doing nothing will ultimately lead the aggregate-supply curve to shift right from $S_1$ back to $S_0$. The problem for policymakers is that a long period of high unemployment and high inflation may be politically unbearable.

# RATIONAL EXPECTATIONS AND MONETARY AND FISCAL POLICIES

When the level of GNP differs from the potential level, forces are set into motion that shift aggregate supply to the left or right until potential GNP is restored. To understand the nature of these forces, consider the labor market in the period immediately following an outward shift in the aggregate-demand curve. The rise in the price level will lead to reduced real wages. With nominal wages fixed, the purchasing power of workers' incomes declines. Ultimately this causes workers to demand nominal wage increases to restore their living standard. As nominal wages rise, the rise in input costs causes the aggregate-supply curve to shift left. It continues to shift until potential GNP is restored.

## Friedman's Fooling Model

Why should workers provide the labor necessary to produce a level of GNP above the potential level if their real wages have gone down? According to one theory put forth by Nobel-prize-winning economist Milton Friedman, they may be fooled by nominal wage increases which are lower than the rate of inflation. If workers are not aware of the inflation rate, this could make them think that their real wages have increased when they have has decreased. Because workers think their real wages have risen, they supply more labor. Fiscal and monetary policy are useful in the short run—until workers come to understand that they have been fooled.

## Rational Expectations

According to the theory of *rational expectations*, in making decisions affecting their economic well-being, individuals use all possible data based on past information, experience, and the current state of affairs. If workers have previously experienced a similar outward shift in aggregate demand and the corresponding decline in their real wage or have some other means of knowing that their real wage will fall, they will *immediately* ask for nominal wage increases to restore their real wage. In this case, after an outward shift in aggregate-demand, the aggregate-supply curve shifts left immediately to restore the potential level of GNP. Thus, if the outward shift in aggregate demand was due to expansionary monetary or fiscal policy, that policy would be totally ineffective in altering the level of GNP and would lead only to a higher price level.

More generally, according to rational expectations theory, familiarity with a model of how the economy works will guide individuals in the decisions they make and lead them to avoid decisions that reduce their welfare. It is not necessary that every citizen have such knowlege; individuals can follow the advice of experts in making decisions. For example, changes in the Index of Leading Indicators are always announced in television network news broadcasts and newspapers. Interpretation of the changes by economists and business leaders usually accompanies the news story.

## RATIONAL EXPECTATIONS AND REAL-WORLD MARKETS

The theory of rational expectations is thought to work best in financial markets where prices of stocks and bonds change with each news story and rumor relating to the market. In labor and other input markets, it is unlikely that rational expectations play much of a role in the short run. Long-term contracts (written and oral agreements concerning the rate at which wages and other input prices will rise) prevent daily, weekly, and sometimes yearly fluctuations in factor prices from taking place. This suggests that monetary and fiscal policy can be effective for the length of time it takes until all existing contracts expire and are renegotiated.

*In this chapter the precise effects of shifts in the aggregate-demand curve due to fiscal and monetary policy have been examined. Both expansionary and contractionary fiscal and monetary policies cause changes in the price level and can affect GNP in the short run. They have no long-term effects on GNP because the economy ultimately works its way back to the potential level. This leads some economists to believe that the economy would be more stable without the fluctuations caused by expansionary or contractionary fiscal and monetary policies.*

*Fiscal policy can cause rearrangement in the mix of private and public expenditure. With expansionary fiscal policy, government spending rises while investment and consumption fall. In a free-market economy, this rearrangement is sometimes considered an undesirable by-product of government interference. When expansionary fiscal policy leads to a crowding-out of private investment, it may lower future rates of economic growth. Less investment expenditure reduces the rate at which the economy's production possibilities frontier will shift out. This reduces future consumption possibilities.*

*Selected Readings*

Lucas, Robert E., Jr. "Understanding Business Cycles," in *Studies in Business Cycle Theory*. Cambridge, MA: MIT Press. 1983.

Shaw, G.K. *Rational Expectations*. New York: St. Martin's Press. 1984.

# 11

# *International Trade and the Macro Model*

*O*ver the past two decades, international trade has become increasingly important in affecting the U.S. economy's macroeconomic performance. The increased significance of trade can be seen by looking at the increase in exports measured in real 1982 dollars. In 1970, exports accounted for $178.3 billion; in 1990, exports were $630.3 billion. Seen in another light, exports accounted for 6.8 percent of GNP in 1970, 12.3 percent in 1990.

As imports and exports grow, they have an increased effect on other economic aggregates, including employment and GNP. When net exports are ignored, predictions concerning the effects of fiscal and monetary policies on the level of economic activity are less precise. Therefore, to model the workings of the macro economy realistically, it is not sufficient to consider aggregate expenditure as only the sum of consumption, investment, and government spending. Net exports must be included.

In this chapter, the basic macro model is expanded to incorporate the effects of international trade. Consideration of trade effects allows for a better understanding of the determinants of the level of imports and exports. It also allows a complete picture of all major macroeconomic interrelationships to be developed. Inclusion of imports and exports involves a slight complication of the model developed in previous chapters. It adds greatly to the model's real-world relevance.

# NET EXPORTS AND THE BALANCE OF PAYMENTS

International transactions include the sale of U.S. goods and services to foreigners and the purchase of foreign goods and services by Americans. In addition, money and financial assets are exchanged. These exchanges are considered in the *balance of payments accounts*. The balance of payments measures the currency and commodity flows that take place between the U.S. and other countries in any year. These accounts consist of two major categories: the *current account* and the *capital account*.

## The Current Account

The *current account* measures the difference between U.S. imports and exports of goods and services. That part of the current account balance reflecting merchandise transactions is known as the *balance of trade*. If U.S. imports exceed U.S. exports, a current-account deficit occurs.

Net exports were negative throughout 1983–1990. In 1990 this current-account deficit equaled $38 billion. The size and persistence of the trade deficit has been the source of great concern during the past decade. Many believe it reflects a decline in the degree of American competitiveness in world markets. When there is a current-account deficit, foreigners must be holding American dollars because the value of goods purchased from foreigners by Americans exceeds the value of goods purchased by foreigners from Americans.

## The Capital Account

The *capital account* measures the difference between foreign purchases of American assets (such as land, stocks, and bonds issued by U.S. companies, or bonds issued by the federal government) and American purchases of foreign assets. A capital-account deficit occurs when American purchases of foreign assets exceed foreign purchases of American assets.

### THE BALANCE BETWEEN THE CURRENT ACCOUNT AND THE CAPITAL ACCOUNT

Current-account and capital-account deficits refer to situations where there are more U.S. purchases of foreign goods, services, and assets than corresponding purchases of American goods, services, and assets by foreigners. In other words, the presence of a deficit in the current account or the capital account implies that foreigners (or their central banks) wind up holding American currency. However, the current and capital accounts cannot be in deficit simultaneously. In fact, current-account deficits are closely matched by capital-account surpluses and vice versa.

When U.S. imports exceed U.S. exports and the current account is in deficit, foreigners use their dollars to purchase American financial assets. They thereby earn a positive rate of return on their excess dollar holdings. Therefore, the current account deficit is associated with a capital-account surplus of approximately the same magnitude. Actual differences between the capital-account surplus and current-account deficit are measured by two additional components of the balance-of-payments accounts: the *official reserve transactions* and the *statistical discrepancy* that arises because of unrecorded exchanges of goods, services, and assets between countries.

## The Determinants of Imports and Exports

Imports represent goods produced by foreigners and purchased by Americans. Exports are goods produced by Americans and sold to foreigners. There are a number of factors underlying the exchange of goods between countries. These factors include tastes for foreign-made goods, income levels of trading countries, and relative prices. Each of these factors plays a role in determining the level of imports and exports a country will experience.

### CURRENCY EXCHANGE AND THE FOREIGN EXCHANGE RATE

One factor affecting the relative prices of foreign and domestic goods is the rate at which the currency needed to purchase these goods can be exchanged. Because each country has its own currency, foreign currency is needed to purchase a foreign good. When purchasing one currency with another, the price involved is known as the *exchange rate*. Exchange rates exist between the U.S. dollar and all other currencies in the world. They express the value of one country's currency in terms of another country's currency. For example, if two American dollars exchange for one British pound, the exchange rate of the dollar is half a pound per dollar. The exchange rate of the pound is two dollars per pound.

**Appreciation and Depreciation of the Dollar.** The exchange rate can be stated with dollars in the numerator or denominator. Therefore, it is not clear whether an increase in the exchange rate means that the dollar can purchase more or fewer units of foreign currency. To avoid confusion, the dollar *appreciates* when it can purchase more units of a foreign currency and *depreciates* when it can purchase fewer units of a foreign currency.

For example, the dollar appreciates when the number of dollars it takes to purchase a British pound falls from $2.00 per pound to $1.50 per pound. Equivalently, the number of pounds it takes to puchase a dollar rises from one-half to two-thirds. Appreciation of the dollar makes foreign goods less expensive to Americans and causes U.S. imports to increase. At the same time, American goods become more expensive to foreigners, and U.S. exports decline. Hence, when the dollar appreciates, net exports (exports minus imports) will fall.

## METHODS OF DETERMINING THE EXCHANGE RATE

To obtain foreign currency, domestic currency is traded. The nature of this trade can vary with the type of exchange-rate system. Historically, the most important exchange-rate systems have been the gold standard, pegged exchange rates, and free-floating exchange rates.

**The Gold Standard.** Under a *gold standard*, all currencies are denominated in *ounces* of gold. For example, the U.S. rate might be $35.00 an ounce while the British rate might be £7 (pounds) per ounce. Under such a system, one British pound will exchange for five U.S. dollars. If the British accumulate a large number of dollars because Americans have purchased large quantities of British goods, gold will be exported from the U.S. to Britain to maintain the trade balance.

**Pegged Exchange Rates.** Under a *pegged exchange rate*, currencies are denominated in terms of one another; however, they are not necessarily convertible into gold. One British pound might be the equivalent of five U.S. dollars, but no reference is made to the price of currencies in gold.

**Free-Floating Exchange Rates.** Under a *free-floating system*, the exchange rate is determined by market forces in a *foreign exchange market*. As with any other market, buyers and sellers of currency meet and based on the interaction between supply and demand, determine an equilibrium price. This is the predominant way exchange rates are determined today, although the amount by which the values of currency are allowed to float is *managed* to avoid destabilizing fluctuations.

*Determining the Exchange Rate under a Free-Floating System*

The price of dollars in a foreign exchange market is based upon the intersection of a *supply-of-dollars* curve and a *demand-for-dollars* curve. In terms of supply and demand, this market is similar to the market for any commodity. Dollars are the quantity on the horizontal axis, and the price of dollars is measured on the vertical axis. This price is stated in the number of units of foreign currency it takes to purchase one dollar.

## THE SUPPLY OF DOLLARS

The supply-of-dollars curve indirectly represents the desire by Americans to purchase foreign goods. This desire will increase when the dollar appreciates. As it comes to command more units of foreign currency, the appreciated dollar enables Americans to purchase more foreign goods less expensively. Hence, assuming that prices of foreign goods remain constant, Americans have a greater incentive to purchase foreign goods. They will therefore supply more dollars on the foreign-exchange market.

For example, if the dollar appreciates from an initial exchange rate of half a British pound per dollar to one British pound per dollar, British goods become half as expensive to Americans. In response, Americans will seek to purchase greater quantities of British goods. As a result, a greater supply of American currency finds its way to the foreign-exchange market. It follows that the supply-of-dollars curve in a foreign-exchange market is upward-sloping.

## THE DEMAND FOR DOLLARS

The demand for dollars represents the desire of foreigners to purchase American goods. That is, as foreigners wish to purchase more American goods, they require more units of American currency. Foreigners will wish to purchase more American goods when the exchange rate (stated in units of foreign currency per dollar) falls. With prices of American goods constant, American goods become less expensive to foreigners because fewer units of their currency must be given up to obtain an additional dollar. It follows that the demand-for-dollars curve in a foreign-exchange market is downward-sloping.

## EQUILIBRIUM IN THE FOREIGN-EXCHANGE MARKET

A typical foreign-exchange market is portrayed in Figure 11.1. Here British pounds are traded for U.S. dollars. The supply-of-dollars curve represents American demand for British currency to purchase British goods. The demand-for-dollars curve represents British demand for American dollars to purchase American goods. These curves intersect at a price of half a pound per dollar. A total quantity of $20 billion is traded at this rate.

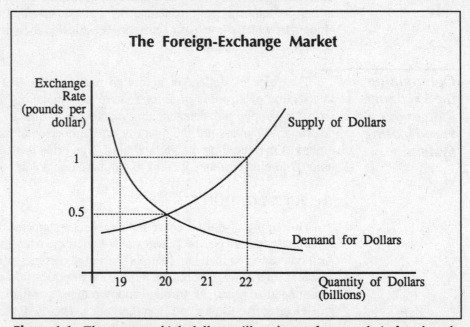

**Figure 1.1** *The rate at which dollars will exchange for pounds is found at the intersection of the supply and demand curves for dollars. If for some reason the dollar appreciates from 0.5 pounds per dollar to 1 pound per dollar, disequilibrium will occur, as the quantity of dollars supplied exceeds the quantity of dolars demanded.*

Should the dollar appreciate to one pound per dollar, the American quantity of dollars supplied would increase to $22 billion, and the quantity of dollars demanded would fall to $19 billion. For Americans, the appreciation of the dollar would make British goods a greater bargain. To the British, appreciation of the dollar would make American goods more expensive. In a free-floating exchange market, given this excess supply of $3 billion, the exchange rate would fall back to the equilibrium level of half a pound per dollar. The dollar would depreciate. If the exchange rate fell below the equilibrium level, an opposite set of forces would cause the dollar to appreciate.

## FACTORS AFFECTING EXHANGE-RATE DETERMINATION

The intersection of the supply and demand curves for dollars determines the exchange rate. The locations of the supply and demand curves determine exactly where this intersection will occur. Aside from the exchange rate, factors affecting the supply of dollars include American tastes for foreign goods and American income. A stronger preference for foreign goods means that Americans will offer more dollars at all exchange rates. Increases in American income lead Americans to consume more of all goods, including foreign goods. Changes in either of these variables cause the supply of dollars curve to shift out; the dollar will depreciate.

From the foreign perspective, these same factors underlie the demand for dollars. Increases in foreign income will lead foreigners to consume more of all goods, including American goods, and changes in foreign tastes for American goods will also lead to increased consumption of American goods. Because the increased consumption of U.S. goods requires dollars, both factors will cause the demand for dollars to increase. This leads to an appreciation of the dollar.

**Financial Assets and the Role of the Interest Rate.** From the macroeconomic perspective, one of the most important American "goods" desired by foreigners is American financial assets such as bonds issued by the government. The U.S. interest rate reflects the rate of return on these assets. An increase in the American rate of interest relative to foreign interest rates means that a greater return can be achieved by holding U.S. assets rather than foreign assets. This will lead to increased demand by foreigners for the American dollars needed to purchase such assets. The resulting appreciation of the dollar will cause imports to rise and exports to fall. Thus, a rise in the American interest rate causes net exports to fall (the increased level of imports is subtracted from the decreased level of exports).

**Purchasing-Power Parity.** *Purchasing-power parity* is thought to determine exchange rates in the long run. The concept of purchasing power parity can be best understood by considering a world in which only one homogeneous product is produced using an identical production process regardless of where it is produced. In such a world, the exchange rate between two countries would equal the ratio of the price of the product in one country relative to the price of the product in the other.

For example, suppose coal is the single homogeneous good produced by the U.S. and Great Britain. If coal costs $200 per ton in the U.S. and 100 pounds per ton in Great Britain, the exchange rate between dollars and pounds will equal the ratio of the price of coal in the U.S. to the price of coal in Britain. It will equal two dollars per British pound (the ton units in the ratio of U.S. to British coal prices cancel).

With the price of coal constant, should the exchange rate be greater than two dollars per pound, it would make sense for the British to purchase all their coal from the U.S. For example, suppose the exchange rate rises from $2 per pound to $3 per pound (the dollar has depreciated, the pound has appreciated). Regardless of the exchange rate, 100 British pounds can purchase one ton of British coal. But, by exchanging pounds for dollars at the going rate, 100 pounds would puchase $300 or 1.5 tons of U.S. coal (at $200 per ton). However, the increased demand for U.S. coal will cause increased demand for U.S. dollars; the pound will depreciate; the dollar will appreciate. Ultimately this will result in the establishment of *parity*, with the exchange rate at two dollars per British pound. Similarly, an exchange rate *less* than two dollars per pound will lead Americans to purchase all their coal from Great Britain. This will lead to depreciation of the dollar and simultaneous appreciation of the pound that ultimately restores the exchange rate to two dollars per pound.

For real-world economies, purchasing power parity implies that exchange rate changes depend upon relative changes in the price levels between countries. For example, under purchasing-power parity, a doubling of the price level in the U.S., given a stable price level in Britain, will cause the dollar to depreciate by one-half in terms of the pound.

## NET EXPORTS AND THE EXPENDITURE FUNCTION

Understanding how the exchange rate is determined and what causes it to appreciate and depreciate is important because imports and exports are both affected by the exhange rate. Imports and exports are also affected by the factors underlying exchange-rate determination: income, tastes, relative prices between countries, and relative rates of interest. The relationship and interaction of these factors can be built into the simple macro model to allow analysis of international trade in the economy. These effects are normally modeled in terms of *net exports*, exports minus imports. A macro model that includes net exports is said to be *open*.

The determinants of foreign tastes for American goods and American tastes for foreign goods are considered to be beyond the realm of macroeconomic analysis, as is the determination of income levels and interest rates in foreign countries. In other words, these factors are exogenous in modeling the macro economy open to foreign trade. However, exchange rates, U.S. income or GNP, the U.S. price level, and the relationship between U.S. and foreign interest rates are all explicitly considered in the open macro model.

## The Exchange Rate and Net Exports

Holding all other factors constant, appreciation of the dollar will lead to increased imports for the U.S. because foreign goods become relatively less expensive for Americans to purchase. Appreciation of the dollar will lead to decreased exports for the U.S. because American goods become relatively more expensive for foreigners to purchase. Therefore, with the fall in exports and rise in imports, appreciation of the dollar means that net exports will fall. Holding all other factors constant, when the dollar depreciates, imports fall and exports rise. Therefore, when the dollar depreciates, net exports will rise.

### GNP AND NET EXPORTS

All else constant, a rise in GNP implies that American income has increased and that Americans will want to purchase more of all goods, including foreign goods. Imports will rise and net exports will fall. As a secondary effect, the rise in American incomes and the increased demand for foreign goods that comes with it leads to an outward shift in the supply-of-dollars curve in foreign-exchange markets. This causes the dollar to depreciate. This depreciation partially offsets the rise in imports due to increased GNP, somewhat increasing U.S. exports. The final effect of a rise in GNP is that net exports will fall.

### THE INTEREST RATE AND NET EXPORTS

All else constant (including foreign interest rates), a rise in the U.S. interest rate will make U.S. financial assets more attractive to foreigners. To purchase these assets, foreigners must purchase U.S. dollars. The demand-for-dollars curve will shift out, and the dollar will appreciate. Appreciation of the dollar implies that imports will rise and exports will fall. Therefore, net exports will decline.

**The Price Level and Net Exports.** With all else constant, a rise in the U.S. price level has the direct effect of making U.S. goods relatively more expensive than foreign goods. It thereby causes net exports to fall. In addition, a rise in the U.S. price level will lead to an increased U.S. interest rate because the demand for money rises. Consistent with the effects of a rising interest rate, the dollar will appreciate, and net exports will fall.

## Incorporating Trade into the Simple Macro Model

Net exports decrease with increases in GNP and increases in the interest rate. They are affected by other exogenous factors such as foreign tastes for American goods. The macro model can easily be expanded to include these effects. A simple net export function might take the form

*Net Exports* $= (Ex - Im) = N - m$ (GNP)(11.1)

The letter $N$ captures the effects of all the autonomous and exogenous factors affecting the level of net exports, such as American tastes for foreign goods, foreign tastes for American goods, and foreign incomes. Price level and interest-rate effects are also embodied in $N$. For example, a rise in the U.S. price level working through the U.S. interest rate causes the dollar to appreciate. An appreciated dollar will cause $N$ to decline in value.

The coefficient $m$ represents the *marginal propensity to import*. Given an increase in GNP, it is expected that imports will rise by $m$ times the GNP increase. For example if $m$ equals 0.08, imports will rise by eight cents for every dollar increase in GNP. Therefore, net exports will decline by 8 cents.

### NET EXPORTS AND THE EXPENDITURE FUNCTION

Aggregate expenditure in an economy open to foreign trade is equal to the sum of consumption, investment, government, and net-export expenditure. Symbolically,

$$E = C + I + G + (Ex - Im)$$

Net exports are added because aggregate expenditure represents the total value of all final goods and services purchased in the U.S. economy in one year. Aggregate consumption, investment, and government spending all contain purchases of imports. Therefore, imports must be subtracted to avoid counting goods produced outside the U.S. Even though they are not consumed in the U.S., exports are added because they are produced in the U.S. economy. They therefore represent part of expenditure on U.S. goods.

With the assumption that the proportional tax rate is zero, the consumption function takes the form

$$C = a - mpc\ (T) + mpc\ (GNP)$$

From the definitions and assumptions used in previous chapters, government spending, taxes, and investment are autonomous with respect to GNP. Combining these relationships with the net-export function (Equation 11.1), total expenditure is written out in full form as

$$E = [a - mpc\ (T) + mpc\ (\text{GNP})] + I + G + [N - m\ (\text{GNP})]$$

(The consumption function and net-export function are presented in brackets for clarity.) Combining terms containing the level of GNP yields

$$E = [a - mpc\ (T) + I + G + N] + (mpc - m)\ \text{GNP} \qquad (11.2)$$

The presence of net exports reduces the slope of the expenditure function because the marginal propensity to import is subtracted from the marginal propensity to consume. Terms within brackets represent the intercept of the expenditure function.

### EQUILIBRIUM WITH NET EXPORTS

As in the simple Keynesian model without net exports, equilibrium occurs when GNP equals the level of expenditure. As shown in Figure 11.2, equilibrium is determined at the point of intersection between the 45-degree line and the aggregate-expenditure function. The dashed line represents the expenditure function without international trade. Because the marginal propensity to import is subtracted from the marginal propensity to consume, the trade adjusted expenditure function is more horizontal than the expenditure function without trade.

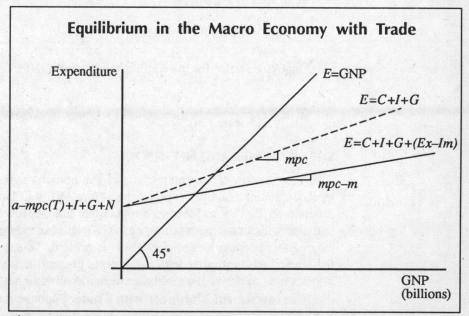

**Equilibrium in the Macro Economy with Trade**

*Figure 11.2  With trade, the expenditure function becomes more horizontal because the marginal propensity to import (m) is present. Depending on whether autonomous net exports are positive or negative, the intercept of the expenditure function may be above, below, or the same as the intercept without trade.*

The trade-adjusted expenditure function is shown with the same intercept as the expenditure function without trade. The actual effect of trade on the intercept depends on the relative size of $N$. A surge in demand for American products by foreigners would cause $N$ to increase and the intercept to rise. An increase in American demand for foreign goods would cause $N$ to decrease and the intercept to fall.

**Finding Equilibrium GNP Using Algebra.** In equilibrium, GNP equals expenditure. This familiar condition appears as

$$GNP = E$$

When the $E$ is substituted with the trade-adjusted expenditure equation, we have

$$GNP = [a - mpc\,(T) + I + G + N] + (mpc - m)\,GNP$$

Collecting terms containing GNP on the left leaves us with the following:

$$GNP - (mpc - m)\,GNP = [a - mpc\,(T) + I + G + N]$$

Next, GNP is factored out:

$$(1 - mpc + m)\,GNP = [a - mpc\,(T) + I + G + N]$$

Finally, we solve for the equilibrium level of GNP:

$$GNP = \frac{1}{(1 - mpc + m)}\,[a - mpc\,(T) + I + G + N] \quad (11.3)$$

## THE MULTIPLIER AND NET EXPORTS

A rise in any of the components of autonomous expenditure, which now includes autonomous net-export expenditure ($N$), will cause the expenditure function to shift up and lead to a higher equilibrium level of GNP. As in the situation without net exports, the rise in GNP will exceed the rise in autonomous expenditure because a multiplier effect is present. To see this and to estimate the size of the multiplier with net exports present involves the same simple algebra used to derive the multiplier formulas without net exports.

**The Investment Multiplier with Trade.** Suppose there is an increase in autonomous investment expenditure. Such a change in investment on the right side of Equation 11.3 will result in an increase in GNP on the left side. Because autonomous consumption, taxes, government spending, and autonomous net exports have not changed, this change in GNP is defined as

$$\Delta \text{GNP} = \left( \frac{1}{1 - mpc + m} \right) \Delta I$$

The investment multiplier is defined as the change in GNP that occurs because of the change in investment. Rearranging terms to solve for this value,

$$\frac{\Delta \text{GNP}}{\Delta I} = \frac{1}{(1 - mpc + m)}$$

**The Size of the Multiplier with Trade.** In the absence of international trade, the marginal propensity to import equals zero and this multiplier becomes the same as the simple investment multiplier used in previous chapters. With trade, $m$ is a positive fraction. When added to 1 minus the marginal propensity to consume, the denominator becomes larger and the value of the overall multiplier is reduced. Intuitively, this makes sense because in an open model consumers can purchase both American and foreign goods with their income. This leakage or outflow from the domestic economy results in a smaller increase in GNP.

**Other Multipliers with Trade.** Multipliers for autonomous consumption expenditure, $\frac{\Delta \text{GNP}}{\Delta a}$; government spending, $\frac{\Delta \text{GNP}}{\Delta G}$; autonomous taxes, $\frac{\Delta \text{GNP}}{\Delta T}$; and autonomous net exports, $\frac{\Delta \text{GNP}}{\Delta N}$, can be obtained in a manner similar to that for the derivation of the investment multiplier. By repeating the steps used in deriving the investment multiplier for each type of autonomous expenditure, it is seen that every other multiplier will be equivalent to the investment multiplier:

$$\frac{1}{(1 - mpc + m)}$$

The one exception is the autonomous tax multiplier. Because the tax level ($T$) is multiplied by $-mpc$, the autonomous tax multiplier will equal

$$\frac{\Delta \text{GNP}}{\Delta T} = \frac{-mpc}{(1 - mpc + m)}$$

As with the tax multiplier in the absence of trade, the denominator is the same as for the other spending multipliers. The sign of the tax multiplier is negative because taxes represent withdrawals from the expenditure flow. The numerator is also smaller because tax changes must first pass through the hands of consumers. They tend to spend a fraction (equal to the marginal propensity to consume) of any change in income they receive.

# THE COMPLETE MODEL WITH TRADE

With a basic understanding of how interest rates and GNP affect the level of net exports, it is possible to extend the aggregate supply-demand model developed in previous chapters. The impact of changes in net exports on the overall economy including GNP, the price level, the interest rate, and each of the components of aggregate expenditure can be considered. It is also possible to analyze the effects of changes in other variables in the model on net exports, especially those associated with monetary and fiscal policy.

In conducting analysis with net exports present, the connections between variables and the changes the economy undergoes are fundamentally the same as when international trade is absent. To capture the effects of trade on the model, it is merely necessary to determine how a change in net exports affects aggregate expenditure and aggregate demand. All other changes, including the feedback effects on net exports, stem from changes in the price level and GNP and their consequences.

## Aggregate Supply and Appreciation of the Dollar

Appreciation of the dollar reduces the effective price that Americans must pay for foreign goods. Because some imported goods like crude oil are used as inputs into production processes, appreciation of the dollar can cause the aggregate supply curve to shift right, just as it would given a decrease in the price of any factor of production. If the supply curve shifts right, it will lower the price level. It will also cause the level of GNP to rise. The magnitude of the supply shift will be greater if foreign inputs to domestic production processes are a large component of total production costs. Depreciation of the dollar will have the opposite effect.

## A Rise in Net Exports

An autonomous rise in net exports might occur because of a change in tastes by Americans in favor of domestically produced goods, a change in tastes by foreigners for American goods, a rise in foreign income, or a rise in foreign interest rates. Given such change, the expenditure curve in the expenditure-GNP diagram will shift up to intersect the 45-degree line at a higher level. The economy's aggregate demand curve will shift out simultaneously. Given an upward-sloping aggregate supply curve, the price level and GNP will rise.

These effects are shown in Figure 11.3. The original expenditure curve is $E_0$ while the original demand curve is $D_0$. Equilibrium GNP is \$5,000 billion. Holding the price level constant at 100, the rise in net exports causes the expenditure function to shift up to $E_1$ and aggregate demand shifts out to $D_1$.

As seen in the new intersection of aggregate supply and aggregate demand, the price level rises to 125. This rise in the price level will cause the expenditure function to shift down from $E_1$ to $E_2$. This occurs because the rise in the price level and GNP causes the interest rate to rise (the transactions demand for money is increased). After these adjustments, the equilibrium level of GNP established by the intersection of the 45-degree line, and expenditure line $E_2$ is equal to $5,300 billion, the level of GNP established at the interesection of aggregate demand and supply. The effects of the rise in GNP, the rise in the price level, and the rise in the interest rate can now be considered in more detail.

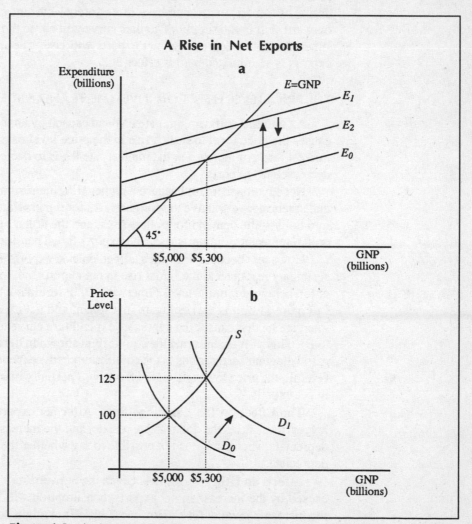

**Figure 1.3** *An increase in net exports causes aggregate expenditure to rise from $E_0$ to $E_1$ and aggregate demand to shift right from $D_0$ to $D_1$. Because GNP and the price level are higher, the interest rate will rise; investment and net exports will fall. This partially offsets the initial upward shift in expenditure and explains the expenditure shift from $E_1$ to $E_2$.*

## THE GNP EFFECT ON NET EXPORTS

From the net-export function, Equation 11.1, the higher level of GNP that occurs at the intersection of aggregate supply and demand curve $D_1$ implies that imports will increase. Increased GNP leads Americans to consume more of all goods, including foreign goods. Therefore, the initial increase in net exports that caused the outward shift in demand will be somewhat reduced, but it is not totally offset.

The increase in GNP also has an effect on the exchange rate. An increase in U.S. GNP causes the supply-of-dollars curve to shift out. This reflects the desire by Americans to purchase more foreign currency to buy imports. An outward shift in the supply-of-dollars curve will cause the dollar to depreciate. When the dollar depreciates, net exports will rise. The initial increase in net exports is accentuated by this effect.

## THE PRICE-LEVEL EFFECT ON INVESTMENT AND NET EXPORTS

An outward shift in aggregate demand caused by an increase in net exports causes the price level to rise. A rise in the price level causes an increase in the interest rate. An increase in the interest rate leads to decreased investment and decreased net exports.

Net exports decrease because a higher U.S. interest rate makes U.S. financial assets more attractive to foreigners. As foreigners transform their currency into dollars, the demand for dollars rises, and the dollar appreciates. When the dollar appreciates, imports rise, and exports fall. Therefore, net exports fall.

However, because the price effect on net exports in this example is a secondary response to the initial rise in net exports, net exports do not decline or fall below their initial level. Otherwise, GNP would fall below its initial level. In Figure 11.3, it is the decline in investment and net exports due to the rising interest rate that causes the aggregate expenditure curve to shift down from $E_1$ to $E_2$. This shift ensures that the equilibrium shown in the aggregate supply-demand diagram corresponds to the equilibrium in the expenditure-GNP diagram. Overall, the price level and GNP effects will partially offset the initial increase in net exports.

**The Effect on the Exchange Rate.** After net exports increase, the price level effect causes the dollar to appreciate, and the increase in GNP causes it to depreciate. Therefore, it is not possible to say whether the dollar appreciates or depreciates.

**Effects on Other Variables.** Given the outward shift in aggregate demand caused by the increase in net exports, consumption will be higher because of the increased level of GNP. However, this effect might be partially offset. The value of assets tied to the value of money decreases when the price level increases; therefore, consumption could be lower because of the real-balance or wealth effect. In Figure 11.3, the presence of such an effect would help explain the downward shift in expenditure from $E_1$ to $E_2$.

Because they are autonomous, government spending and taxes have not changed. As discussed under the price effect for net exports, investment will be lower because of the higher interest rate.

## Fiscal Policy and Net Exports

Through its effect on the other variables of the model, expansionary and contractionary fiscal policies will also have an effect on net exports. Depicted graphically, shifts in aggregate expenditure and aggregate demand are the same regardless of which component of autonomous expenditure changes. Therefore, Figure 11.3 can be used for this analysis. The economy is in initial equilibrium with aggregate-expenditure curve $E_0$, aggregate-demand curve $D_0$, and aggregate supply-curve $S$.

The intersection of the aggregate expenditure curve and the 45-degree line corresponds to the equilibrium level of GNP found at the intersection of aggregate supply and demand, $S$ *and* $D_0$. A rise in government spending or a cut in taxes will lead to an upward shift in aggregate expenditure to $E_1$ and an outward shift in aggregate demand to $D_1$. The price level increases to 125 on the aggregate-supply curve and the final level of GNP is $5,300 billion.

As the demand curve shifts out, the aggregate expenditure curve shifts from $E_0$ to $E_1$. The rise in the price level and GNP cause the interest rate to increase because of the transactions demand for money. This causes aggregate expenditure to shift from $E_1$ to $E_2$. Along expenditure function $E_2$, equilibrium GNP is $5,300 billion, the same equilibrium level found at the intersection of aggregate supply and the new aggregate-demand curve.

### THE EFFECT ON INVESTMENT AND NET EXPORTS

Higher levels of GNP lead Americans to consume more of all goods, including imports. Thus, the rise in GNP that comes with increased government spending or decreased taxes works directly to decrease net exports. However, the increased GNP causes the dollar to depreciate somewhat as the supply of dollars increases in foreign-exchange markets. This secondary effect is assumed not to be strong enough to cause net exports to rise.

The rise in the interest rate lowers investment and net exports. Specifically, by improving their relative rate of return compared with foreign assets, the higher U.S. interest rate leads to increased demand by foreigners for American financial assets. To purchase American financial assets requires dollars that must be purchased in foreign-exchange markets. The increased demand for dollars causes the dollar to appreciate. Exports fall, imports rise, and therefore net exports fall.

**Ultimate Effects on Net Exports.** An expansionary fiscal policy's ultimate impact on trade is to reduce the value of net exports. This is true because the interest rate and the level of GNP rise under the expansionary fiscal policy. Thus, with an initial imbalance of trade in which imports exceed exports, expansionary fiscal policy will enlarge the trade deficit. Contractionary fiscal policy will have the opposite effect.

### EFFECTS ON OTHER VARIABLES

Rising GNP will lead to increased consumption spending. Given that GNP is above its initial level, it must be the case that the increases in consumption (and government spending if this expansionary fiscal policy is used) are large enough to offset the decline in investment and net exports. The rise in the price level might lead to a wealth or real-balance effect and cause consumption to decline. However, it can be expected that the ultimate level of consumption will be higher after the expansionary fiscal policy because of the higher level of GNP.

## Monetary Policy and Net Exports

Though the reasons for the shifts in the aggregate-expenditure and aggregate-demand curves will be different, Figure 11.3 also allows analysis of an increase in the money supply. The economy is in initial equilibrium with aggregate-expenditure curve $E_0$, aggregate-demand curve $D_0$, and aggregate supply curve $S$. The intersection of the aggregate-expenditure curve $E_0$ and the 45-degree line corresponds to the equilibrium $5,000 billion level of GNP. This GNP level is also found at the intersection of the initial aggregate demand and supply curves.

An increase in the money supply lowers the interest rate and raises investment. In addition, the fall in the interest rate causes foreigners and Americans to seek higher rates of return in other countries. Both foreigners and Americans will use their dollars in foreign-exchange markets to purchase the currency necessary to buy assets in other countries with higher interest rates. The demand for dollars will fall, and the supply of dollars will increase; this causes the dollar to depreciate. Depreciation of the dollar causes net exports to rise: exports rise, and imports fall. The higher levels of investment and net exports brought on by the decline in the interest rate cause the aggregate-expenditure function to shift up to $E_1$. This upward shift corresponds to the outward shift in aggregate demand to $D_1$.

The economy's final equilibrium occurs at a GNP level of $5,300 billion with a price level of 125. The rise in the price level and GNP that comes with the outward shift in aggregate demand causes money demand to increase. This increases the interest rate to a level somewhat above that established when the Fed increased the money supply, but the interest rate is still below its initial level. Otherwise, GNP could not have increased. However, the rise in the interest rate causes the aggregate expenditure curve to shift down to $E_2$. Once again, final equilibriums match in both the aggregate-expenditure and aggregate-demand-supply diagrams.

### ULTIMATE TRADE EFFECTS OF MONETARY POLICY

Monetary policy's ultimate effects on net exports are ambiguous compared with the effects of fiscal policy. While the fall in the interest rate will definitely lead the dollar to depreciate and stimulate net exports, the rise in GNP implies that imports will be higher. If the decreased interest-rate effect and resulting depreciation dominates the GNP effect, net exports will be higher. However, if the rise in GNP dominates, net exports could fall. These ambiguous effects will occur in reverse if the money supply is cut.

## EFFECTS ON OTHER VARIABLES

The rise in the money supply will lead to increased GNP. The rise in GNP will lead to higher levels of consumption. Consumption expenditure might be partially offset because of the wealth or real-balance effect—the decline in the value of assets tied to the value of money that comes with the price level increase. When asset values decline, consumers are not as willing to consume. Because the interest rate is lower, investment is higher.

## *Aggregate Supply and Long-Run Effects in the Open Model*

In each of the above examples, if it is assumed that the economy was initially in equilibrium at the potential level of GNP, the expansionary forces at work lead to a level of GNP above the potential level when aggregate demand shifts out. GNP levels above potential imply high levels of demand for inputs. This ultimately leads to higher input costs and leftward shifts in aggregate supply. These forces continue to operate until aggregate supply crosses the new aggregate-demand curve at the price level associated with potential GNP. Thus, in the long run, after any *outward* shift in aggregate demand, the economy returns to the potential level of GNP at a higher price level. After any *inward* shift in aggregate demand, there are forces that shift aggregate supply to the right. The economy eventually returns to the potential level of GNP at a lower price level.

## LONG-RUN ADJUSTMENT

The nature of the long-run adjustment process is shown in Figure 11.4. Initial equilibrium occurs at the intersection of supply curve $S_0$ and demand curve $D_0$, above the potential GNP level of \$5,000 billion. Demand curve $D_1$ has shifted out because of either increased net exports, increased government spending, decreased taxes, increased investor confidence, increased consumer confidence, or an increased money supply. This establishes an equilibrium level of GNP at \$5,300 billion, \$300 billion above potential GNP.

Given the long-run rise in input costs caused by a GNP level above potential, supply curve $S_1$ has shifted back to intersect demand curve $D_1$ at the potential level of GNP. The price level has moved from a value of 125 to 150. The only long-term effects of the outward demand shift is a possible rearrangement in the components of aggregate expenditure at the potential level of GNP.

## LONG-RUN EFFECTS ON EXPENDITURE COMPONENTS

When the rightward shift in aggregate demand is brought about by a change in some component of aggregate expenditure (such as increased autonomous consumption, autonomous investment, autonomous net exports, government spending, or decreased taxes), the leftward shift in aggregate supply will lead

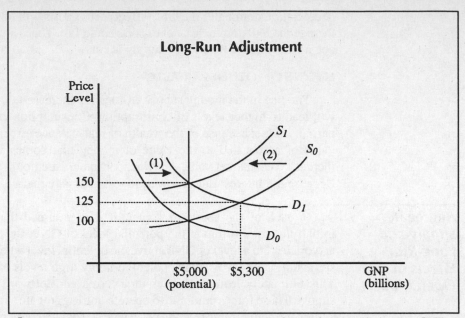

**Figure 11.4** *An outward shift in the aggregate-demand curve (1) causes GNP to rise above potential. In the long run, as input costs rise, aggregate supply shifts left to restore the potential level of GNP (2).*

to a higher price level when potential GNP is restored. The increase in the price level will lead to increased money demand and a higher interest rate. Compared with the initial level before the outward shift in demand, the higher interest rate causes investment to decline. A rising U.S. interest rate will also cause the dollar to appreciate; this causes net exports to fall. As in the model without foreign trade, a higher price level may also lead to declines in consumption through a wealth or real-balance effect as the value of assets tied to money declines. Because GNP has returned to potential, its effects on expenditure components are negated.

## LONG-RUN MONETARY EFFECTS

When aggregate demand shifts out because of an increase in the money supply, GNP rises because the interest rate declines. As the aggregate-supply curve shifts left to restore potential GNP, the interest rate begins to rise to its previous level because money demand increases. When potential GNP is restored, changes brought on by monetary expansion and a lower interest rate are exactly offset by the rise in the interest rate due to the increase in the price level. Thus, in the long run, expansionary monetary policy has no effect on the components of aggregate expenditure; it results only in inflation.

# *THE COMPLETE MACRO MODEL AND THE TRADE DEFICIT*

This chapter has expanded the model of the macro economy to include net exports. It also represents the complete development of the macro model at the introductory level. Through use of this model, the effects of virtually any change in real-world variables can be analyzed, and predictions of how consumption, investment, net exports, the interest rate, and the price level will change can be made. As an example of its ability to deal with real world circumstances, the model will be used to show how a simultaneous solution to the trade and budget deficits can be achieved.

## *Dealing with the Trade and Budget Deficits*

The trade deficit and the budget deficit have been viewed as major macroeconomic problems facing policymakers. To avoid unemployment and inflation, the policy response to these problems requires that GNP remain at the potential level. With GNP fixed at this level, a rearrangement in the mix of fiscal and monetary policy could lead to reductions in both the trade and budget deficits.

To reduce the trade deficit, expansionary monetary policy can be used. A lower U.S. interest rate will cause the dollar to depreciate, thereby causing net exports to increase. However, GNP will rise. To reduce the budget deficit, taxes must be increased or government spending cut. However, GNP will fall. Using an expansionary monetary policy simultaneously with a contractionary fiscal policy could cancel the GNP effects. Aggregate demand would shift out because of the expansionary monetary policy and would shift in because of the contractionary fiscal policy. The inward and outward shifts would cancel. The price level would not change. This simultaneous use of an expansionary monetary policy and a contractionary fiscal policy would leave GNP at the potential level and would lower both the budget and trade deficits. This is exactly the opposite mix of fiscal and monetary policy that has been in use for the 1980s and early 1990s.

### EFFECTS ON OTHER VARIABLES

The simultaneous use of an expansionary monetary policy, which shifts aggregate demand out, and a contractionary fiscal policy, which shifts aggregate demand in, implies that policies can be coordinated so that aggregate demand will not shift. Hence, the price level and GNP will not change. Expansionary monetary policy, with GNP held at the potential level, will lead to increased investment and net exports because the interest rate declines. The increases in investment and net exports can be exactly offset with a decrease in government spending to leave consumption, the remaining component of aggregate expenditure, unchanged. If government spending cannot be cut, taxes could be increased. To maintain GNP at the potential level, increased taxes imply that consumption must fall by an amount equal to the increase in investment and net exports.

Aside from curing the trade deficit and budget defict, an expansionary monetary policy combined with a contractionary fiscal policy could help increase productivity in the U.S. The nation's capital stock will be increased as investment increases. However, this policy mix is not without costs. If government spending is cut, worthwhile social programs could suffer. Tax increases imply less private consumption. In addition, coordination of such a policy requires precise determination of the appropriate monetary stimulus and fiscal restraint. Miscalculation would cause unemployment or inflation.

*In this chapter the importance of international trade and the effects of net exports on the macro model have been considered. In the context of the international balance of payments, imbalances in net exports, captured by the current account, are offset by imbalances in ownership of financial assets, captured by the capital account. These imbalances result in variations in the exchange rate as the dollar appreciates and depreciates.*

*Among the forces affecting trade are many of the variables considered fundamental to macroeconomic analysis, such as the price level, the interest rate, and the level of GNP. Therefore, integration of net exports into the macro model provides a comprehensive means of analyzing the impact of trade effects on the economy. By considering the determinants of net exports, analysis can be extended to cover the effects of changes in other components of the macro model on trade.*

*Understanding the complete macro model with trade is important, for at least three reasons. First, understanding the connections between the various macroeconomic variables and using the graphs and equations which describe them improve analytical and reasoning skills. Second, the complete model can be used to make predictions, given potential changes in policy or unexpected real-world events. For example, in deciding between political candidates, the model allows verification of whether a candidate's planned outcomes, are consistent with his or her platform. In a democratic society, such knowledge is vital in making informed decisions. Third, awareness of the interconnections between macroeconomic variables can lead to more profitable business decisions and better handling of personal financial assets in response to changing economic circumstances.*

## Selected Readings

Rock, James M. *Debt and the Twin Deficits Debate.* Mountain View, CA: Mayfield Publishing Co. 1991.

# APPENDIX

**Proportional Taxes and Trade: Equilibrium and the Multiplier**

If proportional taxes are present along with international trade, the economy's consumption function is written as

$$C = a - mpc\,(T) + mpc\,(1 - t)\,\text{GNP}$$

As always, equilibrium occurs when GNP is equal to expenditure. When the complete expenditure function is used, including trade effects from Equation 11.1, this condition appears as

$$\text{GNP} = [a - mpc\,(T) + (1 - t)\,mpc\,\text{GNP}] + I + G + [N + m\,(\text{GNP})]$$

Moving terms containing GNP to the left side and then solving for GNP yields

$$\text{GNP} = \frac{1}{[1 - (1 - t)\,mpc + m]}\,(a - (mpc)T + I + G + N)$$

Given a change in investment with all other autonomous components constant, the investment multiplier will equal

$$\frac{\Delta\text{GNP}}{\Delta I} = \frac{1}{[1 - (1 - t)mpc + m]}$$

This is the most complicated multiplier usually encountered in introductory economics classes. It contains elements common to the multiplier with proportional taxes and the multiplier for an economy open to trade. Because the range of values on the proportional tax rate is between zero and 1, the proportional tax rate multiplied by the marginal propensity to consume results in a fraction smaller than the marginal propensity to consume. Subtracting this fraction from 1 therefore yields a larger denominator. Adding the marginal propensity to import increases the denominator even more. Therefore, the multiplier that includes the effects of proportional taxes and trade is smaller than the multiplier that would exist in their absence.

Except for the autonomous tax multiplier, the other expenditure multipliers will again be equivalent to the investment multiplier. The tax multiplier will once again have the same denominator, but it will carry a minus sign times the marginal propensity to consume in the numerator.

# 12

# IS-LM *Analysis and the Complete Macro Model*

*W*hen both the money and commodity markets are in equilibrium, the economy's equilibrium level of GNP and interest rate are uniquely determined. Because of the simultaneous way changes in one market affect the other, viewing each market separately does not clearly reveal how all of the variables in the macro model are interrelated. This chapter develops a means of showing how actions in the commodity and money markets interact and lead to the equilibrium interest rate and level of GNP.

The simple model of supply and demand shows how the intersection of the supply and demand curves determines an equilibrium price and quantity. The IS-LM model shows how the economy's IS and LM curves intersect to determine the equilibrium interest rate and level of GNP. The IS and LM curves are derived from equilibrium relationships in both the money market and the commodity market. The letters I and S, respectively, represent investment and savings. Equilibrium in the simple model of the commodity market without government occurs when investment and savings are equal. The letters LM stand for equilibrium in the money market. L represents the money-demand curve, or "liquidity preference schedule" as Keynes called it. M represents the money-supply curve. Equilibrium in the money market occurs at the point where the money-supply and money-demand curves cross. When graphed together, the IS and LM curves capture and summarize all the information contained in graphs of the economy's money-supply and money-demand curves, the investment-demand curve, and the expenditure-GNP diagram.

*In this chapter, the* IS *and* LM *curves are each derived. They are then used to find the level of GNP and rate of interest that leaves both the money and commodity markets in equilibrium. Next, as with standard supply-demand analysis, the factors causing shifts in the curves are considered. Then the effects of shifts in the* IS *and* LM *curves are analyzed. Finally, the connection between the* IS-LM *model and the model of aggregate supply and demand is developed.*

# THE IS CURVE

The *IS* curve is defined as all possible combinations of the interest rate and level of GNP that keep the economy's commodity market in equilibrium. With this definition, deriving the *IS* curve is a simple matter. The commodity market is the market in which the equilibrium level of GNP is determined. Graphically, the commodity market is represented by the expenditure function and the 45-degree line. Because it shows a relationship between the interest rate and the level of GNP, the graph of the *IS* curve is drawn with the interest rate on the vertical axis and the level of GNP on the horizontal axis.

## Deriving the IS Curve

Figure 12.1 shows graphs of the expenditure-GNP diagram and the *IS* curve. Increases in the interest rate lead to lower levels of investment (and net exports in a model open to trade) and cause the expenditure function to shift down. The three expenditure functions in Figure 12.1a differ in their locations because of assumed differences in the rate of interest. The top expenditure function $E_0$ ($r = 4\%$) will exist when the interest rate is 4 percent. A rise in the rate of interest to 8 percent leads to the next lower expenditure function $E_1$ ($r = 8\%$). Finally, a rise in the rate of interest to 12 percent leads to expenditure function $E_2$ ($r = 12\%$). The equilibrium levels of GNP associated with these expenditure functions are \$5,500 billion, \$5,000 billion, and \$4,500 billion, respectively.

The *IS* curve is the graphed relationship between these equilibrium GNP levels and the rates of interest that lead to them. For example, one point on the *IS* curve is found at an interest rate of 4 percent and a GNP level of \$5,500 billion. When all possible interest rates are considered, the *IS* curve emerges. As can be seen, the *IS* curve is downward-sloping. This is because a higher interest rate lowers the level of investment (and net exports). A lower level of investment will shift the expenditure function down. Through the multiplier, this will lower the equilibrium GNP level that prevails in the commodity market.

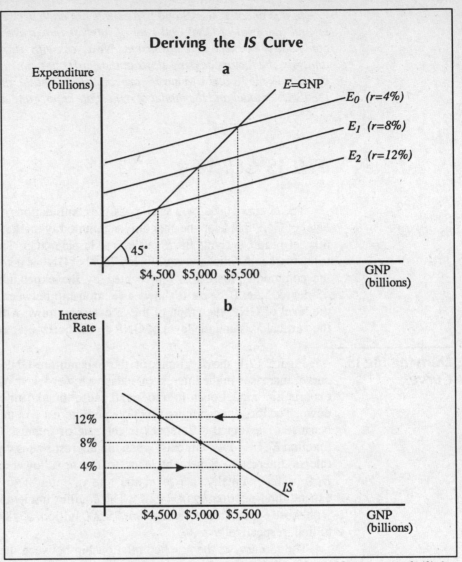

**Figure 12.1**  *As the interest rate rises from 4 to 8 to 12 percent, declining investment (and net exports) cause downward shifts in the expenditure function and lower levels of equilibrium GNP. The relationship between these equilibrium GNP levels and the interest rate is the IS curve.*

## *Shifting the* IS *Curve*

In deriving the *IS* curve, the level of government spending, taxes, autonomous consumption expenditure, and investor confidence were all assumed to be fixed at some predetermined level. Aside from taxes, if any one of these factors increased, the expenditure functions shown in Figure 12.1 would all shift up. This would lead to intersection with the 45-degree line at a point farther from the origin. Therefore, higher levels of GNP would be associated with each given rate of interest. If higher levels of GNP correspond with given rates of interest, the *IS* curve must be located farther to the right.

Given these considerations, the *IS* curve shifts out with increases in government spending, autonomous consumption expenditure, or investor confidence. The *IS* curve will also shift out with a decrease in taxes. Finally, if the model is open to international trade, the *IS* curve will shift out with a rise in autonomous net exports.

### STABILITY AND THE *IS* CURVE

Suppose that the economy is operating at an interest rate of 4 percent and a level of GNP equal to $4,500 billion. As seen in Figure 12.1b, this point lies to the left of the *IS* curve. The low rate of interest will stimulate investment expenditure. However, given the low level of GNP, expenditure will be too high.

At the 4 percent rate of interest, the relevant expenditure function in Figure 12.1a is $E_0$. If GNP equals $4,500 billion, on expenditure curve $E_0$ expenditure is greater than GNP. Because purchases of goods exceed production of goods, ~ventories will be drawn upon to make up the difference; there is unintended unplanned inventory disinvestment. As in the simple Keynesian model, such situation will signal producers to increase production, which causes GNP to crease. In Figure 12.1b, this adjustment is seen as a rightward movement vard the *IS* curve at the 4 percent rate of interest. Eventually the economy 'l find its way to the *IS* curve; GNP increases until it equals $5,500 billion. 'h upward pressure on GNP will occur anywhere to the left of the *IS* curve.

Should the economy be operating to the right of the *IS* curve, opposite ; are set into motion. For example, if the interest rate is twelve percent, expenditure curve $E_2$ will determine the equilibrium level of GNP in Figure 12.1a. But if the level of GNP is $5,500 billion, the high rate of interest leads to too little investment expenditure; aggregate expenditure will be below GNP. Because the amount produced exceeds the amount being purchased, inventories will build up. This unintended inventory investment signals firms to reduce production, thereby lowering GNP. In Figure 12.1b equilibrium will finally occur on the *IS* curve at an interest rate of 12 percent and a level of GNP equal to $4,500 billion. The leftward force of unintended inventory investment will exist everywhere to the right of the *IS* curve.

The return to equilibrium for points off the *IS* curve involves increases or decreases in the level of GNP. The rate of interest does not change because the interest rate is not determined in the commodity market; it is taken as given after it is determined in the money market.

# THE LM CURVE

The *LM curve* is defined as all combinations of the interest rate and level of GNP that keep the economy's money market in equilibrium.

**Deriving the LM *Curve***

Figure 12.2 shows the economy's money market and *LM* curve. Increases in the level of GNP lead to an increased transactions demand for money and cause the money-demand curve to shift out. This raises the equilibrium rate of interest. The three money-demand curves shown in Figure 12.2a have all been affected by changes in the level of GNP. With the money supply fixed, money demand curve *Md*(GNP = $4,500) leads to an equilibrium rate of interest of 4 percent. A rise in GNP to $5,000 billion causes the money-demand curve to shift out to *Md*(GNP = $5,000); this causes the equilibrium interest rate to rise to 8 percent. Finally, a rise in the level of GNP to $5,500 billion causes a further outward shift in money demand to *Md*(GNP = $5,500) and leads to an equilibrium rate of interest of 12 percent.

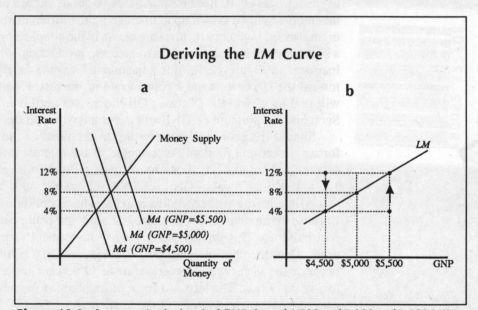

**Figure 12.2**  *Increase in the level of GNP from $4,500 to $5,000 to $5,500 billion lead to increased money demand for transaction purposes. As the money-demand curve shifts out, the equilibrium rate of interest rises. The relationship between GNP and these equilibrium interest rates is the LM curve.*

These GNP levels and the equilibrium rates of interest they lead to are graphed in Figure 12.2b. When all equilibrium interest rates arising from all possible GNP levels are considered, the economy's *LM* curve is derived. As can be seen, the *LM* curve is upward-sloping. This reflects the effects on interest rates of higher levels of GNP; higher GNP levels lead to increased transactions demand for money and a higher equilibrium rate of interest.

### STABILITY AND THE *LM* CURVE

Suppose the economy is not operating on its *LM* curve. For example, in Figure 12.2b, suppose the economy is operating at a point below the *LM* curve with a rate of interest of 4 percent and a GNP of $5,500 billion. Given the GNP level, as seen in Figure 12.2a, the relevant money-demand curve is *Md* (GNP = $5,500). Money demand is too far to the right for 4 percent to be the equilibrium rate of interest. If *Md* (GNP = $5,500) is the money demand curve when the interest rate is 4 percent, the quantity of money demanded exceeds the quantity of money supplied. This means that there is excess demand in the money market; the interest rate will rise. Equilibrium in the money market will occur when an interest rate of 12 percent prevails. In Figure 12.2b, points below the *LM* curve are therefore associated with excess demand for money and upward pressure on interest rates.

For points above the *LM* curve, opposite forces are at work. At an interest rate of 12 percent and a GNP level of $4,500 billion, money demand is too low to achieve a 12 percent equilibrium interest rate. In Figure 12.2a, the relevant money-demand curve is now *Md* (GNP = $4,500). At 12 percent, the quantity of money demanded falls short of the quantity of money supplied; downward pressure on the rate of interest will exist. Ultimately, the rate of interest will fall to its equilibrium value of 4 percent.

For the *LM* curve, the interest rate adjusts to restore equilibrium The force of excess money demand or supply puts upward or downward pressure on the interest rate because GNP cannot be determined in the money market. Instead, GNP is taken as given after its value is set in the commodity market.

## Shifting the LM *Curve*

Held constant in the derivation of the economy's *LM* curve are the money supply, the price level, and the fraction of income that individuals desire to hold as cash. Changes in any of these variables will cause the *LM* curve to shift. The nature of such shifts is as follows.

### SHIFTING *LM*: THE MONEY SUPPLY

Suppose the money supply had been higher in Figure 12.2a. For any money-demand curve, the corresponding equilibrium rate of interest would be lower. Graphing these lower interest rates against the level of GNP associated with each money-demand curve would lead to an *LM* curve farther to the right of the curve shown in Figure 12.2b. It follows that a rise in the money supply will cause the *LM* curve to shift out.

## SHIFTING *LM*: THE PRICE LEVEL

A rise in the price level will cause the money-demand curve to shift out (more money is needed for transactions purposes). This leads to ·a higher equilibrium rate of interest for any given level of GNP. This is shown in Figure 12.3, where a price level of 100 is consistent with a level of GNP equal to $4,500 billion and an equilibrium interest rate of 4 percent. This is a point on the *LM* curve labeled *LM* (*P* = 100). A rise in the price level with GNP held constant causes the money-demand curve to shift out from *Md* (GNP = $4,500, P = 100) to *Md* (GNP = $4,500, P = 125). The GNP level of $4,500 billion is now associated with an equilibrium interest rate of 8 percent. If the *LM* curve was derived based on this higher price level, one point on the new *LM* curve would be located at an interest rate of 8 percent and a GNP level of $4,500 billion. This is a point on the *LM* curve labeled *LM* (*P* = 125). After the price level increase, higher equilibrium interest rates are associated with each level of GNP. It follows that higher price levels cause the *LM* curve to shift up while lower price levels cause it to shift down.

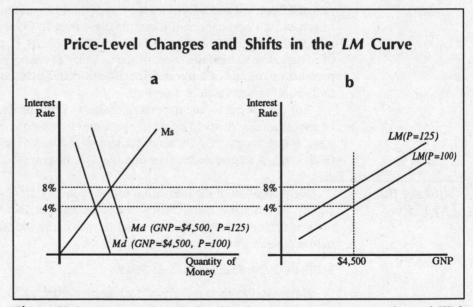

**Figure 12.3** *A raise in the price level leads to an increase in money demand. With a GNP level of $4,500 billion, the equilibrium rate of interest rises from 4 to 8 percent when the price level rises from 100 to 125. Because a higher equilibrium interest rate is associated with the level of GNP, the LM curve has shifted up.*

### SHIFTING *LM*: THE PROPORTION OF INCOME HELD AS CASH

Through the transactions demand for money, higher levels of GNP are assumed to lead to larger cash holdings. With higher incomes, it is expected that a greater volume of daily transactions will occur. Should individuals decide at every level of GNP to hold more income in the form of cash, the money-demand curve will shift out. The effect of this shift is the same as that occurring with a rise in the price level. Each level of GNP will now correspond with a higher equilibrium interest rate. This means that the *LM* curve has shifted up. Should individuals decide to hold less cash at all GNP levels, the *LM* curve will shift down.

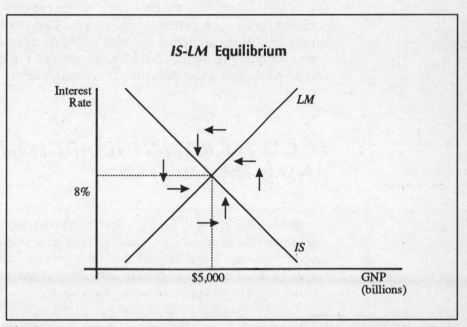

**Figure 12.4**  *The rate of interest and level of GNP leading to equilibrium in both the commodity and money market are found at the IS-LM intersection. Upward pressure on interest rates exists for points lying below the LM curve, while downward pressure exists for points lying above it. There is upward pressure on GNP for points lying to the left of the IS curve and downward pressure for points to the right.*

# EQUILIBRIUM IN THE IS-LM MODEL

When graphed together, the *IS* and *LM* curves will intersect at a single interest rate and level of GNP. By definition, the *IS* curve represents all interest rate and GNP combinations that keep the economy's commodity market in equilibrium. Therefore, because the point of intersection between *IS* and *LM* is on the *IS* curve, the commodity market must be in equilibrium. Similarly, because the *LM* curve represents all interest rate and GNP combinations that keep the economy's money market in equilibrium, the point of intersection between *IS* and *LM* will also be consistent with equilibrium in the money market. In Figure 12.4, the equilibrium rate of interest equals 8 percent and equilibrium GNP is $5,000 billion.

## The Stability of IS-LM Equilibrium

What happens if the economy is operating off both the *IS* and *LM* curves? Points off the *IS* curve bring forth leftward or righward forces that affect GNP because of unintended inventory investment or disinvestment in the commodity market. These forces push the economy back toward the *IS* curve. Because of excess money demand or supply, points off the *LM* curve bring forth upward or downward forces that affect the interest rate. These forces push the economy back to the *LM* curve. Because of both sets of forces, the overall economy is stable. As shown in Figure 12.4, a whirlpool effect centered around the equilibrium point ensures that deviations from equilibrium are corrected.

# FISCAL POLICY, MONETARY POLICY, AND IS-LM ANALYSIS

Because it captures all the factors present in both the money and commodity markets, the *IS-LM* model allows analysis of the effectiveness of both fiscal and monetary policies. The effectiveness of these policies depends greatly upon the shapes of the *IS* and *LM* curves. In turn, these shapes depend on the characteristics of the commodity and money markets.

## Fiscal Policy and IS-LM Analysis

Fiscal policy takes the form of increases and decreases in government expenditure and taxes to bring about some desired policy objective. Government expenditure increases and tax decreases lead to outward shifts in the *IS* curve, while government expenditure decreases and tax increases have the opposite effect.

To analyze the relationship between the upward shift in the aggregate expenditure curve and the outward shift in *IS*, Figure 12.5 presents both curves. In Figure 12.5a, equilibrium initially occurs at the intersection of expenditure curve $E_0$ and the 45-degree line at a $5,000 billion level of GNP. In Figure 12.5b, this equilibrium corresponds to the point on curve $IS_0$ and the *LM* curve above $5,000 billion at an interest rate of 8 percent.

An expansionary fiscal policy causes the expenditure function to shift up from $E_0(r = 8\%)$ to $E_1(r = 8\%)$. Through the simple multiplier, this causes GNP to increase from $5,000 billion to $5,500 billion in Figure 12.5a. In Figure

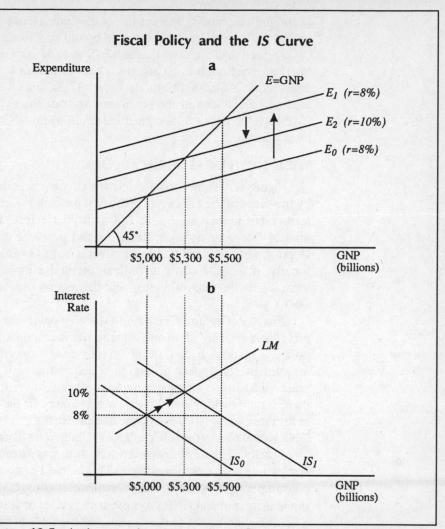

**Figure 12.5** *An increase in government spending or a decrease in taxes causes the expenditure function to shift up from $E_0$ to $E_1$. This corresponds to the IS curve's shift right by the full-multiplier effect. If the interest rate did not increase, GNP would rise from $5,000 billion to $5,500 billion. However, because of the increased money demand that comes with higher levels of GNP, the interest rate will rise, as seen in the movement along the LM curve. The rise in the rate of interest causes the downward shift in the expenditure function from $E_1$ to $E_2$. Final equilibrium GNP is $5,300 billion.*

12.5b, the point above $5,500 billion at an interest rate of 8 percent will be on the new *IS* curve after the expansionary fiscal policy. This point is consistent with the definition of the *IS* curve; it is an interest rate-GNP combination that keeps the commodity market in equilibrium. Hence, an expansionary fiscal policy shifts the *IS* curve to the right by the simple multiplier effect.

As seen in the intersection of the *IS* and *LM* curves, the equilibrium rate of interest rises from 8 to 10 percent. The equilibrium level of GNP at the *IS-LM* intersection is $5,300 billion. In Figure 12.5a, the effect of the increase in the interest rate is seen in the downward shift of the expenditure function from $E_1(r = 8\%)$ to $E_2(r = 10\%)$. The final equilibrium GNP levels in both diagrams must match.

### THE EFFECTIVENESS OF FISCAL POLICY

Figure 12.6 shows how the relative effectiveness of fiscal policy is affected by the shape of the *LM* curve. In the first panel, a perfectly horizontal *LM* curve leads GNP to increase by the full multiplier effect. This occurs because the interest rate does not rise. In the second panel, if the *LM* curve is upward-sloping, part of the full multiplier effect is lost as a result of rising interest rates. Finally, if the *LM* curve is vertical, the entire multiplier effect is offset by increases in the rate of interest, and there is no overall change in equilibrium GNP.

**Fiscal Policy and Crowding-Out.** *Crowding-out* refers to the decrease in private expenditure when interest rates rise in response to an expansionary fiscal policy. Changes in the rate of interest have important implications for the investment component of aggregate expenditure. If an expansionary fiscal policy leads to no change in the interest rate, investment is not affected, and there is no crowding-out. This is seen in Figure 12.6a. In Figure 12.6b, the rise in the rate of interest leads to some decrease in the level of investment; otherwise GNP would rise by the full-multiplier effect. Thus there is partial crowding-out.

Finally, if the *LM* curve is vertical, the expansionary fiscal policy must completely crowd out investment. This is true because GNP equals the sum of consumption, investment, and government spending. When government spending is increased and GNP stays the same, either consumption or investment, or a combination of the two, has declined by a corresponding amount. Because investment is inversely related to the rate of interest, it bears the brunt of the increase in government expenditure by being completely crowded out. It is reduced in magnitude by the same amount as the increase in government expenditure. If consumption is assumed to be a function of the interest rate, it too will decline.

**The Effect on Net Exports.** If net exports are present in the model, rising interest rates will cause the dollar to appreciate and lead to reduced net exports. As long as the *LM* curve is upward-sloping or vertical, in addition to the decline in investment, the economy will find its trade balance going into deficit following an expansionary fiscal policy.

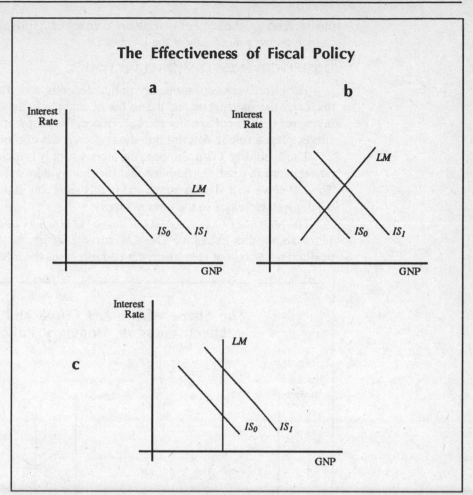

**Figure 12.6** *Depending on the shape of the LM curve, the same outward shift in IS can have very different effects. A horizontal LM curve implies that GNP rises by the full-multiplier effect because there is no change in the interest rate. When the LM curve is upsloping, the rise in the interest rate that comes with the outward shift in IS reduces the rise in GNP somewhat. In the extreme case, if LM is vertical, the rise in the interest rate totally offsets the effects of the IS shift, and GNP will not rise.*

**Monetary Policy and IS-LM Analysis**

Monetary policy involves increasing or decreasing the money supply to bring about a desired change in the level of economic activity. An expansionary monetary policy shifts the *LM* curve outward. This leads to lower interest rates at every level of GNP. By shifting the *LM* curve to the left, contractionary monetary policy raises the interest rate. Through monetary policy's effect on the interest rate, the level of investment is changed. Through the multiplier, this change in investment affects the level of GNP.

## THE EFFECTIVENESS OF MONETARY POLICY

The effectiveness of monetary policy depends upon the ability of the Fed to change the interest rate and the ability of changes in the interest rate to affect investment in the commodity market. Hence, the shape of both *LM* and the *IS* curves plays a role in determining the effectiveness of monetary policy.

**The Liquidity Trap.** Suppose the money supply is increased; if the interest rate remains the same, it implies that the money-demand curve is horizontal. The *LM* curve will also be horizontal in this situation. It therefore cannot shift right, given increases in the money supply.

The presence of a horizontal *LM* curve is known as a *liquidity trap*. Figure 12.7a shows this situation. The *LM* curve remains in the same horizontal position regardless of how much the Fed increases the money supply. Because

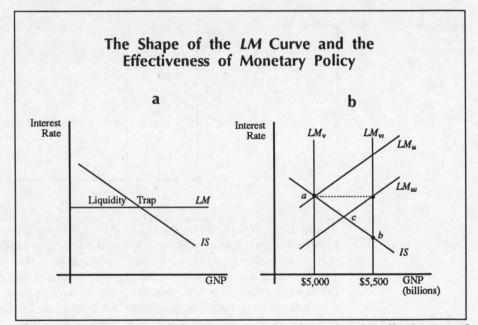

*Figure 12.7   The shape of the LM curve helps determine the effectiveness of monetary policy in changing GNP. In Figure 12.7a the LM curve is horizontal; changes in the money supply do not affect the rate of interest, GNP will not change. In Figure 12.7b with equal rightward shifts of the vertical and upsloping LM curves, the vertical curve leads to a larger decline in the interest rate. Investment is stimulated more, leading to a greater change in GNP. The shifted vertical LM curve intersects the IS curve at point b, to the right of the shifted upward-sloping LM curve's intersection at point c.*

it cannot change the interest rate, monetary policy is ineffective in bringing about changes in the equilbrium level of GNP.

## UPWARD-SLOPING AND VERTICAL *LM* CURVES

A shift in the *LM* curve will have its greatest effect on GNP when the *LM* curve is vertical. Figure 12.7b shows an upward-sloping *LM* curve labeled *LM*$_u$ and a vertical *LM* curve labeled *LM*$_v$. Both curves intersect the *IS* curve above an equilibrium level of GNP of $5,000. This occurs at point *a*. The *LM* curves are then shifted by the same *horizontal amount*, $500 billion. The vertical curve moves to *LM*$_{v1}$ and the upward sloping curve moves to *LM*$_{u1}$. The new vertical *LM* curve intersects the *IS* curve at point *b* above a GNP level of $5,500 billion. The new upward-sloping *LM*, curve intersects the *IS* curve at point *c*. The equilibrium level of GNP established by the intersection at point *c* falls short of $5,500 billion.

The shift in the vertical curve leads to a larger increase in GNP because its rightward shift causes a greater reduction in the interest rate. In fact, for a given rightward shift, the vertical curve causes the greatest possible decline in the interest rate. Therefore, the reduction in the interest rate will lead to the largest possible increase in investment, given an increase in the money supply. Finally, through the multiplier, the largest possible increase in investment given an expansionary monetary policy will lead to the largest possible increase in equilibrium GNP when *LM* is vertical. Thus, when the *LM* curve is vertical monetary policy will be most effective.

**Monetary Policy and the *IS* Curve.** Aside from its ability to influence the rate of interest, the effectiveness of monetary policy depends upon the shape of the *IS* curve. Monetary policy is more effective when a decline in the rate of interest leads to a larger increase in the level of investment. Should investment be unresponsive to the rate of interest, changes in the interest rate will have no effect on GNP. In this case, the *IS* curve will be vertical, shifts in the *LM* curve will not cause equilibrium GNP to change, and monetary policy will be useless. Thus, the more vertical the *IS* curve, the less effective is monetary policy.

As seen in Figure 12.8a, an outward shift in the *LM* curve causes the equilibrium rate of interest to fall from 8 percent to 4 percent. However, because *IS* is vertical, there is no change in GNP. The decline in the interest rate has not stimulated investment, so GNP will not rise. In Figure 12.8b, the *LM* curve also shifts right because of an expansionary monetary policy. Again the interest rate falls from 8 to 4 percent. GNP rises from $5,000 billion to $5,300 billion. The decline in the interest rates has caused investment to rise. Through the multiplier, the level of GNP increases.

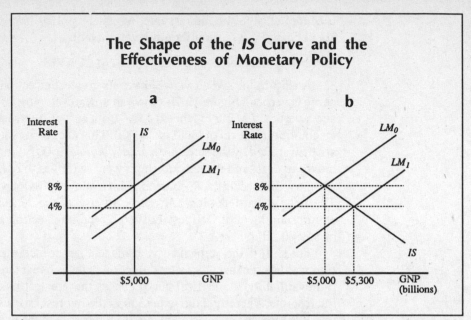

**The Shape of the *IS* Curve and the Effectiveness of Monetary Policy**

**Figure 12.8** *In both graphs, an increase in the money supply reduces the equilibrium rate of interest from 8 to 4 percent. However, when the IS curve is vertical, investment does not respond to changes in the interest rate, so GNP does not change. A downward-sloping IS curve reflects the inverse relationship between investment and the interest rate. When the interest rate falls, investment rises. Through the multiplier, GNP also rises. The more horizontal the IS curve, the more effective monetary policy will be.*

# IS-LM *AND AGGREGATE DEMAND*

The *aggregate-demand curve* is defined as all combinations of the price level and level of GNP that keep the economy's money and commodity markets in equilibrium. It can be derived using the *IS-LM* diagram. This derivation is shown in Figure 12.9, where the economy is assumed to be in initial equilibrium at a GNP level of $5,000 billion along *LM* curve $LM(P = 100)$ and the *IS* curve. From its defintion, one point on the aggregate-demand curve is found when the price level is 100 and the level of GNP is $5,000 billion. A rise in the price level from 100 to 115 will lead to increased money demand and cause the *LM* curve to shift up to $LM(P = 115)$. The new intersection of the *IS* and *LM* curves reduces equilibrium GNP to $4,500 billion and determines another point on the aggregate-demand curve. Continued increases in the price level cause continued upward shifts in *LM* and continued reductions in the equilibrium level of GNP. Consideration of all such points leads to the complete aggregate-demand curve.

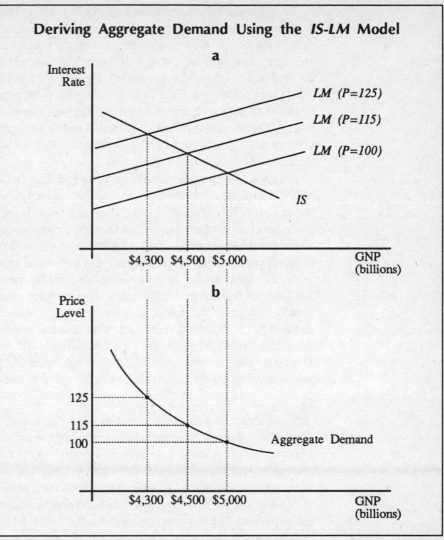

**Figure 12.9** *Increases in the price level cause the LM curve to shift up, lowering the equilibrium level of GNP. When all price-level–equilibrium-GNP levels are condsidered, the aggregate-demand curve is derived.*

## SHIFTING THE AGGREGATE-DEMAND CURVE

Changes in variables in both the commodity and the money market will lead to shifts in the aggregate-demand curve. The relationship between these variables and the shifts they cause are the same as for the aggregate-demand curve derived without the *IS-LM* curves.

**Aggregate-Demand Shifts and the *IS* Curve.** The *IS* curve shifts out with increases in the level of government spending, autonomous consumption expenditure, and investor confidence. It will also shift out if taxes are reduced. If the aggregate-demand curve in Figure 12.9 was derived using an *IS* curve located to the right of the one shown, higher levels of GNP would be associated with every price level. Graphing these relationships would lead to an aggregate-demand curve located to the right of the one shown. Hence, any factor that causes the *IS* curve to shift out will cause aggregate-demand to shift out. Conversely, factors causing the *IS* curve to shift in will cause the aggregate-demand curve to shift in.

**Aggregate-Demand Shifts and the *LM* Curve.** The *LM* curve shifts out when the money supply is increased, when individuals decide to hold less money at all levels of GNP, and when the price level decreases. Because the price level appears on the axis of the aggregate-demand curve, changes in its value cause movements along the curve, not shifts. In deriving the aggregate-demand curve in Figure 12.9, if each *LM* curve had been located to the right of its initial position (because of an increase in the money supply or decreased holdings of money by individuals), the resulting equilibrium levels of GNP would be higher, and points on the aggregate-demand curve would be further to the right. It follows that the aggregate-demand curve will shift out whenever the *LM* curve shifts out, unless the *LM* curve shifts out in response to a price level decrease. Inward shifts in *LM*, except those due to price level increases, will correspond with inward shifts in aggregate demand.

*I*S-LM *analysis is usually covered in great detail in intermediate macroeconomics courses. However, the overview of the basic IS-LM model presented here provides important details for understanding the complete macro model. By making explicit the relationship between GNP and interest rates in the money and commodity markets, the IS-LM model summarizes the many effects present. Used in conjunction with the aggregate demand-supply diagram, this model provides an important link between changes in the price level, changes in GNP, and changes in the individual components of aggregate expenditure sensitive to the interest rate.*

# Part III

*Microeconomic Theory*

# 13

## *Microeconomics and the Role of Supply and Demand*

*Economics at the macro level is the study of broad aggregates such as the level of GNP, the price level, the money supply, and the overall level of taxes. At the micro level, economics is concerned with the actions of individuals and firms. While macroeconomic analysis might consider how an increase in the price level will affect aggregate investment, microeconomic analysis addresses the question of how the typical individual, household, or firm will react to a price increase for a single product. Aside from the commodity whose price had risen, which commodities within the household's budget will be affected most? How will consumer satisfaction be affected by the price increase? From the perspective of the firm, microeconomic analysis examines how profits can be maximized and how profits change with changes in the price of the firm's output. It also examines how changes in input prices affect the firm's use of inputs.*

*While often considered to be distinct disciplines, micro- and macroeconomics are clearly connected in that the microeconomic actions of individuals and firms are reflected in macroeconomic measures. Macroeconomic policies must not ignore how individuals will react to them. It is the determination of such individual responses, whether induced by policy or other forces, that microeconomic analysis focuses upon.*

*The study of microeconomics is divided into two broad categories: the theory of consumer behavior and the theory of the firm. As consumers, individuals and households purchase goods and services from firms and derive satisfaction or utility from their consumption. Analysis of these activities constitutes consumption theory. Firms produce and sell goods and services to earn a profit. The theory of the firm involves examination of how firms can maximize profits.*

*The actions of individuals and firms are interrelated in two ways. First, to derive funds for consumption activities, consumers sell their labor, capital, land resources, or entrepreneurial services to firms in input markets. Firms use these inputs to produce the output purchased by consumers. Second, goods produced by firms are exhanged for the money previously paid to factor owners in input markets. This takes place in output markets. Beginning with a detailed treatment of supply-demand analysis, this chapter and those that follow will investigate the factors underlying and resulting from the behavior of consumers and firms.*

# SUPPLY AND DEMAND

For conducting analysis and making predictions, both the theory of the firm and the theory of consumer behavior ultimately rely upon the supply-demand model. In *output markets*, decisions made by consumers regarding what goods to consume and in what amounts are reflected in the demand curves for the various products produced in the economy. The supply of these products originates with the decisions firms make regarding what to produce and in what amounts. In *input markets*, the sale of labor or other factors of production to firms is manifested in the form of an input supply curve. This curve shows how much of a particular input will be offered for sale at each possible price. Firms use inputs to produce output. The relationship between an input's price and purchases of the input by firms is represented by the factor-demand curve.

In the following sections, the simple overview of supply-demand analysis presented in Chapter 2 is extended. This extension provides a deeper understanding of the forces underlying supply and demand curves and their interaction. By working with hypothetical representations of supply-demand relationships, additional insight is gained into the use of supply-demand analysis in addressing real-world problems. Special attention is paid to developing *elasticity* measures which show the responsivness of quantity supplied and demanded to changes in price.

# THE DEMAND CURVE

The demand curve shows the relationship between the quantity of a good consumers are willing and able to purchase at each possible price of the good. According to the *law of demand*, as the price of a good falls, the quantity demanded will increase. With price measured along the vertical axis and quantity measured along the horizontal axis, it follows that demand curves are downward sloping. The position of the demand curve depends on the number of consumers in the market for the product as well as consumer tastes, income, the prices of other related goods, and expectations of price changes.

From the perspective of the firm, aside from the position of the demand curve, the precise shape of the demand curve is extremely important, especially around the prevailing price. For example, suppose the firm knew that quantity demanded would remain the same even if it raised the product's price. In all probability, the firm would raise its price and earn higher profits. Such a response by consumers will occur if the demand curve is vertical, but a demand curve with this extreme shape is not the only interesting one for the firm or economists. A measure of the shape of the demand curve with regard to the responsiveness of the quantity demanded to changes in price is discussed next.

## The Elasticity of Demand

The output of different products is measured in different units. Eggs are sold by the dozen; wheat by the bushel. Even individual products can be sold in different units. Wheat can be sold by the ton. The existence of different units for the same or different products can make measurement of how quantity demanded changes when price changes difficult. When a 50 cent decline in the price of wheat leads to a half-unit increase in sales, it makes a big difference for farmers whether that unit is a bushel or a ton. Similarly, when a price declines by 50 cents, it is of some importance to both buyers and sellers whether the original price is $1 or $1,000.

To account for these measurement problems, economists have developed a unit-free measure of the shape of demand curves known as the *elasticity of demand*. The elasticity of demand captures the response of quantity demanded to changes in price. Technically, it is the ratio of the percentage change in quantity demanded to the percentage change in price that leads to the change in quantity.

### PERCENT CHANGES

A *percentage change* or *percentage rate of change* forms the basis of the elasticity measurement. When variables change from some initial value to some new value, it is convenient to have a standardized way of measuring the change. A percentage rate of change refers to the difference between the initial value of a variable and its new value, expressed as a percentage of its initial value. For example, if the price of eggs rises from $1 per dozen to $1.25 per dozen, the percentage rate of change in that price is

$$\frac{\$1.25 - \$1.00}{\$1.00} \times 100 = 25\%$$

The percentage change is always unit-free; in this example, the dollar units in the numerator cancel the dollar units in the denominator. The ratio is multiplied by 100 to transform it into a percentage.

In percentage terms, it is possible to compare the price increase in eggs with a price increase that might occur for any commodity. This avoids the confusion that comes when dealing with different units and prices that differ by wide margins. For example, suppose the price of an automobile rises from $10,000 to $10,500. This price increase is far more than the increase in the price of eggs. However, relative to the original price of the automobile, the percentage change equals

$$\frac{\$10,500 - \$10,000}{\$10,000} \times 100 = 5\%$$

For quantities, the percentage change formula works in the same way. If the rise in the price of eggs caused consumers to reduce their egg consumption from 1 million dozen per year to 850,000 per year, the percentage change in quantity demanded would be

$$\frac{850,000 - 1,000,000}{1,000,000} \times 100 = -15\%$$

Observe that the initial value (1 million dozen) is always subtracted from the new value and divided by the initial value. Again, because the units (dozens of eggs) appear in both the numerator and denominator, the percentage change in quantity is unit-free.

## PERCENTAGE CHANGES: ANOTHER VERSION

The simple formula shown above for calculating percentage rates of change is often used by economists. However, a problem in interpretation arises when differences between inital and final values are large. This is true because the percentage change in going from the initial value to the new value does not equal the percentage change in going from the new value to the initial value. In the previous example, suppose that the initial quantity of eggs demanded was 850,000 dozen when a decrease in their price caused the quantity demanded to increase to 1 million. The percentage change, using the formula shown above, would equal

$$\frac{1,000,000 - 850,000}{850,000} \times 100 = 17.65\%$$

Neglecting the difference in the positive and negative signs, the discrepency between the two percentage changes is obvious. To ensure consistency in moving from smaller initial values to larger final values and vice versa, the approach taken by economists is to use the average of the initial and final values in the denominator of the percentage change formula. The percentage change in quantity demanded will then appear as

$$\frac{1,000,000 - 850,000}{\left(\dfrac{1,000,000 + 850,000}{2}\right)} \times 100 = 16.22\%$$

The sign of this percentage change formula will differ depending on whether quantity increases or decreases; however, its absolute value will always remain the same. The general formulas and simplified notation for percentage changes used to calculate elasticities are therefore

$$Percentage\ Change\ in\ Price = \%\Delta P = \frac{P_1 - P_0}{\left(\dfrac{P_0 + P_1}{2}\right)} \times 100$$

$$Percentage\ Change\ in\ Quantity = \%\Delta Q = \frac{Q_1 - Q_0}{\left(\dfrac{Q_0 + Q_1}{2}\right)} \times 100$$

## THE DEMAND-ELASTICITY FORMULA

By definition, for any good, the elasticity of demand represents the ratio of the percentage change in quantity demanded divided by the percentage change in price that caused the percentage change in quantity. Making use of the percentage change formulas presented above, and using $E$ to represent demand elasticity, demand elasticity appears as

$$E = \frac{\dfrac{Q_1 - Q_0}{\left(\dfrac{Q_0 + Q_1}{2}\right)}}{\dfrac{P_1 - P_0}{\left(\dfrac{P_0 + P_1}{2}\right)}}$$

In simplified notation, the elasticity formula, the percentage change in quantity divided by the percentage change in price, is written

$$E = \frac{\% \Delta Q}{\% \Delta P}$$

**The Sign of Demand Elasticity.** Because of the law of demand, the demand curve is downward-sloping; therefore, an increase in a product's price will always lead to a decrease in the quantity demanded. Conversely, a price decrease will cause the quantity demanded to increase. Therefore, the numerator and the denominator of the elasticity ratio will always have opposite signs; when one value is increasing, the other will be decreasing. It follows that the elasticity of demand will always have a negative sign. However, because it is more convenient to speak in terms of positive values, the negative sign associated with demand elasticity is not considered when demand elasticities are discussed. In other words, the absolute value of demand elasticity is used in analyzing the shape of the demand curve. For this reason, a negative sign often appears as a multiplicative factor in the elasticity formula.

**The Elasticity of Demand: An Example.** Given a 22.2 percent rise in the price of eggs from $1 to $1.25 and the resulting 16.2 percent decrease in the quantity of eggs from 1 million units to 850,000 units, the elasticity of demand is seen to equal 0.73. This result can be easily verified by making use of the elasticity formula:

$$E = -\frac{\dfrac{8,500,000-1,000,000}{\left(\dfrac{1,000,000+850,000}{2}\right)}}{\dfrac{1.25-1.00}{\left(\dfrac{1.25+1.00}{2}\right)}} = -\frac{\dfrac{-150,000}{925,000}}{\dfrac{.25}{1.125}} = \frac{.162}{.222} = .73$$

## DEMAND-ELASTICITY AND TOTAL REVENUE

For a firm producing a particular product, *total revenue* represents the product of the quantity sold and the price at which it sold. For example, if an automobile dealership sells 500 cars at $10,000 each, its total revenue will equal $5 million. Total revenue is written as

$$Total\ Revenue = Price \times Quantity = P \times Q$$

There is a unique set of relationships that exist between changes in a firm's total revenue and its elasticity of demand. In absolute value, the elasticity of demand can take on any value from zero to infinity. The magnitude of this value describes in percentage terms the change in quantity due to a change in price. It therefore captures the responsiveness of quantity changes to price changes. Extreme values occur as the elasticity approaches zero or infinity. However, other ranges of elasticity values can be interpreted with regard to their relationship to total revenue.

**A Zero Elasticity Value.** Given the simple elasticity formula

$$E = \frac{\%\Delta Q}{\%\Delta P}$$

a zero value occurs when a given percentage increase in price leads to no change in quantity. In such a situation, with price increased and quantity demanded unchanged, sellers of the product must find their total revenue increased. Mathematically this is so because total revenue is defined as the product of price and quantity. When one element in the product grows while the other remains fixed, the product must increase. If a firm sells just as many units of output after a price increase as it does before the increase, its total revenue must rise.

As seen in Table 13.1, the intial price of some product equals $1 per unit and the initial quantity equals 100 units. In the first row of the table, a rise in the product's price to $2 per unit causes no reduction in quantity demanded; it still equals 100 units. Making use of the demand-elasticity formula, it is easily verified that the demand elasticity is zero. Before the price change, total revenue equals $100 ($1 × 100); after the price change, total revenue equals $200 ($2 × 100). The rise in price has led to a rise in total revenue because the elasticity of demand equals zero.

Demand for products with zero elasticity values is said to be *perfectly inelastic* and is associated with vertical demand curves. For consumers, such products are considered necessities, such as water where no substitutes exist. The lack of substitutes explains why quantity demanded does not change in response to price changes. In addition, demand may be highly inelastic for some products in the short run because consumers may not be aware of substitutes for them. A totally or perfectly inelastic demand curve is shown in Figure 13.1a.

**Elasticity Values Between Zero and 1.** A zero elasticity value occurs when a given price increase or decrease is associated with no change in the quantity demanded. For elasticity values greater than zero but less than 1, the elasticity formula shows that

$$\frac{\%\Delta Q}{\%\Delta P} < 1$$

or

$$\%\Delta Q < \%\Delta P$$

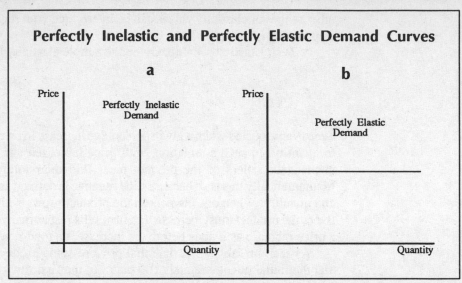

**Figure 13.1**  *A vertical demand curve is said to be perfectly inelastic because no matter how much the product's price may rise, the same quantity is demanded. A perfectly elastic demand curve is horizontal. If the product's price rises above the level of the demand curve, quantity demanded will fall to zero*

The percentage decline in quantity demanded is less than the percentage increase in price. For total revenue (the product of price and quantity), an elasticity value between zero and 1 means that a price increase will not be totally offset by a decrease in the quantity demanded. Hence, total revenue will rise. If price is cut, the increase in quantity demanded will not compensate for the decrease in price, and total revenue will fall. While not as extreme as the case of a perfectly inelastic demand, demand curves with elasticity values between zero and 1 are said to be *inelastic*.

The case of inelastic demand is considered in Table 13.1, when a price rise from $1 to $2 per unit causes the quantity demanded to fall from 100 units to 95 units. Making use of the formula, the elasticity of demand equals 0.077. With this inelastic demand, given the rise in price, total revenue rises from $100 ($1 × 100) to $190 ($2 × 95).

Goods consumers consider to be extremely important and without close substitutes generally have inelastic demands. Gasoline used for transportation and electricity used for lighting are examples. In addition, inexpensive goods that are relatively small parts of a consumer's overall budget may have inelastic demand because price increases do not matter a great deal to the consumer.

**Demand Elasticity Values Equal to 1.** When the elasticity of demand equals 1, the percentage change in quantity is exactly equal to the percentage change in price that caused it. The elasticity of demand in this situation is said to be *unitary*. For total revenue, the price increase is exactly offset by the quantity decrease; this leaves total revenue unchanged. Conversely, price decreases will lead to quantity increases that exactly offset each other in the total-revenue formula. Again, total revenue will remain unchanged. This fact is observed in Table 13.1. A unitary elasticity value implies that the the percentage change in quantity exactly equals the percentage change in price that causes it. A rise in price from $1 to $2 represents a 66.7 percent increase. A fall in quantity demanded from 100 units to 50 units represents a 66.7 percent decrease. The ratio of these values equals 1. Total revenue begins at $100 ($1 × 100) and ends at $100 ($2 × 50).

**Elasticity Values Greater than 1.** When the elasticity of demand is greater than one, manipulation of the elasticity formula shows that

$$\%\Delta Q > \%\Delta P$$

In the total-revenue formula, the percentage decrease in quantity more than offsets the increased price effect. This causes total revenue to fall. If the price of the product should fall, total revenue will rise because the quantity response is so large.

When the demand curve for a good has an elasticity greater than 1, it is said to be *elastic*. Goods with elastic demand are not necessities and often have close substitutes, goods that can be readily used in their place as prices rise. A good which composes a large part of the consumer's budget is more likely to have an elastic demand; if its price increases, failure to reduce the quantity demanded implies a greater sacrifice of other goods in the budget. In Table 13.1, demand is seen to be elastic when a rise in the product's price from $1 to $2 causes quantity demanded to fall from 100 units to 45 units. The demand elasticity equals 1.14. Total revenue begins at $100 before the price increase but falls to $90 after the increase.

**An Infinite Elasticity Value.** The elasticity of demand is defined as the ratio of the percentage change in quantity to the percentage change in price. The elasticity value will approach infinity when a percentage increase in price leads to an extemely large percentage reduction in the quantity demanded. In such a situation, the firm must find its total revenue declining. Relative to its initial value, the product of a slightly increased price and a greatly decreased quantity will be lower. When demand is infinitely elastic, the demand curve is horizontal, or *perfectly elastic* at some price. Figure 13.1b shows a perfectly elastic demand curve.

As an example, consider a firm that attempts to raise the price of its output above the price charged by other firms. If the firm's product is very similar to that produced by other firms, consumers will see no reason to pay more for it. Quantity demanded for the firm's product should drop to zero. This fact is shown in Table 13.1. A rise in the price of the product from $1 to $1.01 causes demand for the product to fall from 100 units to zero units. Making use of the elasticity formula, the elasticity of demand equals 201. This is not quite infinity, but a price rise of even a tiny fraction of a cent would have caused demand to drop to zero. This would make the elasticity value larger. Because such small changes in price cause such a large change in the quantity demanded, the elasticity value will skyrocket. Because output falls to zero, total revenue falls from $100 to zero.

| | **Elasticity Values and Total Revenue** | | | |
|---|---|---|---|---|
| **Elasticity** | **New Price** | **New Quantity** | **New Total Revenue** | **Elasticity Value** |
| Zero | $2.00 | 100 | $200.00 | 0.0 |
| Inelastic (0 < E < 1) | 2.00 | 95 | 190.00 | 0.077 |
| Unitary (E =1) | 2.00 | 50 | 100.00 | 1.0 |
| Elastic (E > 1) | 2.00 | 45 | 90.00 | 1.14 |
| Infinite | 1.01 | 0 | 0.00 | 201.0 |

*Table 13.1  Starting with an initial price of $1.00 and an initial quantity demanded of 100 units, total revenue will equal $100.00. Given a change in price and the resulting change in quantity, the effects of different demand elasticities on total revenue are shown. Price rises lead to increases in total revenue when the demand elasticity is less than one. A price elasticity greater than one implies that total revenue falls as price rises. When the elasticity value exactly equals one, a change in price causes no change in total revenue.*

## ELASTICITY VALUES AND THE SLOPE OF THE DEMAND CURVE

In extreme cases it is easy to get an idea of a product's elasticity of demand by looking at the slope of its demand curve. Therefore, the concepts of slope and elasticity are often confused. For example, a perfectly vertical demand curve reflects the fact that a change in price has no effect on the quantity demanded. The elasticity of demand is clearly zero, or perfectly inelastic. However, depending on the scale of the graph, pictures can be deceiving.

Figure 13.2 shows that just because a curve looks more horizontal it is not necessarily more elastic than a steeper looking curve. At every price, the more vertical-looking demand curve is more *elastic* than the more horizontal looking curve. For example, as the price of output rises from $4 to $5 per unit along the curve that appears more vertical, quantity demanded falls from 10 to 8 units. The elasticity of demand is unitary, equal to 1. Along the seemingly more horizontal curve, this price increase leads to a one-unit decrease in quantity demand from 9 to 8 units. The elasticity of demand is 0.53, inelastic because it is less than 1.

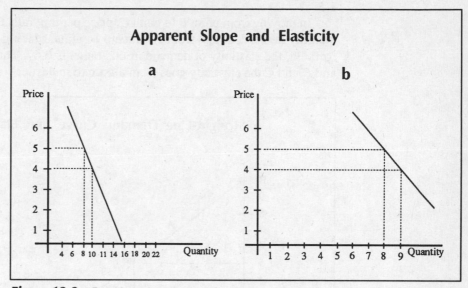

**Figure 13.2** *Despite appearances, the curve on the right is more inelastic at each price than the curve on the left. On the left, as price rises from $4 to $5, output falls from 10 to 8 units. Using the elasticity formula, the demand elasticity equals 1. On the right, the same rise in price leads to a one-unit decrease in output. The demand elasticity is 0.53.*

For the sake of exposition, it is often convenient to draw relatively horizontal demand curves to represent elastic demand and relatively vertical demand curves to show inelastic demand. However, except when the demand curve is perfectly vertical or horizontal, it is not possible to tell whether demand is truly elastic or inelastic. The problem is that the units in which quantity is measured may make the demand curve look elastic (or inelastic) when use of the elasticity measure would reveal that it is not. To be sure that a demand curve is elastic or inelastic over the points of interest, use the elasticity formula and see whether the value is greater than or less than 1.

**Straight-Line Demand Curves and Elasticity.** Aside from drawing inferences based on the rough shape of the demand curve, problems of determining elasticity values also arise because the elasticity of demand may be different at every point on the demand curve. This is especially true for straight-line demand curves, which by defintion have a constant slope. Although the slope may be constant, the elasticity of demand changes at every point. This fact is verified in Figure 13.3, which portrays a straight-line demand curve and shows three points on it. Given that the price intercept equals 10 and the quantity intercept equals 20, the slope of the line (the rise over the run) is equal to minus one-half.

In moving from point *A* to point *B*, price per unit of output declines from $7 to $5, while quantity demanded rises from 6 to 10 units. Through use of the demand-elasticity formula, the elasticity over this range of the demand curve is 1.5.

In moving from point *B* to point *C*, price per unit falls from $5 to $3, while quantity demanded rises from 10 units to 14 units. Making use of the elasticity formula, the elasticity of demand in this range is 0.67. Thus between *A* and *B* and *B* and *C* the elasticity goes from elastic to inelastic.

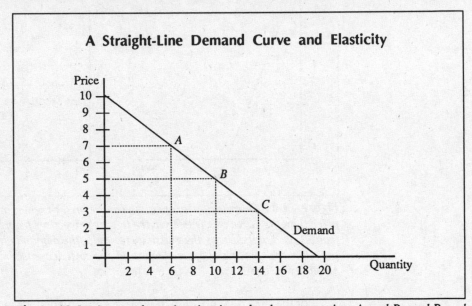

**A Straight-Line Demand Curve and Elasticity**

**Figure 13.3**  *As seen by estimating its value between points A and B, and B and C, the elasticity of demand along a straight-line demand curve is not constant. Above point B, the midpoint of the curve along the quantity axis, the demand curve is elastic. Below point B, the curve is inelastic.*

**A Constant Elasticity of Demand.** Except when it is vertical or horizontal, a straight line demand curve, even with its constant slope, will not yield a constant demand elasticity. Instead, a demand curve curved in a special way can have a constant elasticity. Along a curved line, the slope changes continuously. If the elasticity of demand is to be constant, slope changes must be exactly offset by changes in the ratio of average price and quantity values everywhere along the demand curve.

An important example of a demand curve with constant elasticity throughout its range arises when the demand curve is represented by the function

$$P = \frac{a}{Q}$$

Here, *a* is a constant that determines the precise location of the curve. Graphically, as shown in Figure 13.4, this demand curve appears as a *rectangular hyperbola*. Its elasticity can be shown to equal 1 at every point along the curve. Therefore, changes in price along this demand curve lead to changes in quantity that keep total revenue the same.

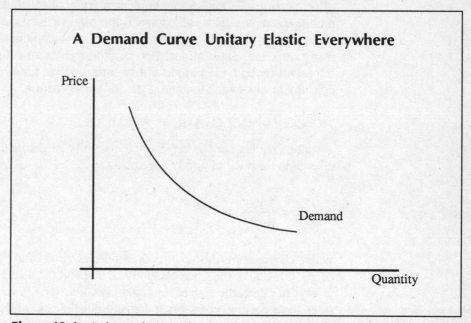

**Figure 13.4** *A demand curve that is everywhere unitary elastic (an elasticity of 1) will arise if percentage changes in price are exactly offset by percentage changes in quantity, The equation for such a demand curve is P = a/Q. Demand curves based on this formula are known as a rectangular hyperbolas.*

## SHORT-RUN VERSUS LONG-RUN DEMAND ELASTICITY VALUES

A good that is seen as a necessity in the short run may lose that status in the long run. In the short run, immediately following a price increase, consumers may not be familiar with substitutes for the product. However, the higher price makes searching for a substitute worthwhile, and as time passes, consumers may become acquainted with other products serving nearly the same function. In addition, the rise in price may lead other producers to develop substitutes for the good. In such circumstances, the elasticity of demand becomes more elastic through time.

*Cross-Price Elasticities of Demand*

Aside from the price elasticity of demand, economists are also interested in the responsiveness of demand for goods given price increases in other goods. By definition, the *cross-price elasticity of demand* measures the percentage change in the quantity demanded of one good in response to a given percentage price change in another. In this context, goods can be either *complements* or *substitutes*. One good is a substitute for another if its demand increases in response to an increase in the price of the other good. Examples include butter and margarine or tea and coffee.

A complementary good's demand curve will shift in if its complement's price increases. Examples of complementary goods include gasoline and automobiles, compact discs and compact-disc players. Knowledge of the degree to which one good can be substituted for or used in conjunction with another has many important applications. For example, given an oil-price increase, it is important for both oil and gas utility companies to know the degree to which consumers will switch to natural gas for home heating.

## THE CROSS-PRICE ELASTICITY FORMULA

The formula for the cross-price elasticity of demand for good $i$ given a change in the price of good $j$ appears as

$$E_{ij} = \frac{\%\Delta Q_i}{\%\Delta P_j}$$

where $Q_i$ represents the quantity demanded of good $i$ and $P_j$ represents the price of good $j$. Unlike the price elasticity of demand for a single product, which is always negative, the *sign* of the cross-price elasticity is very important. Substitutes have positive cross-price demand elasticities, while complements have negative cross-price demand elasticities. If these goods are substitutes, a price increase for good $j$ implies that good $i$ will experience an increase in demand. Therefore, the percentage change in the quantity of good $i$ will be positive; because the price and quantity changes are positive, the cross-price elasticity will be positive. If these goods are complements, a price increase for good $j$ implies that good $i$ will experience a reduction in demand. Therefore, the percentage change in the quantity of good $i$ will be negative, implying that the cross-price elasticity will be negative. The strength of the positive or negative relationship is determined by the magnitude of the cross-price elasticity. A cross-price elasticity value of zero implies that the increase in the price of good $j$ has no effect on good $i$; they are therefore unrelated, neither complementary nor substitute goods.

## The Income Elasticity of Demand

Increases in income will also have an effect on the quantity demanded. An increase in consumer income causes the demand curve for a product to shift out, which in turn will cause the quantity demanded to rise. The response of quantity demanded to the change in income reveals how consumer demand changes for specific products. By definition, the income elasticity of demand is the percentage change in quantity demanded given a 1 percent change in income. It is expressed as

$$E_y = \frac{\% \Delta Q}{\% \Delta Y}$$

where $Y$ represents income.

### INCOME-ELASTICITY VALUES

Values of the income elasticity of demand between zero and 1 imply that as income increases, the proportion of the consumer's budget allocated to purchases of the good decreases. Income-elasticity values equal to 1 imply that as income increases the good maintains its share in the budget. Income-elasticity values greater than 1 imply that the good assumes a larger fraction of the household budget as income increases. Products like rice and potatoes are likely to have income elasticities of demand less than 1; shrimp, filet mignon, and lobster are likely to have income-elasticities in excess of 1. If the income-elasticity is negative, it implies that the quantity purchased has decreased given an increase in income. Because income increases should lead to increased demand for all normal goods, commodities with negative income-elasticities are said to be inferior goods. Second-hand clothing or travel by bus (versus airplane) may be examples of inferior goods.

## THE SUPPLY CURVE

The supply curve shows the relationship between the price of a product and the amount of the product that producers will offer for sale. Because of the *law of supply*, a higher price will induce producers to offer more of the product for sale. The location of the supply curve is determined by the number of producers in the market, the price of inputs used in the production of output, and technology. As with the demand curve, the shape of the supply curve is described in terms of its elasticity.

**The Elasticity of Supply**

The *elasticity of supply* measures the responsiveness of the quantity of a product offered for sale to a change in its price. Rather than reflecting the response of consumers to a higher price, the supply elasticity shows the response of sellers to a price change. The formula for the elasticity of supply is almost the same as the demand elasticity:

$$E_S = \frac{\%\Delta Q}{\%\Delta P} = \frac{\dfrac{Q_1 - Q_0}{\left(\dfrac{Q_0 + Q_1}{2}\right)}}{\dfrac{P_1 - P_0}{\left(\dfrac{P_0 + P_1}{2}\right)}}$$

However, as the product's price changes, quantities are naturally taken from the supply curve rather than the demand curve. Suppose the supply curve shown in Figure 13.5 represents the quantities of wheat that will be offered for sale at various prices. A price increase from $3 per bushel to $3.50 per bushel causes the quantity of wheat supplied to rise from 12 to 16 million bushels. The supply elasticity over this range of the supply curve will equal

$$\frac{\left(\dfrac{16 - 12}{14}\right)}{\left(\dfrac{3.5 - 3}{3.25}\right)} = 1.86$$

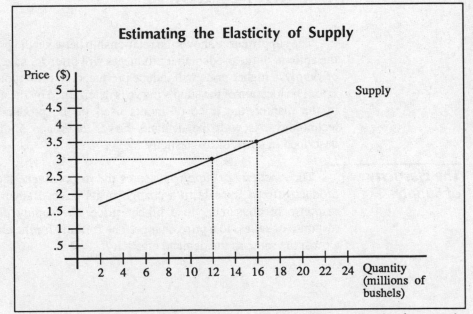

**Estimating the Elasticity of Supply**

**Figure 13.5** *A price rise from $3.00 to $3.50 induces a rise in the quantity supplied from 12 to 16 million bushels. From the formula, this implies a supply elasticity of 1.86 over this part of the supply curve.*

Because the supply elasticity is greater than one, the supply curve is said to be *elastic* over the range of values between 12 and 16.

## ELASTICITY AND A VERTICAL SUPPLY CURVE

As shown in Figure 13.6a, if the supply curve is vertical, the quantity supplied will remain the same regardless of the product's price. The prime example of a commodity with a fixed supply is land. Although small additions are possible by filling in coastal areas to acquire more, the available quantity of land is not subject to much expansion, regardless of how high its price is. When supply is vertical, quantity supplied is unresponsive to price changes; a change in price leads to no change in quantity. The elasticity of supply is zero in this case; supply is said to be perfectly inelastic.

**Time and Supply Elasticity.** Time plays an important role in determining the elasticity of supply. In the very short run, the supply of many products may be perfectly inelastic because of the time it takes to increase production. Given an increase in demand, the product's price will increase, but the quantity supplied remains fixed. Over the longer run, additional production capacity can be brought on line, and supply will respond positively to price increases. An example of a relatively inelastic short-run supply curve is seen in the supply of oil after the first Arab oil embargo of 1973 and 1974. In the short run, even as the price of oil was rising to four times its original level, supply was limited to

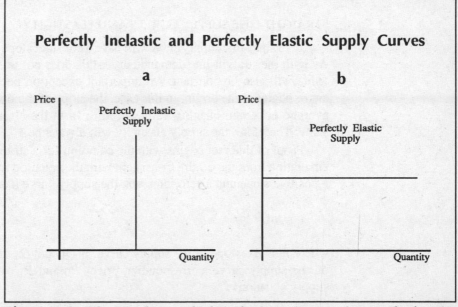

**Figure 13.6** *When supply is perfectly inelastic, no increase in a product's price can induce firms to sell more output. The supply elasticity is zero, or perfectly inelastic. When the supply curve is horizontal, consumers can purchase as many units of the product as they like at the prevailing price.*

in response to this massive price increase, a great deal of new capacity, including production from Alaska and the North Sea, found its way to the market.

## ELASTICITY AND A HORIZONTAL SUPPLY CURVE

As shown in Figure 13.6b, when supply is horizontal, any price below the supply curve causes the quantity supplied to drop to zero. Only at a price equal to or above the supply curve's level will output be forthcoming. However, the supply curve's horizontal shape implies that regardless of how far to the right the demand curve is located, the quantity necessary to satisfy that demand will be supplied and at the same price.

Because the shape of a supply curve reflects the per-unit cost of producing output, a horizontal supply curve signifies that per-unit production costs are constant. Two assumptions ensure this. First, technology must allow output increases to occur in proportion with input increases; there must be constant marginal productivity. Second, input or factor prices must be fixed as output expands; the increase in output does not place any strain on input markets that could lead to input price increases. Otherwise, if input costs are affected as output rises, the supply curve would shift up parallel to itself. Supply curves for mass-produced commodities may be horizontal throughout certain portions of their range.

## STRAIGHT-LINE SUPPLY CURVES AND ELASTICITY

A straight-line supply curve will have a constant slope throughout its range. As with the straight-line demand curve, this does not imply that the elasticity value will also be constant. An important exception occurs when the supply curve begins at the origin. In this case, the slope of the line and the ratio of the average price and quantity values used to form the elasticity are exactly the same. Therefore, the supply elasticity will always be 1.

Proof of this fact begins with the equation for a straight line supply curve emanating from the origin. Consistent with the equation for a straight-line with a positive slope and a zero intercept, the supply curve has the form

$P = mQ$

where $m$ is the slope of the supply curve. If $Q_0$ and $Q_1$ are any two quantities on the supply curve, corresponding prices $P_0$ and $P_1$ can be found from the supply equation:

$P_0 = mQ_0$

and

$$P_1 = mQ_1$$

Letting the initial price be $P_0$ and the new price be $P_1$, according to the supply-elasticity formula and the straight-line supply equation,

$$E_s = \frac{\%\Delta Q}{\%\Delta P} = \frac{\dfrac{Q_1 - Q_0}{\left(\dfrac{Q_0 + Q_1}{2}\right)}}{\dfrac{P_1 - P_0}{\left(\dfrac{P_0 + P_1}{2}\right)}} = \frac{\dfrac{Q_1 - Q_0}{\left(\dfrac{Q_0 + Q_1}{2}\right)}}{\dfrac{mQ_1 - mQ_0}{\left(\dfrac{mQ_0 + mQ_1}{2}\right)}} = 1$$

The elasticity equals 1 because the slope coefficient $m$ in the denominator can be factored out and canceled. Then both the numerator (the percentage change in quantity) and the denominator (the percentage change in price) are the same.

# SUPPLY, DEMAND, AND THE EFFECTS OF EXCISE TAXES

An *excise tax* is a tax on a single commodity. Examples include taxes on gasoline, liquor, and cigarettes. Such taxes are applied to each unit of the item sold. For example, the tax on gasoline might be set at 20 cents per gallon. In the supply-demand model, such a tax is likely to have an effect on a product's equilibrium price and quantity. These effects are considered next.

## The Excise Tax and Supply

The imposition of an excise tax raises the price at which commodities can be offered for sale. Such a tax causes the supply curve to shift up by the amount of the tax. This is shown in Figure 13.7 where a tax of $1 per pack has been imposed on cigarettes. The tax acts like an increase in the per-unit cost of production. Without the tax, 30 million packs of cigarettes would be offered at a price of $1 per pack. Because of the tax, 30 million packs can now be offered only at a price of $2 per pack; $1 per pack goes to cover the costs of producing cigarettes, and the other dollar goes to the government.

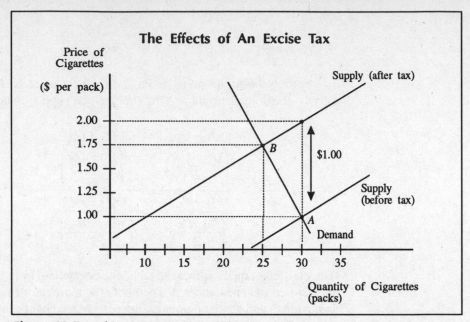

**Figure 13.7**  *A $1 tax on cigarettes shifts the supply curve vertically by the amount of the tax. However, because demand is downward-sloping, the price of cigarettes is raised by on 75 cents. The remaining 25 cents of the tax on each pack sold is paid by producers.*

## EQUILIBRIUM AND THE EXCISE TAX

On hearing that the government had imposed a $1 per-pack tax on cigarettes, most individuals would probably think that the price of cigarettes would rise by $1. However, as seen in Figure 13.7, the excise tax causes the intersection of supply and demand to move from point *A* to point *B*. Because demand is not vertical, increases in price lead to a reduction in the quantity demanded. Therefore, the tax does not lead to a full $1 increase in price because some consumers are not in the market at a price of $2 per pack. Instead, the price of cigarettes rises from $1.00 to $1.75.

## THE INCIDENCE OF THE TAX

The *incidence* of a tax refers to who actually pays the tax. On the surface, because consumers wind up paying more after the tax, it seems that they bear the full burden of the tax. However, closer examination of the situation before and after the tax reveals that this is not necessarily the case. Referring to Figure 13.7, the price paid by consumers rises by only 75 cents. The full tax is $1 per pack. Since the government is unlikely to be shortchanged on its tax receipts, 25 cents of the tax must be paid by the firms. In this situation, the incidence of the tax falls on both producers and consumers.

**Tax Incidence and Vertical Demand.** As shown in Figure 13.8a, if the demand curve is perfectly inelastic, a tax increase that causes an upward shift in supply leads to a price increase equal to the magnitude of the tax. Because the product's price rises by the full amount of the tax, the incidence of the tax is entirely upon consumers.

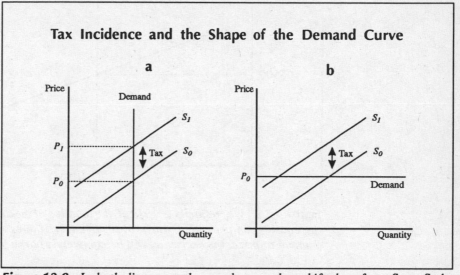

**Figure 13.8** *In both diagrams, the supply curve has shifted up from $S_0$ to $S_1$ by the full amount of an excise tax. When demand is totally inelastic, or vertical, the product's price rises by the full amount of the tax, and consumers bear the full burden. With a perfectly elastic, or horizontal, demand carve, the product's price will not rise, and firms bear the burden of the tax.*

**Tax Incidence and Horizontal Demand.** In Figure 13.8b, the demand curve is perfectly elastic. The upward shift in supply due to the tax causes no change in the product's price. The government receives the full tax on each unit sold. Therefore, producers pay the full tax.

## ECONOMIC RENT AND A VERTICAL SUPPLY CURVE

*Rent* is the payment received by owners of land in return for the use of their property. More generally, *economic rent* refers to a payment received by the owner of a factor of production over and above the minimum price necessary to obtain that factor's services. As shown in Figure 13.9, when supply is vertical, the location of the demand curve determines the equilibrium price, and quantity supplied will not increase with price increases. Thus, even at a zero price, the same quantity of output is supplied. It follows that the entire price received by an owner of a factor of production with a perfectly inelastic supply is economic rent.

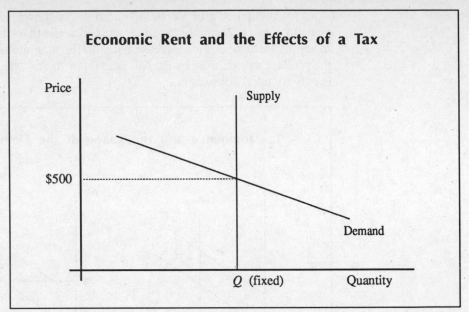

**Economic Rent and the Effects of a Tax**

*Figure 13.9*  *When supply is vertical, the location of the demand curve determines the equilibrium price that will prevail. Because it does not affect the product's demand or price, the excise tax will be completely borne by suppliers.*

**Vertical Supply and the Incidence of a Tax.** If the government imposes an excise tax on a resource with a perfectly inelastic supply, the upward shift in supply is not discernible. Since the tax does not affect the demand curve and the government is expected to receive the full revenues from the tax, the supplier bears the full burden of the tax. For example, in Figure 13.9, if a tax of $100 per acre is placed on land, consumers continue to pay a price of $500 per acre. Because the government receives $100 per acre, suppliers will find their rent decreased from $500 to $400; they thereby experience a loss in rent exactly equal to the amount of the tax.

*E*xtended to include elasticity measures, supply-demand analysis allows determination of the precise response of quantities supplied and demanded to changes in price. Because of its relation to total revenue, demand elasticity helps firms predict the implications of price changes. The shapes of supply and demand curves, as reflected in elasticity values, provide an important means of analysis in the supply-demand context. In textbook case studies, extreme values of demand and supply elasticities provide a fast and convenient means of making predictions and analyzing the range of potential effects from changes in prices. Because there is uncertainty concerning actual elasticities for real-world products, economists spend a great deal of time trying to estimate them empirically.

*The extension of supply-demand analysis presented in this chapter provides basis for further consideration of the microeconomic topics presented in future chapters. As will be seen again and again, interaction between supply and demand curves underlies much of this analysis. A thorough knowledge of the supply-demand model simplifies understanding of the seemingly varied topics to come.*

# APPENDIX

## The Arc Elasticity versus the Point Elasticity of Demand

When the elasticity of demand is measured over a range of values using the elasticity formula presented in this chapter, the *arc elasticity of demand* is calculated, However, it is possible to imagine the distance between the points over which the demand elasticity is measured becoming smaller and smaller. Interest finally centers on a single point on the demand curve, rather than over some range of values. To find the demand elasticity at a point on the demand curve, the slope of the curve is estimated using the rules of calculus to find the derivative of the equation describing the demand curve. Multiplying by a minus sign to make the demand elasticity positive, the *point elasticity of demand* is then defined as

$$E = -\frac{dQ}{dP}\left(\frac{P}{Q}\right)$$

The values of $P$ and $Q$ associated with the point of interest are then used to calculate the point elasticity value. In this formula, $dP$ corresponds to $\Delta P$, the change in price. The change in quantity caused by the change in price is $dQ$. This expression can be reformulated as the ratio of the percentage change in quantity to the percentage change in price:

$$E = -\frac{\left(\dfrac{dQ}{Q}\right)}{\left(\dfrac{dP}{P}\right)}$$

## The Point Elasticity: An Example

Suppose the relationship between price and quantity for a demand curve is given by the equation

$$P = 10 - 0.5Q$$

Rewriting the equation in terms of $Q$ so that a derivative with respect to $P$ may be taken yields

$$Q = 20 - 2P$$

The derivative of this equation is

$$\frac{dQ}{dP} = -2$$

To estimate the elasticity of demand, a particular point on the demand curve must be chosen. Suppose that the point of interest is $P = 5$ and $Q = 10$. (Plugging these values into the demand equation confirms that this point is on the demand curve.) The elasticity of demand (expressed as a positive value) will be

$$E = -\frac{dQ}{dp}\left(\frac{P}{Q}\right) = 2\left(\frac{5}{10}\right) = 1$$

This example can be used to illustrate an important fact regarding elasticity values. The equation used to estimate the demand elasticity is a straight line and therefore possesses a constant slope. The presence of a constant slope for the demand curve does not imply a constant elasticity value. For example, suppose interest is focused at the point on the demand curve where $Q = 4$ and $P = 8$. Making use of the elasticity formula, it is seen that the elasticity at this point is 4.

# 14

## Consumer Choice and Utility Maximization

*This chapter introduces the basic model of consumer choice. Here the basic building blocks of utility analysis are presented. The fundamental assumptions and the importance of the model in drawing inferences concerning consumer behavior are discussed. In later chapters, it will be seen that the development of the theory of the firm is closely patterned after the theory of the consumer. Therefore, careful attention to the subject matter discussed here will pave the way for easy understanding of future material.*

## THE MODEL OF CONSUMER CHOICE

Because the goals, aspirations, and other factors that guide human actions are so varied and numerous, it might seem impossible ever to formulate a theory of individual behavior capable of explaining the nature of choices made by individuals. Economic theory does just that by making certain assumptions about how individuals weigh alternatives to reach desired objectives. Individuals are assumed to be rational and to act in a manner consistent with deriving the greatest level of satisfaction from their activities. When combined with information concerning the resources individuals have to work with and the constraints they face in making decisions, these simple behavioral assumptions provide a powerful means of explaining observed behavior. Even though the focus of economics is on that subset of human activities related to the purchases and production of goods and services, the basic precepts of economic theory extend well beyond this realm.

## Consumer Choice and Utility

In the basic model of consumer behavior, economists assume that individuals attempt to maximize satisfaction from consumption. They do so by consuming the most ideal combination of goods they can purchase with their income. Stated more succinctly, consumers maximize utility, or satisfaction, subject to a budget constraint. Understanding just how this process works involves understanding what economists mean when they speak of utility and maximizing utility.

### THE CONCEPT OF UTILITY

It is possible to gauge the level of many forms of activity. For example, a car's speeds are shown by the speedometer. In a jet, altitudes can be measured by an altimeter. While it is possible to measure such quantities precisely, no such measures exist for the satisfaction or *utility* that an individual receives from consuming various quantities of a product. Despite this fact, individuals can rank satisfaction they obtain from various levels of consumption. An individual may feel a certain level of satisfaction or utility from his or her first compact disc. Purchase of a second disc will also provide satisfaction, and the individual can at least gauge whether this satisfaction exceeds or falls short of that associated with the first disc.

**Cardinal and Ordinal Utility.** In using economic theory to analyze the behavior of consumers, economists sometimes assume that utility can be measured in units that reflect the actual level of satisfaction received from consumption. These utility or satisfaction units are known as *utils*. Such measurement uses *cardinal numbers*, numbers that designate a certain quantity of utils. Utility measured in this manner is called *cardinal utility*.

When utility is measured *ordinally*, only the relative level of satisfaction is important; a certain level of utility will be higher or lower than another. An increase in the quantity of goods consumed will lead to a greater degree of satisfaction, but no attempt is made to determine the precise satisfaction gained.

### TOTAL AND MARGINAL UTILITY

*Total utility* refers to the total satisfaction derived from the consumption of all goods and services purchased by an individual. For an individual commodity, it is possible to speak of the total utility derived from all the units consumed of that commodity. *Marginal utility* refers to the addition to total utility derived from consuming one more unit of the commodity.

**Marginals and Totals.** The definition of marginal utility and the relationship between marginals and totals is of extreme importance in economic analysis. In moving from the theory of the consumer to the theory of the firm, it will be seen that whenever the adjective *marginal* appears, it implies that an extra amount has been added to or subtracted from some total. As with the definition of marginal utility, the factor ultimately causing the increase or decrease in the total is implicit in the definition. Thus, when speaking of the marginal utility derived from some good, the change in total utility is brought about by a one-unit increase or decrease in the consumption of the good.

## THE LAW OF DIMINISHING MARGINAL UTILITY

The *law of diminishing marginal utility* is really an assumption. It concerns the additional satisfaction that individuals receive from consuming additional units of some good. The law states that eventually, marginal utility declines with each additional unit of a good consumed. From personal experience, it is easy to see the basis for this law. Consider the satisfaction that comes during a meal with the first morsel. Additional consumption during the meal generally leads to greater overall satisfaction, but additional amounts tend to provide less and less addition to overall satisfaction. Ultimately, if consumption continues for too long, discomfort may lead to negative marginal utility and a decline in total utility.

**Diminishing Marginal Utility: An Example.** The law of diminishing marginal utility is illustrated in Table 14.1. The good consumed is compact discs. Although utility cannot be exactly measured, the numbers shown are assumed to reflect the level of satisfaction for the individual as subsequent discs are purchased. The first disc purchased yields a utility equal to 100. The second provides an additional 75 units of utility. Thus the marginal utility of the second disk is 75 units, and the total utility associated with consumption of the first two disks is 175. As more disks are purchased, marginal utility continues to fall while total utility continutes to increase. Even though marginal utility is declining, it remains positive; it continues to add to total utility as more and more units of the good are consumed.

## Diminishing Marginal Utility and the Relationship Between Marginal and Total Utility

| Quantity of Disks Purchased | Marginal Utility of an Extra Disc | Total Utility from all Discs |
|:---:|:---:|:---:|
| 1 | 100 | 100 |
| 2 | 75 | 175 |
| 3 | 60 | 235 |
| 4 | 50 | 285 |
| 5 | 45 | 330 |

*Table 14.1*

*Optimal Consumer Choice and Marginal Utility*

With a solid grasp of the definitions of *marginal utility* and the *law of diminishing marginal utility*, the foundation is established for understanding how consumers optimally or ideally allocate their incomes among the goods and services they can purchase. This *optimality condition*, or rule for maximizing utility, is derived for a typical consumer. This consumer is assumed to have a fixed budget, a finite amount of income measured in dollars.

As the consumer begins his or her shopping expedition, a constant comparison is made between the additions to utility from purchasing goods and the loss of utility that comes with giving up dollars to purchase goods. Some goods may seem extremely desirable, but prices that involve too large a fraction of income may reduce their attractiveness, especially when considering other goods that must be given up if expensive goods are purchased. At the checkout counter, no other market basket of goods that could be purchased with his or her income could lead to a higher level of satisfaction. If one or more goods still on the shelves provided a higher level of utility than one or more goods in the market basket, the consumer would merely substitute goods until the highest level of utility was achieved without exceeding the budget.

### OPTIMALITY AND MARGINAL UTILITY PER DOLLAR

When the consumer is finished shopping, maximization of utility requires an equal marginal utility per dollar of expenditure on each good purchased. This is the optimality condition for the consumer's choice problem. If the consumer derives more utility by spending a dollar on cereal rather than hamburger, more cereal should be purchased. Letting $MU_i$ stand for marginal utility derived from good $i$ and $P_i$ stand for the price of good $i$, optimality requires that

$$\frac{MU_i}{P_i} = \frac{MU_j}{P_j}$$

between all pairs of goods.

**Interpreting the Optimality Condition.** The optimality condition that must hold between all pairs of goods states that the marginal utility per dollar of each good purchased must be equal across all goods. To make sense of the formula that symbolizes this condition, it is essential that the units involved be clearly understood. The marginal utility of good $i$, $MU_i$, has units of utility per unit of good $i$ consumed. The price of good $i$ will have units equal to dollars per unit of good $i$. The ratio of the marginal utility of good $i$ to the price of good $i$, $\dfrac{MU_i}{P_i}$ will have units of utility per dollar spent on good $i$; the units of good $i$ in the numerator and the demoninator cancel. Similarly, the ratio of the marginal utility of good $j$ to the price of good $j$ will have units of utility per dollar spent on good $j$.

Suppose now that the optimality condition is violated, so that

$$\frac{MU_i}{P_i} > \frac{MU_j}{P_j}$$

In this situation, the utility received by spending a dollar on good $i$ exceeds the utility received by spending a dollar on good $j$. Because more satisfaction comes from buying good $i$, it makes sense for the consumer to spend the dollar on good $i$. At this point, the law of diminishing marginal utility takes effect. When an additional dollar's worth of good $i$ is purchased, its marginal utility declines. It follows that $\dfrac{MU_i}{P_i}$ decreases in value and becomes closer in value to $\dfrac{MU_j}{P_j}$.

If the utility derived from spending an additional dollar on good $i$ still exceeds that derived from spending a dollar on good $j$, another dollar should be spent on good $i$. Again, because of the law of diminishing marginal utility, the extra utility that comes with a dollar's worth of good $i$ will decline, and the ratio of marginal utilities to price will come closer to equality. Ultimately the point of equality, or *indifference* is reached. At this point, the consumer is indifferent between spending an extra dollar on good $i$ or spending it on good $j$. Each good will yield the same marginal utility in return for the dollar. No rearrangement in the consumption of these goods will lead to higher utility.

# CONSUMER DEMAND AND THE MARKET-DEMAND CURVE

The law of diminishing marginal utility and the assumption that consumers arrange their purchases so that total utility is maximized provide the basis for deriving the downward-sloping demand curve. From the optimality condition that must hold between any two goods, $i$ and $j$,

$$\frac{MU_i}{P_i} = \frac{MU_j}{P_j}$$

*Ceteris paribus*, other things equal, a decrease in the price of good $i$ means that the ratio of the marginal utility of good $i$ to its price will exceed the ratio of the marginal utility of good $j$ to its price. To rectify this situation, more units of good $i$ should be purchased. The marginal utility of good $i$ will then decline, and the equality condition will be restored.

Thus, to maintain the optimality condition, a price decrease must lead to decreases in marginal utility. Such decreases are brought about by additional purchases of the good whose price has fallen. This result is entirely consistent with the law of demand, which states that a price decrease leads to an increase in the quantity demanded.

## The Income and Substitution Effects

Starting from an initial situation in which the consumer is maximizing utility, it will be the case for any two goods, $i$ and $j$, that the marginal utility per dollar will be equal:

$$\frac{MU_i}{P_i} = \frac{MU_j}{P_j}$$

If the price of good $i$ declines, this equality is upset, and the marginal utility per dollar of $i$ will exceed the marginal utility of $j$:

$$\frac{MU_i}{P_i} > \frac{MU_j}{P_j}$$

From the consumer's perspective, $i$ has become more attractive relative to $j$ because its price has declined. The decline in the price of good $i$ will induce the consumer to purchase more of it in order to restore the equality of marginal utilities per dollar. The actual changes in consumption of $i$ and other goods can be considered in terms of measures known as the *income effect* and the *substitution effect*.

## THE INCOME EFFECT

It is assumed that the consumer is working with a fixed budget. After a decline in its price, additional units of good $i$ can be purchased with funds from two hypothetical sources. First, a decline in the price of good $i$ implies that the same quantity of good $i$ can be purchased for less money. The consumer will reap a cost savings equal to the difference between the previous level of expenditure on good $i$ and the new level after the decline in its price. This cost savings can be used to purchase more of good $i$ and more units of all other goods. In a sense, the consumer's income has been increased because of the decrease in the price of good $i$. The increase in the quantity of good $i$ purchased because of the consumer's increased spending power after a price decline is known as the *income effect*.

## THE SUBSTITUTION EFFECT

In addition to the income effect, the decline in the price of good $i$ might induce consumers to purchase fewer units of the other goods because they are now relatively more expensive. More units of the good whose price has fallen will be purchased. Increased purchases of a good because it has become a relatively more attractive purchase because of a decrease in its price are known as the *substitution effect*.

# THE MARKET-DEMAND CURVE

The discussion of the downward slope of a consumer's demand curve is based on utility-maximizing behavior for a single individual. However, in analyzing demand for each of the many products produced in the economy, it is more useful to consider a single representation of demand by all consumers. The market-demand curve is based upon the demand curves for each individual in the market for the product. For each particular price, it shows the sum of the quantities demanded by all individuals in the market.

Given individual demand curves for all consumers in the market for a product, the derivation of the market-demand curve involves the horizontal summation of curves. To understand why the demand curves are added horizontally (instead of vertically), consider the axes of a typical demand curve. Price, in units of dollars per unit of output, is measured on the vertical axis. Quantities of the good are measured on the horizontal axis. Points on the demand curve for an individual consumer show the quantities he or she is willing to purchase at each price. Points on the market-demand curve show the relationship between the quantities all consumers wish to purchase at each price. Because each price will be associated with a certain quantity demanded by each consumer, adding these quantities yields the total quanity demanded at that price. In terms of the overall demand curve for the product, the relationship between this price and the quantity demanded by all consumers is depicted as a single point on the market-demand curve. Consideration of all possible prices and quantities yields the market-demand curve.

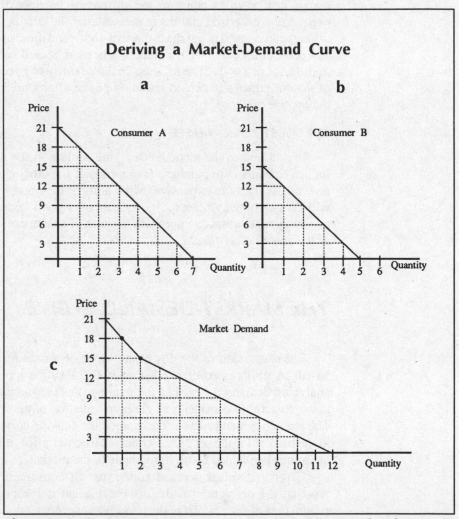

**Figure 14.1**   *The market-demand curve is found by adding together the quantity demanded by all consumers at each price. When the market price is $9, consumer A will demand 4 units of the good, while consumer B will demand 2 units. Market demand therefore equals 6 units.*

## Deriving a Market-Demand Curve

For simplicity, assume that the economy is composed of only two consumers. Consumer A's demand curve is shown in Figure 14.1a while consumer B's demand is shown if Figure 14.1b. Figure 14.1c shows the combined demand of consumers A and B. At a price of $21 per unit, the quantity demanded by each consumer, as well as overall demand, is zero. As the product's price reaches zero, a total of 12 units will be demanded, 7 by consumer A and 5 by consumer B. Points on the market-demand curve between a zero price and $21 also reflect the sum of quantities demanded by consumers. At a price equal to $15 per unit, consumer A demands 2 units the product; consumer A is the only consumer who demands any of the good. A kink in the total demand curve appears at a price of $15; this occurs because decreases in price below this level cause both consumer A and consumer B to desire quantities of the product.

Demand curves used in economic analysis are typically drawn without kinks; if the individual demand curves of all consumers for real-world products were added, kinks would tend to be smoothed out.

## Consumer Surplus

*Consumer surplus* represents the difference between the maximum amount an individual is willing to pay for each unit of a commodity and the price actually paid for the product. Referring back to Figure 14.1a, note that consumer A is willing to pay $18 for the first unit of the good, $15 for the second unit, and $12 for the third unit. Suppose the market price is established at $12 per unit. This price is associated with a $6 difference between what consumer A was willing to pay for the first unit and the market price; consumer surplus is $6 for this unit. There is a $3 difference between what was actually paid for the second unit and what consumer A was willing to pay; consumer surplus for the second unit is $3. For the third unit, there is no difference between what consumer A is willing to pay and what consumer A must pay; consumer surplus for this unit is zero. Thus, for consumer A, a total of $9 of consumer surplus is achieved when the product's price is $12.

Figure 14.2 shows a typical demand curve for a product. With a market price of $5 per unit, 100,000 units are demanded. The total amount paid by consumers equals $500,000 and is represented by the rectangular area under the $5 price to 100,000 units. The *total* consumer surplus is represented by the area of the triangle below the demand curve, to the right of the vertical axis, and above the $5 price. As in the case of an individual consumer, consumer surplus for any unit of the commodity is found by subtracting the market price from the amount consumers are willing to pay for that unit. Total consumer surplus is found by adding this result for all quantities. Consistent with the downward shape of the demand curve, the consumer surplus for each unit declines with each additional unit of the commodity sold.

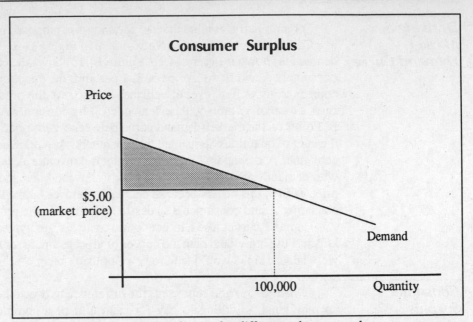

**Figure 14.2**   *Consumer surplus is the difference between what consumers are willing to pay for a product, found along the demand curve, and what they have to pay, seen in the market price. For any quantity, consumer surplus is the vertical distance between the demand curve and the product's price. Given a price of $5 per unit, the total consumer surplus for all units of output sold is the area below the demand curve and above the $5 price.*

*F*rom the economist's perspective, individuals constantly seek to maximize their utility by making choices consistent with this goal. In deciding on what quantities of available products to purchase, consumers take into account the constraint imposed by their budget. They then make purchases to the point at which the satisfaction derived per dollar of expenditure is equalized across commodities. Results of this process, when combined with the law of diminishing marginal utility, yield the downward sloping demand curve consistent with the law of demand. The demand curve for an individual therefore reflects optimizing behavior, as does the overall market demand curve for a product. Market demand is nothing more than the horizontal sum of all individual demand curves for a product.

The market-demand curve for a product provides half the necessary ingredients required for supply-demand analysis. Subsequent chapters deal with the entire range of problems involved in supplying the products that consumers demand. The theory of consumer behavior is of special importance in discussing labor markets, where individuals exchange their labor power for money. Here, in maximizing their utility, individuals must decide how much of *their available time they wish to spend earning the income that enables them to consume goods.*

*The economist's basic model of consumer behavior spills over to describe the actions of individuals in activities other than the buying or selling of goods and services. In virtually all forms of activity, individuals are faced with constraints and must make choices to achieve their goals. Just as it is possible to discuss the responses of consumers to relative price changes, it is often possible to draw inferences concerning likely outcomes given existing and changing circumstances by applying the tools of economic analysis to problems not expressly in the realm of economics.*

# 15

# *Production, Output, and Costs*

*F*rom the economist's perspective, individuals consume output to achieve the highest level of utility, subject to a budget constraint. Firms, on the other hand, are thought to consume or use inputs to achieve the highest level of output, subject to a cost constraint. Given the similarities between these approaches, many of the same concepts underlying the study of consumer behavior also apply to the study of the firm.

In this chapter, the factors underlying the production problems faced by the firm are examined in detail. Beginning with a discussion of the basic characteristics of the production process, attention is focused on the technological assumptions economists make concerning the transformation of inputs into outputs. Next, the production problem is discussed in terms of the cost relationships used as a foundation in many forms of economic analysis. Aside from assumptions and their implications, the material is mostly definitional. It serves as the analytical basis for the input-demand problem and the various forms of market structure discussed in later chapters.

# CHARACTERIZING THE NATURE OF PRODUCTION

The *production function* is one of the most important means of characterizing the relationship between the inputs used and the output produced by firms. By definition, a production function is a graph, table, or mathematical function that shows the relationship between inputs and the output that can be produced efficiently with those inputs. The term *efficiently* implies that production takes place in a manner consistent with the existing range of technological possibilities; methods of production are chosen so that inputs are not used needlessly.

Table 15.1 presents data representing a production function over a very small range of input and output possibilities. The numbers from the production function reflect an engineering relationship between input requirements and output possibilities, given the state of technology. The inputs considered are labor and capital; the output is chairs. Through the substitution of one input for another, different combinations of inputs can lead to the same level of output. When more of one or both inputs is used, more output is produced. For example, 4 chairs can be produced using 8 units of labor and 3 units of capital, or they can be produced using 6 units of labor and 4 units of capital. In this case, the amount of labor has been decreased, and capital has increased, in such a way that the output produced remains constant. If labor is held constant at 8 units, chair output can be increased from 4 to 8 units by raising capital use from 3 to 7 units. When both labor and capital rise, say from 5 units of labor and 6 units

## Input Combinations and Output: A Typical Firm's Production Function

| Labor Input | Capital Input | Chair Output |
|:-----------:|:-------------:|:------------:|
| 8 | 3 | 4 |
| 6 | 4 | 4 |
| 5 | 6 | 4 |
| 10 | 3 | 8 |
| 8 | 7 | 8 |
| 6 | 9 | 8 |

**Table 15.1** *The production function shows the input combinations required to produce various levels of output. Input substitution implies that different combinations of labor and capital can be used to produce the same number of chairs. If either or both the capital and labor inputs are increased, chair production will rise.*

of capital to 6 units of labor and 9 units of capital, output will also rise. Substitution among inputs and the idea that greater levels of input lead to higher levels of output are important characteristics of the production functions used by economists.

Data for a more complete production function might fill many pages. Therefore, to express the relationship between inputs and outputs more succinctly, a mathematical function might be used, or the relationship could be graphed to display visually the relationship between all input and output combinations.

In order to make more effective use of the information conveyed in production functions, assumption are made regarding the relationship between the output produced and the inputs that are free to vary. Assumptions concerning the time frame under consideration, the number of inputs the firm is allowed to increase or decrease during this time frame, and the measured relationship between changes in output and changes in the quantity of input used are all important.

## The Production Time Frame

The production function allows measurement of the effects on output of simultaneous changes in all inputs used by the firm. However, depending on the length of time, it may not be possible for the firm to alter the quantity of all inputs. When the firm is constrained by this time factor or the firm simply wishes to expand its use of one input holding constant the other available inputs, a number of important measures can be developed to reveal the relationship between input use and output. Through use of these measures, additional insight concering the nature of production and technology is gained.

### THE SHORT RUN AND THE LONG RUN

The two basic time frames used in economic analysis are the *short run* and the *long run*. These time frames do not refer to periods of any specific length; they reflect the options for changes in input use at the disposal of the firm. The time it would take a small company to double the number of computers it uses is far shorter than the time it would take an airline to double the number of planes it flies; however, economists might consider both examples of long-run changes.

**The Short Run.** The short run refers to a period of time so short that it is not possible for the firm to vary the level of at least one input. The input that is generally assumed to be fixed in the short run is the capital stock (buildings and machines). If output is to be increased, firms are able to do so only by using existing plant and equipment. This is because of the large expense typically associated with capital purchases and building lags involved in producing certain types of capital equipment. In the short run, the firm can make additional use of inputs that can be readily hired, such as labor.

**The Long Run.** In the long run, it is assumed that the time frame is of sufficient duration that the firm can change the use of any or all of its inputs. Thus, the firm can change the scale of its operation to any degree; it can double or triple its size. It does so in order to produce the desired level of output most efficiently.

## Production Measures

When a firm varies its use of a single input, with all other inputs held constant, the precise output response to changes in the level of this input can be measured and interpreted in several useful ways. Depending on the purpose of analysis, one or all of these measures may be useful.

### TOTAL PHYSICAL PRODUCT

*Total physical product* refers to the total quantity of output produced with a given amount of some input, such as labor. All other inputs are assumed to be held constant. The adjective *physical* refers to the fact that actual output is being considered, not output valued in dollar terms; this adjective is often omitted and reference is made merely to *total product*. In accordance with standard assumptions regarding the production function, use of greater amounts of input lead to production of higher levels of output, a higer total product. Although only one input is considered in determining the total product, the level of other inputs is not zero. However, their level remains fixed, so that the relationship between total product and the input considered can be measured.

Columns one and two of Table 15.2 show the relationship between a firm's total product and the labor input necessary to produce it. If 4 laborers are employed, the firm's total product of labor is 50 chairs. When the number of laborers employed increases to 5, holding constant the machinery and other tools the workers have at their disposal, the total product of labor is 60 chairs.

### Total, Average, and Marginal Products

| Labor Employed ($L$) | Total Product ($Q$) | Average Product $\left(\dfrac{Q}{L}\right)$ | Marginal Product $\left(\dfrac{\Delta Q}{\Delta L}\right)$ |
|---|---|---|---|
| 1 | 7 | 7 | |
| 2 | 23 | 11.5 | 16 |
| 3 | 38 | 12.7 | 15 |
| 4 | 50 | 12.5 | 12 |
| 5 | 60 | 12 | 10 |

**Table 15.2**

## AVERAGE PHYSICAL PRODUCT

The *average physical product*, or *average product*, is the firm's total product divided by the amount of the variable input used to produce it. Suppose labor is the input under consideration. Using $Q$ to denote the total product and $L$ to represent the amount of the variable labor input used, the average product of labor is written

$$Average\ Product = \frac{Q}{L}$$

Column three of Table 15.2 shows the average product associated with various levels of input use. When 4 laborers are employed, 50 chairs are produced. The average product of labor is 12.5 chairs per worker.

## MARGINAL PRODUCT

*Marginal product* refers to the *change* in the total product given a change in the variable input. It represents the extra output produced given a 1-unit increase in the amount of the variable input. Again letting $Q$ represent the total product and $L$ represent the quantity of labor, the marginal product of labor takes the form

$$Marginal\ Product\ of\ Labor = \frac{\Delta Q}{\Delta L}$$

The delta sign refers to the change in the variable that it precedes. In this definition, it is the change in the amount of labor used that causes output to increase or decrease. Therefore, causality in the marginal-product formula runs from the denominator to the numerator. This is consistent with the idea that input use is a prerequisite for the production of output.

From Table 15.2, as the amount of labor increases from 4 to 5 units, the quantity of output rises from 50 to 60. Thus, the 1-unit increase in labor input is associated with a 10 unit increase in output. The marginal product in moving from 4 to 5 laborers is therefore 10 chairs. The marginal product of labor is shown in the last column of Table 15.2.

## The Law of Diminishing Returns

An important assumption regarding the nature of the change in output given a change in the level of one input is classified under the *law of diminishing returns*. As additional units of the variable input are employed, it is assumed that a point will be reached when the marginal product will begin to decline. The law of diminishing returns is also referred to as the *law of diminishing marginal productivity*.

As seen in Table 15.2, when additional units of labor input are used, the total product rises, but in decreasing increments. In other words, the marginal product of labor is declining. In moving from the employment of 3 to 4 laborers, total product rises from 38 to 50 units of output. The marginal product of the fourth laborer is therefore 12 units of output. When the fifth worker is hired, the total product rises to 60 units. The marginal product of the fifth worker equals only 10 units, 2 less than the marginal product of the fourth worker. This occurs even though all workers are assumed to possess the same skills. Because all other inputs are fixed, labor becomes less productive as more laborers are hired; there are fewer machines and other inputs per worker.

## COST IMPLICATIONS OF DIMINISHING RETURNS

Diminishing marginal productivity, or diminishing returns, has an important implication when the firm decides to increase its output by increments of a fixed size. With diminishing marginal productivity, each additional unit of output requires more of the variable input than the preceding unit of output. As seen in Table 15.2, if the firm is producing 23 units of output using 2 laborers and desires to produce 15 extra units, it must hire one additional worker. Employment rises to 3 laborers and output increases to 38 units. Should the firm now desire to increase output by another 15 units, more than one worker must be hired; the marginal productivity of the fourth worker only equals 12 units of output. Because of the law of diminishing marginal productivity, increasing output in fixed increments will result in higher and higher costs for each output unit produced.

## Marginals and Averages

Table 15.2 reveals an interesting fact concerning the relationship between average and marginal values. When the average value is rising, the corresponding marginal value is greater than the average. Similarly, when the average value is falling, the marginal value is below the average. For example, in moving from use of 1 to 2 units of labor, total output rises from 7 to 23 units, and the marginal product equals 16. Because the average output produced by the first worker equals 7 units, if the second worker produces 16 additional units, the average output of both the first and second workers must increase. The fact that it does so is seen in the rise in the average product of labor from 7 (7/1=7) for the first worker to 11.5 (23/2=11.5) for the first and second workers. It follows that when new marginal values are greater than previous average values, the new average value will increase.

Alternatively, in moving from employment of 4 to 5 workers, the marginal product of the fifth worker is only 10 units. Before this worker was employed, average output per worker was 12.5 units. Because the last worker hired adds less to total output than the average output produced by previously hired workers, employment of the fifth worker reduces the average output of the firm to 12 units per worker. When new marginal values are smaller than previous average values, the new average value will decrease.

*The Production Function and Returns to Scale*

While the law of diminishing returns deals with the effects of output changes given a change in the use of a single input, the concept of *returns to scale* deals with the impact on output of proportional increases or decreases in the use of all inputs simultaneously. Underlying this concept is the nature of the production process and the question whether proportional changes in *all* inputs lead to increased, decreased, or the same level of efficiency. Diminishing returns is a short-run concept; returns to scale deal with the long run. The production of some outputs becomes more efficient when the scale of operation is increased. Examples include electricity generation using nuclear power and automobile manufacture.

Other outputs grow in proportion to the inputs used. For example, by doubling the number of trucks and drivers, a delivery firm can be expected to double the deliveries it is able to make. Finally, there are cases in which increasing all inputs by a given proportion results in a less than proportional increase in output. A manufacturing operation may become so large that it cannot be effectively run when management is increased in proportion to other inputs. These three cases are classified below.

### INCREASING RETURNS TO SCALE

The presence of increasing returns to scale signifies that a scaling-up of all inputs by the same proportion leads to a more than proportional increase in the amount of output produced. If all input quantities are doubled, increasing returns to scale implies that output will more than double.

### CONSTANT RETURNS TO SCALE

Returns to scale are constant if a proportional change in input use leads to a change in output of exactly the same proportion. If output doubles when all input quantities are doubled, returns to scale are constant.

### DECREASING RETURNS TO SCALE

Decreasing returns to scale are present when a proportional change in input use leads to a less than proportional change in output. Here, a doubling of all input quantities leads to less than a doubling in the level of output.

## COST CURVES

Once a decision has been made to produce a certain level of output, it is assumed that the firm will choose inputs so that the overall costs of production are minimized. In examining the costs faced by firms for the inputs they use, assume that input prices are not affected by the firm's decision to employ more or less units of any particular input; the firm faces an established market price for the wages, interest, and rent it must pay for the labor, capital, and land resources it uses. This fact means that doubling the *inputs* used by the firm will double the cost.

The cost implications of a firm's decision to double its *output* are not so obvious. Over the long run, nonconstant returns to scale imply that input requirements, and therefore total cost, might be more than doubled or less than doubled when the firm doubles its output. In the short run, a decision to increase the level of output implies that the law of diminishing returns will affect cost. Diminishing returns cause cost to increase at an increasing rate. More and more units of the variable input are required to produce given increments of additional output. These considerations are addressed in the following sections, along with various ways of measuring costs incurred.

## The Components of Cost

In examining the relationship between cost and output, it is useful to divide costs into those that vary with the level of output and those that remain fixed as output changes. In addition, as with the various measures of output, the concepts of total, average, and marginal cost provide an important means of analyzing the implications of the firm's activities.

### FIXED COSTS

In producing output, certain inputs are often necessary before production can begin. They have nothing to do with the quantity of output produced. The firm incurs a cost for these inputs, but once they are purchased, there is no need for additional expenditure, regardless of how much output is produced. For example, a factory requires a building to house machines and to provide a place for laborers to work. The factory owners must incur the cost of the building to produce any output, but this cost remains the same whether the firm produces one or a million units.

**Average Fixed Costs.** *Average fixed cost* is defined as total fixed cost divided by the quantity of output. Letting TFC represent total fixed cost and AFC represent average fixed cost, the formula for average fixed cost is

$$AFC = \frac{TFC}{Q}$$

If the total fixed cost of constructing a factory is $1 million and if the firm's total output equals 500,000 units, average fixed cost will equal $2 per unit. If output expands to 2 million units, average fixed cost is reduced to 50 cents. Average fixed cost will always decline as the level of output rises because total fixed cost does not vary with output. Hence, as the output produced by the firm increases, a fixed numerator is divided by an ever-increasing denominator.

## VARIABLE COSTS

Production of larger quantities of output requires larger quantities of some inputs. *Total variable cost* refers to costs that vary directly with the level of output. For example, a trucking company will incur fuel and labor costs for each mile that goods are transported. If goods are to be transported over longer distances, greater labor and fuel costs must be paid. As additional miles are traveled, the number of labor hours increases, and the amount of fuel used rises. Traveling more miles does not raise the price of fuel or labor; input prices are assumed to be fixed. Note that fixed costs in this example would be reflected in the cost of the trucks required before the firm can conduct business.

**Average Variable Cost.** *Average variable cost* is defined as average total cost divided by the level of output. Letting TVC represent total variable cost and AVC represent average variable cost, the formula for this measure is

$$AVC = \frac{TVC}{Q}$$

As output rises, both the numerator and denominator of this fraction rise. Therefore, it is not possible to say whether average variable cost will rise or fall with output. However, under the assumption of diminishing returns, cost increases at a faster rate than output because input use grows faster than output. Therefore, average variable cost will increase as output increases.

## TOTAL COST

For any level of output, total cost represents the total expenditure by the firm on the inputs used for production. The total-cost function relates total cost to the level of output. By definition, total cost equals the sum of total fixed cost and total variable cost. Letting TC represent total cost,

$$TC = TFC + TVC$$

**Average Total Cost.** When total cost is divided by the level of output, *average total cost* is defined. For example, if production of 100 units of output entails a total cost of $500, average total cost will equal $5 per unit of output. If $Q$ represents the level of output and ATC average total cost, the formula for this measure is

$$ATC = \frac{TC}{Q}$$

To account for the fact that total cost equals the sum of total fixed and variable costs, this definition can be expanded as

$$ATC = \frac{TFC}{Q} + \frac{TVC}{Q} = AFC + AVC$$

Average total cost equals the sum of average fixed cost and average variable cost.

## MARGINAL COST

*Marginal cost* represents the change in total cost that occurs with a one unit change in output. For example, if the total cost of producing 50 units of output is $300 and the total cost of producing 51 units is $315.00, marginal cost will equal $15. Except for the specific reference to cost, the nature of marginal cost as a change in one variable caused by a change in another corresponds exactly to the definition of marginal product and the other marginals that have been introduced. Using MC to represent marginal cost, the formula for marginal cost is

$$MC = \frac{\Delta TC}{\Delta Q}$$

**Marginal Cost Equals Marginal Variable Cost.** Marginal cost has nothing to do with fixed cost; fixed cost does not change with the level of output. Thus, marginal fixed cost always equals zero. On the other hand, by definition, total variable cost does change with the level of output. Hence, marginal cost and marginal variable cost measure exactly the same thing. This is easily shown. By definition,

$$TC = TFC + TVC$$

Making use of delta notation to define the change in total cost,

$$\frac{\Delta TC}{\Delta Q} = \frac{\Delta TFC}{\Delta Q} + \frac{\Delta TVC}{\Delta Q}$$

By definition, $\frac{\Delta TC}{\Delta Q}$ equals marginal cost, and marginal fixed cost, $\frac{\Delta TFC}{\Delta Q}$, equals zero. Therefore, marginal cost and marginal variable cost, $\frac{\Delta TVC}{\Delta Q}$, are the same.

## The Shape of the Firm's Short-run Cost Curves

The production of higher levels of output requires greater amounts of input. Thus, the firm's total-cost curve will always be upward-sloping. However, depending on whether the marginal product of the variable input rises, falls, or remains the same as output increases, the *slope* of the total-cost curve can increase, be constant, or decrease.

In producing additional increments of output, the law of diminishing returns implies that the quantity of the variable input must increase because greater and greater quantities of the input are required to produce each extra unit of output. In this situation, total cost will increase at an increasing rate; the total-cost curve will become steeper and steeper as the level of output increases. Conversely, if the firm operates in a range where marginal productivity increases as output expands, the total-cost curve will become more and more horizontal as output rises; the quantity of the variable input required to produce given increments of output becomes smaller and smaller. Finally, if the marginal product of the variable input remains the same over some range of output, cost will increase at a constant rate with output, and the slope of the total-cost curve will be constant.

### TOTAL COST: GRAPHIC PORTRAYAL

To represent the shape of cost curves based on real-world experience, economists assume that over the initial range of output produced by a typical

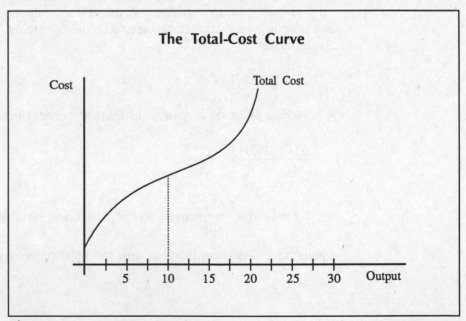

**Figure 15.1** *As output rises from zero to 10 units, total cost increases at a decreasing rate, reflecting increasing marginal productivity for the variable factor. After 10 units of output, diminishing marginal productivity takes hold, and total cost increases at an increasing rate.*

firm, marginal product actually increases. Hence, total cost increases at a decreasing rate and the slope of the cost curve decreases. However, economists generally agree that at some point diminishing returns begin to take effect, causing the cost curve's slope to increase.

Figure 15.1 portrays a typical total-cost curve (TC) as envisioned by economists. The total-cost curve does not intersect the vertical axis at a zero cost because of the presence of fixed costs, costs incurred even if the firm produces zero output. Over the range of outputs between zero and 10 units, cost increases at a decreasing rate. This reflects the fact that marginal productivity is increasing; the cost curve becomes more horizontal; its slope decreases. However, the law of diminishing returns takes hold at 10 units. The cost curve begins to rise more steeply beyond this point. The curve becomes more vertical; its slope increases.

## GRAPHING AVERAGE COST

When total cost appears as shown in Figure 15.1, average-cost curves graphed as a function of output must be shaped consistently with the total cost curve's shape.

**Graphing Average Fixed Cost.** Because total fixed cost is independent of

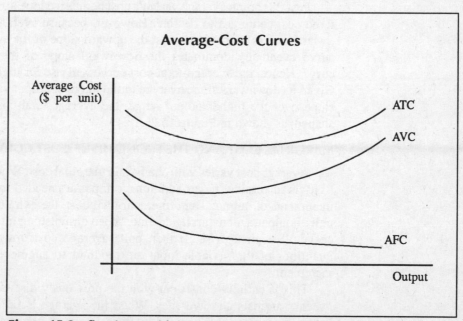

**Figure 15.2** *Consistent with increasing marginal productivity over the first 10 units of output, average variable cost (AVC) declines. When diminishing marginal productivity takes hold, average variable cost begins to rise, Because fixed cost does not change, average fixed cost (AFC) declines as output rises. As the sum of average variable and average fixed costs, average total cost (ATC) lies above average variable cost and is U-shaped.*

the level of output, average fixed cost will decline as output increases. The average fixed cost curve is the lowest curve shown in Figure 15.2. It decreases throughout its entire range.

**Graphing Average Variable Cost.** For output values where the marginal product of the variable input increases, average variable cost will decrease. Greater and greater quantities of output can be produced with each additional unit of the variable input used. These efficiency gains mean less average variable cost. When diminishing returns take hold, efficiency falls as more output is produced. Average variable cost therefore increases because a greater quantity of input must be used to produce a given amount of additional output. Combining the downward-sloping segment associated with increasing returns with the upward-sloping segment associated with decreasing returns, the average variable cost curve will have a U-shape, as shown in Figure 15.2.

**Graphing Average Total Cost.** Average total cost is equal to the sum of average fixed cost and average variable cost. Therefore, the shape of the average-total-cost curve depends on the shape of both the average-fixed and the average-variable cost curves. Because both average variable cost and average fixed cost are downward-sloping over a certain portion of their ranges, average total cost will also be downward-sloping over this range.

Past this point, average variable cost begins to slope upward, while average fixed cost continues to decline. However, because average fixed cost moves toward zero as output increases, the upward slope of the average variable cost curve eventually dominates the downward slope of the average-fixed-cost curve. Hence, the average-total-cost curve will rise for higher levels of output. Given its downward slope over the initial range of output values and its upward slope over the higher output range, the average-total-cost curve will be U-shaped, as shown in Figure 15.2.

## MARGINAL COST AND THE ECONOMIST'S COST CURVE

Average cost varies with changes in marginal cost. When marginal productivity is increasing, fewer additions to input are needed to produce additional increments of output. Therefore, marginal cost, the extra cost of an additional unit of output, will naturally decline. When diminishing returns set in, marginal cost will begin to rise. It then pulls average cost upward because greater quantities of the variable input are required to augment output by a given increment.

This is entirely consistent with the previously discussed relationship between marginals and averages. When the average is falling, the marginal is below the average. When the average is rising, the marginal is above the average. Marginal cost will equal average cost at the point where average cost has ended its decline and has begun its ascent. As shown in Figure 15.3, this occurs at the bottom of the U-shaped average-total-cost curve.

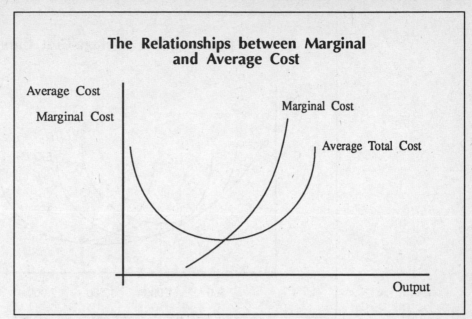

## The Relationships between Marginal and Average Cost

Average Cost

Marginal Cost

Marginal Cost

Average Total Cost

Output

*Figure 15.3  When marginal cost is below average total cost, average total cost falls as output expands. Marginal cost equals average total cost when average total cost is constant at its minimum point. Finally, when marginal cost is above average total cost, average total cost is rising.*

## The Long-Run Cost Curve

In the long run, firms are able to adjust the amounts of all inputs to desired levels. Thus, the firm would not be constrained to the single set of cost curves shown in Figures 15.1 and 15.2. Instead, depending upon the level of output to be produced, the firm can alter its input combinations so that the input levels chosen lead to the lowest average cost.

### DERIVING THE LONG-RUN AVERAGE-COST CURVE

To derive the long run average-cost curve, it is necessary to visualize the ideal short-run U-shaped average cost curves associated with every level of output. Individually, these short-run cost curves will all share the characteristic of achieving their minimum level above the level of output for which they are optimal. In Figure 15.4, these curves are labeled SRAC. In moving from one level of production to a slightly higher or lower level, it is assumed that short-run average costs do not change erratically. Thus, the boundary of all possible short-run average-cost curves can be drawn as a smoothly curved continuous line. This boundary, or *envelope* represents the long-run average-cost curve.

This envelope does not represent the locus or set of all minimum points on the individual short-run average-cost curves. For example, in Figure 15.4 the minimum cost associated with producing 1,000 units of output occurs at a point

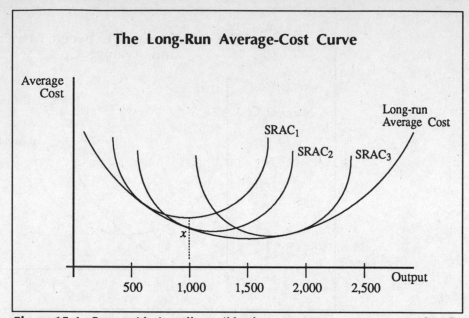

**Figure 15.4** *By considering all possible short-run average-cost curves (SRAC), the long-run average-cost curve is derived. It is tangent to each of the short-run average-total-cost curves.*

$x$ on the long-run average-cost curve. This point is also found on the cost curve labeled $SRAC_2$, but it is not the minimum point on curve $SRAC_2$. Nevertheless, it is below the minimum point on cost curve $SRAC_1$, which achieves a minimum when 1,000 units of output are produced.

**The Effects of Returns to Scale.** Returns to scale will determine the ultimate shape of the firm's long run cost curve. Unlike diminishing returns, which refer to the decreasing additions to output in the short run with increases in the level of a single variable input, returns to scale refer to the relationship between proportional changes in all inputs and the corresponding output response. Changes in the level of all inputs are assumed to occur only in the long run.

If the firm experiences increasing returns to scale, a proportional increase in all inputs will lead to a more than proportional increase in output. It follows that increasing output by given increments requires the use of fewer and fewer additional input quantities. Total cost then increases at a decreasing rate. Because the proportional increase in cost is less than the proportional increase in output, long-run average cost will fall. Mathematically, long-run average cost falls because total cost, located in the numerator of the average cost formula, grows more slowly than total output in the denominator.

If constant returns to scale prevail, proportional increases in output must be met with matching proportional increases in the quantity of inputs used. In this case, total cost (in the numerator) increases at a constant rate with output (in the denominator); long-run average cost will be constant. Finally, with decreasing returns to scale, proportional increases in output require more than proportional increases in inputs. Cost rises more than proportionately with changes in output. The long-run total-cost curve will increase at an increasing rate; long-run average total cost will rise.

The relationship between long-run total cost, long-run average cost, and output is shown in Figure 15.5. In Figure 15.5a, the efficiency gains that come with increasing returns to scale lead to a total-cost curve that becomes less steep as output increases; long-run average total cost slopes downward. In Figure 15.5b, constant returns lead to a total-cost curve with a constant slope; the long-run average cost curve is horizontal. Finally, in Figure 15.5c, decreasing

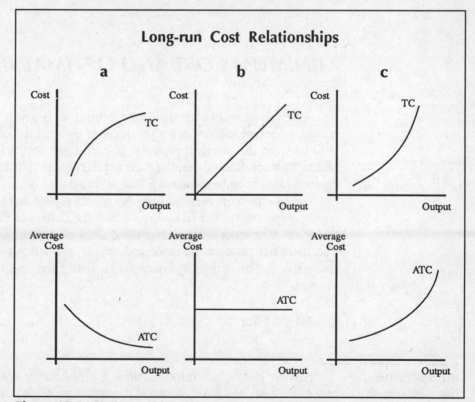

**Figure 15.5**  *In Figure 15.5a, long-run returns to scale are increasing because total cost increases at a decreasing rate. Therefore, average total cost declines as output increases. Constant returns result in the cost function with constant slope seen in Figure 15.5b and lead to a constant level of average total cost. Finally, decreasing returns to scale will cause long-run total cost to increase at an increasing rate and lead average total cost to rise as output rises as in 15.5c.*

returns to scale are represented by a long-run total-cost curve with an ever-increasing slope; the long-run average-cost curve rises throughout its range.

## Shifting Cost Curves

The long-run and short-run cost curves developed in this chapter are based on the assumption that input prices are fixed and the level of technology is given. Given an increase in the price of some factor of production, the total cost and average-total-cost curves will shift upward. Technological changes that allow firms to produce more output through use of the same quantitites of input will cause the total-cost- and average-total-cost curves to shift downward.

Because of the unique relationship between total, marginal, and average cost curves, upward or downward shifts in total cost will be associated with corresponding shifts in average and marginal cost curves. There is one exception to this rule. If factor price changes or technological changes affect only fixed costs, average variable cost and marginal cost will not shift.

# MINIMUM COST AND OPTIMAL INPUT USE

When firms minimize their cost subject to a given level of output or maximize output subject to a given level of cost, an important condition will hold between the marginal products of each input factor and the price of the factor. This condition states that the marginal product per dollar of expenditure on each input must be the same across all inputs.

Suppose the firm makes use of the inputs capital and labor, denoted by $K$ and $L$, respectively. The letter $r$ represents the dollars of interest paid per unit of capital. The letter $w$ represents the dollars of wages paid per unit of labor. The marginal products of labor and capital are written as $MP_L$ and $MP_K$, respectively. The optimality condition regarding the cost-minimizing level of inputs is

$$\frac{MP_L}{w} = \frac{MP_K}{r}$$

## Interpreting the Optimality Condition

At first glance, the information in the optimality condition is not at all obvious. However, by remembering the definition of marginal productivity and considering the units involved in measuring $w$ and $r$, the common sense of this equation is readily apparent. The marginal product of labor is expressed in units of output per laborer. The wage rate represents the dollars paid per laborer. The ratio of the marginal product of labor to the wage therefore represents the additional output produced when an extra dollar is spent on labor. Similarly, the ratio of the marginal product of capital to the dollars of interest paid per unit of capital represents the output produced when an additional dollar is spent on capital.

Suppose that equality between these ratios does not hold. For example, suppose that

$$\frac{\text{MP}_L}{w} > \frac{\text{MP}_K}{r}$$

An additional dollar spent on labor leads to the production of more output than an additional dollar spent on capital. If the owners of the firm are rational, they should spend additional dollars on labor; it leads to the production of more output than a similar expenditure on capital. As additional units of labor are employed, the law of diminishing returns takes hold; that is, the marginal product of labor will fall. Ultimately, as more dollars are spent on labor, the output per dollar spent on labor will equal the output per dollar spent on capital. When this occurs, the firm will have allocated its expenditure on these two inputs to minimize cost. In general, firms should allocate expenditure on inputs so that the output produced from a dollar of expenditure on a factor is maximized.

*Explaining the relationship between output and cost provides a solid basis for further analysis of the behavior of firms. The definitions and concepts presented here will be seen repeatedly in coming chapters that deal with profit-maximizing behavior and different types of market structure. The characteristics of production experienced by the firm, reflected in its cost curves, will ultimately be combined with the decisions and potential actions of consumers, reflected in demand curves. This will lead to an equilibrium state in output markets. This equilibrium determines both the equilibrium price and the equilibrium quantity of goods and is consistent with optimizing behavior of firms and individuals.*

# 16

## The Model of Perfect Competition

*P*revious chapters have focused on the factors underlying the demand for products by consumers and the factors firms consider in supplying output to the market. In this chapter, elements from both the supply side and the demand side are combined in the determination of a product's equilibrium price and quantity. The context in which supply and demand considerations are analyzed is very special. In the model of perfect competition, the long run forces that lead to equilibrium are assumed to work so that products reach the market at their lowest price.

Perfect competition is one of several important models used to explain the nature of competition among firms. It represents an ideal case in which competition leads to the most beneficial outcome for consumers. Of all the models used by economists in analyzing the behavior of firms, the model of perfect competition is the most important. It does not apply to every market in the real world, but it provides a base-line case against which all other types of competition can be compared.

The model's construction begins and proceeds in a manner similar to that of most other forms of economic analysis. First, definitions and assumptions are made to identify clearly the specific points of interest. Next, relevant components are combined through the use of graphs to form a stationary model. Supply, demand, and cost curves are plotted together, and their interrelation leads to establishment of market equilibrium. Finally, assumptions used to set up the model are relaxed, and the implications of these changes are analyzed. In other words, curves are shifted, and the effects on equilibrium in a perfectly competitive market are observed.

# THE PERFECTLY COMPETITIVE FIRM

Although the model of perfect competition deals with the relationship between buyers and sellers, the foundation of this model lies in assumptions concerning the characteristics of a typical firm in a perfectly competitive industry. Such a firm operates within the confines of a market structure where it has no control over the price of its output. The firm's production characteristics are represented by the standard U-shaped average-cost curve. With these relationships, it is possible to represent geometrically the revenue, cost, and profit levels for the firm at various levels of output and to determine where its profits are maximized. It is also possible to derive the firm's supply curve.

## Perfect Competition: Underlying Assumptions

For the model of perfect competition, assumptions deal with the nature of costs, the nature of the product produced, and the degree to which firms can compete. There are assumed to be many firms in the industry. These firms produce a single homogeneous or standardized commodity. The objective of each firm is to maximize its profit. No firm has any advantage over any other firm; in producing output, information is freely available concerning technology, input prices, output price, and other factors that might affect production decisions. In addition, there are no barriers to entry into or exit from the perfectly competitive industry. It is easy to set up or close down a business. Regulations limiting entry or extremely high start-up costs are not present.

## The Firm as a Price Taker

The presence of many firms in the market, each producing a homogeneous product with no advantage over other firms, implies that no firm can control the market price of output. Firms are said to be *price takers*. An attempt by a firm to raise its price above the market price would result in the loss of all its customers. Who would pay more when an identical product could be bought for less from another firm? The typical firm takes the market price as given and adjusts output so that its profit is maximized.

### THE FIRM'S HORIZONTAL DEMAND CURVE

The fact that firms are price takers means that individual firms can sell as much output as they like without affecting the market price of output. At first glance, this appears to violate the law of demand, which states that lower prices are necessary to increase the quantity demanded. Demand curves are typically downward-sloping. However, within the context of a perfectly competitive industry, no firm is assumed to produce a significant amount of total industry output; therefore, no single firm has any effect on output price.

The relationship between a typical firm's demand curve and the industry demand curve for some product is portrayed in Figure 16.1. The firm's demand curve in Figure 16.1a is shown as a horizontal line intersecting the vertical axis at a price of $10. This price is determined by the intersection of the industry's supply and demand curves in Figure 16.1b. Although the firm adds to the overall supply of industry output, its contribution is very small relative to total industry output. In the industry, the supply of and demand for millions of units determine equilibrium price. The firm produces only hundreds of units, a small fraction of total output. Therefore, the price established within the industry will not change, regardless of how much or how little the individual firm produces.

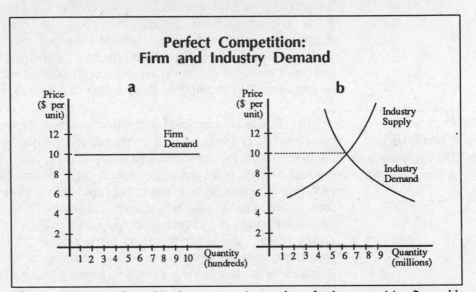

**Figure 16.1** *As reflected in the output units, each perfectly competitive firm adds only a small amount to the total quantity produced in the industry. Therefore, individual firms cannot affect the price of output by increasing or decreasing their output. Because price is taken as given, the firm's demand curve is horizontal. When demand is horizontal, price, marginal revenue, and average revenue are equivalent.*

As an example of what the horizontal demand implies for the firm, consider the $10 per unit market price established at the intersection of the industry demand and supply curves. Should the firm try to sell its output at a price greater than $10, it would sell nothing; consumers would find plenty of other sellers willing to provide the homogeneous product at the market price. The firm can sell its output for less than $10, but this would not be rational. Because it can sell as much as it likes at the prevailing price of $10, the firm would lose money if it lowered its price.

**Shifting the Firm's Demand.** Shifts in the industry demand or supply curves will lead to the establishment of a new equilibrium price for the commodity. A change in price causes the demand curve (the price line) for the individual firm to shift up or down, depending upon whether the commodity price rises or falls. A horizontal demand curve is said to be *infinitely* or *perfectly elastic.*

## The Firm's Revenues

The *total revenue* a firm receives from the sale of its output equals the product of the price of the commodity and the quantity sold. If a firm sells a single unit at a price of $10, its total revenue is $10. Similarly, if it sells 100 units at a price of $10 per unit, its total revenue is $1,000. Letting $P$ stand for a product's price and $Q$ stand for the quantity sold, total revenue is

$$Total\,Revenue = PQ$$

The definition of total revenue serves as the basis for development of two other important revenue measures: *average revenue* and *marginal revenue*. Conceptually, except for the fact that they refer to revenues, these measures correspond to the average-cost and marginal-cost measures developed in the previous chapters.

### AVERAGE REVENUE

*Average revenue* is defined as total revenue divided by the quantity of output produced. The average revenue the firm receives from the sale of its product is equivalent to the price of the product. Because total revenue is equal to the product of price and quantity, dividing total revenue by the quantity of output leaves only price.

$$Average\,Revenue = \frac{Total\,Revenue}{Quantity} = \frac{PQ}{Q} = P$$

If the firm's total revenue equals $1,000 and the firm has sold 100 units, average revenue equals $10. This is equal to the price of the product.

### MARGINAL REVENUE

*Marginal revenue* refers to the change in total revenue that occurs with a change in the quantity of output produced. Marginal revenue can be written as

$$Marginal\,Revenue = \frac{\Delta(Total\,Revenue)}{\Delta(Quantity)} = \frac{\Delta(PQ)}{\Delta Q}$$

where the delta sign refers to the change in the variable that follows it. More intuitively, marginal revenue is the extra revenue received by the firm from the sale of an extra unit of output. For example, suppose the firm's total revenue from the sale of 100 units equals $1,000. If the firm sells 101 units of output, total revenue might rise to $1,025. The firm's marginal revenue, the change in total revenue given a one-unit increase in sales, equals $25.

## DEMAND, AVERAGE REVENUE, AND MARGINAL REVENUE

Under perfect competition, the firm is a price taker. Over the range of output it can produce, its demand curve is equivalent to the price established by the intersection of *industry* supply and demand. By definition, price and average revenue are the same. Thus, aside from representing the firm's demand curve, the price established at the intersection of the industry's supply and demand curves also represents the typical firm's average-revenue curve.

**Marginal Revenue and Price.** When the demand curve is horizontal, price does not change with changes in quantity. In Figure 16.1, price for the typical firm equals $10 whether the firm produces 1 or 100 units. In this situation, marginal revenue and price will be the same. To see this fact, suppose the firm sells an extra unit of output. The extra revenue received by the firm from the sale of this extra unit is the price of the product. If 9 units of output are sold at a price of $10 per unit, total revenue equals $90. If 10 units are sold, total revenue equals $100. Marginal revenue, the change in total revenue that comes with the sale of an extra unit of output, equals $10.

Because price does not change as the perfectly competitive firm sells more or less units of output, the equivalence of marginal revenue and price is seen as follows:

$$Marginal\ Revenue\ (Perfect\ Competition) = \frac{\Delta(PQ)}{\Delta Q} = \frac{P(\Delta Q)}{\Delta Q} = P$$

Therefore, for the perfectly competitive firm, the horizontal line at the product's price is equivalent to the demand, average revenue, and marginal revenue curves.

**Some Facts Concerning Revenue Curves.** Important facts should be noted about the relations between price, demand, average revenue, and marginal revenue for the perfectly competitive firm and firms in general. First, it is not always true that price and the demand curve are the same. With a downward-sloping demand curve, a different price corresponds to each unit of output. Only when the demand curve for a product is horizontal, as in the case of the perfectly competitive firm, will one price be associated with all levels of output that the firm might offer for sale.

On the other hand, from the firm's perspective, its demand curve can be thought to represent its average revenue curve as well. The demand curve shows the relationship between the quantity of output that will be sold and the product's price. Given the quantity of output to be produced, the corresponding price along the demand curve represents the number of dollars the firm will earn from each unit of output it sells. This is average revenue.

Finally, the marginal revenue curve will equal the average revenue curve only when the demand curve is horizontal. When demand is downward-sloping, different quantities of output are associated with different prices, and price must decline to sell more output. Because price and average revenue are the same, average revenue declines. Given the relationship between marginals and averages, if average revenue is falling, marginal revenue must be below average revenue.

## The Firm's Cost Curves

Under perfect competition, industry demand shows how the output demanded by consumers will change in response to price changes. The single price determined through the intersection of industry supply and demand is the price taken by each firm in the industry. This price is equivalent to the demand, average-revenue, and marginal-revenue curves faced by individual firms. Moving from revenues to costs, the characteristics of production for an individual firm are reflected in its average-cost and marginal-cost curves.

Figure 16.2 shows the average-cost and marginal-cost curve for a typical firm. The average cost curve is U-shaped. This symbolizes the standard assumption concerning how average cost changes with output. The presence of declining average cost over the initial range of output is associated with increasing marginal productivity; average cost falls as output rises. The higher output range is associated with diminishing marginal productivity; average cost rises as output increases.

The marginal-cost curve shown is consistent with the relationship between average and marginal values. When average cost is falling, the marginal-cost curve is below the average-cost curve. When the average cost is rising, the marginal-cost curve is above the average-cost curve. At the minimum point on the average-total-cost curve, where the average neither rises nor falls, marginal-cost equals average total cost.

### FINDING COSTS ON COST CURVES

For any quantity of output, the corresponding marginal cost is found at the point on the marginal-cost curve directly above the quantity considered. Its value is read on the vertical axis. In Figure 16.2, the marginal cost of producing the sixth unit of output is $14. Similarly, to find the average cost associated with some quantity of output, the point on the average-cost curve above that quantity is found; the value of average cost is then read from the vertical axis. In Figure 16.2, the average cost of producing 6 units of output is $8 per unit. Average and marginal cost are equal only at the minimum point on the average-cost curve. In Figure 16.2, this occurs at 4 units of output where marginal cost and average cost each equal $6.

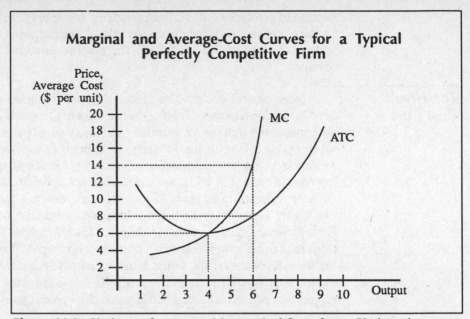

### Marginal and Average-Cost Curves for a Typical Perfectly Competitive Firm

**Figure 16.2** *Under perfect competition, typical firms face a U-shaped average-total-cost curve (ATC) and corresponding marginal-cost curve (MC). When six units of output are produced, the firm incurs an average total cost of $8 per unit of output and a marginal cost of $14 per unit.*

## PROFIT MAXIMIZATION AND PERFECT COMPETITION

A typical firm in a perfectly competitive industry is assumed to maximize its profit. By definition, *profit* equals total revenue minus total cost. Through use of the firm's revenue and cost curves, the quantity of output that maximizes the firm's profit can easily be found. But first it is essential to understand the relationship that must exist between marginal cost and marginal revenue for profit to be maximized. This relationship is the basis for the optimality condition or profit-maximizing rule that firms should follow if their goal is to maximize profit.

*Profit, Marginal Revenue, and Marginal Cost*

To develop and understand the condition that must be satisfied for profit maximization, it is necessary to recall the definitions of *marginal revenue* and *marginal cost*. It is also necessary to think in terms of *additions* to profit rather than the overall level of profit.

*Marginal revenue* refers to the extra revenue earned from selling an extra unit of output. *Marginal cost* refers to the extra cost of producing an extra unit of output. When marginal revenue is greater than marginal cost, the revenue the firm takes in from the sale of a unit of output exceeds the amount it must pay out to factors of production. For any quantity of output produced and sold, as long as marginal revenue exceeds marginal cost, there will be an addition to profit. As long as additions to profit are positive, total profit must rise.

Suppose the firm is considering production of a unit of output for which marginal cost is above marginal revenue. The extra cost of producing that unit exceeds the extra revenue the sale of the unit brings to the firm. The addition to profit will be negative and total profit will fall.

Finally, suppose the quantity of output produced and sold is associated with the equality of marginal cost and marginal revenue. If marginal cost equals marginal revenue, the addition to cost from producing an additional unit of output is exactly equal to the revenue obtained through its sale. The addition to profit is zero.

## Maximum Profit and the Perfectly Competitive Firm

In Figure 16.3 the typical perfectly competitive firm's marginal-cost and average-cost curves are graphed along with its demand curve. The demand curve is equivalent to the firm's marginal revenue curve. For now, the average-total-cost curve is not important. Marginal revenue and marginal cost intersect at 300 output units. Marginal revenue is above marginal cost for each quantity below 300 units. When marginal revenue exceeds marginal cost, additions to profit are positive. Total profit therefore rises with each additional unit produced in the output range below 300 units.

As the quantity of output produced and sold increases, marginal cost also increases because of the law of diminishing returns. When the firm produces its 300th unit of output, the marginal cost and marginal revenue associated with that quantity are exactly equal. There is no addition to profit at this point. Beyond 300 units, additional costs will exceed additional revenues. For example, if production is carried out to the 301st unit, marginal cost will rise above marginal revenue; the addition to profit will be negative. Because a negative value is added to profit, total profit will diminish.

Based on these considerations, profit is maximized when all the positive additions to profit have been exhausted. This occurs when the 300th unit of output is produced. The firm should produce the quantity associated with the intersection of marginal cost and marginal revenue. This is the firm's optimality rule for determining the profit-maximizing quanity of output: Produce where marginal cost equals marginal revenue.

## Portraying the Firm's Profit Graphically

To show the firm's total revenues, total costs, and total profit in a graph, it is necessary to use the definitions of the various revenue and cost concepts. *Average cost* is defined as total cost divided by quantity. *Average revenue* equals total revenue divided by quantity. If average revenue and average cost are each multiplied by the quantity of output, *total revenue* and *total cost* will be determined. Finally, *profit* equals total revenue minus total cost.

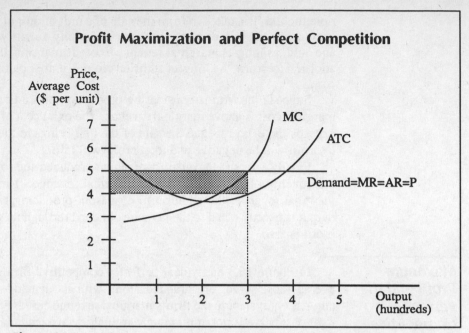

**Figure 16.3** *As long as marginal revenue (MR) exceeds marginal cost (MC), additions to profit are positive. The firm maximizes profit by producing 300 units of output. Total revenue, the product of price and quantity, is the area of the rectangle enclosed by the axes, the $5 price, and 300 units of output. When the profit-maximizing 300 units are produced, average total cost is seen to equal $4 per unit. Total cost, the product of average total cost (ATC) and output, is represented by the area enclosed within the $4 average total cost and 300 units of output. Profit, the difference between total revenue and total cost, is shaded.*

These relationships can be readily used to determine total revenue and total cost in terms of geometric areas. First, one area consistent with the definition of total revenue is found. Second, another area consistent with the definition of total cost is located. Finally, by subtracting the total-cost area from the total-revenue area, a third area consistent with the definition of profit is found.

### FINDING TOTAL REVENUE

In Figure 16.3, the intersection of marginal cost and marginal revenue determines the quantity of output that will maximize profit—300 units. The price at which this quantity of output will be sold is found by looking at the demand curve, which happens to be equal to the marginal-revenue curve under perfect competition. The profit-maximizing price is $5 per unit of output.

The area of a rectangle is equal to the product of two adjacent sides. Consider the rectangle represented by the area enclosed by the axes and found under the demand curve between zero and 300 units of output. One of its sides has a length equal to the distance from the origin to the prevailing price of $5.

The adjacent side's length is equal to the distance from the origin to the profit maximizing quantity of 300. The area of this rectangle is equal to the product of price and profit-maximizing quantity. This is total revenue. With a market price of $5 per unit, given that 300 units of output are sold, the total revenue represented by the area of the rectangle is $1,500.

## FINDING TOTAL COST

The average cost associated with any particular quantity of output is located by finding the point on the average-cost curve directly above the quantity of interest. The corresponding average cost is then found on the vertical axis. In Figure 16.3, to produce 300 units of output, this average cost is $4 per unit. A rectangle with one side's length equal to the average cost of $4 and a length for an adjacent side equal to 300 units of output can then be formed. The area of this rectangle is the product of average cost and quantity, which equals total cost. Total cost therefore equals $1,200.

## FINDING PROFIT

*Profit* is defined as total revenue minus total cost. The difference between the areas representing total revenue and total cost is the shaded area in Figure 16.3. It is the area between $4 and $5 and between zero and 300 units of output. Since total revenue equals $1,500 and total cost equals $1,200, the area representing profit must equal $300.

The area representing profit is also contained within a rectangle. One of its sides is output (300 units). The adjacent side is the difference between average revenue and average cost ($5 – $4). Therefore, it is possible to estimate total profit as the product of quantity times the difference between average revenue and average cost, defined as *average profit*. Using the Greek letter $\pi$ (pi) to represent total profit, this is estimated as

$$\pi = (\$5 - \$4) \times 300 = \$300$$

More generally, profit can be estimated as follows:

$$\pi = (Average\ Revenue - Average\ Cost) \times Quantity$$

or

$$\pi = (Average\ Profit) \times Quantity$$

Using the definitions of total and average revenue, total and average cost, and profit,

$$\pi = \left( \frac{Total\,Revenue}{Quantity} - \frac{Total\,Cost}{Quantity} \right) \times Quantity$$

or

$$\pi = Total\,Revenue - Total\,Cost$$

# THE SUPPLY CURVE UNDER PERFECT COMPETITION

By definition, a firm's supply curve represents the relationship between a product's price and the quantity of output the firm is willing to supply for sale at that price. Through use of this definition, it is possible to derive the supply curve for a perfectly competitive firm.

## Supply, Price, and Output

The perfectly competitive firm has no control over the sale price of its output. Given the price of output, the firm adjusts the output it produces (supplies) in a manner consistent with the maximization of its profits. Under perfect competition, price is equivalent to both marginal revenue and demand. Because the firm constantly seeks to maximize profit, it will always produce the quantity of output at which marginal cost is equal to marginal revenue. Thus the profit-maximizing quantity of output the firm produces can be read from the quantity axis directly below the intersection of the marginal-cost curve and horizontal demand/marginal revenue curve.

### DERIVING THE FIRM'S SUPPLY CURVE

The price of the commodity produced by the perfectly competitive firm is determined by the intersection of the *industry* supply and demand curves. If changes in the location of the supply and demand curves at the industry level lead to a change in the commodity's price, the location of the horizontal demand curve faced by individual firms will also change. A rise in the commodity's price leads to an upward shift in the firm's demand curve; a fall in the commodity's price leads to a downward shift. Such shifts are shown in Figure 16.4.

Three separate demand curves are presented, consistent with three prices for the commodity produced by the firm. The firm's marginal-cost curve is also shown. If price equals $5 per unit of output, the profit-maximizing level of

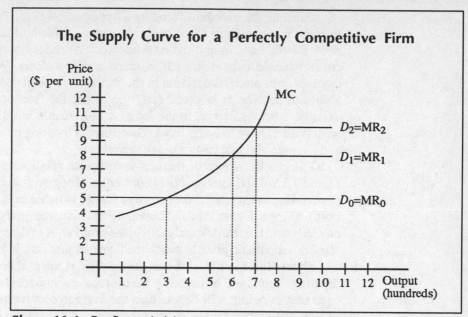

**Figure 16.4** *Profit-maximizing output expands along the marginal-cost curve as the price of output rises. Because it shows the relationship between price and output offered for sale, the firm's marginal-cost curve is equivalent to its supply curve.*

output is 300 units. A price of $5 per unit is equivalent to a marginal revenue of $5 per unit; the marginal-cost curve intersects this level of marginal revenue when 300 units of output are produced. A rise in price to $8 per unit implies that the demand curve has shifted up at all output levels. The equivalence of demand, price, and marginal revenue means that marginal revenue has also risen to $8 per unit. The intersection of marginal cost and marginal revenue now occurs at 600 units. Finally, if price rises to $10 per unit, marginal cost and marginal revenue intersect at a still higher level. Profit will be maximized at 700 units.

**Marginal Cost and Supply.** As seen in Figure 16.4, a rising product price causes the firm to increase the output it offers for sale along its marginal-cost curve. Because supply is the relationship between the price of a product and the quantity offered for sale, the marginal-cost curve for a perfectly competitive firm is equivalent to its supply curve.

## SUPPLY IN THE SHORT RUN AND LONG RUN

The derivation of the firm's supply curve must account for the relationship between price and average costs. To stay in business, the price or average revenue earned from the sale of a product must at least cover the cost of producing the product. Otherwise, the firm will experience a loss or negative profit.

Consider the problems faced by a hypothetical firm. To go into business, the firm must cover its fixed costs, the expenses for buildings and machinery needed before any output can be produced. To produce output, the firm has to cover variable expenses, such as labor and fuel costs. With buildings and machinery in place, production in the short run depends only upon the firm's ability to pay for its laborers, fuel, and so on; the firm only has to cover its variable costs. However, in the long run, the firm's building and machinery wear out and have to be replaced. Therefore, in the long run both average fixed and average variable costs must be covered.

The precise nature of these cost and price relationships is illustrated in Figure 16.5. Total average cost is presented along with average variable cost. (Recall that average total cost equals average variable cost plus average fixed cost.) Marginal cost is also shown. Given that the marginal cost curve is equivalent to the firm's supply curve, the problem is to determine the particular level of output and price at which the firm can just stay in business.

**Short-Run Supply.** If the product's price is lower than average total cost, the firm's profit will be negative; the average revenue received from producing each unit of output will be less than the average cost incurred. However, this fact alone is not sufficient to cause the firm to go out of business, at least in the short run.

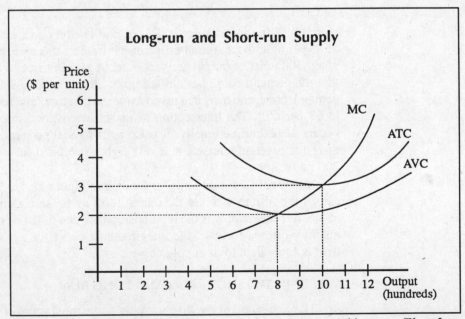

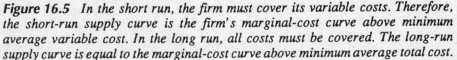

*Figure 16.5 In the short run, the firm must cover its variable costs. Therefore, the short-run supply curve is the firm's marginal-cost curve above minimum average variable cost. In the long run, all costs must be covered. The long-run supply curve is equal to the marginal-cost curve above minimum average total cost.*

In Figure 16.5, the lowest level of output at which the firm can produce and still cover its variable costs is found at the minimum point on its average-variable-cost curve. This occurs at 800 units of output and a price of $2 per output unit. This $2 price equals both marginal cost and *minimum* average variable cost. If the price of output also equals $2, the firm will maximize profit by producing 800 units, the level of output associated with the intersection of marginal revenue and marginal cost. Should price fall below $2 per unit, variable costs are no longer covered. The firm will go out of business. Therefore, in the short run, the firm's supply curve equals its marginal-cost curve above minimum average variable cost.

**Long-Run Supply.** In the long run, the firm must cover both its fixed and variable costs. The minimum point on the firm's average total cost curve therefore represents the beginning of the firm's supply curve in the long run. In Figure 16.5, this occurs at a price of $3 per unit and 1,000 units of output.

Actual production will take place at the intersection of the marginal cost and price-marginal-revenue line. If the price of output is lower than minimum average total cost and above minimum average variable cost, the firm can cover variable costs in the short run; it cannot cover fixed costs. Hence, as buildings and machinery fall into disrepair and are not replaced, the firm will go out of business.

## THE INDUSTRY SUPPLY CURVE

In the short run, the firm's supply curve is equivalent to its marginal-cost-curve at and above minimum average variable cost. Industry output at any price comprises the output of all firms producing in the industry. Therefore, the industry supply curve is the horizontal summation of the supply curves of individual firms in the industry. This implies the horizontal summation of the marginal-cost curves above minimum average variable cost for the firms. Because average costs rise for quantities above minimum average cost, marginal cost will also rise. The industry supply curve will be upward-sloping.

The derivation of the industry supply curve corresponds conceptually to the derivation of the demand curve for a commodity from the model of consumer behavior. Summation of curves is horizontal rather than vertical because the quantity of output offered for sale by each firm varies with the market price. For example, consider an industry composed of two firms. If a market price of $6 per unit leads to the production of 3,000 units by the first firm and 8,000 units by the second, the total quantity offered for sale at the $6 price would be 11,000 units. This is one point on the industry supply curve. Consideration of all other prices and quantities leads to the entire industry supply curve.

It is also possible to discuss the determinants of a perfectly competitive industry's long-run supply curve. However, the shape of this curve depends on long-run adjustments within the industry; these have not yet been covered. The industry's long-run supply curve is discussed after the development of the complete model of perfect competition.

# THE COMPLETE MODEL OF PERFECT COMPETITION

With revenue, cost, profit, and supply characteristics established, it is possible to consider the effects on the perfectly competitive industry of positive, zero, and negative profit levels. When experienced by typical firms in the industry, the presence of positive or negative profits causes price and quantity changes that lead profit levels to move toward zero in the long run. The complete model of perfect competition explains the nature of this adjustment and the implications for firms and consumers.

## Opportunity Cost and Factor Mobility

Economists predict that whenever rates of return are higher in one industry than in another, factors of production will move into the industry that yields the higher rate of return. Thus, if workers with the same training, experience, and education are being paid a higher wage in the steel industry for doing the same kind of work as workers in the shipbuilding industry, it is expected that workers from the shipbuilding industry will seek employment in the steel industry. Expanded to the more general case, if profits in one industry are higher than in another, it is expected that entrepreneurs will shift their organizational efforts to the industry where profits are higher. This is true because the opportunity cost of not shifting resources is the profit that would be earned by doing so. Such movements are expected to occur as long as information is freely available and there are no barriers to entry.

### THE ECONOMIST'S DEFINITION OF PROFIT

From an accounting perspective, profit is the revenue that remains after payments have been made for the inputs of the production process. For economists, profit represents the difference between revenues received by a firm and revenues required by the firm to stay in business. In other words, profit represents a premium paid to entrepreneurs and resource owners. This premium is above the amount necessary to command the services of the inputs. This view of profit is based on the idea that payments to a factor of production should be no greater than the minimum amount necessary to obtain the services of that factor. When only these minimum payments are made, profit will be zero. In an industry where profit is greater than zero, new firms will be started because entrepreneurs shift their resources to obtain the excess rate of return.

## Profit and the Perfectly Competitive Firm

It is assumed that resources will be drawn to those activities that yield the highest rate of return. The presence of profits will draw new entrants into an industry experiencing positive profit levels. With more producers, the industry supply curve shifts to the right. Similarly, negative profits imply that resources are earning a lower rate of return than they could earn in another industry. Firms will leave the industry. With fewer producers, the industry supply curve shifts to the left. Only when profits are zero is there no incentive for firms to enter or leave an industry. When profits are zero for typical firms, the industry is said to be in *long-run equilibrium*.

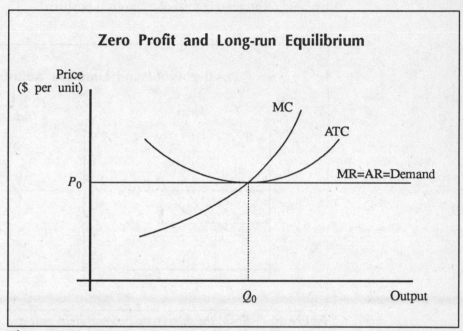

**Figure 16.6** *In the long run, price will be pushed to the level of minimum average total cost. At this point, price also equals marginal cost. Total revenue and total cost are equal, and typical firms earn zero profit.*

In Figure 16.6, profits for the typical firm equal zero when price equals minimum average cost. This occurs at price $P_0$ and quantity $Q_0$. At this price and quantity, the area of the rectangle representing total revenue is exactly equal to the area of the rectangle represting total cost. In this long-run situation, price equals marginal cost.

## POSITIVE PROFIT AND LONG-RUN EQUILIBRIUM

Given positive profits, the nature of the adjustment process that takes place within typical perfectly competitive firms and the perfectly competitive industry is shown in Figure 16.7. In Figure 16.7b, the market price $P_0$ is established at the intersection of industry supply curve $S_0$ and industry demand $D$. The typical firm shown in Figure 16.7a takes price $P_0$ as given, considers it to be the same as its demand and marginal-revenue curves, and maximizes its profit by producing at the quantity associated with the intersection of marginal cost and marginal revenue. The profit-maximizing quantity produced is $Q_0$. Because the area of the rectangle representing total revenue exceeds the area of the rectangle representing total cost, profit is positive.

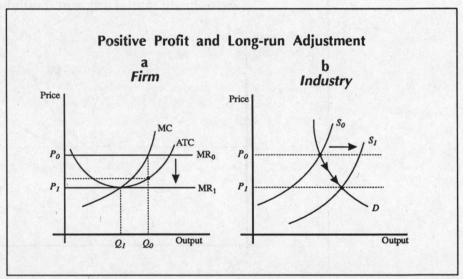

**Figure 16.7**  *From the intersection of marginal cost and marginal revenue, $Q_0$ units of output will by produced by the typical firm. At this level of output, price is greater than average total cost. The existence of profit for typical firms in the industry causes industry supply to shift right because new firms enter the industry. Equilibrium price falls, and individual firms find their demand curves shifting down. Downward pressure on the price ceases when price equals minimum average total cost for typical firms.*

**Positive Profit: Long-Run Adjustment.** The existence of profit for typical firms in the industry will be a fact known to entrepreneurs throughout the economy. Such information is assumed to be freely available under perfect competition. Because there is free entry into and exit from a perfectly competitive industry, new firms will be established in hopes of earning profit. As new firms enter the industry, consistent with the shift factors discussed in the elementary model of supply and demand, the industry supply curve will begin to shift to the right. As it does so, the price of the commodity will fall. For the typical firm in the industry, the horizontal price–demand–marginal-revenue curve will begin to shift downward. This leads to lower intersections with the marginal-cost curve. The firm produces lower levels of output and earns lower levels of profit.

Entry of new firms into the industry continues until profits for typical firms equal zero. In Figure 16.7b, this occurs when the industry supply curve has shifted out to $S_1$ and the price of output has fallen to $P_1$. As seen in Figure 16.7a, at a price of $P_1$, profit for the typical firm is zero; price and average total cost are the same. The typical firm will product $Q_1$ units of output.

**Factors Leading to Positive Profit.** Starting in a position of long-run equilibrium (with firms experiencing zero profits because price equals minimum average total cost) factors that will lead to lower average-cost curves and short-run profits for typical firms include declines in the price of inputs and technological change. These changes reduce the input quantities required to produce given levels of output.

Aside from declines in cost, short run profits for typical firms will also arise when demand for the industry's product increases. An outward shift in industry demand causes price to increase. The average-revenue–marginal-revenue–demand curve shifts up for typical firms. Such a shift in demand could be caused by a change in tastes, a rise in consumer income, increases in the prices of substitute goods, decreases in the prices of complements, increased population, or expectations that the price will rise in the future.

## NEGATIVE PROFIT AND LONG-RUN EQUILIBRIUM

The two panels of Figure 16.8 show a situation in which the equilibrium price established at the intersection of industry supply $S_0$ and industry demand $D$ leads to negative profit for the typical firm. In Figure 16.8a, the profit-maximizing quantity of output is associated with the intersection of marginal cost and marginal revenue. This corresponds to a situation in which the average cost of each unit of output produced, $ATC_0$, exceeds average revenue, $P_0$. Hence, profits are negative. The area representing total cost, given by the formula ($ATC_0 \times Q_0$), exeeeds the the area representing total revenue, given by the formula ($P_0 \times Q_0$).

**Negative Profit and the Long-Run Adjustment Process.** Negative profits cause resource owners to seek employment in other industries where the rate of return is higher. As firms go out of business and leave the industry, the industry supply curve shifts to the left. The equilibrium price established through the intersection of industry supply and demand will therefore rise. This implies that horizontal demand curves for typical firms will rise, resulting in a smaller difference between average revenue and average cost. As long as profit is negative, firms will continue to leave the industry, industry supply will continue to shift left, and price will rise. Profits will ultimately reach zero when revenues just cover costs; at this point, there will be no further incentive to

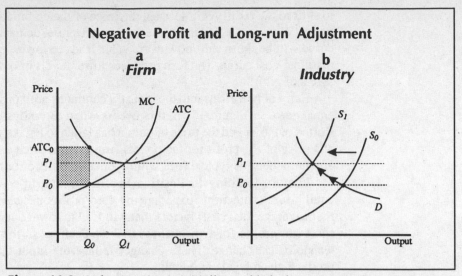

**Figure 16.8** *Industry price is initially established at price $P_0$ through the intersection of supply curve $S_0$ and demand curve D. For the typical firm, marginal cost equals marginal revenue at $Q_0$ units of output. Because average total cost is above price, firms experience the negative profit shown as the shaded region. Profit is still maximized in that any other output level will lead to greater losses. Negative profit causes firms to leave the industry. This shifts industry supply left toward $S_1$ raising equilibrium price. Eventually, price $P_1$, equal to minimum average total cost, will be established along with zero long-run profits.*

leave. In the long run, as seen in Figure 16.8b, supply will shift left to $S_1$. The commodity's price will rise to $P_1$. As seen in Figure 16.8a, this is equal to minimum average cost and marginal cost.

**Other Factors Leading to Negative Profit.** Starting in a position of long-run equilibrium, inward shifts in industry demand cause price to decline. Profits for typical firms become negative because of decreases in average revenue. Specifically, each firm's demand–marginal revenue–average revenue–price line will shift downward, decreasing revenues relative to costs. Such industry demand shifts are caused by changes in tastes, declines in income, declines in the prices of substitute goods, increases in the prices of complements, decreased population, or expectations that the price will fall in the future. From the cost side, factors that can lead to negative profits include increases in factor prices or technological changes that require use of more inputs to produce output. For example, government regulation might require that firms use certain equipment to reduce pollution emissions. Such changes lead to negative profit by causing average and marginal cost curves to shift up.

## Pure Competition and Long-Run Industry Supply

In the long run, the price of output established in a perfectly competitve industry is equal to minimum average total cost. This minimum level is the same for all firms. Suppose there is an increase in industry demand. Output in the industry will be increased as new firms enter the industry. If this occurs without leading to price increases for factors of production, average costs will be constant as the industry's output level increases. In other words, new entrants will face the same cost characteristics as existing firms. While the existence of profits will induce firms to enter the industry, the long-run price adjusts downward to equal minimum average total cost, regardless of the quantity of output produced by the industry. It follows that the industry supply curve will be horizontal, or perfectly elastic.

If expansion in the industry causes the price of one or more factors of production to increase, the long-run industry supply curve will slope upward. As factor prices increase, the average-cost curves for typical firms within the industry will shift upward. Aside from increasing factor prices, the presence of fixed or semifixed factors of production can cause costs to increase through the law of diminishing returns. For example, in response to an increase in oil prices, more firms might enter the oil-drilling business. While the quantity of output will increase, the presence of additional drillers on a given number of oil fields can lead costs to rise because marginal productivity declines.

## Efficiency and Long-Run Equilibrium under Competition

Long-run equilibrium in a perfectly competitive market leads to a situation in which two important types of efficiency are achieved. This occurs because equilibrium involves the equality between the price of a product, the minimum average cost of producing it, and marginal cost. For the typical firm, the equivalence of these measures is seen in Figure 16.6. The equality of cost and revenue measures connects the actions of producers and consumers in a way that achieves optimality for both.

### TECHNICAL EFFICIENCY

The typical firm in competitive long-run equilibrium sells output at a price equal to minimum average total cost. For consumers, this results in prices at their lowest level. Any lower price would cause firms to go out of business. *Technical* or *productive* efficiency refers to this cost-efficient use of resources.

Production at the minimum level of average cost implies that resource use per unit of output is minimized, given the prevailing valuation of inputs. All other levels of output except that associated with minimum average total cost must involve a higher level of expenditure per unit of output for at least one input. Because the average-cost curve represents the costs associated with the most efficient use of resources at each level of output, rearrangements in the mix of inputs used to produce long-run profit-maximizing output will lead only to higher costs.

## ALLOCATIVE EFFICIENCY

Under pure competition, the equality between output price and marginal cost connects the actions of firms with the actions of consumers. *Allocative efficiency* refers to the overall state of optimization that occurs when price is equal to marginal cost.

**Utility Maximization by Consumers.** For consumers, the price of a product represents the dollars that must be given up to gain an additional unit of the good. For the last unit purchased, the satisfaction or utility the consumer derives must be worth exactly the number of dollars paid for the product. Suppose that, after purchasing a unit of the good, the consumer would still derive more satisfaction from purchasing another unit than from holding dollars to purchase other goods. Additional units of the good should be purchased. Under the law of diminishing marginal utility, additional purchases yield less and less utility. Purchases should continue until a state of equality exists between the satisfaction obtained from the purchase of an extra unit and the satisfaction that comes from holding onto the dollars. In this way, the consumer's utility is maximized.

At the utility-maximizing level of output, no additional units of the good can be purchased without causing the utility valuation of the money spent to exceed the utility valuation of the good gained. In this optimal state, let $P$ represent the price of the good and MU represent the marginal utility obtained from the purchase of the last unit. If it were possible to measure marginal utility in terms of dollars, it would be the case that

$$P = \text{MU}$$

At the optimal state, the extra dollar's worth of utility obtained through acquisition of the last unit is exactly equal to the price paid for the good. It is in this sense that the price of a good reflects optimization for consumers.

**Profit Maximization by the Firm.** From the perfectly competitive firm's perspective, when price equals marginal cost the firm is maximizing its profit; marginal revenue and price are the same. When price equals marginal cost, it is also true that the extra cost of employing the resources used to produce the last unit of output (marginal cost) is exactly equal to the price the commodity sells for in the market. Letting MC stand for marginal cost,

$$P = \text{MC}$$

**Overall Optimization.** Combining the optimal relationship between price and marginal utility for consumers ($P = \text{MU}$) with the optimal relationship between price and marginal cost for firms ($P = \text{MC}$). The correspondence between the utility received from consuming an additional unit of a good and the marginal cost of its production is expressed as

$$MU = MC$$

The extra value consumers receive from purchase of the product is exactly equal to the extra value of the resources used to produce the last unit of the product.

If the price established in the market is greater than marginal cost, the valuation consumers place on the product exceeds the cost of resources used to produce it. Consumer satisfaction and profit can be increased by producing more units. Under the law of diminishing returns, increased output will lead to increased marginal costs. Under the law of diminishing marginal utility, consuming extra units leads to declines in the utility gained. Thus, expansion of output will bring marginal cost, marginal utility, and price into equality.

*In this chapter the assumptions and definitions underlying the model of perfect competition have been presented, and the basic model has been developed. As captured in the definitions of technical and allocative efficiency, in an economy where perfect competition prevails, prices are pushed to their lowest possible level, goods are produced in a manner which uses resources most efficiently, and the valuation consumers make for products is equivalent to value of the resources used in producing them. Although it represents an ideal state, this model provides a means of explaining price adjustments and changes in the level of output for a number of products in both the short run and the long run. In dealing with real-world problems, public policy is often focused on ensuring the efficiency that emerges when the assumptions underlying the model of perfect competition are satisfied. Aside from this, the model of perfect competition serves as a basis of comparison with other types of market structure considered in the next several chapters.*

## Selected Readings

Layard, P. R. G. and A. A. Walters. *Microeconomic Theory*. New York: McGraw Hill. 1978.

Mansfield, Edwin. *Microeconomics, Theory and Applications*. New York: W. W. Norton. 1991.

# 17

## The Monopoly Model

*M*onopoly and perfect competition lie at opposite ends of the competitive spectrum. Rather than many competitive firms acting as price takers, under monopoly there is only one firm producing and selling output to consumers at a price it establishes. In this chapter, the factors leading to domination of an entire industry by a single firm are discussed. Modification of the assumptions underlying the model of perfect competition provides the basis for analyzing monopolistic behavior. A model is developed that shows how the monopolist determines the profit maximizing price and quantity of output sold and the nature of the conditions the monopolist finds optimal. The monopolist's failure to achieve allocative and technical efficiency is also examined. The model is then extended to cover the case of natural monopoly, a form of monopoly that can be beneficial to consumers.

## THE COMPONENTS OF THE MONOPOLY MODEL

As in the development of the model of perfect competition, analysis of monopoly behavior begins with assumptions regarding the market in which the monopolist operates. Next, assumptions regarding the nature of demand and cost are made, so that the shapes of the various revenue and cost curves used can be ascertained. Finally, assumptions concerning the optimizing behavior of the monopolist are made. Like perfectly competitive firms, monopolists are assumed to maximize profit. Given this assumption, the relationship between cost and revenue curves reveals the optimal quantity and the price of output from the monopolist's perspective.

## Assumptions Underlying the Monopoly Model

Under pure competition, it is assumed that many firms produce a homogeneous product making use of freely available information concerning costs and production techniques. Firms can enter or exit the perfectly competitive industry at will. Under monopoly, there is only one firm. A single product is produced, and there are no close substitutes for it. If consumers desire the product, they have no alternative but to purchase it from the monopolist. In addition, information is not freely available; the monopolist can have trade secrets. Finally, it is not possible for other firms to enter freely into competition with the monopolist. In other words, there are barriers to entry that limit competition.

## The Monopolist's Revenue Curves

The assumptions underlying the monopoly model have important consequences for the determination of profit maximizing price and output. As in the model of perfect competition, supply considerations are based on cost curves, and demand for the monopolist's product underlies development of revenue curves. The shapes of the cost and revenue curves play an important role in analyzing the behavior of the monopolist. In the subsections that follow, important features of the monopoly demand and revenue curves are discussed, with special attention to the straight-line demand curve.

### THE MONOPOLIST'S DEMAND CURVE

Demand curves are based on the utility-maximizing behavior of consumers. The industry demand curve represents the quantities of output demanded by all consumers at different prices. Under perfect competition, the quantity demanded and the equilibrium price are determined at the intersection of the industry's supply and demand curves. Each firm in the industry shares in producing a small portion of the total industry output. Under monopoly, since there is only one producer, the firm and the industry are the same. Therefore, industry and firm demand are identical. The monopolist's demand curve is still based on utility-maximizing decisions of consumers and still provides information on average and marginal revenues. When combined with information concerning marginal and average costs, it is possible to determine the monopolist's profit maximizing level of output and to identify total revenue, total cost, and the total level of profit.

**Average Revenue and Demand.** Figure 17.1 shows a typical monopolist's demand curve. Consistent with the law of demand, it is downward-sloping; higher prices lead consumers to demand fewer units of output. Because there is only one firm in the industry, the industry demand curve also represents the monopolist's average revenue curve. This is easily seen by recalling and making use of the definitions of *total* and *average revenue*. For example, if the price of output is $15 per unit, the monopolist will sell 10,000 units. Total revenue, the product of price and quantity, will equal $150,000. Average revenue, equal to total revenue divided by quantity, is therefore equivalent to the price of $15.

**Marginal Revenue and Demand.** The shape of the firm's average-revenue curve implicitly provides information concerning the location of the firm's marginal-revenue curve. Recall that when the average value is falling, as it does along the demand curve, the marginal value will be located below the average. Consistent with this relationship, as shown in Figure 17.1, the marginal-revenue curve is below the demand curve.

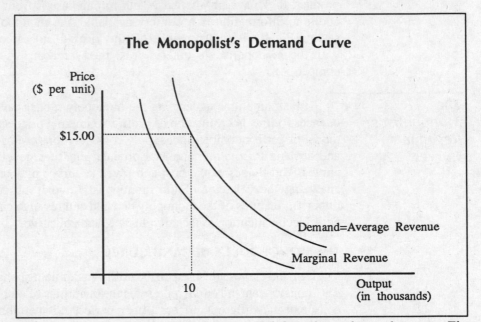

*Figure 17.1 Under monopoly, industry and firm demand are the same. The demand curve is equivalent to the average-revenue curve. Consistent with the downward slope of the average-revenue curve, marginal revenue is below the average-revenue curve.*

### THE STRAIGHT-LINE DEMAND CURVE

In analyzing the behavior of the typical monopolist, use is often made of a straight line demand curve. The downward-sloping straight line is the simplest representation of demand and has a number of interesting implications for elasticity values, the marginal-revenue curve, and the total-revenue curve. If demand is drawn as a straight line with price (*P*) on the vertical axis and quantity (*Q*) on the horizontal axis, as an equation it can be represented by

*Straight–Line Demand:* $P = B - mQ$

*B* represents the vertical intercept, the price at which quantity demanded drops to zero; *m*, along with the minus sign, represents the slope of the demand curve. Suppose *B* equals 2,000 and *m* equals 4. The demand equation is then

$$P = 2,000 - 4Q$$

This demand function is graphed in Figure 17.2a. The intercept of the demand curve is $2,000 and the slope of the curve is minus 4.

**Total Revenue and Straight-Line Demand.** By definition, total revenue is equal to price times quantity. Multiplying both sides of the straight-line demand equation by *Q* yields

$$Total\,Revenue = PQ = BQ - mQ^2$$

This equation will give rise to a total-revenue curve shaped like an inverted U. Based on the demand curve shown, Figure 17.2b shows the inverted U shape of the firm's total-revenue curve when demand is a straight line. This total-revenue curve is estimated using the equation

$$PQ = 2,000Q - 4Q^2$$

Total-revenue values can be estimated by considering different levels of output. When output is zero, total revenue equals zero. If 250 units of output are produced and sold, total revenue equals $250,000 [(2,000 × 250) − (4 × 250$^2$)] Over the initial range of output to 250 units, the positive product BQ outweighs the negative $mQ^2$ effect. Hence, total revenue rises. For levels of output above 250 units the magnitude of 4 times quantity squared, ($mQ^2$), begins to dominate the product of 2,000 times $Q$, ($BQ$). This causes total revenue to decline and to fall eventually to zero at 500 units of output.

**Marginal Revenue and Straight-Line Demand.** Whenever the demand curve is a downward sloping straight line, the marginal-revenue curve will possess the same intercept as the demand curve, but it will be twice as steep. The marginal-revenue curve for a straight-line demand curve will always intersect the quantity axis halfway between the origin and the point of intersection of the demand curve.

*Marginal revenue* is defined as the change in total revenue brought about by a change in total output. For total revenue to increase, marginal revenue must be positive. In Figure 17.2b, total revenue rises continuously from zero to 250 output units. Hence, as shown in Figure 17.2a, marginal revenue is positive between zero and 250 units. Because total revenue grows at a decreasing rate, marginal revenue becomes smaller and smaller. Because total revenue stops growing at 250 units, marginal revenue is zero there. Beyond 250 units, total

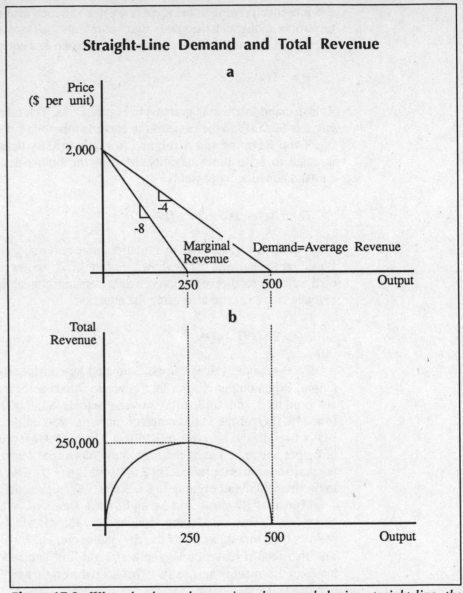

## Straight-Line Demand and Total Revenue

**a**

Price
($ per unit)

2,000

-4

-8

Marginal
Revenue

Demand=Average Revenue

250        500        Output

**b**

Total
Revenue

250,000

250        500        Output

***Figure 17.2*** *When the demand curve is a downward-sloping straight line, the marginal-revenue curve will also be a downward-sloping straight line twice as steep as the demand curve. Marginal revenue intersects the price axis at the same point as the demand curve. It intersects the quantity axis at a point halfway between the origin and the point of intersection of the demand curve. When the demand curve is a straight line, the total-revenue curve has an inverted U shape. Total revenue rises as long as marginal revenue is positive. After 250 units of output, total revenue falls because marginal revenue is negative beyond this output level.*

revenue falls continuously. Hence marginal revenue is negative beyond 250 units.

Note that marginal revenue and demand both intersect the price axis at $2,000. The quantity intercept of the demand curve is found at 500 output units. The quantity intercept for marginal revenue is located at 250 units of output, halfway between zero and the quantity intercept of the demand curve. Consistent with the relationship between marginals and averages, the marginal revenue curve is below the downward-sloping average-revenue–demand curve. The marginal revenue curve shown in Figure 17.2a is a straight line. This follows directly from the fact that the demand curve upon which it is based is a straight line. Because the marginal-revenue curve intersects the quantity axis halfway between the origin and the point where the demand curve intersects the quantity axis, the marginal-revenue curve is twice as steep as the demand curve. Since the demand curve's slope is minus 4, the slope of the marginal-revenue curve is minus 8.

**Elasticity Values and Straight-Line Demand.** The elasticity of demand represents the percentage change in quantity that occurs with a 1 percent change in the price of a product. Elasticity values help to determine whether changes in a product's price lead to increases or decreases in total revenue. If demand is elastic, the elasticity value is greater than 1; a decline in the price of a product

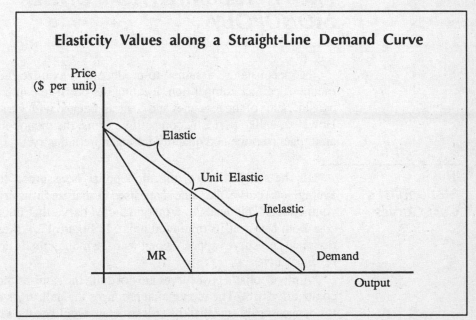

**Figure 17.3** *When a price decrease leads to an increase in total revenue, marginal revenue must be positive, and demand is elastic. Price decreases leading to a negative marginal revenue imply that total revenue falls. Hence demand is inelastic. When marginal revenue is zero, demand is unitary elastic.*

will cause total revenue to increase because the percentage increase in quantity sold offsets the effects of a lower price. Demand is inelastic when the elasticity value is less than 1. A decline in price causes total revenue to fall; the rise in output sold is more than offset by the decline in price.

For the straight-line demand curve, declines in price are associated with increases in total revenue as long as marginal revenue is positive. In Figure 17.2, this occurs between zero and 250 output units. The range of output values associated with positive marginal revenue therefore corresponds to elasticity values greater than 1. Conversely, over the range of output values where marginal revenue falls below zero (where marginal revenue falls below the quantity axis), declines in price cause total revenue to decline. Therefore, demand is inelastic over this range. Finally, at the point on the demand curve where marginal revenue is just equal to zero, a decrease in price must be exactly offset by an increase in quantity sold. Hence, the elasticity of demand equals 1. The range of elasticity values along the straight-line demand curve and the relationship between marginal revenue and elasticity values are shown in Figure 17.3.

# PROFIT MAXIMIZATION UNDER MONOPOLY

Monopolists are assumed to produce to maximize their profit. As in the model of perfect competition, locating the profit-maximizing output involves consideration of the revenues and costs associated with various levels of output. However, unlike perfectly competitive firms, the monopolist's decisions have an impact on price and quantity for an entire industry.

## The Monopolist's Cost Curves

In the standard case, the monopolist is assumed to face a U-shaped average-cost curve, the same shape used to analyze firms in the model of perfect competition. This leads to a marginal-cost curve that intersects average total cost from below at its minimum point. In Figure 17.4, these average cost and marginal cost curves appear, along with the monopolist's demand and marginal revenue curves.

A monopolist's cost curves are not quite the same as those for the perfectly competitive firm. The monopolist produces the industry's entire output, and it is not necessarily true that the cost structure would be the same if the industry's output was spread out and produced by many small firms. Differences in economies of scale may affect the shape of the cost curves. In the case of *natural monopoly*, as output increases, average cost falls. Thus there are cost advantages to producing large quantities of output.

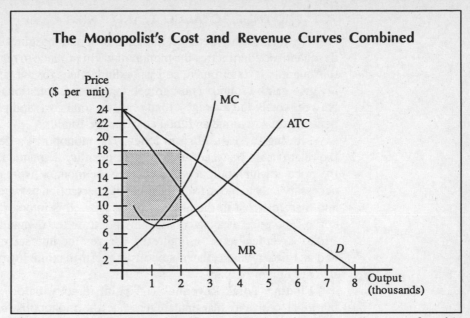

## The Monopolist's Cost and Revenue Curves Combined

**Figure 17.4** *Monopolists face the same U-shaped average-cost curves found in the model of perfect competition. When combined with its revenue curves, the monopolist's profit-maximizing output is found on the quantity axis below the point where marginal cost equals marginal revenue. Profit-maximizing price is then found at this quantity using the demand curve. Total revenue is the area represented by the product of price and quantity. Total cost is the area represented by the product of average total cost and quantity. Profit, the difference between total revenue and total cost, is shown as the shaded area. When the monopolist maximizes profit, price is greater than marginal cost.*

**Profit Maximizing Conditions for the Monopolist**

In the model of perfect competition, the profit-maximizing level of output is found at the intersection of the firm's marginal-revenue and marginal-cost curves. This condition holds true for the monopolist. In Figure 17.4, consider the marginal-cost and marginal-revenue curves. Over the initial range of output, the marginal-revenue curve is above the marginal-cost curve; marginal revenue exceeds marginal cost. Therefore, additions to revenue obtained through production and sale of extra units of output exceed additions to cost. Hence, additions to the monopolist's profit are positive. Given the upward slope of the marginal-cost curve and the downward slope of the marginal-revenue curve, additions to revenue are ultimately offset by additions to cost. Producing beyond the point at which marginal cost equals marginal revenue implies that more costs would be incurred in producing extra units than the revenues received through sale of those units. Hence, the addition to total profits would be negative. The profit-maximizing quantity associated with the intersection of marginal cost and marginal revenue equals 2,000 units of output.

## TOTAL REVENUE, TOTAL COST, AND PROFIT

The relationship between marginal cost and marginal revenue determines the quantity of output that the monopolist will produce to maximize profit. Once this quantity is determined, corresponding values for average cost and average revenue can be found. Through geometric representations of the relationship between totals and averages, total revenue, total cost, and profit (the difference between total revenue and total cost) can be found.

**Finding the Equilibrium Price.** The monopolist's demand curve shows the relationship between price and the quantity demanded. Therefore, to find the price at which output will sell when the monopolist maximizes profit, it is necessary only to move from the point of intersection between marginal revenue and marginal cost to the point directly above this intersection on the demand curve. The price associated with this point on the demand curve is then read from the vertical axis. In Figure 17.4, given the intersection of marginal cost and marginal revenue, the monopolist's profit-maximizing price is seen to equal $18 per unit of output.

**Finding Total Revenue.** The point directly below the intersection of marginal cost and marginal revenue is the monopolist's profit-maximizing output. Total revenue is the product of price and quantity. Therefore, the monopolist's profit-maximizing total revenue is represented by the rectangle formed by enclosing the area below profit-maximizing price, to the right of the vertical axis, to the left of profit maximizing quantity, and above the horizontal axis. Given the profit-maximizing price of $18 per unit of output and the profit maximizing quantity of 2,000 units, this area can be seen in Figure 17.4. Total revenue will equal $36,000.

**Total Costs.** The average cost of producing the profit-maximizing output is represented as the vertical distance between that quantity and the point on the average-cost curve directly above it. The actual value of average cost is read from the vertical axis. In Figure 17.4, the average cost of producing the profit-maximizing output of 2,000 units is $8 per unit. Total cost equals the product of average cost and quantity. It is represented by the rectangle formed using these values as its sides. Total cost equals $16,000.

**Profit.** Total profit is the difference between total revenue and total cost. It is represented by the difference between the area representing total revenue and the area representing total cost. In Figure 17.4, the shaded area represents this difference. Given the monopolist's total revenue of $36,000 and total cost of $16,000, total profit equals $20,000. Because marginal cost equals marginal revenue at 2,000 units of output, no higher level of profit can be achieved by the monopolist.

*Profit Maximization: Monopoly versus Perfect Competition*

In comparing the profit-maximizing condition of the monopolist and the perfectly competitive firm, there are both similarities and differences. Because both monopolists and perfect competitors maximize profit, both produce at the output level corresponding to the intersection of marginal cost and marginal revenue. However, because the monopolist faces a downward-sloping demand curve, marginal revenue and average revenue are not the same. Therefore, the intersection of marginal revenue and marginal cost does not lead to equality between marginal cost and price.

## DIFFERENCES IN PRICE AND OUTPUT

Under perfect competition, firms produce where price equals marginal cost. For price to equal marginal cost, the quantity of output and the price must correspond to the intersection of the marginal-cost curve and the demand curve. In Figure 17.4, the monopolist's marginal-cost curve intersects the demand curve to the right of the profit-maximizing output and below the price the monopolist will charge. The monopolist therefore charges a higher price and produces a lower output than would prevail in a perfectly competitive industry.

Seen from another perspective, under perfect competition, the industry supply curve represents the horizontal summation of marginal-cost curves for the firms in the industry. Output is produced at the point where industry supply intersects industry demand. At this point, marginal cost equals price. The monopolist's marginal-cost curve can be viewed as the supply curve of a perfectly competitive industry taken over by a single firm. When the monopolist maximizes profit by producing the output associated with the equality of marginal cost and marginal revenue, price is increased above the perfectly competitive level, and output is reduced.

**Monopoly and Efficiency.** Price is greater than marginal cost under monopoly. Because the monopolist's price does not equal marginal cost, allocative efficiency is not present. This implies that consumer valuation of an additional unit of the product exceeds the cost of producing an additional unit of the product. Society's welfare could be increased by producing more units. In other words, society values the product more than it values the resources used to produce the product. Use of the additional resources necessary to produce extra units of output would lead to greater overall utility, but monopoly prevents this.

There is no guarantee that the monopolist's profit-maximizing output will be produced at minimum average total cost. Even if technical efficiency is achieved under monopoly, consumers do not benefit because they pay a price greater than minimum average total cost.

**The Long Run and the Short Run.** In the model of perfect competition, nonzero profits cause firms to enter the industry; entrepreneurs and resource owners attempt to acheive the highest rates of return. Because of barriers to entry, this does not occur in the monopoly model; profits can persist in both the long run and the short run.

## Price Discrimination

In the model discussed so far, all buyers willing to pay the one prevailing market price can obtain as many units of output as they desire at that price. Under a system of *price discrimination* , the seller of a product is able to charge different prices to different consumers. This occurs even though producing the units of output sold to each customer does not involve distinguishable differences in cost. Examples of price discrimination are common. As means of increasing sales, new customers are sometimes given special prices. The post office charges lower rates to non-profit organizations and to advertisers than to the general public. Lawyers and doctors might charge one rate for well-to-do clients and another, lower rate for poorer clients. Electric utilities are able to vary their prices depending upon the quantity of electricity purchased. Large customers pay lower prices per kilowatt hour than do small customers.

### THE CONDITIONS NECESSARY FOR PRICE DISCRIMINATION

For price discrimination to exist, consumers must have no alternative except to buy the product from the price discriminator. This implies that all firms in an industry must cooperatively engage in price discrimination. Otherwise, the presence of competition would drive the product's price down to a single level for all output sold and for all customers. Achieving such cooperation among firms is unlikely. Therefore, a monopolist is in an excellent position to regulate the prices charged to different customers. However, once the product is sold to a consumer, it must not be possible to sell it to someone else. Otherwise, "secondary" markets would develop. Individuals who paid low prices for the product would attempt to resell it to others who might have to pay more if they purchased it directly from the price-discriminating monopolist. In addition to these requirements, the price discriminator must be able to identify or somehow sort out those buyers willing to pay higher prices from those willing to pay less.

### PRICE DISCRIMINATION AND THE MONOPOLIST

The existence of price discrimination alters the analysis of monopoly behavior somewhat. The monopolist will still maximize profits. However, because the price charged to different customers varies, there are modifications to the monopolist's marginal-revenue curve and profit-maximizing output. In the extreme case, the price-discriminating monopolist is able to extract all *consumer surplus*, the difference between what consumers are willing to pay and what they actually have to pay for a good. This is accomplished by charging consumers the price on the demand curve associated with each unit of output sold.

As shown in Figure 17.5, the highest price that someone is willing to pay for a unit of output is $35, while the customer purchasing the one-thousandth unit will buy it only if its price is $5. Under price discrimination, units in between are also sold for whatever price they command on the demand curve. Marginal revenue, the extra revenue the firm receives from the sale of an extra

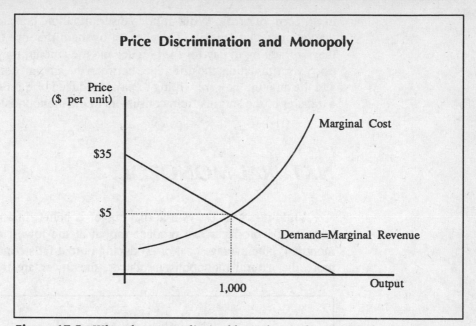

**Figure 17.5** *When the monopolist is able to charge the price on the demand curve for each separate unit, demand and the marginal-revenue curve become one and the same. Profit is maximized when marginal revenue and marginal cost are equal. Here, the buyer most willing to pay faces a price of $35 per unit, while the last buyer will pay $5 per unit. Because a single price is not established in the market, total revenue equals the entire area below the demand curve. Consumer surplus, the area below the demand curve and above the price of $5, is lost by consumers and gained by the monopolist.*

unit of output, is now found along the demand curve; the sale of an extra unit of output does not involve a decline in the price of *all* other units of output sold. Therefore, the demand curve for the price discriminator is also the price discriminator's marginal-revenue curve.

**Price Discrimination and Profit Maximization.** Profit maximization involves equating marginal revenue and marginal cost. This occurs at the point where the marginal-cost curve crosses the price discriminator's marginal-revenue–demand curve. Before this point, marginal revenue is greater than marginal cost. Hence, additions to profit are positive. Beyond the intersection of the marginal-cost and -demand curves, extra revenues exceed extra costs, and additions to profit are negative. As seen in Figure 17.5, profit is maximized for the price discriminator when output equals 1,000 units. The price of the last unit sold is $5; each unit below 1,000 commands its corresponding price on the demand curve.

The monopolist's profits will be higher than without discrimination. Profit now consists of the entire area below the demand curve and above the marginal-cost curve because the monopolist is able to extract the entire consumer surplus in the form of profit. Without price discrimination, consumers pay the single market price that prevails. They benefit by the difference between the amount they are willing to pay for the product and the amount they have to pay. With price discrimination, the difference between the amount consumers have to pay and the amount they are willing to pay is reduced or eliminated. There is thus a transfer of the surplus from consumers to the monopolist.

# NATURAL MONOPOLY

While it is not always true that bigger is better, in a *natural monopoly* a large single producer can produce output at the lowest cost. Under natural monopoly, the average cost of producing output falls continuously. Thus, the more the natural monopolist produces, the lower are the average costs of

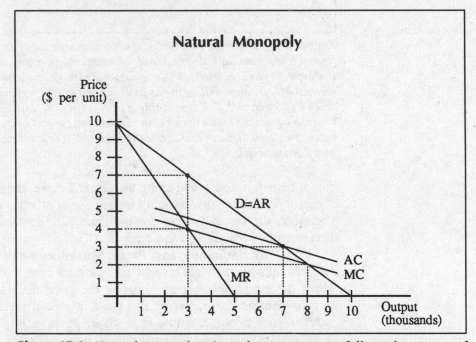

**Figure 17.6** *Natural monopoly arises when average cost falls as the amount of output produced rises. Marginal cost will lie below average cost. Profit is maximized at the level of output where marginal cost equals marginal revenue; a price of $7 per unit would be established, and 3,000 units would be produced and sold. Through regulation, output can be expanded and price lowered until average cost equals average revenue. Price would equal $3 per unit, and seven thousand units would be sold. Allocative efficiency is achieved when price equals marginal cost. Price would equal $2 per unit, and 8,000 units would be sold.*

production. The problem that arises with natural monopoly involves finding ways of ensuring that consumers benefit from the lack of competition and the decreasing costs that come with increased scale.

## Cost and Profit Under Natural Monopoly

The relationship that holds between marginals and averages is as follows: When the average is rising, the marginal is above the average, and when the average falls, the marginal is below the average. With regard to cost, when the average-cost curve declines over the entire range of output, the marginal-cost curve will always lie below the average-cost curve. This situation is shown in Figure 17.6. The monopolist, the only firm in the industry, faces a downward-sloping demand curve. If the monopolist is free to choose any level of output, profits are maximized at the intersection between the marginal-revenue and marginal-cost curves. This occurs when 3,000 units of output are produced. As usual, price will be determined on the demand curve at the point directly above the optimal quantity, and its magnitude is read from the vertical axis. The natural monopolist will charge $7 per unit of output.

### REGULATION, ALLOCATIVE EFFICIENCY, AND NATURAL MONOPOLY

Allocative efficiency is not automatically achieved with a downward-sloping average-cost curve. As in the standard monopoly situation, when freely determined by the natural monopolist, price is observed to be greater than marginal cost. To achieve allocative efficiency, output and price must correspond to intersection between the demand curve and the marginal-cost curve; only at this point does price equal marginal cost. Because marginal cost is less than average cost, under natural monopoly this would occur at a price lower than average total cost. Such a price would cause profits to be negative; the natural monopoly would go out of business in the long run.

**The Role of Regulation.** Natural monopolies, such as telephone companies and electric utilities, are often regulated to compensate for the inequity thought to exist when there is no competition and to insure that consumers share in the benefits created by declining average costs. Regulation ensures that lower prices are maintained and a greater quantity of output produced than would occur under pure monopoly. However, from the regulatory point of view, the problem of determining the price that should be charged remains.

A price equal to average cost, found at the intersection of the demand curve and the average-cost curve, will enable the natural monopolist to cover all costs at the going rate of return. In Figure 16.6, output would be expanded to 7,000 units, and price would fall to $3 per unit. But because this price exceeds marginal cost, overall welfare can be increased by lowering the price further, so that it equals marginal cost. Because it is below average cost, a price equal to marginal cost will not enable the monopolist to cover all costs. In Figure 16.6, price equals marginal cost at a price of $2 per unit; 8,000 output units will be produced. However, there is a loss on each unit produced. Eventually the monopolist would go out of business; the benefits of both marginal-cost pricing and size would be lost.

**Subsidizing Natual Monopoly.** One way to achieve allocative efficiency under natural monopoly is to pay the monopolist a subsidy that covers the costs of production when the price charged for output equals marginal cost. If the size of the subsidy is less than the value derived from consuming extra units of the natural monopolist's output at a lower price, it is in society's interest to pay such a subsidy.

Figure 17.7 portrays the variables and points of concern. The demand curve shows the relationship between price and quantity demanded. A price set at A allows the monopolist to break even because the price charged is exactly equal to average cost. One thousand units would be produced and profit would be zero. However, allocative efficiency is achieved at price F where price equals marginal cost. This price corresponds to point E where the marginal cost curve intersects the demand curve. At this point 1,500 units would be produced. Point D on the average cost curve is located directly above point E. It determines the average cost, G, of producing the output at which allocative efficiency is achieved. The difference between average cost G and price F represents the loss

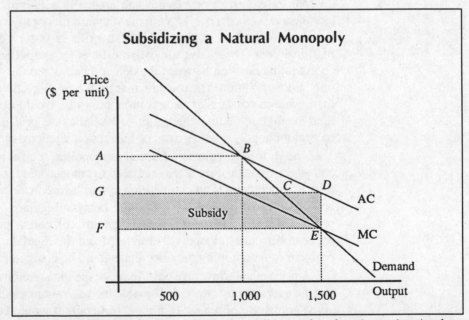

**Figure 17.7** *The monopolist could cover all costs by charging price A where average cost and average revenue are equal. Allocative efficiency is achieved at price F where price equals marginal cost. However, average cost will then exceed average revenue by the difference between G and F. To ensure that the natural monopolist can stay in business, a subsidy equivalent to the area G–D–E–F must be paid.*

the natural monopolist will incur on each unit of output. When all units of output up to the demand curve at point $E$ are considered, the area $D$–$E$–$F$–$G$ represents the subsidy that must be paid to the natural monopolist so that total costs can be covered.

   *Consumer surplus* refers to the difference between what consumers are willing to pay for a product and the amount they actually have to pay. The area $A$–$B$–$E$–$F$ under the demand curve represents the gain in consumer surplus that occurs when price is lowered from $A$ to $F$. The gain totally encloses the area representing the subsidy except for the triangular area enclosed by $C$–$D$–$E$. The consumer surplus in excess of the subsidy is represented by the area $A$–$B$–$C$–$G$. Because area $A$–$B$–$C$–$G$ exceeds area $C$–$D$–$E$, the gain in consumer surplus exceeds the cost of the subsidy. A net gain in welfare is possible by paying the subsidy, having the monopolist produce the output associated with the intersection of marginal cost and demand, and charging a price equal to marginal cost.

*The monopoly model predicts that monopolists will restrict output and raise the price of output compared to the situation that would prevail under perfect competition. Therefore, allocative efficiency is not achieved under monopoly. Extending the monopoly model to the monopolist who is also a price discriminator, the output the monopolist offers for sale will increase, but so will the monopolist's profit. This profit comes at the expense of lost surplus to consumers. Under natural monopoly, the benefits of lower costs at higher levels of output can be achieved when there is a single seller. To ensure that consumers benefit from these lower costs, regulation can reduce price to the level of average cost or marginal cost. However, because marginal cost is below average cost when average cost is falling, if the price is set at marginal cost, the monopolist must be subsidized to stay in business.*

   *In the following chapter, models of other market structures are developed that capture the characteristics of competition between the extremes of perfect competition and monopoly. Analysis occurs in the same general framework as that used to study perfect competition and monopoly. Attention is again focused on the nature of competition and the attainment of efficiency.*

**Selected Readings**

Layard, P. R. G. and A. A. Walters. *Microeconomic Theory*. New York: McGraw Hill. 1978.

Mansfield, Edwin. *Monopoly Power and Economic Performance*. New York: W. W. Norton. 1978.

Mansfield, Edwin. *Microeconomcs, Theory and Applications*. New York: W. W. Norton. 1991.

# *APPENDIX*

## *Finding Marginal Revenue Using Calculus*

*Marginal revenue* is defined as the change in total revenue that comes with a one-unit increase in the quantity of output sold. It represents the derivative of total revenue with respect to output. Given a straight-line demand curve described by the equation

$$P = B - mQ$$

total revenue is defined as

$$PQ = BQ - mQ^2$$

Marginal revenue is found by taking the derivative of the total revenue function:

$$Marginal\ Revenue = \frac{d(Total\ Revenue)}{d(Quantity)} = \frac{d(BQ - mQ^2)}{dQ} = B - (2m)Q$$

There are two important details to notice. The marginal-revenue curve has the same intercept, (B), as the demand curve. It is also negatively sloped. However, the absolute value of the slope of the demand curve is $m$ while the absolute value of the slope of the marginal-revenue curve is $2m$. The marginal-revenue curve is therefore twice as steep as the demand curve. If $m$, the slope of the demand curve, is minus 4, the slope of the marginal revenue curve will be minus 8.

# 18

## Imperfect Competition: Monopolistic Competition and Oligopoly

*B*etween the extremes of perfect competition and monopoly lie a variety of market structures. Oligopoly and monopolistic competition are the two categories studied most often within this range. Unlike the model of perfect competition, under monopolistic competition and oligopoly, firms have some control over the price of their output. Through advertising, they may also have some ability to control the demand for their product. Unlike the monopoly model, under monopolistic competition and oligopoly, firms must be concerned about the presence and actions of other firms in the industry.

To explain how equilibrium prices and quantities are determined in monopolistically competitive and oligopolistic markets, models using cost and revenue curves are developed. This is the same approach used to study perfect competition and monopoly. However, the presence of different underlying assumptions results in new equilibrium states for monopolistic competitors and oligopolists. Once these optimal states are established, they are compared with the efficiency conditions achieved under perfect competition.

# MONOPOLISTIC COMPETITION

As the name implies, firms within a monopolistically competitive industry share some of the characteristics of perfectly competitive firms and some of the monopoly. Consistent with the model of perfect competition, monopolistic competition is characterized by the presence of many firms, the availability of complete information, and freedom of exit and entry. Unlike perfect competition, the products produced by monopolistically competitive firms are not homogeneous. Because each firm in the industry produces a product that differs in some slight way from the products of its competitors, individual firms are similar to monopolies. However, because competitor's products are close substitutes, firms do not have real monopoly power.

Wheat farming usually serves as an example of perfect competition and electrical power as an example of monopoly. Monopolistic competition is exemplified by the presence in most cities and towns of many small retail outlets selling similar products, such as gasoline or dry-cleaning services. Product differentiation under monopolistic competition does not always involve actual differences between products. Instead it involves perceived differences due to factors such as location and quality of service. Firms in the industry may engage in advertising or other forms of nonprice competition to increase demand for their product.

## Monopolistic Competition: Short-Run Profit Maximization

As with analysis of other forms of competition, understanding the market characteristics experienced by monopolistic competitors requires that the cost and revenue curves faced by the typical firm be specified. Because monopolistic competitors are assumed to maximize their profits, the relationship between marginal cost and marginal revenue determines the optimal quantity of output: Given this quantity, the demand curve determines the price at which output will be sold. The presence of free entry and exit implies that positive profits in the short run will lead to greater competition. This competition results in a long-run state of zero profit.

### REVENUE CURVES FOR THE MONOPOLISTICALLY COMPETITIVE FIRM

The good produced by a monopolistically competitive firm is assumed to differ in some way from the goods produced by other monopolistic competitors. Because of this *product differentiation*, the typical firm will find that it can alter the price of its product to affect the quanity of output sold. Therefore, like a monopolist, the monopolistic competitor will face a downward-sloping demand curve. Recall, there are no close substitutes for the product produced by a monopolist. This is not the case under monopolistic competition; competitors sell products that are similar in all but a few respects. The typical demand curve for a monopolistically competitive firm will be more horizontal or elastic than that for a typical monopolist.

**Demand and Marginal Revenue.** By definition, a firm's demand curve is equivalent to its average-revenue curve. Because the monopolistically competitive firm's demand curve is downward-sloping, the marginal-revenue curve will lie below the demand curve. (When the average is falling, the marginal is below the average.)

## SHORT-RUN PROFIT MAXIMIZATION UNDER MONOPOLISTIC COMPETITION

Figure 18.1 presents the revenue and cost curves for a typical monopolistically competitive firm. The firm's average-cost curve has the standard U shape used for the model of perfect competition. Consistent with the relationship between marginal cost and average cost, the marginal cost curve is below average cost when average cost is falling; it intersects the average cost curve at its minimum point, where average cost neither rises nor falls; it rises above average cost when average cost is rising.

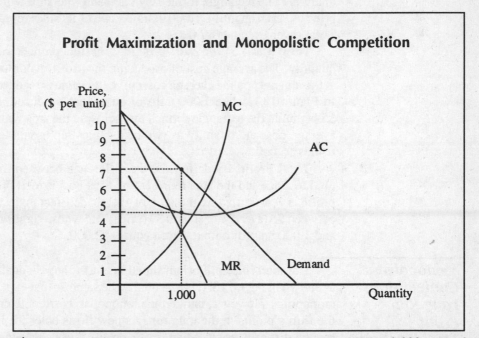

**Figure 18.1** *Marginal cost (MC) equals marginal revenue (MR) at 1,000 units of output. Given this quantity, the firm can charge a price of $7 per unit. At 1,000 units, average cost (AC) is seen to equal $5 per unit. Profit is $2,000.*

**Profit-Maximizing Output.** Additions to a firm's profit are positive as long as the marginal revenue received from the sale of an additional unit of output exceeds the marginal cost incurred in producing that unit. Profit is maximized when marginal cost equals marginal revenue. Given the downward slope of the marginal-revenue curve and the upward slope of the marginal-cost curve, in Figure 18.1 marginal revenue exceeds marginal cost until their intersection at a quantity of 1,000 units of output. Production past this output level leads to cost additions that exceed revenue additions. Hence, beyond 1,000 units, additions to profit will be negative; total profit will be less compared with that attained at the intersection of marginal cost and marginal revenue.

**Profit-Maximizing Price.** The marginal-revenue curve used to determine profit-maximizing output is based on the firm's demand curve. Marginal revenue explicity captures the effects on the firm's revenues of selling various levels of output at the corresponding prices on the demand curve. Therefore, to find the equilibrium price, we find the point on the demand curve directly above the profit-maximizing quantity and read this price from the vertical axis. As seen in Figure 18.1, the price corresponding to the profit-maximizing quantity of 1,000 units is $7 per unit of output.

**Total Revenue.** *Total revenue* is defined as the product of price and quantity. The rectangle formed by enclosing the area with profit-maximizing price ($7) and quantity (1,000 units) as two of its sides represents total revenue. Total revenue equals $7,000.

**Total Cost.** *Total cost* is defined as the product of average cost and quantity. The average cost of producing the profit-maximizing output is found at this quantity on the average cost curve. Its value is read from the vertical axis. In Figure 18.1, when 1,000 units of output are produced, average cost equals $5 per unit. The rectangle formed by enclosing the area with profit-maximizing average cost and quantity as two of its sides represents total cost. Total cost equals $5,000.

**Total Profit.** By definition, the difference between the area representing total revenue and the area representing total cost is total profit. In Figure 18.1, profit is represented as the area of the shaded rectangle whose left side lies between $5 (average cost) and $7 (price) and whose right side lies between zero and 1,000 units of output. Profit equals $2,000.

*Monopolistic Competition: Long-Run Profit Maximization*

The short-run equilibrium situation of a monopolistically competitive firm, as shown in Figure 18.1, is essentially the same as that experienced by a typical monopolist. However, unlike the monopolist, barriers to entry will not protect the firm's profits in the long run. As new firms enter the industry, the typical monopolistically competitive firm's profits will be driven to zero. The lack of barriers to entry ensures that rates of return from factors of production will be no greater in the monopolistically competitive industry than those prevailing in other sectors of the economy.

### THE EFFECTS OF ENTRY ON THE MONOPOLISTIC COMPETITOR

Given the presence of profits for typical producers, new firms will enter the monopolistically competitive industry. The goods and services provided by the new firms will closely correspond to those already produced in the market. The greater availability of substitutes will entice some customers of existing firms to make their purchases from the new entrants. Hence, as new firms enter, the *demand curves* for existing firms begin to shift inward and may also become flatter. Given the relationship between marginal revenue and demand, marginal revenue also shifts inward; it will intersect marginal cost at a lower level of output. Because the inward shift in the demand curve results in lower levels of average revenue at all levels of output, profit declines. Ultimately, profit equals zero.

## PORTRAYING LONG-RUN EQUILIBRIUM GRAPHICALLY

For profit to be positive, average revenue (demand) must be above average cost at the level of output produced. When profits are zero, average cost is exactly equal to average revenue. For profits to be zero under monopolistic competition, the entry of additional firms into the industry must finally lead to a situation where the typical firm's demand curve is just tangent to a point on the downward-sloping portion of the average-cost curve.

As shown in Figure 18.2, this occurs when the quantity of output equals $Q^*$. All other points on the average cost curve are above the demand curve; no other quantity of output allows the firm to cover all its costs. Because other quantities of output lead to lower (in fact, negative) profits, profit is maximized. Therefore, marginal cost and marginal revenue must intersect just below the point of tangency between the demand curve and the average total cost curve.

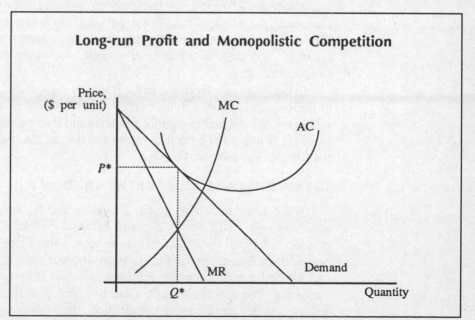

*Figure 18.2* *Profit-maximizing output is found at the intersection of the marginal-revenue and marginal-cost curves. Because average cost is tangent to demand at this quantity, price equals average cost, and profit is zero.*

With profits equal to zero, there is no incentive for additional firms to enter the industry. Should they do so, the typical firm's demand curve will shift further inward, causing average costs to exceed average revenues at all levels of output. In this situation, the firm will still maximize its profit (minimize its losses) by producing the quantity of output associated with the intersection of marginal cost and marginal revenue. However, because profits are negative, resources can be allocated to other industries and earn a higher rate of return. Thus the presence of negative profit for a typical monopolistically competitive firm also represents a short-run situation. Firms will leave the industry, and demand curves for individual firms will shift out. Only zero profit is associated with long-run equilibrium.

## CHARACTERISTICS OF LONG-RUN EQUILIBRIUM

As seen in Figure 18.2, the monopolistically competitive firm's profit-maximizing output is found at the point of tangency between its demand curve and the downward sloping portion of its U-shaped average-cost curve. This level of output is to the left of the output level corresponding to minimum average total cost. The difference between these two output levels is known as *excess capacity*. Because of excess capacity, the monopolistically competitive firm does not achieve technical or productive efficiency in the long run. Average production costs (and therefore resource use per unit of output) can be decreased by producing more output.

**Allocative Efficiency.** At the long-run optimal quantity of output, the price charged by the monopolistically competitive firm is greater than marginal cost. Therefore, the marginal valuation of output by consumers exceeds the resource costs of producing an extra unit; overall well-being can be enhanced by expanding output.

In the long run, compared to the perfectly competitive firm, there is a loss of both allocative and technical efficiency. However, compared to monopoly with respect to the higher equilibrium price and lower equilibrium quantity, the situation is likely to be far less severe because of the highly elastic nature of the typical firm's demand curve.

## THE BENEFITS OF PRODUCT DIFFERENTIATION

When firms maximize profit, allocative and technical efficiency can be achieved only if the firm's demand curve is perfectly horizontal. But the presence of a horizontal demand curve means that price differentials are the only factor affecting consumers' decisions to purchase output. Thus, if technical and allocative efficiency are achieved, product differentiation is no longer important. Therefore, although allocative and technical efficiency are not achieved under monopolistic competition, the presence of a wide variety of differentiated products means that a better match is possible between consumer preferences and the goods and services available in the market. Consumers may derive extra utility from the choices available to them. This characteristic of monopolistically competitive long-run equilibrium suggests that the loss of allocative and technical efficiency may be offset by the benefits derived from the variety of goods and services.

# OLIGOPOLY

*Oligopoly* represents a type of market structure in which a few firms dominate in the production of a good or service. Examples include the airline, automobile, steel, and tobacco industries. The fact that industries may produce a homogeneous product, such as steel, or differentiated products, such as the various brands of cigarettes and models of automobiles, implies that the degree of product differention in the market does not matter in classifying an industry as oligopolistic. Instead, the degree of *market power* possessed by the industry's leading firms is important.

The domination of an industry by a few major producers can occur with the presence of economies of scale. In this circumstance, in order for new entrants to compete effectively, high start-up costs must be incurred. Other barriers to entry, such as lack of brand-name recognition and the inability to obtain patent rights, can also lead to oligopoly. Regulation may also play a role, as seen in the domination of the airwaves for many years by the three major television networks. In addition, firms do not ordinarily reveal marketing strategies, production techniques, or other proprietary information; complete information is not available under oligopoly.

Because the actions of each firm in an oligopoly can have a large impact on the output and profits of others in the industry, there is a far greater degree of interdependence among firms than under perfect or monopolistic competition. Capturing the nature of this interdependence is the main goal of economic models of oligopoly. However, the complicated ways firms can interrelate and react to one another's actions make modeling the behavior of typical oligopolists quite difficult.

Under perfect and monopolistic competition, the presence of a large number of sellers precludes the possibility of implicit or explicit cooperation or collusion. Firms have few options but to accept prevailing market conditions and to act independently. It would be impossible for a single firm to affect the behavior of all or even a small number of other firms. Under monopoly, there is only one decision-maker; the reactions of rivals are not a factor. Under oligopoly, the total demand for output is split among a few large sellers. Therefore, before a firm engages in any action likely to affect existing market shares, it must consider the reactions of its competitors. These actions and reactions must also be incorporated into the models used by economists to study oligopolistic behavior.

Attempts to capture the effects of the actions and reactions that rival firms might initiate have led to a variety of approaches in modeling oligopolistic behavior. The *kinked-demand-curve-model* of oligopolistic behavior is probably the most widely known. Other approaches examine the effects of dominant firms, price leadership, and collusion. Game theory, which involves consideration of the expected payoffs associated with various market stategies, is another way of analyzing the behavior of oligopolists.

## The Kinked-Demand-Curve Model

The kinked-demand-curve model, often used to explain the presence of relatively stable prices under oligopoly, is based on assumptions concerning how firms in an oligopolistic industry respond to a price change by one firm. Except for the assumptions concerning the shape of the demand curve, the oligopoly model follows the pattern and makes use of the theoretical structure used to analyze the behavior of perfect competitors, monopolistic competitors, and monopolists.

### REACTIONS TO PRICE CHANGES

In estimating its share of market demand for the product it produces, an oligopolistic firm must consider the reactions of its rivals if a decision is made to raise or lower price.

**Reactions to Price Decreases.** If the actions of firms were totally independent of one another, the decision by one firm to lower the price of its output would be expected to increase the quantity of output the firm sells. However, an increase in sales for one firm in an oligopolistic industry can result in significant sales reductions for the other firms. Hence, rather than ignoring the initial oligopolist's decision to lower its price, other oligopolists are logically expected to follow suit and lower their prices. They do so to maintain or increase their market shares. Although the quantity of output demanded increases in the industry, each firm's share of the increase is less than would be the case if the other firms had not also lowered their prices.

**Reactions to Price Increases.** If an individual firm in an oligopoly raises its price, it will naturally expect the quantity of output sold to decrease. The decline in the quantity of output sold would be much less if other firms in the industry followed along and raised their prices too. Customers desiring the product would face a higher price from all sellers. However, other oligopolists will not necessarily follow. Their overall level of sales will increase if they do not raise their prices because, compared with the oligopolist that raises its price, their price is lower. This implies that the decline in sales for a firm that raises its price could be substantial.

### THE OLIGOPOLIST'S KINKED-DEMAND-CURVE

To see how the reactions of other firms in an oligopolistic industry affect the demand for a typical firm, two demand curves are shown in Figure 18.3. Demand curve I is more horizontal than demand curve II; it reflects the relationship between price and quantity demanded if the other oligopolists in the industry do not react to price changes by the firm. Assume initially that equilibrium price and quantity are established at point *B*, the point where the two demand curves cross. If the firm's actions induce no response from its rivals, a drop in price from $P_b$ to $P_c$ will move the firm along curve I from point *B* to point *C*. There is a relatively large increase in quantity demanded. Similarly, an increase in price from $P_b$ to $P_a$ will move the firm along demand curve I from point *B* to point *A*. Quantity demanded falls by a relatively large amount. However, if the price decrease induces other oligopolists to lower their prices, the increase in the quantity of output sold will be less than that shown along demand curve I. Instead of moving from point *B* to point *C*, the oligopolist will find sales increasing only to the level associated with point *c* on demand curve II.

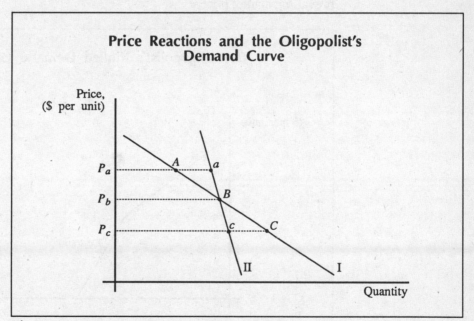

**Figure 18.3** *The shape of a typical oligopolist's demand curve depends on the reaction of its rivals. Beginning at point B, when other oligopolists follow suit, a decline in price from $P_b$ to $P_c$ leads to increased quantity demanded along demand curve II. When other oligopolists fail to follow suit, raising price from $P_b$ to $P_a$ leads to decreased quantity demanded along demand curve I.*

If the firm decides to raise its price, it would prefer to see its rivals follow suit. This would lead to the reduction in output from point *B* to point *a* on demand curve II; quantity demanded would not fall by much. However, because the other oligopolists in the industry are more than happy to see declining sales among their rivals, this response does not occur. Instead, the firm's decision to increase price leads to the larger decrease in quantity seen in the movement from point *B* to point *A* along demand curve I.

The fact that other oligopolists match price decreases with corresponding price decreases but fail to match price increases implies that the typical oligopolist faces a demand curve composed of two sections. Above the price that prevails in the market, a firm's price increases lead to relatively large (or elastic) quantity decreases because rivals respond by not raising their prices. Below the price that prevails in the market, a firm's price decreases lead to relatively small (or inelastic) quantity increases because rivals respond by lowering their prices. The complete demand curve for the typical oligopolist is therefore more horizontal or elastic over its inital output range than over the range beyond the point on the demand curve associated with the prevailing market price. As seen in Figure 18.4, the typical oligopolist's demand curve is kinked at $P^*$, the prevailing market price.

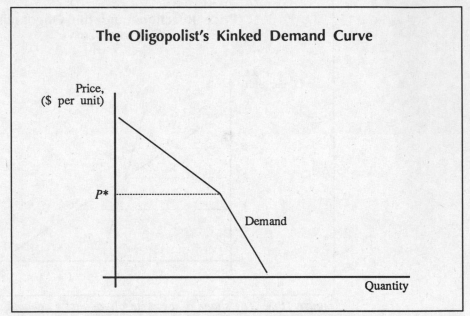

**Figure 18.4** *Consistent with the price response of its rivals, increases in price above the established market price P\* lead to large sales reductions; decreases in price below the established level lead to small sales increases.*

**Marginal Revenue and the Kinked-Demand Curve.** Recall that the firm's demand curve is equivalent to its average-revenue curve. Because marginal revenue lies below average revenue when average revenue is falling, the marginal-revenue curve can be found under the downward-sloping average-revenue (demand) curve. The presence of a kink in the oligopolist's demand curve has a special effect on the nature of the marginal-revenue curve. This effect is best understood by recalling the relationship between demand and marginal revenue when the demand curve is a downward sloping straight line: The marginal-revenue curve is also a downward-sloping straight line twice as steep as the demand curve. This means that the marginal-revenue curve intersects the horizontal axis exactly half the distance between the origin and the intersection of the demand curve with the horizontal axis. The steeper the demand curve, the steeper the marginal-revenue curve.

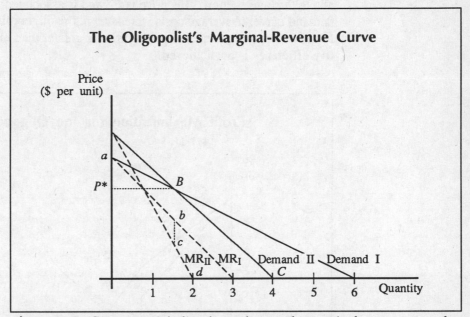

**Figure 18.5** *Given a straight-line demand curve, the marginal-revenue curve has the same price intercept but is twice as steep. The oligopolist's effective demand curve is denoted a–B–C. The corresponding marginal revenue curve is shown as the dotted line a–b–c–d.*

In Figure 18.5, the relevant demand curve for a typical oligopolist is composed of the portion of curve I from point *a* to point *B* and the portion of curve II beyond point *B* to point *C*. Consistent with the oligopolist's kinked demand curve, the marginal-revenue curve is also seen to possess two distinct portions. Marginal-revenue curve I is effective for levels of output up to the kink, from points *a* to *b*. Marginal revenue curve II, from points *c* to *d*, is effective for levels of output beyond the quantity associated with the kink. The vertical gap or discontinuity that exists between these two marginal revenue curves is considered part of the oligopolist's overall marginal revenue curve. The oligolopist's entire marginal-revenue curve is the line formed by *abcd*.

## PROFIT MAXIMIZATION AND THE KINKED-DEMAND CURVE

Figure 18.6 portrays the typical oligopolist's kinked-demand curve and associated marginal-revenue curve. In addition, the oligopolist's marginal-cost curve is shown. Under the assumption that oligopolists seek to maximize profits, output is produced to the point at which marginal cost equals marginal revenue. As shown Figure 18.6, marginal cost intersects marginal revenue in its vertical range. The oligopolist charges the price on the demand curve directly above this intersection. This price is $P^*$ and is associated with the kink in the demand curve. If average costs were shown, the oligopolist's profits could be found in the usual manner. Because price is greater than marginal cost, allocative efficiency is not achieved.

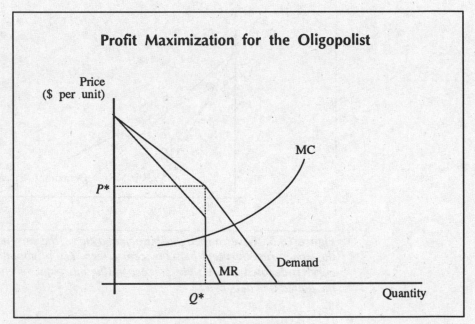

**Figure 18.6** *The vertical segment of the marginal-revenue curve is consistent with the kink in the oligopolist's demand curve. Profit is maximized when marginal cost intersects marginal revenue. As long as shifts in marginal cost lead to intersection with marginal revenue in its vertical range, profit-maximizing output and price remain unchanged.*

**Price Stability under Oligopoly.** In terms of price stability, the kinked demand curve and the vertical portion of the marginal-revenue curve indicate that shifts in marginal cost may not lead to a change in the quantity of output produced or the price. As long as shifts in the marginal-cost curve lead to an intersection with the marginal-revenue curve in its vertical range, the desire to maximize profits dictates that no change in price or quantity will occur.

## Price Leadership and Implicit Collusion

Another model of oligopolists' behavior is based on the assumption that the price of output for the industry is determined by the the price-setting actions of one firm in the industry. Serving as the basis for models of this type is the assumption that other firms in the industry follow suit even without *explicit collusion* (written contracts or verbal agreements designed to reduce competition). Acceptance by firms of *tacit price leadership* (an understanding by all firms in the industry that the price leader's price will be followed) precludes the necessity of developing stategic responses to the actions of other firms. If the price leader raises its price, so do all other firms in the industry. It is not necessary for the same firm always to initiate price changes. The understanding is that a price increase by any firm will be followed by all other firms.

### NON-COLLUSIVE PRICE LEADERSHIP

If the major firms in an oligopoly experience similar cost and revenue characteristics, following a price leader can represent an optimal pricing strategy. In this situation, cost increases or demand shifts are likely to affect all firms simultaneously. Because the underlying reasons for price changes will be known to all firms, a price change by one firm will be seen as a means of maintaining existing market shares if all firms follow suit.

**The Dominant Firm.** In some oligopolistic industries, production of total market output is split between one large producer controlling a significant portion of the market and many other smaller producers. The large producer is known as the *dominant firm*; the many small producers are known as the *competitive fringe*. The demand curve for the dominant firm is estimated as follows: at each price, the quantity of output that would be *supplied* by the firms in the competitive fringe is subtracted from the overall industry demand curve. The remaining quantity demanded at each price represents the dominant firm's demand curve. The dominant firm uses this demand curve to estimate its marginal revenue curve; it then acts like a monopoly in setting price and determining its level of output. The price established by the dominant firm is taken as given by the firms in the competitive fringe.

### EXPLICIT COLLUSION

Though prohibited by law, cooperation among oligopolists in establishing market price can lead to higher profits and greater stability for firms that participate. Through such cooperation, firms can achieve an outcome similar to that found under monopoly. Therefore, monopoly-like models are often used to analyze the gains from cooperation. Aside from a desire to maximize profits, firms might also collude to reduce competition. For example, prices might be set high enough to ensure acceptable profit levels but low enough to keep potential new entrants out of the market. Collusive firms therefore forgo short-run profits to ensure continued profits in the long run.

**Cartels.** A *cartel* exists when collusive behavior between oligopolists takes the form of written agreements or other formal arrangements regarding output price and quantity. OPEC, the Organization of Petroleum Exporting Countries, is the most notable cartel in recent times. Because of cooperation among its members, oil prices were quadrupled in the early 1970s, and then this increase was doubled in the late 1970s. Because OPEC members had control over such a large fraction of the world's oil reserves and the agreement involved pricing practices established by soverign governments, there was little that countries adversely affected by OPEC's actions could do to prevent the cartel's actions. During the height of OPEC's power, smaller producers around the world acted as a competitive fringe accepting the price established by the dominant "firm," the OPEC cartel.

The circumstances created with the formation of cartels tend to lead to their disintegration in the long run. While OPEC managed to raise the price of crude oil above competitive levels, the resulting high profits caused other producers to enter the industry. For example, with the development of North Sea oil reserves, Great Britain has become self-sufficient in crude oil, and other non-OPEC oil producers have also expanded output. In addition, high prices led many members of OPEC to cheat on their production quotas to increase profits. These actions, substitution away from petroleum products caused by their high price, and lower oil demand during the major recession of 1982 finally led to significant crude-oil price decreases in the mid and late 1980s. OPEC has not yet recovered.

## Game Theory

*Game theory* provides another means of modeling the behavior of oligopolists. Under the game theory approach, firms within an oligopoly consider their actions regarding price changes or changes in other variables along with the possible reactions of their competitors. The combination of a given action and a competitor's reaction leads to a certain payoff or profit for the firm. Given its predictions of all such reactions and payoffs, the firm uses a *decision rule* to determine its optimal action.

### THE PAYOFF TABLE

The process of decision-making used in game theory is often portrayed through use of a *payoff table*. For oligopolistic decision making, the rows of the payoff table represent possible actions by a firm; the columns represent actions or reactions by its rivals. Column headings are also referred to as *states of nature* because the firm has no direct control over them.

Table 18.1 shows a typical payoff table. Here an oligopolist is assumed to have three choices: the price of output can be raised, or it can be lowered; in addition, the oligopolist can engage in nonprice competition through advertising. As represented by the column headings, in reaction to the decision made by this oligopolist, rivals will either raise their prices, lower their prices, or engage in advertising. At the intersection of rows and columns is the change in profit, or the payoff, that the firm will experience from each action given the response of its rivals. For example, if the firm decides to lower its price and its rivals respond by engaging in advertising, the firm that lowers its price will find its profits increased by $400.

| Possible Payoffs from Changing Price or Advertising | | | |
|---|---|---|---|
| | Other Oligopolists' Reactions | | |
| **Firm's Action** | Raise Price | Lower Price | Advertise |
| Raise Price | $1,100 | –$2,100 | –$1,000 |
| Lower Price | $900 | $700 | $400 |
| Advertise | $600 | $1,000 | $500 |

*Table 18.1*

## THE MAXIMIN CRITERION

To determine what action the oligopolist should undertake, a decision rule is needed. Under the decision rule known as the *maximin criterion*, the *worst* possible payoff for each possible action is determined. The firm then chooses the action that leads to the largest of the worst possible payoffs.

In Table 18.1, first find the worst payoffs associated with each action. If the firm raises its price above the current level, at worst it will lose $2,100 if other firms lower their prices. If the firm lowers its price, at worst its profits increase by $400, if other firms respond by advertising. If the firm engages in an advertising campaign, the worst outcome will add $500 to its profit. Because it leads to the best of the worst possible payoffs, the optimal strategy under the maximin criterion is to start an advertising campaign.

## THE MINIMAX REGRET CRITERION

An alternative decision rule involves calculation of the loss, or *regret*, the firm will experience by chosing a certain action. Under each possible reaction by other oligopolists, the firm will experience regret when an outcome other than the best outcome occurs. For example, when other firms decide to raise their prices, the only action that leads to no loss or regret occurs if the firm raises its price. In this case, the firm earns $1,100 and experiences the best outcome, given the reaction of its rivals. If it had lowered its price and other firms had decided to raise theirs (row two, column one), the firm would add $900 to its profit, but it loses out on the extra $200 that could have been earned if it had raised its price instead; its regret is $200. Similarly, a decision to advertise, with other firms raising their prices, brings in $600. But this is $500 worse than if it had raised its price along with other firms.

The entire regret table is shown in Table 18.2. Under the minimax-regret criterion, the firm should choose the action that minimizes its maximum regret. When the firm decides to raise its price, the maximum regret that occurs is $3,100. This is the largest or maximum value in the action row labeled Raise Price. The maximum regret from lowering price is $300. The maximum regret from advertising is $500. The smallest of these maximum values is $300. The firm should choose to lower its price under the minimax criterion.

| Possible Regrets from Changing Price | | | |
|---|---|---|---|
| | Other Oligopolists' Reactions | | |
| Firm's Action | Raise Price | Lower Price | Advertise |
| Raise Price | $0 | $3100 | $1,500 |
| Lower Price | $200 | $300 | $100 |
| Advertise | $500 | $0 | $0 |

**Table 18.2**

## THE PRISONER'S DILEMMA

By altering the shape of the payoff matrix, another means of portraying the interconnectedness of oligopolistic decision-making is seen in the *prisoner's dilemma game*. Each of the four squares in Figure 18.7 represents payoffs associated with the actions of two firms. Each firm has the option of raising price or holding price constant. As seen in the lower-right square, a decision to hold price constant will lead to no change in either firm's profits. However, if

| The Prisoner's Dilemma | | |
|---|---|---|
| | B raises price | B holds price constant |
| A raises price | Payoff (A) = $200<br>Payoff (B) = $200 | Payoff (A) = -$100<br>Payoff (B) = $100 |
| A holds price constant | Payoff (A) = $100<br>Payoff (B) = -$100 | Payoff (A) = 0<br>Payoff (B) = 0 |

**Figure 18.7**   *The payoff an oligopolist can expect from any action depends on the reaction of its rivals. If both firms hold prices constant, there is no gain to either firm. If firm A holds its price constant in response to firm B's price increase, firm A earns $100, while firm B loses $100. Should both firms agree to raise prices, each gains $200.*

firm A raises price while firm B holds price constant (the upper-right square), A loses $100 and B earns $100. Similarly, a decision by firm B to raise price while firm A holds price constant (the lower left square) leads to a $100 loss for B and a $100 gain for A. If both firms raise their prices, each will gain $200.

This model of oligopolistic behavior points out the benefits of tacit price leadership in an industry and the benefits of explicit collusion. Without some form of collusion, it is in the interest of both firms to keep price constant because of the possible losses involved in raising price. However, an implicit or explicit agreement to match price increases with price increases leads to increased profits for both firms. It simultaneously reduces the risk associated with noncollusive strategic pricing (independent pricing decisions designed to offset the negative impact of a rival's pricing decision).

*In this chapter various models of competition between the extremes of perfect competition and monopoly have been presented. These models attempt to explain the behavior of firms where factors other than price are relevant. Because most output generated in modern economies is produced by firms that are neither monopolists nor perfect competitors, such models are extremely important in understanding, describing, and making predictions about business activity. They explain why prices tend to be fairly stable for some products and why prices often move simultaneously in the same direction. These models also explain why firms engage in advertising and why the conditions leading to free competition are sometimes violated.*

**Selected Readings**

Chamberlin, Edward. *The Theory of Monopolistic Competition*. Cambridge, MA: Harvard University Press. 1933.

Layard, P. R. G., and A. A. Walters. *Microeconomic Theory*. New York: McGraw Hill. 1978.

Mansfield, Edwin. *Microeconomics, Theory and Applications*. New York: W. W. Norton. 1991.

Robinson, Joan. *The Economics of Imperfect Competition*. London: Macmillan. 1933.

Scherer, F. M. *Industrial Market Structure and Economic Performance*. Chicago: Rand McNally. 1980.

Von Neuman, John, and Oskar Morgenstern, *The Theory of Games and Economic Behavior*, New York: John Wiley & Sons, 1944.

# 19

## The Organization, Financing, and Regulation of Business

*Economic classifications of business activity depend upon the nature of competition in the production of particular goods. The characteristics that define perfect competition, monopolistic competition, oligopoly, and monopoly allow analysis of pricing and output decisions made by firms in a given market structure and the evaluation of profit-maximizing states in terms of technical and allocative efficiency. Another useful way to classify businesses is according to their legal form of organization. This categorization allows us to consider the advantages and disadvantages of different forms of business organization in terms of decision-making, financing, and liability.*

*In addition to the laws concerning ownership and control of businesses, regulations are imposed by government regarding what constitutes acceptable business behavior. It is here that legal forms of organization and the competition-based classifications used by economists overlap to some degree. This chapter provides an overview of the forms of business organization, discusses methods by which businesses are financed, and covers the nature and range of business regulation.*

# THE ORGANIZATION OF BUSINESS

Three forms of organization are used to classify firms in the business world. The most popular form is the *single* or *individual proprietorship*, seen in the many small privately owned businesses found in every city and town. Intermingled with these are *partnerships*, businesses owned by two or more individuals. Finally, there are *corporations*. These are sometimes so small as to be indistinguishable from single proprietorships, but they are also represented by automobile manufacturers and the other giant companies that are highly visible producers in our economy. For those involved in business activity, each form of organization has advantages and disadvantages. These are generally placed into the categories of *control*, *financing*, and *liability*.

## The Individual Proprietorship

The most simple and most numerous type of business organization is the individual proprietorship. Under this form of business organization, one individual owns and generally runs a company.

### CONTROL

Beginning an individual proprietorship requires individual initiative, a salable product or service, and enough money to get things going. Decisions concerning business operations are not shared; as long as no laws are violated, the owner is answerable to no one concerning the firm's activities. All profits from the business belong to the owner and need not be shared with partners or shareholders. For tax purposes, these profits are treated as income, and normal income-tax rates apply.

### LIABILITY

While the proprietor reaps all profits when times are good, if things do not go well for the business, the owner is responsible for all losses. In fact, the proprietor has *unlimited liability* for the debts incurred in running the business. Aside from losing whatever capital may be invested in the firm, the owner's personal assets, such as a house or automobile, can be used to settle claims against the firm.

### FINANCING

While being one's own boss has certain advantages, an individual proprietor will generally experience financial constraints. Financing for expansion of the firm depends solely upon the personal resources of the owner and loans.

## The Partnership

The partnership is a more complicated form of business organization than the simple proprietorship. More than one individual is involved, and a written legally binding contract is usually drawn up stating each partner's responsibility. Aside from this, there are few other legal complications involved in establishing a partnership.

### CONTROLLING THE PARTNERSHIP

Partners can run the business themselves, or they can hire a manager to run the business. Disadvantages to partnership arrangements occur when partners disagree about how the business should be run. Management of the firm can become inefficient when squabbling over who is in charge occurs. In addition, legal complications can arise when a partner dies or no longer wishes to be associated with the business. Such events can lead to dissolution of the partnership.

### LIABILITY

As with the single proprietor, partnerships face unlimited liability for their business. Should some partners not be able to cover their share of liabilities, other partners must bear the burden, even if this includes the loss of personal property. The existence of *limited partnerships* offsets this disadvantage somewhat. Under this form of partnership, only the *general partner* is fully responsible for the business's liabilities. Other partners, known as *limited partners,* have liability only to the extent of their holdings in the firm.

### FINANCING THE PARTNERSHIP

The presence of more than one partner means that the business has access to more funds for establishing, operating, or expanding the business. Profits from the enterprise are split among the partners in accordance with their contract. For tax purposes, these profits are treated as income, and normal tax rates apply. Thus the firm's profits are taxed only once. Although partnerships are generally able to finance larger operations than individual proprietorships, funding limitations are still likely to constrain expansion.

## The Corporation

In terms of overall sales, the corporation is the most important form of business activity. To incorporate, a charter is obtained for a fee from the state in which the business plans to operate. Businesses organized as corporations have a number of advantages. Because the corporation can sell ownership shares (stocks) to individuals or to the general public, it has access to a large pool of funds for financing expansion. These shares can be freely traded in the *stock market*, so that the problems of ownership transfer experienced by partnerships are avoided. When someone no longer wishes to be an owner of the corporation, the shares are sold.

The disadvantages of incorporation center mainly around the *double taxation* of corporate profits. When a corporation earns profits, they are, at least in part, distributed to the corporation's shareholders. However, the profits are taxed both before and after distribution. The profits the corporation earns are first subject to the *corporate income tax*. Once the remaining profits have been distributed to the corporation's shareholders, they are treated as individual income and taxed again.

## CONTROL OF THE CORPORATION

The owners of the corporation are the shareholders. However, in most large corporations there are so many shareholders that it is impossible for all of them to be involved in running the business. Therefore, managers are generally hired to run things; ownership and control of the corporation are thereby split.

Ownership of shares of stock entitles one to participate in the control of the corporation. In corporate elections, shareholders cast votes on issues affecting the corporation and vote for members of the board of directors. However, the control a shareholder possesses is directly proportional to the number of shares held. One share corresponds to one vote; ownership of 1,000 shares entitles the owner to 1,000 votes. For most large corporations, individual shareholders own a very small fraction of the total stock. Therefore, the control by any one shareholder is likely to be limited. The positions advocated by management are generally supported in elections.

Management and shareholders do not always have the same objectives. For example, shareholders might be most interested in long-run profit maximization, while managers might focus on short-run sales maximization or activities designed to further their personal gain. For individual shareholders, the costs of understanding management's motives or organizing a sufficient number of votes to change management's behavior may be too high to produce any action. Should management act in a manner that reduces the profitability of the corporation or otherwise leads to dissatisfaction, individuals are free to sell their stock and purchase others from companies that look out better for their shareholders' interests.

## LIABILITY

Legally the corporation is treated as an individual. Therefore, aside from issuing stock to finance its activities, it can also borrow funds, either from a bank or by selling bonds. Should the corporation fail, liability is limited to the assets owned by the corporation. Shareholders cannot lose amounts greater than the value of their stock in the corporation.

## FINANCING CORPORATE ACTIVITY

There are two basic ways a corporation can finance its activities. First, it can use funds generated through product sales. It does so by withholding profits from shareholders. Withheld profits are known as *retained earnings*. A second means of acquiring funds involves looking outside the corporation for financial support. The corporation can borrow money from a bank, issue stock, or issue bonds.

**Stock.** Both borrowing money and issuing bonds increase the debt of the corporation because the acquired funds must be paid back with interest. However, if stock is issued, the corporation is selling certificates of ownership in itself, and there is no debt. Buyers have obtained a share of the assets of the corporation in exchange for their money. In return, dividends are paid to shareholders. Dividends are payments similiar to interest earned on a savings account. The corporation's rate of profit determines the amount that can be paid; this amount varies from year to year. The total dividend payment any individual recieves is proportional to the amount of stock owned. In other words, a fixed dividend per share of stock is paid. The *dividend yield* is the dividend divided by the price of the stock. The dividend yield is a measure of the rate of return on the stock to its owner. For example, suppose a share of stock costs $100. If the dividend on this stock is $8, the dividend yield is 8 percent.

Stock is bought and sold in a stock market, such as the New York Stock Exchange. Once a corporation's new issue of stocks is purchased, the corporation is not involved in further sales of that stock. Such transfers take place among participants in the stock market. Stock prices depend upon the number of shares individuals are willing to purchase or desire to sell. Thus, stock prices do not remain stable. They may rise or fall depending upon how potential buyers view the present and future performance of the corporation. If the company's profits are expected to rise in the future, its stock price will rise. Although ownership of stock entitles an individual to part of the corporation's assets if the corporation goes bankrupt, payment does not occur until all other claims on the corporation's assets have been satisfied. Thus ownership of stock in a company is not as risk-free as placing money into an insured savings account.

**Bonds.** A corporation can also issue bonds to finance its activities. Unlike stock, a bond is not a certificate of ownership in the corporation but a loan to the corporation. It represents an obligation to the bondholder that will be repaid by the corporation. Should the corporation go bankrupt, bondholders have prior claim over shareholders to the assets of a corporation. Therefore, holding a bond is less risky than holding stock.

A bond gives the holder no control over the policies of the corporation. Instead, as long as the corporation is not in default, the bondholder is entitled to an interest payment each year the bond is held. Unlike a dividend payment, this interest payment is specified in a contract (the bond certificate) between the corporation and the bondholder. For example, in exchange for $10,000, a corporation might pay $500 per year. This payment does not depend in any way on the profits of the corportion. Bonds are issued for fixed periods of time. The end of this period is known as the *maturity date*. At this time, the original amount, or *principal*, paid to the corporation for the bond is returned to the bondholder.

**The Bond Market.** Just as stocks can be bought or sold in the stock market, there is a market for bonds. Thus, an individual who purchases a bond with a 10-year maturity date can sell that bond to another individual (generally not the corporation that issued it) before ten years are up. Determining the market price of a bond at any point in time depends upon the *market rate of interest*. To induce a person to purchase a bond in the first place, the corporation must offer yearly interest at least equal to the interest the individual could earn elsewhere. If the corporation requires $1000 and the prevailing rate of interest is 5 percent, at least $50 ($1000 × .05) per year must be paid to the potential buyer. *Ceteris paribus*, all else being equal, no rational buyer would purchase a bond offering a return less than the amount that can be earned elsewhere.

**Bond Prices and the Market Interest Rate.** Because the bond is like a loan contract, once an individual has purchased it, the $50 payment comes year in and year out, regardless of the market rate of interest prevailing later on. However, changes in the market rate will affect the *price* (the market value) of the bond. To other potential buyers, the bond represents a promise by the corportion to pay $50 per year to its holder. These buyers ask, "How much does it cost *at the prevailing rate of interest* to generate a return of $50 per year?" If the interest rate has risen to 10 percent, the answer is $500. A bond purchased from a corporation for $1000 when the prevailing interest rate was 5 percent is worth only $500. *The bond's price falls when the market interest rate rises.* On the other hand, if the market rate fell to three percent, $50 per year could be earned only if $1,666.67 were placed in an interest-bearing account. The fall in the rate of interest is associated with a rise in the amount someone would be willing to pay for the right to $50 per year. That is, *the price of the bond rises when the market interest rate falls*. Bond prices and interest rates are *inversely* related.

**The Bond Price Formula.** The formula used to determine the price of bonds maturing far into the future is

$$Bond\ Price = \frac{Annual\ Interest\ Payment}{Market\ Rate\ of\ Interest}$$

The annual interest payment is similar to any interest payment while the bond price is the sum it takes to achieve this payment. The annual interest payment is assumed to be known; it is determined when the bond is initially issued. To determine the present bond price, divide the annual payment by the market rate of interest.

# THE REGULATION OF BUSINESS

With the the growth of large corporations has come increased regulation by government. This regulation is designed to ensure that the benefits of competition are maintained and the rights of individuals protected. As seen in the discussion of monopoly and oligopoly, the presence of a dominant firm in an industry can lead to higher prices and lower output than would prevail under competition. Thus, whether achieved through diligent and honest effort or through collusion, the concentration of market power in the hands of one or several firms can have adverse effects for consumers. Aside from concern over bigness, regulation also deals with product safety, worker safety, the safety of consumers, the preservation of plant and animal species affected by productive activities and their by-products, and the effects of production on finite resources. The rationale and effects of each of these types of regulation are discussed next.

## Controlling Monopoly Power

One of the most important forms of government regulation concerns the limitation of market power, usually a function of the relative size of firms in an industry. The laws to control monopoly power and ensure fair business conduct are discussed in this section. Attention is first focused on the way firm size and potential monopoly power are measured. Next, specific laws are discussed.

### MERGERS, CONCENTRATION, AND MONOPOLY POWER

In the monopoly model, a single firm has sole control of output in an industry. In viewing problems associated with the development of monopoly power in the real world, a number of factors must be examined. First is the question of merger activity. When two firms join together, does it always follow that competition will be reduced? Second is the question of size. Does an extremely large dollar volume of sales indicate the presence of monopoly power? In analyzing monopoly power, both economists and the courts have paid special attention to these matters.

**Market Share and the Concentration Ratio.** A firm's *market share* is the ratio of its total sales to total industry sales. Under monopoly, market share is 100 percent. Firms producing under pure competition have minute market shares. The *concentration ratio* measures the market power of the leading firms in an industry. The concentration ratio is the fraction of total industry sales composed of the sales of the largest firms in the industry. The four leading firms in the industry are usually used to form the concentration ratio. For example, the top four firms in an industry might have market shares of 20, 15, 10 and 8 percent. The concentration ratio based on the leading four firms equals 53 percent.

While market share and monopoly power are not the same thing, a large market share is a prerequisite for monopoly power. It is also much easier for a few firms to collude than for many. Therefore, the market share for particular firms and the degree of concentration in an industry are often used as measures of the degree of monopoly power. Because absolute size does not necessarily reveal market power, these relative measures provide a means of determining just how big "big" is.

**Horizontal Mergers.** There are at least three basic forms of merger activity. A *horizontal merger* is said to occur when two firms producing the same or similiar products merge. Because such mergers increase the market share of the combined firm, it can be expected that competition will be reduced. Horizontal mergers are generally prohibited except in cases where one participant in the merger is near bankruptcy. However, given the presence of economies of scale, it is not clear whether prohibition of such mergers is always justified. By combining production activities, per unit costs can be lowered, and consumers may benefit through lower prices.

**Vertical Mergers.** *Vertical mergers* involve the combining of firms involved in different stages of the *same production process*. For example, coal is used as an input in steel manufacturing. The merger of a firm producing steel and a producer of coal represents a vertical merger. Such mergers can greatly increase efficiency for the firms involved; they provide both a guaranteed source of supply and enable the streamlining of activities to the special requirements of the final product. However, competition is also affected; other sellers of inputs to the firm may be forced out of business. The resulting lack of resource suppliers may be detrimental to new firms attempting to enter the market.

*Conglomerate Mergers.* If two firms that are not related merge, a *conglomerate merger* results. Because such mergers do not have a direct effect on any one market, it can be argued that competition is not reduced. The combination of firms producing diverse products provides protection for the different branches of the conglomerate; negative profits for one firm in the conglomerate will not cause the conglomerate or the firm to go out of business. However, it is not clear whether this is beneficial to society. Resources continue to be used in an unprofitable enterprise, one that would go out of business under competitive conditions, and there is concern about the efficiency that may be lost in managing diverse enterprises.

## REGULATION OF MONOPOLY POWER

Starting in the late 1800s, a number of acts were passed to control the means and extent to which firms could gain monopoly control of an industry.

**The Sherman Act.** Passed in 1890, the Sherman Antitrust Act is composed of two important sections. The first prohibits contracts or other agreements that inhibit trade or commerce among the states. The second expressly prohibits attempts to monopolize a market.

**The Clayton Act.** The Clayton Act of 1914 disallowed the purchase of stock in competing companies if such purchases would have the effect of reducing competition. *Tying contracts* were also prohibited; such contracts are imposed by the buyer of a product and require that the seller purchase particular goods from the buyer. The Clayton Act also made price discrimination illegal when such discrimination inhibited competition. The Clayton Act overlooked the possibility of anticompetitive mergers, resulting when one firm acquired the assets of another rather than its stock. This practice was outlawed by the Celler-Kefauver Antimerger Act of 1950.

**The Federal Trade Commision Act.** The Federal Trade Commision Act, passed in 1914, created the Federal Trade Commision and gave it responsibility to investigate unfair and deceptive business practices. Based on the Wheeler-Lea Act of 1938, the Federal Trade Commision was given the responsibility of protecting consumers against false or misleading advertising.

## Other Reasons for Regulation

Protecting the public from the evils of monopoly is not the only reason the government regulates business. In modern economies governments also take responsibility for ensuring worker, consumer, and environmental safety.

### WORKER SAFETY

Economists prefer to assume that individuals are fully rational and well informed. As such, they should be aware of the dangers involved in the occupations they choose and intelligent enough to know whether the rewards are worth the risks. *Ceteris paribus*, all else being equal, if a particular occupation is especially hazardous, it should command a high wage to compensate the worker for the risk taken. If a high wage is not offered, it is assumed that the worker will choose to work somewhere else and avoid the risk.

Arguments in favor of regulation to ensure worker safety are based on the degree to which workers and firms can be expected to understand the risks in particular occupations. They are also concerned with the costs to society of paying compensation to those whose health is adversely affected by job-related activities.

Given the many new discoveries concerning the safety implications of the workplace environment, it is possible to argue that workers cannot be expected to understand the risks they face in certain forms of employment. Employers may not be aware of the risks they subject their workers to, or they may not inform workers of risks; in either case, workers may accept risk in return for inadequate compensation. In addition, imperfect markets can affect a worker's decision to accept risk. For example, when one industry provides a major source of employment in a region, such as coal mining in West Virginia, workers may have few options but to accept the given wage and the dangerous employment.

An even stronger argument for regulation involves the long-term health or other costs incurred by society in caring for victims of occupational hazards or their dependents. Because of these costs, it is in the public's interest to ensure that safety regulations are established and abided by, even if firms could find individuals willing to accept the risks. The Occupational Health and Safety Administration is responsible for developing proposals regarding the regulation of working conditions and the monitoring of businesses to ensure that laws are obeyed. While most states had enacted worker-safety legislation, in 1971 the Occupational Safety and Health Act was passed by the federal government to ensure that health and safety regulations would be promoted, implemented, and enforced.

## PRODUCT SAFETY

*Caveat emptor* (let the buyer beware) has long been the prevailing attitude in markets for most goods and services. Under this precept, once a transaction is complete, consumers bear all responsibility for injuries resulting from the use of a product. As seen in the establishment of the Consumer Products Safety Commission, this approach to product liablity has been challenged. Because sellers are assumed to have more complete information on the possible dangers of using their products, they are now often considered responsible for injuries that result from their use. Notable examples of this new attitude are seen in Ralph Nadar's campaign in the 1960s against the Chevrolet Corvair, which Nadar deemed an unsafe product. The Ford Motor Company experienced lawsuits in the 1970s when rear-end collisions led the gas tanks on a number of its Pintos to explode. More recently, some individuals have brought tobacco companies to court claiming that their adverse health effects from smoking are the cigarette companies' responsiblility.

## ENVIRONMENTAL REGULATION

Without environmental regulation, firms can use the air or water as a dumping ground for wastes without regard for the costs imposed on other users of these resources. These costs include cleanup expenses for areas where toxic chemicals have been dumped and the medical and lost-productivity costs due to adverse health effects from air or other pollution. To remedy such problems, the Clean Air Act and the Clean Water Act have been passed, and the Environmental Protection Agency has been empowered to ensure that environmental quality is maintained. Legislation has been expanded to ensure that economic activity does not destroy certain threatened species such as the spotted owl, whose habitat has become the victim of logging operations. The goal of such regulation is to ensure that all the costs of economic activity are accounted for. When this is the case, product prices are more reflective of the actual costs involved, and allocative efficiency is more nearly achieved. The issue of environmental protection is discussed more fully in Chapter 21.

*This chapter has examined the various legal forms of business organization and the costs and benefits associated with each. For modern economies, the corporation represents the most important form because of the large sums it is able to raise to fund its operations and the limited liability enjoyed by its owners. The large size of firms within many industries, as measured by concentration ratios and market share, gives rise to concern over monopoly power. Beginning with the Sherman Act, the government has sought to control this power through* regulation. In recent times the government has expanded its regulation of business to protect workers, consumers, and the environment more fully.

The models of perfect competition, monopolistic competition, oligopoly, and monopoly are based on conceptually different views of the firm than the legal forms presented in this chapter. Nevertheless, economic and legal classifications can easily be integrated in real-world analysis when addressing questions of competition and efficiency. As seen in the rationale underlying regulation of a monopoly, legal institutions are concerned with ensuring the existence of competition. Regulation to ensure safe labor practices, consumer safety, and environmental quality are also based on improving overall economic efficiency, ensuring that the total costs to society of private business decisions are accounted for. Economic analysis also allows evaluation of the various limitations placed on business activity by government regulation. It provides a means of analyzing the appropriateness, effectiveness, and likely consequences of this regulation.

## Selected Readings

Devine, P.J., N. Lee, R.M. Jones, and W.J. Tyson. *An Introduction to Industrial Economics*, London: George Allen & Unwin. 1985.

Kahn, Alfred. *The Economics of Regulation: Principles and Institutions*. New York: Wiley. 1970

Malkiel, Burton G., *A Random Walk Down Wall Street*. New York: W. W. Norton and Co. 1981.

# 20

## The Labor Market

*Economic activity is classified into two basic market types. Output markets are associated with the sale to consumers of final products such as automobiles, radios, and refrigerators. By consuming these goods and services, individuals obtain utility or satisfaction. Input markets involve the sale of land, labor, and capital services to firms. Through the use of these inputs, the goods and services sold in output markets are produced. The demand for inputs is said to be derived from the demand for output. In other words, the decision to employ specific quantities of land, labor, and capital is based upon the amount of output the firm plans to sell. Hence, there is a connection between the quantity of goods supplied in output markets and the demand for inputs in input markets.*

*There is also a connection between the quantity of inputs supplied in input markets and the quantity of output demanded in output markets. In a free-market economy, the services of factors of production can be obtained only by offering remuneration sufficient to obtain desired input levels. The amounts of factor services offered for sale at various payment levels are reflected in factor-supply curves. Factor payments—composed of rent, wages, and interest—provide the consumer income necessary to purchase the output produced. The specific amounts of output that will be purchased at various prices are seen in the output-demand curve.*

*The special characteristics of the labor market are explored in this chapter. The fact that labor is supplied by human beings and that it is such a large fraction of the typical firm's total costs makes it an especially interesting factor of production. With labor used as a representative input, a theory of input demand is developed based on the concept of marginal productivity. As a part of this theory, a decision rule for determining optimal levels of input demand is formulated. In discussing the demand for capital in Chapter 23, this optimality rule is extended and reformulated to deal with the fact that capital, unlike labor, is productive for periods beyond the date it is purchased. Because of the potentially ambiguous nature of its response to wage increases, attention is also focused on the characteristics of labor supply. Next, the role of unions is examined. Finally, various models of discrimination in the labor market are considered.*

## THE LABOR MARKET

At the theoretical level, the market for labor functions through the interaction of supply and demand, just like any other market. The price of labor is wages. The quantity of labor can be measured by considering the number of hours individuals work or counting the number of individuals employed. The quantity of labor employed may also be represented by *full-time equivalents*. Under the assumption that a full-time worker works 40 hours per week and 50 weeks per year, one full-time equivalent equals 2,000 hours. Finally, labor supply is sometimes measured by the *labor-force participation rate*, the fraction of the working age population that is in the labor force.

The intersection of the labor supply and demand curves determines the equilibrium wage and the equilibrium quantity of labor. Underlying the demand for labor are a number of factors, including the amount of output the firm plans to sell and the technology that determines how labor and other inputs are transformed into output. Underlying labor supply is the utility-maximizing behavior of consumers.

## THE DEMAND FOR LABOR

The quantity of labor demanded by a typical firm depends upon the relationship between the productivity of labor, output price, and the wages the firm must pay workers. Productivity depends upon the state of technology, the ability to transform inputs into output, as reflected in the firm's production function. Output price may be fixed, or it may vary with the level of output sold. If the firm operates in a perfectly competitive output market, the price of output is fixed because the firm is a price taker. If imperfect competition prevails, the firm faces a downward-sloping output-demand curve; price must decrease if additional output is to be sold. Wages may or may not vary with the quantity of labor employed. If the total quantity of labor employed is small compared to the overall labor market, the firm may be a wage-taker: It must accept the prevailing market wage if it expects to hire any laborers. However, if the firm employs a significant fraction of the total labor in a particular area, it will find that its decisions to employ more or fewer workers can lead to changes in the market wage.

## The Demand for Labor: Competitive Markets

The simplest way to derive the typical firm's labor-demand curve is to assume that the firm takes as given the price at which it sells its output and the wage of its labor input. Deciding on the optimal quantity of labor involves a comparison of costs and revenues. Hiring workers involves the cost of the wages the firm must pay; however, with more workers, additional output can be produced, and the sale of this output generates revenues for the firm. Therefore, a firm finds its optimal quantity of labor input by comparing the wage it pays for an additional worker and the value of the extra output the firm can produce and sell because of the worker's efforts.

### DIMINISHING RETURNS AND THE VALUE OF THE MARGINAL PRODUCT

Assume that the levels of all inputs other than labor are fixed. Through the firm's production function, increases in the quantity of labor employed will lead to increases in output; when more of an input is used, more output is produced. However, because of the law of diminishing returns, the increase in output that comes with *each additional unit* of labor will decrease. The firm sells the output produced by each additional worker at the prevailing market price. Assuming

## Employment and the Value of the Marginal Product[a]

| Number of Workers | Marginal Product | Value of the Marginal Product |
|:---:|:---:|:---:|
| 1 | 80 | $160 |
| 2 | 70 | 140 |
| 3 | 60 | 120 |
| 4 | 50 | 100 |
| 5 | 40 | 80 |
| 6 | 30 | 60 |
| 7 | 20 | 40 |
| 8 | 10 | 20 |

[a]Assumes that the market price is fixed at $2 per unit of output.

*Table 20.1*

that the price of output is fixed, the value of the extra output produced as additional workers are hired will also decrease because of diminishing returns.

Table 20.1 presents an example of this situation. The market price of output is fixed at $2 per unit. Column one shows the number of workers the firm might employ. Column two shows the marginal product of each worker. In accordance with the law of diminishing returns, the marginal product of each additional worker declines. The first worker produces 80 units of output, the second produces an additional 70 units, and so on. Column three shows the value of the output produced by the additional worker. This value, found by multiplying the $2 per unit price of output by the number of units produced by each worker, is defined as the *value of the marginal product of labor*.

## DETERMINING THE OPTIMAL QUANTITY OF LABOR INPUT

Suppose that the firm must pay a wage equal to $100 per employee. How many workers should the firm hire? Examining the data in Table 20.1, note the decline in the value of the marginal product caused by the law of diminishing marginal productivity. The firm should definitely employ the first worker; it pays only $100 for his or her services, but it earns $160 from the sale of the output he or she produces. The value of the marginal product also exceeds the $100 wage for the second and third workers. They should clearly be hired if profits motivate the firm's actions. The wage paid to the fourth worker is exactly equal to the revenues gained from the sale of the resulting output. Although the firm would technically be indifferent to hiring this worker, the fourth worker represents the limit of profitable employment opportunites. Beyond four workers, the revenues gained from the sale of the output produced by extra workers do not cover their wage. Diminishing returns have taken their toll. Thus, if the fifth worker is hired, the additions to revenue equal $80, $20 less than the $100 that must be paid to acquire this worker's services.

**The Optimal-Input-Use Condition.** Laborers should be hired to the point at which their wage equals the value of the marginal product. This condition appears as

$$W = P \times MP_L$$

$W$ is the prevailing wage for labor; $P$ is the price per unit of output; $MP_L$ is the marginal product of labor, the extra output produced by the last worker hired.

The wage represents the extra cost incurred by the firm when it hires an extra worker. By multiplying the marginal product of labor by the price of output, the value of the marginal product of labor is found—the addition to the firm's revenues by hiring an extra unit of labor. If the value of the marginal product of labor exceeds the wage, the firm adds to its profit by hiring more labor. Given the law of diminishing returns, hiring additional units of labor will reduce marginal productivity, and the value of the marginal product will fall.

The firm should continue to hire addtional units of labor until the additions to revenue no longer exceed the additions to cost, to the point of equality between the wage and the value of the marginal product of labor. Beyond the point of equality, additions to profit will be negative, and total profit will decline.

**An Analysis of Units.** Observe the equivalence of the units found on either side of the equality in the optimality condition. On the left side, the wage has units of dollars per unit of labor. On the right side, the price of output has units of dollars per unit of output, and the marginal product of labor is measured in units of output per unit of labor. Because the output units cancel, the product of output price and the marginal product of labor (the value of the marginal product) is also measured in dollars per unit of labor. The equivalence of units allows both the wage and the value of the marginal product to be measured along the same axis in a graph. This is an important fact in deriving the firm's demand curve for labor.

## THE LABOR-DEMAND CURVE AND THE VALUE OF THE MARGINAL PRODUCT

The demand curve for labor shows how many workers should optimally be hired at each possible wage. Figure 20.1 plots the data shown in Table 20.1. It showns a downward sloping curve representing the value of the marginal product of different quantities of labor. The slope reflects diminishing returns. The wage and the value of the marginal product are measured on the vertical axis; the quantity of labor is measured on the horizontal axis.

At any wage, the optimal quantity of labor is determined by the equality between the wage and the value of the marginal product. If the wage is $80, 5 workers should be hired. If the wage is $40, 7 workers should be hired. By definition, a demand curve represents the amount of a commodity that will be purchased at various prices. Since the wage rate represents the price of labor, it follows that the value of the marginal-product curve is equivalent to the firm's demand curve for labor.

**Shifting the Labor-Demand Curve.** Because the labor-demand curve is equivalent to the value of the marginal-product curve, factors affecting the value of the marginal product simultaneously affect labor demand. In deriving the labor-demand curve, it is assumed that the price of output is fixed, that quantities of all other inputs are held constant, and that the state of technology is fixed. A change in any one of these factors will therefore cause the labor-demand curve to shift.

A rise in output price increases the value of the marginal product for every unit of labor hired. Therefore, an increase in the output price causes the labor-demand curve to shift outward. For example, using the data from Table 20.1, a rise in price from $2 to $4 raises the value of the marginal product of the first worker from $160 to $320. This value lies above the labor-demand curve in Figure 20.1, implying that a shift has occurred. Plotting the new value of the marginal-product schedule that arises at this price verifies this fact.

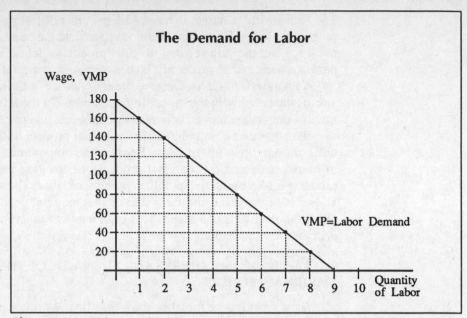

**Figure 20.1** *Laborers should be hired to the point at which the value of the marginal product of labor (VMP) equals the wage. At a wage of $100, four workers should be hired. Because the VMP curve shows the relationship between the price of labor and the quantities that will be hired, it is equivalent to the labor-demand curve.*

If the marginal product of each worker doubles because of a change in technology, the value of the marginal product of each worker will also double. Therefore, a change in technology that increases the marginal productivity of labor results in a higher value of the marginal product and leads to an outward shift in the labor-demand curve.

The same is true for an increase in the use of the other factors of production held constant in deriving the labor-demand curve. If the firm's capital stock increases, the presence of more capital per unit of labor will increase labor productivity. The increased marginal productivity will increase the value of the marginal product for all potential workers. This causes the labor-demand curve to shift out.

## THE REAL WAGE AND LABOR DEMAND

The condition used to determine the optimal quantity of labor is sometimes written in terms of the *real wage*. The real wage is defined as the wage rate divided by the price of output. Rather than the condition

$$W = P \times MP_L$$

both sides are divided by the price of output and

$$\frac{W}{P} = MP_L$$

The optimal quantity of labor requires that the firm's real wage equal the marginal product of labor.

Because of the law of diminishing returns, the marginal product of labor declines as the quantity of labor employed increases. Therefore, the marginal-product curve will be downward-sloping. Once the real wage is known, the optimal labor input associated with that real wage is found along the marginal-product curve. Thus, stated in real terms, the firm's marginal-product curve for labor is equivalent to its labor-demand curve.

Based on the data shown in Table 20.1, the labor demand curve is shown as a function of the real wage in Figure 20.2. At a real wage of 50, 4 workers will be hired. If the real wage drops to 10, 8 workers will be hired.

**Interpreting the Optimality Condition.** The wage is measured in dollars per laborer and the price of output is measured in dollars per unit of output. When their ratio is formed, the output units rise to the numerator, and the dollar units cancel. Therefore, the ratio of wage to price of output has units of output

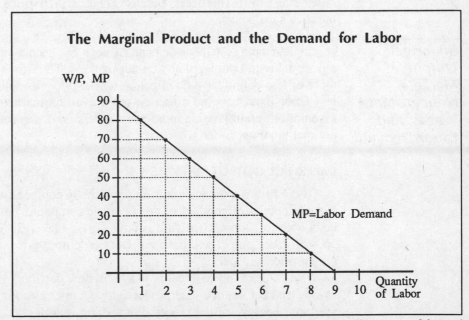

**Figure 20.2** *The optimal labor-input condition can be expressed in terms of the real wage (W/P): Laborers should be hired to the point at which the marginal product of labor (MP) equals the real wage (W/P). At a real wage of 50, four workers should be hired. Because the MP curve shows the relationship between the real price of labor and the quantities that will be hired, it is equivalent to the labor-demand curve.*

per laborer. The ratio of wage to price represents the rate of transformation of labor into output based on prevailing market wages and prices. It measures the output a laborer must produce for the firm to cover the costs of hiring a laborer. If the wage is $50 per laborer and the price of output is $5, the real wage is 10 units of output. A worker must produce at least 10 units of output to be worth hiring.

If the marginal product falls below the real wage, the additional worker is not producing enough output to justify his or her further employment. If the real wage is 10 units of output per laborer and the worker's marginal product is 3 units of output, the firm gains only 3 units of output by hiring an extra worker; it must pay the worker the equivalent of 10 output units. It is not to the firm's benefit to employ this worker.

**Labor-Demand-Shift Factors.** When the real wage is used with the firm's marginal-product curve to determine the optimal level of labor input, the demand-shift factors include changes in technology and changes in the use of other inputs like capital. Changes in the price of output are explicitly captured by the real wage and in no way affect the marginal product of labor. Therefore, unlike the case where the value of the marginal product curve serves as the labor demand curve, changes in output price will lead to movements along the curve rather than a shift. This occurs because a change in the price of output will affect the firm's real wage.

## Imperfect Output Markets, Nonconstant Wages, and Labor Demand

In developing the labor-demand curve, it has been assumed that the firm is a price-taker in both input and output markets. The firm's actions to produce more or less output have no effect on output price; its actions to hire more or less labor input have no effect on the prevailing market wage. When these assumptions are relaxed, a more general version of the condition required for optimal input use is derived.

### IMPERFECT OUTPUT MARKETS

If the firm is a participant in an imperfectly competitive industry (the firm is a monopolist, oligopolist, or monopolistic competitor) its demand curve will be downward sloping. The firm is now a price-maker: Its decision to produce and sell more output will have an effect on output price. As output expands, output price will fall.

The value of the marginal product will now decline, for two reasons. First, as was true before, marginal productivity declines as additional units of labor are hired because of the law of diminishing returns. Second, because of the downward-sloping output-demand curve, output price will decline as output increases. The combined effects of declining marginal product and declining product price mean that the firm's labor-demand curve is still downward sloping, but it is more vertical than where the firm is a price-taker. Increases in the quantity of labor employed now cause larger declines in the value of the marginal product.

**Marginal-Revenue Product.** The presence of imperfect output markets means that the firm's production decisions affect the price of output. Therefore, it is necessary to redefine the extra revenue the firm receives from the sale of the output produced by hiring an extra worker. Instead of the value of the marginal product, the *marginal-revenue product* is measured. The marginal-revenue-product curve is now equivalent to the firm's labor-demand curve. This definition is more general and encompasses the case where the firm is a price taker in the output market. When the firm is a price-taker, the value of the marginal product is the same as the marginal-revenue product. The adjective *marginal* is entirely consistent with the definition of marginal revenue discussed in previous chapters. There is explicit recognition of the fact that changes in the quantity of labor, rather than changes in output, cause changes in the firm's revenues.

## NONCONSTANT WAGES

The firm cannot always obtain additional workers for a fixed wage. If the labor market is small compared with the firm's requirements for labor, hiring additional laborers might require a greater wage. In this situation, hiring more laborers implies moving up along a labor-supply curve. If the firm employs less labor, wages will fall. Because it is assumed that the firm pays a single wage to all workers, hiring even a single additional worker results in a higher wage for all workers.

*Marginal Input Cost.* The presence of nonconstant wages means that the firm's production decisions affect the prices of factor inputs. In the case of labor, instead of the wage, reference is made to the *marginal labor cost.* The adjective *marginal* in this definition is consistent with the definition of marginal cost discussed in previous chapters. In this case, reference is made to the change in cost that occurs when an extra unit of labor is hired. This definition encompasses the case where the firm is a wage-taker in the input market. When the firm is a wage-taker, the wage is the same as marginal-labor cost.

# THE MONOPSONY MODEL

It is not unusual to find regions where one industry provides most of the jobs. If someone in the region wants a job, it is most likely to be found with this industry. The *monopsony model* allows us to analyze the case in which a single firm is the sole employer of labor in a region. It also allows us to use the concepts of marginal-labor cost and marginal-revenue product. The monopsonist can be said to have "monopoly control" over the buyer's side of the input market.

Whereas the monopolist has control over production of output, the monopsonist is able to decide how much of an input will be employed.

## *Optimality for the Monopsonist*

In hiring the optimal quantity of some input, the monopsonist's problem is conceptually no different from the problem faced by any other employer. Extra units of input should be hired until additions to revenue from the sale of output equal the additions to cost from hiring the input. All additions to profit greater than zero should be attained. In seeing how this condition is satisfied for the monopsonist, the primary problem is to locate the curve that shows the additions to cost involved in hiring extra units of input.

### THE MONOPSONIST'S MARGINAL LABOR COST

Figure 20.3 presents a monopsonist's labor demand curve and the labor-supply curve of the market. In a normal market, the intersection of demand and supply determines the equilibrium wage rate and quantity of labor. This is not the case here. For the monopsonist, the labor supply curve represents the *average cost* it incurs in hiring certain quantities of labor. From the relationship between marginals and averages, when average labor cost is rising, marginal labor cost is greater than the average; therefore, the marginal-labor-cost curve

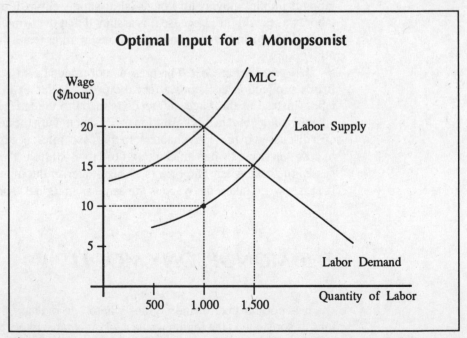

**Figure 20.3**  *For the monopsonist, labor supply represents average labor cost. Optimal input use occurs when marginal labor cost (MLC) and the marginal revenue product/demand for labor are equated at 1,000 units. The wage necessary to bring forth the optimal quantity of labor is $10.*

More intuitively, when the monopsonist decides to hire an extra unit of labor, it pays the wage found on the labor-supply curve to *all* workers. To hire an extra unit of labor means moving up along the supply curve. Therefore, the extra cost incurred when an extra unit of labor is hired is the sum of the wage paid to the additional worker (found on the labor-supply curve) and the pay increase received by existing workers. The marginal-labor-cost curve is denoted as MLC in Figure 20.3.

### THE MONOPSONISTS'S OPTIMAL EMPLOYMENT LEVEL

Revenues from employing additional units of labor will exceed costs as long as the labor-demand curve (equivalent to the marginal revenue product curve) is above the marginal-labor-cost curve. Because the marginal-labor-cost curve is upsloping and the labor-demand (marginal-revenue-product) curve is downsloping, eventually additions to profit are zero. As shown in Figure 20.3, the monopsonist's optimal level of employment is found when 1,000 units of labor are hired.

**The Monopsony Wage.** Without monopsony, the intersection of the labor-demand and labor-supply curves would determine the equilibrium wage and quantity of labor. In Figure 20.3, this would occur at a wage of $15 and a quantity equal to 1,500 units. To determine the wage that must be paid to bring forth 1,000 units of labor, the $10 wage associated with 1,000 labor units is found along the labor-supply curve. The monopsonist reduces wages below the level that would be paid under competitive conditions and lowers the quantity of labor employed. Employing more workers is not optimal for the monopsonist. Marginal labor cost exceeds the marginal-revenue product of labor beyond 1,000 labor units. To increase employment, the increased wage needed to attract extra workers would have to be paid to all workers.

# THE SUPPLY OF LABOR

According to economic theory, to induce worker participation in the labor market, a wage high enough to offset the disutility or dissatisfaction associated with labor must be paid. Different job characteristics require different wage rates to attract workers. Personal achievements required for the job, such as a high level of education or specific training, might require that a high rate of pay be offered. Characteristics of the workplace, including dangers involved, the pleasantness of working conditions, steadiness of work, will all have an effect on the wage required to attract a desired quantity of laborers.

For workers, the income gained from working additional hours must be balanced against the corresponding loss of leisure time. The availability and attractiveness of market goods is also a factor in determining how many hours people will be willing to work. As was discovered in Eastern European countries under communism, pay alone is not sufficient to create productive labor efforts. When store shelves are empty, earning a particular wage has no value. Leisure becomes a more appealing alternative.

## The Shape of the Labor-Supply Curve

For most products, increases in price bring forth an increase in quantity supplied. This is not necessarily true in the labor market. Although higher wages make additional hours of work more attractive, an individual receiving an increased wage simultaneously enjoys a rise in income. Given the desire to consume more of all goods when income rises, this could lead to reduced work effort as individuals seek to enjoy one of the most important of all goods— leisure. To capture the two forces affecting labor supply when wages change, economists make use of the *substitution* and *income* effects.

### THE SUBSTITUTION EFFECT OF A WAGE INCREASE

Economists define the *opportunity cost of leisure* as the wage rate. The hourly wage provides a monetary measure of the amount an individual could earn by reducing leisure activities by one hour. If the prevailing wage is $20 per hour, $20 is given up when a worker decides to work one less hour. A rise in a person's wage increases the opportunity cost of leisure. This might induce a person to spend more time in the labor market because the relative price of leisure has risen. The *substitution effect* of a wage increase measures the increase in labor supplied with a rise in the wage.

### THE INCOME EFFECT OF A WAGE INCREASE

A rise in the wage corresponds to an increase in income. When income rises, consumers are expected to consume more of all goods, including leisure. When more leisure is consumed, fewer hours are supplied for work. The *income effect* of a wage increase measures the decrease in labor supplied with an increase in the wage.

### THE NET EFFECT

Given the presence of the substitution and income effects, it is not clear whether the quantity of labor supplied will increase or decrease with a rise in the wage. If the substitution effect dominates the income effect, as wages rise, more labor will be supplied; the labor-supply curve will have the normal upward slope associated with most products. This is shown in the left panel of Figure 20.4. If the income effect dominates the substitution effect, the labor-supply curve can actually be backward bending, as shown in the right paned of Figure 20.4. If the income and substitution effects cancel each other, the labor-supply curve will be vertical.

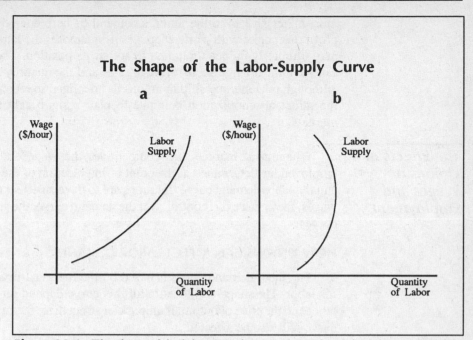

**Figure 20.4** *The shape of the labor-supply curve depends on the relative size of the income and substitution effects. If the substitution effect dominates the income effect, the labor-supply curve will have the usual upward shape shown in the left diagram. Over the range of wages where the income effect dominates the substitution effect, the labor-supply curve bends backward, as shown in the right diagram.*

### THE ACTUAL SHAPE OF THE LABOR SUPPLY CURVE

Empirical estimates of the labor-supply curve find that its shape depends upon the group considered. For older men, the income effect seems to dominate the substitution effect; early retirement has become more attractive in spite of the higher wages that come with years of experience. For women, as reflected in rising female wages and the large rise in female labor-force participation rates, the substitution effect seems to dominate.

## THE ROLE OF UNIONS

Unions provide workers with an organized means of negotiating with employers about the conditions of employment. For economists, unions are viewed as organizations through which workers can gain monopoly power over the supply of labor services. When unions are dissatisfied with employment conditions, this power is manifested in strikes. To counteract a strike, a firm must either give in to the union's demand or be prepared to face the loss of profit that comes with work stoppages. If it chooses the latter strategy, the firm may ultimately induce the union to soften its position. The actions of unions can have important effects on wage rates and the quantity of labor employed. Although total membership in unions has declined in recent years, unions and the threat of unionization continue to play a significant role in many labor markets.

## The Effects of Unions on Wages and Employment

When input markets are competitive, the wage and quantity of labor employed are determined at the point of intersection of the labor-supply curve and the labor-demand curve. If unions are to have an effect on employment and wages, they must exert control over the demand curve, the supply curve, or both curves.

### HOW UNIONS CAN AFFECT LABOR DEMAND

The labor-demand curve is based on the marginal-revenue-product curve for labor. The shape and location of this curve depend on the productivity of labor and the price of output. If unions can affect these factors, the labor-demand curve will also be affected.

**Productivity Effects.** Increased marginal productivity leads to a greater marginal-revenue product of labor. If unions can increase the productivity of workers in an industry, the labor-demand curve will shift out. At the new intersection with an upward-sloping labor-supply curve, more workers will be hired, and the equilibrium wage will increase. Such a circumstance is possible when the presence of a union leads workers to become more satisfied with their jobs. Participation of the union in setting pay scales, improving working conditions, setting guidelines for promotion decisions, and settling grievances accomplish this. If contented or informed workers perform more efficiently than discontented or uninformed workers, productivity will increase. As seen in *efficiency-wage models*, productivity can also be increased if wages are increased. Thus, if the union succeeds in raising wages and the assumptions underlying the efficiency wage models are correct, labor demand would shift out also.

The firm may also play a role in the increased productivity that comes with higher wages. Because it must pay workers more, the firm will naturally seek to employ the most highly qualified individuals who are willing to work for that wage. Hiring processes will be toughened. Over time, the presence of a higher wage established by the union can therefore lead to higher productivity because of employment screening by the firm.

**Price Effects.** Aside from productivity, the labor-demand curve's shape and location are based on the price at which the output sells. If knowledge that goods are union-made causes consumers to purchase them instead of nonunion goods, output demand will rise. Demand increases for union products might come about if union goods are thought to be of higher quality or consumers believe that the union serves a worthwhile function that should be encouraged. This increased demand causes the price of output to rise also. Hence, the firm's marginal-revenue product of labor increases and the demand for labor will rise. This leads to increased wages and increased employment.

## HOW UNIONS CAN AFFECT LABOR SUPPLY

Working through the labor-supply curve, there are two distinct ways unions can affect wages and employment levels. First, unions can restrict labor supply by establishing certain employment criteria. Second, unions can negotiate for minimum pay levels for their members.

**Employment Criteria.** Employment criteria generally involve requiring the acquisition of a license or a period of apprenticeship before membership in the union (and therefore employment) is allowed. If the establishment of a union leads to such restrictions, the labor-supply curve will shift left; it will intersect the demand curve at a higher wage but at a lower quantity of employment. Technically, because labor demand equals labor supply after the supply shift, the union does not create unemployment through this action. It does reduce the number of individuals who will be employed. This is the price paid for the higher wage achieved by those able to meet the membership standards set by the union.

**Union Wage Setting.** Unions can also set minimum wages below which their members will not work. These wages vary for union members, based on

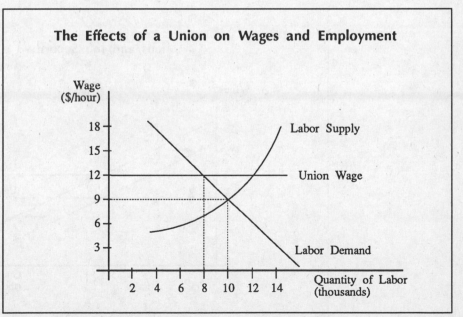

**Figure 20.5** *The equilibrium wage in this industry is $9 per hour with 10,000 workers employed. If a union succeeds in negotiating a wage of $12 per hour, employment falls along the demand curve to 8,000 workers.*

*seniority*, the number of years a worker has been employed by the firm, and the type of job performed. The firm must accept this wage or set of wages to employ any union workers. The establishment of a fixed minimum wage by the union implies that the labor supply curve becomes horizontal. The firm will not be able to hire any workers below the union wage and is assumed to be able to get as many workers as it likes at the union wage. Conceptually, except for the fact that an input rather than an output is involved, this situation corresponds to that experienced by a firm in a perfectly competitive industry facing a horizontal demand curve. The firm is a wage-taker.

The wage set by the union can cause a loss of jobs. In Figure 20.5, the upward-sloping labor-supply curve before unionization is shown, along with the horizontal wage-labor-supply line set by the union. The union manages to raise the wage from the competitive level of $9 per hour to $12 per hour. Because firms cannot be forced to hire more workers than they desire, the quantity of labor employed will be found at the intersection of the union's wage line and the firm's labor-demand curve. Employment falls from 10,000 to 8,000 workers. Two thousand workers will lose their jobs.

**Unions and Job Stability.** Aside from wages, unions can also be concerned with the size of their membership and maintaining union jobs. In Figure 20.6, the union wage is originally $12 and 8,000 workers are employed. Then there is a decrease in the demand for labor. Such a decrease might arise because less

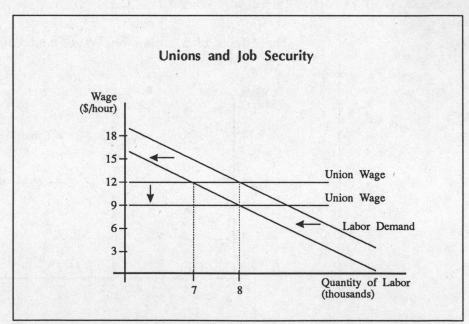

**Figure 20.6**  *At the union wage of $12 per hour, an inward shift in the demand for labor will reduce employment to 7000 workers. If the union wishes to provide job security for its members, the union wage must be reduced to $9 per hour.*

expensive foreign imports reduce demand for American goods (and therefore American workers) or because of changes in consumer tastes for the products of unionized firms. If the union wishes to maintain employment at its previous level, wage cuts must be accepted. A wage of $9 per hour leaves employment at the same level as before the demand shift.

## A Union versus Monopsony: Bilateral Monopoly

Attempts by a union to raise wages to a minimum acceptable level can lead to a loss of jobs for some members. However, this is not always the case. The union has monopoly power over labor supply. When dealing with a monopsony—a firm that has monopoly power over labor demand—a union can actually increase employment and wages. Consideration of the possible effects on employment and wages when a monopsonist deals with a union takes place in the context of the *bilateral monopoly model*.

### THE EFFECTS OF UNIONIZATION ON MONOPSONY

Consider the standard monopsonist's equilibrium, shown in Figure 20.7. Without the union, the monopsonist views the labor-supply curve as its average-labor-cost curve. Because average-labor cost is rising, the marginal-labor-cost curve lies above the supply curve. For the monopsonist, the optimal quantity of labor is found at the point where labor demand (the marginal-revenue product of labor) intersects the marginal-labor-cost curve. This quan-

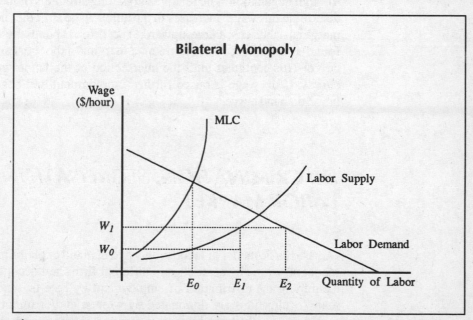

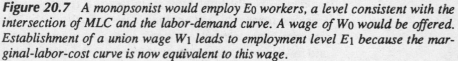

**Figure 20.7** *A monopsonist would employ $E_0$ workers, a level consistent with the intersection of MLC and the labor-demand curve. A wage of $W_0$ would be offered. Establishment of a union wage $W_1$ leads to employment level $E_1$ because the marginal-labor-cost curve is now equivalent to this wage.*

tity is labeled $E_0$. The wage the monopsonist would like to pay equals $W_0$; it is found on the labor-supply curve at the point associated with the optimal quantity.

When a union gains the support of workers composing the monopsonist's labor supply, the situation faced by the monopsonist will change. Suppose the union succeeds though negotiation, strike threats, or actual strikes to raise the wage to $W_1$. Now the firm must hire all the workers it desires at the single wage established by the union. This wage becomes the monopsonist's *effective* marginal-labor cost. Whenever an additional worker is hired, wage $W_1$ is paid for the extra worker. Up to the labor-supply curve, the monopsonist's effective marginal labor cost curve is horizontal; the wage need not be increased as additional workers are hired because it was set by the union.

In Figure 20.7, after the union succeeds in raising the wage from $W_0$ to $W_1$, employment expands from $E_0$ to $E_1$. Because wage $W_1$ is fixed for all workers, the firm would like to hire $E_2$ units of labor. However, an attempt by the monopsonist to hire more than $E_1$ workers will require an increase in the wage paid to all workers. The upward-sloping labor supply curve takes effect for wages above $W_1$. The actual marginal-labor-cost curve determines the extra cost associated with hiring workers beyond this point; it is well above the labor-demand curve there.

The actual wage that prevails under bilateral monopoly is determined through negotiation. The relative bargaining strengths of the union and the firm determine this wage. Increases in the union wage shift the (horizontal) effective marginal-labor-cost curve upward. The firm responds by hiring the quantity found at the intersection of effective marginal-labor cost and the labor-supply curve. This continues until the intersection of the labor-supply- and -demand curves. If the wage is raised further, employment will begin to fall along the labor-demand curve.

# DISCRIMINATION, SEGREGATION, AND THE LABOR MARKET

The basic model of labor supply and demand explains much about employment and wage characteristics in different firms and occupations. However, in examining the distribution of employment by race or sex, it is apparent that many occupations are dominated by women and/or minorities. For example, women typically hold jobs as nurses, secretaries, and telephone operators. Doctors, managers, and engineers are typically men. Blacks and other minorities are disproportionately employed in occupations associated with low pay and low status. There is great debate about the degree to which this *labor market segregation* is due to utility-maximizing and profit-maximizing behavior by individuals and firms involved or to *discrimination* in the labor market.

Labor-market discrimination occurs when individuals with equal qualifications for a particular job are treated unequally because of differences in sex, race, age, and so on. Discrimination adds another dimension to the analysis of labor markets. Important methods of analyzing the effects of discrimination include the *dual-labor-market model and the human-capital model*.

## The Dual-Labor-Market Model

The dual-labor-market model splits the labor market into two major sectors. These sectors differ in terms of pay, promotion opportunities, job security, working conditions, and the predominant type of competition.

### THE PRIMARY LABOR MARKET

The first or primary sector offers jobs with high pay, good promotion opportunities, and the potential for long-term attachment to the firm. Employees in this sector receive high levels of on-the-job training. This leads to greater job security because firms will seek to minimize training costs by reducing labor turnover. Positions are filled through an *internal labor market*; workers are assumed to work their way up in the firm by beginning their employment in certain entry level jobs. Firms in the primary labor market tend to be located in monopolistic and unionized industries.

In the primary market, the productivity characteristics of potential employees are important. It is here that potential discrimination can keep certain groups out of the primary sector. For example, if employers see blacks and women as less productive than white males, only white males will be seriously considered for jobs.

### THE SECONDARY LABOR MARKET

In the secondary labor market, blacks, women, and others turned away from the primary labor market face jobs with poor pay, poor promotion opportunities, and low skill requirements. Such jobs tend to be located in competitive industries. Because required job skills are minimal, firms in the secondary market are not greatly concerned with labor turnover rates. There is a lack of job security. Because workers in the secondary market receive little or no valuable training, movement from the secondary to the primary sector is difficult.

### THE DUAL LABOR MARKET: EMPIRICAL EVIDENCE

Evidence on whether the dual-labor-market model accurately explains labor-market segregation is mixed. It is always possible to divide jobs into those with pleasant and unpleasant characteristics. It is a different matter to explain fully why certain groups wind up in one type of job. Discrimination may be an important factor, but average education levels and other nonracial and nonsexual indicators of productivity are also relevant. Unless these characteristics are somehow accounted for, the degree to which hiring in the primary sector is based on discriminatory behavior cannot be ascertained.

## The Human-Capital Approach

Just as firms make investments in capital to increase their productivity, human beings invest in education and training to increase their earnings. This simple idea forms the basis of the *human capital* approach in explaining wage and occupational differences. Treated purely as making investments, individuals are assumed to calculate the expected benefits and costs derived from undertaking additional education or training. Options resulting in the highest rate of return will be selected.

For example, a high school senior has a choice of entering the job market immediately after graduation or going to college for four years. If the choice is to attend college, four years of earnings will be forgone and tuition costs must be covered. Ignoring the nonmonetary benefits that come with a college education, to determine which choice leads to the highest return, account must be taken of differences in future earnings with and without a college education. Expected future earnings from both choices must be *discounted* (transformed from future into current dollar values). A choice is then made based on the difference.

Under the human-capital model, economists assume that individuals constantly make decisions concerning investments in themselves. In reality, explicit costs and revenues need not be calculated. Rough estimates of the potential returns to various human capital investments can be seen by observing the wage and occupational characteristics of those who have already made such investments. Nonmonetary factors also enter into the implicit calculation. For example, for many women, given the present household division of labor, the utility gained by having a family must be compared with potential monetary and other gains associated with the labor market. If the expected satisfaction derived from full-time participation in the labor market exceeds the expected satisfaction of raising a family, the human-capital model predicts that the labor-market option will be chosen.

### HUMAN CAPITAL AND THE DISCRIMINATORY RESIDUAL

To determine whether discrimination is an important factor in explaining wage differences between whites and blacks and men and women, economists attempt to quantify all the relevant human-captial characteristics of individuals, accounting for years of education, training, years of on-the-job experience, and college major. If all relevant human-capital variables have been considered in explaining wage differences between groups, the unexplained residual is thought to represent the effects of discrimination. Empirically, the human capital approach does not explain all differences in wages between males and females or whites and blacks. This suggests that discrimination is the missing factor in explaining wage differentials.

## THE HUMAN-CAPITAL APPROACH AND FEEDBACK EFFECTS

Even if the human-capital model explained all wage differences between different groups, it could still be true that the effects of discrimination are present. If an individual fears discrimination, the expected rate of return from undertaking certain forms of training or education will be reduced and therefore become less attractive. Why undertake the expense of acquiring education or training if one's job prospects are not significantly enhanced? Because they see such a small potential payoff, blacks and women might avoid such investments. However, without such investments, these individuals are likely to wind up in low-paying, low-status occupations. Their actions are perfectly rational and consistent with the human-capital model.

## Models of Labor-Market Discrimination

Economists use a number of models to analyze discriminatory behavior in labor markets. These models make use of various assumptions that capture the characteristics of observed discrimination. Such models are developed to make predictions concerning the likely implications of discriminatory practices and the effects of policies designed to eliminate discrimination. For example, if perfect competition prevails, discriminatory behavior can raise costs for discriminating firms above those of nondiscriminating firms. This occurs because highly productive workers of the "wrong" color, sex, or age are not hired. Such behavior is expected to lower profits for discriminating firms and drive them out of business in the long run. There is no need for government intervention in this case.

### THE OVERCROWDING MODEL

The overcrowding model seeks to explain the effects of labor-market segregation as the result of discrimination. In Figure 20.8, the economy has two sectors. Because of discrimination, women and men are employed in different sectors. The market for female labor appears in the left graph, and the market for male labor appears in the right graph. For simplicity, the supply of male and female labor is assumed to be vertical, or perfectly inelastic (income and substitution effects cancel for all possible wage rates). Because of the different demand characteristics in each sector, women's wages, $W_w$, are lower than men's, $W_m$.

**Discrimination and the Cost to Society.** Crowding women into one sector of the economy leads to a potential output loss for society. In each sector, the optimal quantity of labor is found at the point where demand (the marginal-revenue-product of labor) is equal to the marginal cost of labor. If women were allowed to enter the male-dominated sector from the female-dominated sector, the labor-supply curve in the women's sector would shift left at the same rate the supply curve in the men's sector shifted right. As long as the wage in the male-dominated sector exceeds the wage in the female-dominated sector, additional employment of women in the male-dominated sector will lead to marginal-revenue-product gains in excess of the marginal-revenue product lost.

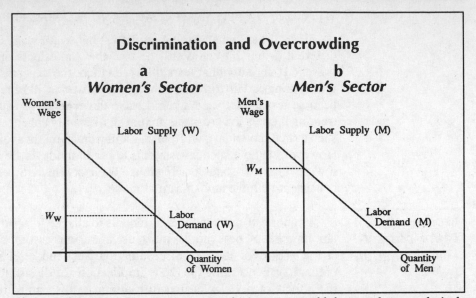

**Figure 20.8**  *When discrimination results in segregated labor markets, a relatively large supply of female workers competes for available jobs in the women's sector; their wage and value of the marginal product fall below that received by men. Society's output could increase by transferring women from the women's to the men's sector.*

This implies a net gain in the value of output for society and shows the potential gains of ending discrimination.

## OTHER MODELS OF DISCRIMINATION

There are many other models used to explain discriminatory behavior, depending on the circumstances being considered. These are classified as the *employer taste for discrimination model*, models of *employee and customer discrimination*, and the model of *statistical discrimination*.

**The Employer Taste for Discrimination Model.** It is usually assumed that firms are in business to maximize their profits. However, individuals might also derive utility from owning a firm and making decisions about how it is run. Some employers might derive utility by hiring workers of a certain sex or from certain racial groups. In the employer taste for discrimination model, employers are assumed to sacrifice profits for the utility gained by discrminating against certain groups.

**Employee Discrimination.** Employee-based discrimination models are founded on the premise that some workers prefer not to work with others with different characteristics. For example, white male workers might not want to work with minorities or women. They must be paid a premium for working with minorities or women.

**Customer Discrimination.** Models of customer discrimination are used to explain situations where customers will not purchase goods produced by firms employing minorities or women unless they receive some price break. For example, if patients have a preference for male doctors, female doctors might have to lower their rates to attract patients.

**Statistical Discrimination.** *Statistical discrimination* occurs when an employer makes use of an average characteristic of a certain race or sex in determining whether an individual is qualified for a position. If white male workers are on average more productive than blacks or women, the employer will ensure higher productivity by hiring just white males. However, this form of discrimination is unfair to individuals. A black or female job applicant far more productive than the average black, female, or white male worker will never be given the opportunity to display his or her productivity.

*In this chapter, the basic elements of labor demand and supply have been examined. The derivation of the firm's labor-demand curve stems from the law of diminishing returns and the relationship between marginal-labor costs and the marginal-revenue product of labor. Units of labor should be hired as long as the additions to revenue derived from sale of the output produced by such units exceed the additions to cost of employing them. This derivation does not apply only to labor. Any other factor of production, such as capital, could have been used.*

*Unlike other inputs, the shape of the labor-supply curve is ambiguous at the theoretical level. Increases in the wage make work more attractive but also increase income. As income increases, individuals desire to consume more of all goods, including leisure. Thus the labor-supply curve may be upward-sloping, vertical, backward-bending, or all three over various portions of its range. When combined together, the labor-demand- and -supply curves allow determination of the market wage and the level of employment.*

*As seen in the monopsony and bilateral monopoly models, extensions of the basic labor-market model allow consideration of various input market structures. When additional information concerning real-world labor-market conditions are incorporated, the labor-market model also provides a means of analyzing various forms of discriminatory behavior.*

**Selected Readings**

Blau, Francine D. and Marianne A. Ferber. *The Economics of Women, Men, and Work.* Englewood Cliffs, New Jersey: Prentice Hall. 1986.

Mansfield, Edwin. *Microeconomics: Theory and Applications.* New York: W. W. Norton. 1990.

Schiller, Bradley R. *The Economics of Poverty and Discrimination.* Englewood Cliffs, New Jersey: Prentice Hall. 1989.

# 21

## *Public Goods and Externalities*

$U$*ntil now, it has been taken for granted that all the goods and services desired by consumers are readily supplied by profit-maximizing producers. It has also been assumed that all costs incurred in production processes are captured by the firm's cost curves. If these assumptions held true, except for imperfect competition, the market system could be expected to function without the need for government interference. However, there are a variety of goods and services that will not necessarily be produced in a free-market system despite the fact that consumers might be willing to pay for them. Such commodities are classified under the heading of public goods. In terms of the costs of production, it is often the case that industrial activity leads to unwanted by-products, such as pollution, noise, or other forms of environmental degradation. These costs are not factored into the private cost curves used to determine optimal output by firms or the prices that consumers pay for products. Such spillover effects are classified under the heading of externalities.*

*Public goods and externalities imply that actions taken in the private sector of the economy do not necessarily lead to maximum societal welfare. Their presence provides a reason for the existence of government and a reason for government's involvement in the economy. In this chapter, precise definitions of public goods and externalities are presented with analyses of their effects on economic activity. Problems of determining the optimal level of output for firms generating external costs or benefits are considered along with the pricing problems that exist in providing public goods.*

# PUBLIC GOODS

Consider an individual eating popcorn and watching a movie at a theater. Each mouthful deprives other potential consumers of the opportunity to enjoy some of the popcorn. The popcorn represents an example of a private good. However, because the movie can be watched by everyone in the theater without decreasing the amount of movie available to anyone, the movie is an example of a public good. A *public good* is a commodity whose consumption by one individual does not preclude consumption of the same commodity by another individual. Such goods therefore have the quality of being *non-rival* in their consumption. Examples of public goods include parks, streetlighting, lighthouse warnings, air, and national defense.

A commodity is said to be a *pure public good* if in addition to being non-rival, it is not possible to exclude individuals from consuming it. Although a movie can be watched by many individuals without affecting the consumption of other individuals (assuming the theater is not overcrowded), it is possible to limit viewing by showing the film in an enclosed area and charging a fee for admission. On the other hand, the protection individuals receive from national defense is neither rivalrous nor excludable. In other words, the condition that additional users do not detract from anyone else's protection is satisfied, and it is not possible to exclude this protection for any citizen.

## The Provision of Public Goods

The provision of public goods in a free-market economy raises several interesting problems. With their non-rival nature, a producer of public goods can sell a unit of output to one or many individuals and still not experience any increase in cost. Each individual receives the benefits of the good, but because the act of consumption by any individual does not deplete the good, it is available to be sold again and again. This fact leads to questions concerning the optimal pricing of public goods. If it is also not possible to exclude individuals from the benefits derived from production of a public good, questions concerning their provision and financing arise. Who will produce such goods? Solutions to these problems can be found by determining the demand for public goods and ensuring their provision through government involvement in the marketplace.

### THE FREE-RIDER PROBLEM

In the case of pure public goods, a problem of financing arises because individuals cannot be excluded from their consumption. Ideally, every individual enjoying the benefits of the good would pay something to finance it. Honest individuals might voluntarily pay some amount for the satisfaction they receive from consuming public goods. But in order to avoid payment, other individuals might claim that they derive no utility from the public good and enjoy its presence anyway. The inability to exclude those individuals who do not reveal their true preferences implies that they will receive benefits without incurring any cost. This is the so called *free-rider* problem. Some individuals who benefit from the public good pay nothing. The full costs of paying for the public good will fall on those honest enough to say they derive utility from it. Because of this problem, private markets for pure public goods cannot exist. If pure public goods are to be provided at all, government action is required to find a means of financing them.

## EFFICIENT PRICING OF PUBLIC GOODS

The fact that additional consumers can enjoy the benefits of public goods without diminishing anyone else's enjoyment means that the marginal cost of public goods is zero. For example, providing national-defense services to another citizen adds nothing to overall defense costs; providing lighthouse services to another passing ship adds nothing to the cost of operating the lighthouse. From the model of perfect competition, efficient pricing of a commodity requires that its price equal its marginal cost. It follows that the price of a public good should be zero if resources are to be allocated efficiently. Because no private firm could stay in business charging a zero price, efficiency cannot be achieved when the private sector provides public goods.

## THE DEMAND CURVE FOR A PUBLIC GOOD

Individuals cannot be expected to reveal their preferences if it means they may have to bear an unfair share of a public good's cost. However, if individuals believed that all potential users of a public good would be assessed their fair share of its costs, they might reveal the prices they would pay for various quantities of the public good. A demand curve represents the relationship between the prices for which a good sells and the quantities of the good individuals are willing and able to purchase at those prices. If the government had knowledge of the demand for a particular public good, it would be better able to determine what quantity to provide and what amount to tax its citizens to pay for the good.

**Deriving a Public Good's Demand Curve.** To simplify the derivation of the public good's demand curve, consider a society of just two individuals. In Figure 21.1, the demand curves for these two potential consumers are shown in a and b. If the good was private, output produced to satisfy the demand of one individual could not serve the dual function of providing satisfaction to the other. Finding the total demand by these consumers would involve the horizontal summation of each individual demand curve; at each price, the quantities demanded by each individual are added.

With public goods, the story is different. The total-demand curve for a public good is derived to determine society's willingness to pay for various quantities. Individual members of society will not pay for particular units of the public good. Because they are non-rival, the production of any quantity of

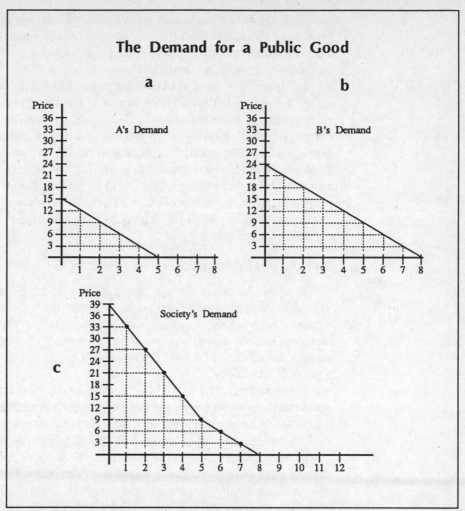

*Figure 21.1  The demand curve of a public good represents the relationship between the quantity of the good supplied and the amount society is willing to pay for its provision. It is found by vertically adding the public good's demand curve for each individual in society.*

public good found at some price can satisfy the demand of all individuals demanding that quantity.

These facts lead to the following considerations in determining the demand curve for a public good. Each individual will be willing to pay a certain amount for a unit of the public good. If this unit of public good is produced, all individuals can consume it, each without affecting the consumption of any other. Because they are able to consume quantities individually, the total amount that can be charged is equal to the sum of the amounts offered for each quantity. Therefore, the public good's demand curve is derived by adding the price each individual is willing to pay for given quantities of the public good. To find society's demand curve for a public good, individual demand curves are added vertically, not horizontally.

In Figure 21.1, person A is willing to pay $12 for the first unit of the public good. Person B will pay $21 for one unit of the good. These amounts represent each person's valuation of the public good. Therefore, in this two-citizen country, society's total valuation of the first unit of public good is $33. To obtain two units of public good, A is willing to pay $9 per unit and B will pay $18. Society's total valuation therefore equals $27 for the second unit. Other points along the total demand curve are found by adding the price each consumer is willing to pay for a quantity of output. The kink shown in Figure 21.1 is assumed to be smoothed out when the demands of the numerous citizens in real-world economies are accounted for.

## THE OPTIMAL PROVISION OF PUBLIC GOODS

Because the prices along a public good's demand curve are based on the valuation of extra units of the public good by individuals, the demand curve represents society's *marginal-benefit schedule* for the public good. The marginal-benefit schedule shows the extra benefits society derives from consuming an extra unit of the public good. Society's *total* benefits from consuming a particular quantity of the public good are represented by the area under the entire demand curve up to the quantity consumed. As the quantity of the public good increases by one unit, the marginal benefit is seen as the additional area under the demand curve associated with that unit of public good.

To find the optimal quantity of the public good, the costs of providing the public good must be considered along with the benefits derived. In Figure 21.2, the marginal-cost curve (MC) associated with producing the public good is shown along with the public good's demand–marginal-benefit curve. The optimal quantity of the public good is found at the point of intersection of these curves. To the left of the intersection, marginal benefits exceed marginal costs. Providing additional units of the public good adds to society's overall welfare because the extra benefits received are valued more highly than the extra costs. As the quantity of the public good increases, the additions to total benefits are reduced along the demand curve, while the addition to costs increase. Ultimately, at the point of intersection, no further additions to total benefits are possible. Moving further to the right, when marginal cost exceeds marginal benefits, total benefits will decrease.

**The Problem of Financing**. From a theoretical standpoint, the intersection of the marginal cost and marginal benefit schedule determines the optimal quantity of the public good; this amount should be provided. However, the problem of financing its production still remains. Imposing a uniform tax on all members of society might ensure that sufficient funds are avaiable to supply the optimal quantity of public good. However, because valuations of the good

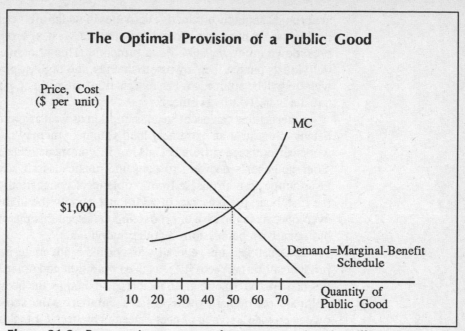

**Figure 21.2** *Because it represents the amount society is willing to pay, the demand curve for the public good represents its marginal-benefit schedule. Net benefits are positive so long as marginal benefits exceed marginal cost. Therefore, the optimal provision of the public good occurs when 50 units are provided.*

differ across individuals, some individuals would pay too much tax for the benefits they enjoy and others would pay too little. Because a rearrangement in the tax burden could make some individuals better off without making other individuals worse off, the uniform tax arrangement is not *Pareto optimal*. Evaluating tax strategies in terms of their effect on efficiency is fully considered in the branch of economics known as public finance.

# EXTERNALITIES

When costs and market prices do not accurately account for the true costs involved in producing or consuming some commodity, *external* economies and diseconomies are said to occur. For example, a firm might make free use of a river to dispose of wastes generated during the production process. Other users downstream will find they are no longer able to use the water for drinking or swimming. They incur unwanted costs due to the firm's actions. Similarly, the adverse health effects of air pollution represent externalities. These externalities are brought about by productive activities in which air is considered a free good, in this case a dumping ground for gaseous wastes. Externalities represent a breakdown in the *invisible hand* principle. This principle suggests that when individuals pursue their own selfish ends, the highest possible state of social welfare will be attained. When externalities are present, pursuing one's self-interest adversely affects others.

Externalities can occur in consumption as well as production. If a neighbor listens to music at an extremely loud volume, you may incur disutility. If your work performance suffers because of it, you incur other more tangible costs. Your neighbor's decision to consume music has an adverse effect on you. Externalities can also arise from problems of congestion. For example, during the rush hour, the presence of additional cars on the highway slows travel for everyone. As in the case of production, it is seen that pursuit of selfish interests has negative repercussions on other individuals.

Externalities are generally associated with undesirable or harmful by-products of certain activities, such as pollution and noise. However, externalities can also be beneficial. In the classic example, the bees kept by a beekeeper pollinate the orchard owner's trees. Similarly, the activities of the orchard owner provide a source of nectar needed by bees for making honey. Here, note that the externality involves interaction between one producer and another; each producer benefits from the actions of the other.

A final type of externality occurs when market activities affect prices, wages, or input costs but not utility functions (through which consumers transform goods into satisfaction) or production functions (through which firms transform inputs into outputs). For example, if a new firm is established in a small town, the wage rates of all workers in the town might increase because of competition for the available labor supply. Existing firms have suffered an external diseconomy; they must now pay a higher wage to their workers. Such externalities are classified under the heading of *pecuniary externalities*. These externalities involve shifts in supply and demand curves within well-established markets and are not of concern in this chapter.

## Externalities, Efficiency, and Optimal Output

In the model of perfect competition, it was shown that private-market activities can lead to a situation in which allocative efficiency is achieved. However, even if all sectors of the economy operated under perfect competition, when market prices do not incorporate the true costs of production or consumption activities, efficiency in the use of inputs and the production of outputs can no longer be taken for granted. When private cost curves no longer capture the true costs of production, the theoretical apparatus used to evaluate efficiency conditions must be altered so that all costs can be considered. As a means of achieving efficiency, government involvement (through regulation or taxes) can ensure that all the costs of productive activities are accounted for by private firms.

## EXTERNALITIES AND THE OPTIMAL LEVEL OF OUTPUT

Accounting for an activity that imposes external costs on other individuals involves augmenting private costs with these external costs. In this way, all costs are accounted for. In Figure 21.3, two marginal-cost curves are shown for a perfectly competitive firm. Aside from producing its own output, the firm introduces cancer-causing pollutants into the atmosphere. The curve labeled MPC represents the firm's marginal-private-cost curve, the firm's supply curve when external costs are ignored. The firm will maximize its profits by producing 1,000 units of output at the market price of $4 per unit. Under conditions of pure competition without externalities, the firm would achieve allocative efficiency because the price charged for output is exactly equal to marginal-private cost. The marginal valuation consumers place on an extra unit of output would be exactly equal to the marginal valuation society places on the inputs used in the production process.

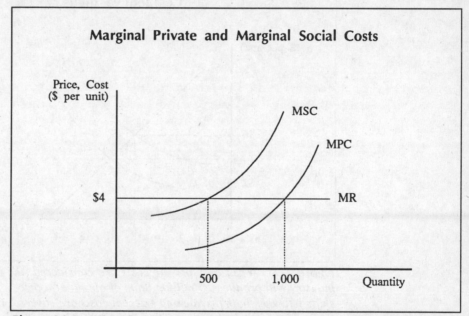

**Figure 21.3** *When firms cover only private costs, profit is maximized at 1,000 units of output, where marginal private cost (MPC) equals marginal revenue (MR). Accounting for both private costs and external social costs leads to an upward shift in marginal cost. From society's perspective, optimal output is 500 units, where marginal social cost (MSC) equals marginal revenue.*

The presence of externalities means that true allocative efficiency is not achieved. The actual costs imposed on society include both the private costs paid by the firm and the costs of pollution. When marginal pollution costs are added to private marginal production costs, the firm's marginal-cost curve shifts up to coincide with the marginal-social-cost curve. Five hundred units of output will be produced when both private and social costs are covered.

**Externalities and Optimal Industry Output.** The effects of accounting for external costs on a perfectly competitive industry are shown in Figure 21.4. Forcing firms in the industry to cover both marginal private costs and marginal social costs leads the industry's supply curve to shift left, from $S_0$ to $S_1$. This reduces the equilibrium quantity of output in the polluting industry from 10 to 8 million units and raises the price of output from $4 to $6 per unit. Once costs and prices have fully adjusted, profits are returned to the zero level for typical firms, and price will equal marginal social cost. The valuation consumers place on additional units of output will exactly equal true resource costs, both private and social; allocative efficiency will be achieved.

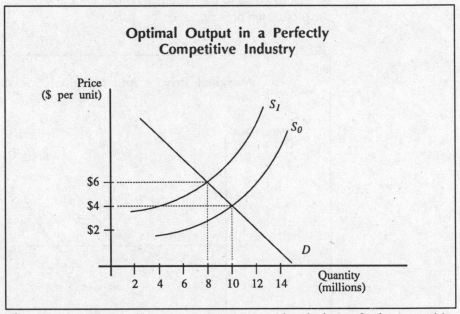

**Figure 21.4** *When only private costs are considered, the perfectly competitive industry will produce 10 million units of output at a price of $4 per unit. Supply shifts left when both private and external costs are covered. Equilibrium output in the industry falls to 8 million units, and equilibrium price rises to $6 per unit.*

*Pollution Costs, Benefits, and the Optimal Level of Pollution*

Many people consider a zero level of pollution the socially optimal level. For economists, determining the optimal level of pollution involves comparing the costs associated with pollution and the benefits derived from producing the products that lead to pollution. The issues involved are portrayed graphically in Figure 21.5. The units on the vertical axis are dollars per ton of pollution; the level of pollution is measured on the horizontal axis. The marginal-pollution-cost curve (MPC) is shown as increasing at an increasing rate, becoming steeper as the quantity of pollution rises. This reflects the idea that smaller levels of pollution are associated with lower costs but higher levels add to society's costs at an increasing rate.

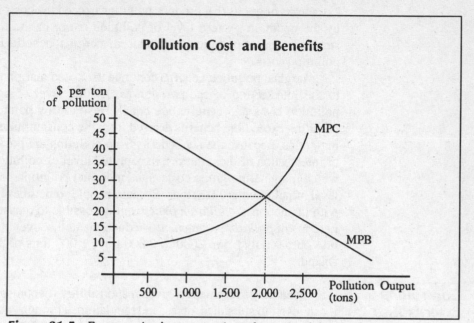

**Pollution Cost and Benefits**

*Figure 21.5 From society's perspective, the optimal level of pollution occurs when the marginal pollution costs (MPC) just equal the marginal pollution benefits (MPB). Benefits are derived from the good whose production causes pollution. Two thousand tons of pollution will be produced.*

At first glance, the concept of a marginal-pollution-benefit (MPB) curve seems like a contradiction of terms. However, pollution is a by-product that comes with the production of goods and services. Think of the fuel that is consumed and transformed into pollution in the course of tranporting people and goods, generating electricity to provide lighting, and burning oil or gas to provide heat. These goods provide utility and are demanded by consumers; if this were not the case, such goods and the associated pollution would not be produced. Through the law of diminishing marginal utility, the marginal benefits of the goods responsible for pollution output are assumed to decline as their output increases. Therefore, the marginal-pollution-benefit curve is downward-sloping.

## THE OPTIMAL LEVEL OF POLLUTION

To find the optimal level of pollution, it is necessary to engage in the standard comparison of marginal costs and marginal benefits. To the left of the point of intersection in Figure 21.5, the extra benefits derived from consuming extra units of goods that produce pollution exceed the costs imposed on society by the pollution. A zero level of pollution is not in society's interest. When small amounts of pollution are produced, marginal benefits far exceed marginal pollution costs.

Marginal pollution benefits continue to exceed marginal pollution costs up to the intersection of the two curves. At this level of pollution, additional pollution costs and benefits are equal. Beyond this point, the extra costs of polluting exceed the benefits derived from the consumption of pollution-creating goods. Because the net benefits from polluting are positive up to the point of intersection of these curves, the optimal level of pollution is the quantity at which marginal pollution costs equal marginal pollution benefits. The optimal level of pollution is 2,000 tons. Because people sometimes have a difficult time with the notion of *pollution benefits*, it is possible to recast the above analysis in terms of *pollution abatement*—reductions in the level of pollution. If pollution output falls from 3,000 to 2,000 tons, 1,000 tons of pollution have been abated.

## Controlling Externalities

When the government is given responsibility for controlling external costs, it can resort to subsidies, taxes, and regulation. Through subsidies, government can pay firms to seek alternate means of production that lead to reduced levels of unwanted by-products. Through taxes, it can charge firms a fee for each unit of by-product produced. This encourages firms to seek production methods that generate fewer undesirable by-products. Finally, the government can impose regulations that set specific acceptable pollution levels for firms and industrial processes.

### TAXES AND SUBSIDIES VERSUS REGULATION

When pollutants are extremely dangerous or deadly, such as radiation emissions from the production of nuclear power or dioxin production in the manufacture of paper, government has little choice but to establish regulations to control them. For pollutants that are not so dangerous, assume that the level of pollution that equates marginal social costs and marginal social benefits has been determined. In deciding between regulation, taxes, and subsidies, the problem is to find the least costly means of reducing pollution consistent with the socially optimal level.

In general, taxes and subsidies are preferable to regulations and standards for all firms. Taxes and subsidies induce firms with the lowest marginal abatement costs to reduce their emissions first. The government can impose a tax on pollution emissions and continue to raise the tax rate until the desired level of pollution has been achieved. Firms whose cleanup costs are less than the tax will reduce their pollution emissions to avoid the tax. As the tax increases, more and more firms will find it in their interest to reduce emissions. On the other hand, firms that experience extremely high cleanup costs will choose to pay the tax. Society will benefit from this arrangement because the real resource costs associated with attaining the desired pollution abatement are reduced compared to those that would arise if all firms had to cut emissions regardless of their costs.

**Taxes versus Regulation: An Example.** Suppose the government has decided that pollution output must be reduced by 1,000 gallons. There are two firms in the economy. Under the regulation plan, the 1,000-gallon decrease is to be achieved by having each firm reduce pollution in proportion to its total pollution emissions. Because Firm A is responsible for 75 percent of all pollution, it must cut its emissions by 750 gallons. Firm B, responsible for 25 percent of all pollution, must cut its emissions by 250 gallons. The total cost of reducing the emissions depends upon the pollution-abatement cost each firm faces. Suppose it costs firm A $20 to reduce its pollution output by one gallon. Its total abatement costs will equal $15,000 (750 × $20). Suppose Firm B incurs a cost of $10 per unit of emission reduction. Its total abatement cost will equal $2,500 (250 × $10). The total cost of the resources used in reducing pollution emissions by 1,000 gallons therefore equals $17,500.

The same amount of pollution reduction could have been achieved by giving each firm the option of cleaning up 1,000 gallons of pollution or paying a tax on pollution emissions equal to $11 per gallon on the 1,000 gallons. Because its cleanup costs are so high, Firm A would continue to pollute and pay the tax on all 1,000 units. The government would receive $11,000. Because the tax charge is greater than its cost of cleanup, Firm B would reduce its emissions by 1,000 units at a cost of $10,000.

The $11,000 in taxes the government has collected from Firm A was not used for pollution cleanup and does not enter into the actual resource costs of pollution abatement. It is an income transfer between Firm A and the government. As a result of the tax, the value of *real resources* used for pollution cleanup has fallen from $17,500 under regulation to the $10,000 paid by firm B. This savings occurs because the firm with the lower marginal cost of cleanup is entirely responsible for the pollution abatement. As a general rule, the use of taxes to achieve emissions goals will lead to lower pollution-abatement costs because those firms able to clean up for the least expense will do so.

Had the government paid a *subsidy* of $11 per gallon for pollution abatement instead of imposing a tax, the result would be the same. Firm A would have no incentive to clean up; its abatement costs of $20 per gallon are too high. Firm B would clean up all 1,000 gallons, incurring a real-resource cost of $10,000. There would be an income transfer from the government to firm B of $11,000. Because firm B's cleanup costs are only $10 per gallon, any tax or subsidy greater than $10 (say, $10.01) could be used by the government to achieve its goal.

**The Bubble Principle.** The *bubble principle* provides means by which regulation can lead firms to reduce emissions with the lowest marginal costs. Rather than set a particular emissions-reduction requirement for all processes within a firm, the bubble principle allows achievement of pollution-reduction goals in two stages. First, the desired amount of overall pollution reduction is determined by the government. Next the government instructs the firm to achieve the goal using any means it likes. Because firms will seek to minimize the costs of compliance associated with any regulation, controls will be placed on those processes with the lowest marginal pollution-abatement costs.

For example, a firm with two smokestacks might face an abatement cost of $15 per ton from one stack and $5 per ton from the other. If the government requires that emissions from each stack be cut by 100 tons, the firm will incur a total cost of $2,000. Instead of this approach, the government can instruct the firm to reduce its emissions by 200 tons in any way it chooses. *Ceteris paribus*, other things being equal, the firm will cut emissions by 200 units in the stack with the lower cost and incur a cost of only $1,000. The government is not concerned about the emissions from every stack used by the firm. In a sense, the government has placed a bubble or dome around the firm and concerns itself only with the aggregate emissions from the bubble.

## The Coase Theorem

Up to this point, it has been assumed that control of externalities requires government intervention. The *Coase theorem* provides a set of circumstances in which externalities can be properly accounted for and dealt with without government intervention. The Coase theorem states that if property rights are well specified and costless negotiation is possible, the amount of pollution will be efficient and identical regardless of how property rights are allocated.

### PROPERTY RIGHTS

The lack of well-defined property rights is one of the main reasons for externalities. For example, the air we breathe belongs to everyone but is not really controlled by anyone. Most people think that polluters should pay the costs associated with their activities. However, the ownership of rights to particular resources plays an important role in determining how externalities can actually be controlled. Property rights provide a basis for negotiation that does not exist when everyone or no one thinks they have control over resources.

If a firm has the legal right to pollute a river, individuals living downstream from the firm might have to pay the firm to reduce its emissions. Here the costs of controlling the externality are borne by those affected by it. Otherwise, the firm has no legal or monetary incentive to stop polluting. If the people downstream have a legal right to clean water, the costs of the externality will be borne by the firm. The firm can either use pollution-reducing equipment or pay the individuals downstream for the right to pollute. Similarly, if loud music is tolerated and uncontrolled in your apartment building, you could always offer to pay your neighbor to lower the volume of his or her stereo. In this case you would bear the cost of controlling the externality. If you have the right to silence, you might consider payment from your neighbor for the right to listen to loud music at certain times of the day. The costs are now borne by the creator of the externality.

## COSTLESS NEGOTIATION

Organizing individuals and getting them to agree on a strategy to deal with the effects of pollution take time and effort. Because of these costs, a community affected by pollution may or may not take action to deal with it. Aside from the problems one side or the other might have in organizing itself, once negotiations take place, agreement between parties may not readily occur. Once again, negotiation costs are incurred. The assumption of costless negotiation sidesteps these problems. Thus, in formulating the predictions of the Coase theorem, it is assumed that the negotiation process involves no costs.

## EFFICIENT POLLUTION LEVELS AND THE COASE THEOREM

Figure 21.6 presents the marginal-pollution cost and marginal-pollution benefit schedules for some pollutant. The pollutant is produced by a factory that

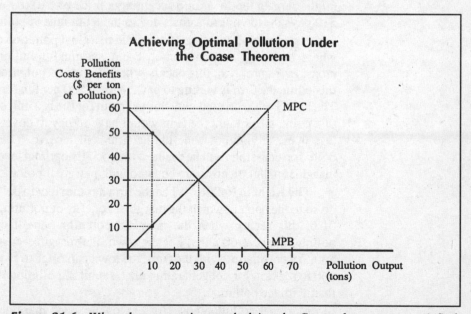

*Figure 21.6  When the assumptions underlying the Coase theorem are satisfied, the socially optimal level of pollution will be produced. Marginal pollution costs (MPC) in excess on marginal pollution benefits (MPB) open the door for payment by the town for the right to clean water when the firm has the right to pollute. MPB in excess of MPC can lead to payment by the firm to the town when the town has the right to clean water.*

dumps it into a river and thereby imposes external costs on a town downstream. To understand how the Coase theorem works, two cases are examined. First, it is assumed that the town has the right to clean water. Next, the firm is assumed to have the right to pollute.

**The Right to No Pollution.** When the town has the right to clean water, the initial amount of pollution allowed is zero. However, through negotiation, it may be possible for the firm to acquire some pollution rights from the town. Consider the range of pollution values lying to the left of the intersection of the marginal-pollution cost and marginal-pollution-benefit schedules. At any level of pollution output in this range, the benefits of polluting for the firm exceed the costs to the town. The firm can therefore cover the town's costs and still experience a postive marginal benefit.

For example, the tenth unit of pollution output brings the firm $50 in benefits but costs the town only $10. If the firm offered the town $11 for the right to generate the tenth unit of pollution, it would be in the town's interest to accept the $11. The payment it would receive for allowing this unit of pollution exceeds the cost. However, tough negotiation on the part of the town could lead to a higher payment than this. It would be in the firm's interest to pay for the pollution right as long as the price is below $50. A price of $49.99 would still leave the firm better off. Similarly, a tough negotiator for the firm might bargain the town into accepting a price of $10.01. Any payment above $10 pays the town for its costs due to the tenth unit of pollution.

Marginal-pollution benefits exceed marginal pollution costs up to the point where the marginal-pollution-cost and marginal-pollution-benefit schedules cross. In Figure 21.6, this occurs when 30 tons of pollution are generated. At this point, the firm is willing to pay the town $30 per ton for the right to pollute. The town is just satisfied with this payment for the last unit of pollution. Beyond this point, the amount the firm would have to pay to cover the town's costs is less than the value of benefits the firm will receive. Therefore, the level of pollution emissions will be found at the socially optimal level, the level at which marginal pollution costs are equated with marginal pollution benefits.

**The Right to Pollute.** When the firm has the right to pollute, it will naturally do so to the point at which the marginal benefits of polluting are zero. In Figure 21.6, this occurs when the marginal-pollution-benefit curve intersects the pollution axis at 60 units. For the town, the marginal cost of the 60th unit is $60. By negotiating with the firm, the town can offer to pay any amount below $60 to the firm for not generating the last unit of pollution and still be better off than with the pollution.

Marginal pollution costs for the town exceed marginal pollution benefits for the firm for all units of pollution to the right of the marginal cost and marginal benefit intersection. Therefore, negotiation and pollution reductions over this range are also possible. However, the town will not rationally pay the firm to reduce its pollution to the left of the point of intersection; marginal costs to the town are below the marginal benefits to the firm. Once again, despite the change in ownership of the property right, the efficient level of pollution—the level associated with equality between marginal pollution costs and marginal pollution benefits—is achieved.

## A MARKET FOR POLLUTION RIGHTS

By stating the conditions necessary to establish a market for pollution rights, the Coase theorem solves the problem of externalities. When the conditions of the Coase theorem are not satisfied, the government can take steps to create them. One means of creating a market in pollution rights involves the printing of certificates by the government. These certificates give the holder the right to emit a certain quantity of pollution. The total number of certificates is limited by what the government determines to be the socially optimal level of pollution.

Firms that pollute bid for the pollution certificates in a pollution-rights auction. The highest bid that any firm would make is limited by the actual costs of abating its emissions. Therefore, the highest bidders at the auction will be those firms with the highest pollution-abatement costs. Those firms outbid for pollution rights find it cheaper to cut back on their pollution levels. As in the case of a tax or subsidy on pollution, firms with the lowest abatement costs will clean up first, thereby reducing the overall costs to society of pollution abatement. The number of certificates issued controls the amount of pollution firms can produce; therefore, the desired limitation of emissions is also achieved.

*Two important exceptions to the smooth running of a free-market economy are seen in public goods and externalities. They join with imperfect competition as examples of situations where allocative efficiency is not necessarily achieved. As with imperfect competition, public goods and externalities provide a rationale for government intervention in the economy. Because public goods may not be provided by the free market at socially optimal levels, government action may be necessary to ensure their availability. The presence of externalities implies that certain costs and benefits are left out of private calculations regarding economic activity. Greater correspondence between marginal social costs and marginal social benefits can be attained through government involvement, by assigning property rights, or by establishing markets that ensure all costs and benefits are considered.*

# 22

## Comparative Advantage and the Gains from Free Trade

*E*xchanges of goods take place both within and between the countries of the world. In the United States, trade with other countries, as measured by exports of goods and services, currently accounts for about 12 percent of gross national product. Although it is not obvious, given the publicity surrounding trade deficits and workers displaced by foreign competition, engaging in international trade offers participating countries important economic gains. By presenting a simple model of exchange, this chapter examines the nature of these gains. The important concept of comparative advantage is defined, and its implications are explored. Next, arguments against free trade are considered along with methods used to inhibit trade.

## COMPARATIVE ADVANTAGE AND THE GAINS FROM SPECIALIZATION

One of the most important distinctions in understanding the basis of international trade is that between the definitions of *comparative* and *absolute advantage*. An *absolute advantage* occurs when one country can produce units of a good using fewer real resources than those required by another country.

*Comparative advantage* requires only that one country be *relatively* better at producing a good. With comparative advantage, even a country that has an absolute advantage in the production of all the goods it consumes will find its consumption possibilities enhanced by engaging in international trade.

The concept of comparative advantage is based on the opportunity costs of producing goods and services in different countries. The presence of different opportunity costs between countries not only opens the door for trade but also allows increased specialization and expanded worldwide production possibilities. These facts are examined by first showing how trade is made possible when production costs differ between countries. These production-cost differentials are then used as a basis for defining absolute and comparative advantage. The effects of trade on production and consumption possibilities are then considered.

## Comparative Advantage and International Trade

If one country produces a commodity using fewer real resources than another, it has an *absolute advantage* in producing that commodity. One country has a *comparative advantage* over another if, with the same quantity of resources, the first country can produce *relatively* more of the commodity than the second. A country can have a comparative advantage without having an absolute advantage in the production of any commodity. As an example, suppose that Japanese workers take 40 hours to produce 1 automobile and 10 hours to produce 1 ton of rice. American workers might require 60 hours to produce 1 auto and 20 hours to produce 1 ton of rice. Given the labor requirements for both automobiles and rice, the relative price of these goods in each country can be found. In Japan, the fact that producing one automobile requires 40 hours of labor and producing one ton of rice requires 10 hours means that 1 automobile is equivalent to 4 tons of rice. If wages are equal across industries and output prices reflect relative input costs, the Japanese price of rice per ton will be one quarter the price of an automobile. In the U.S., because it takes 20 hours to produce one ton of rice and 60 hours to produce one auto, the price of an auto will equal three tons of rice. In Table 22.1, the labor requirements and relative prices in Japan are shown along with the relative prices that prevail in the U.S.

## Trade Based on Comparative Advantage

|  | Labor Hours per Auto | Labor Hours per Ton of Rice | Relative Price (Tons of Rice per Auto) |
|---|---|---|---|
| Japan | 40 | 10 | 4 |
| United States | 60 | 20 | 3 |

*Table 22.1*

As seen in the hours required to produce autos and rice, Japan is a more efficient producer; it has an absolute advantage in both products. Nevertheless, as seen in the relative prices, there are advantages to trade between these countries. An enterprising Japanese trader will observe that 3 tons of rice sold in the U.S. are sufficient to purchase an automobile. Thus, rather than pay 4 tons of rice for one auto in Japan, a one-ton rice savings can be obtained by trading with America. From the U.S. perspective, rather than selling an auto in the U.S. for 3 tons of rice, a trader in possession an of automobile could reap a one-ton rice profit by selling the auto in Japan.

## COMPARATIVE ADVANTAGE AS A BASIS FOR TRADE

As seen in the example, it is not absolute advantage that leads to trade but comparative advantage. Comparative advantage originates with differences between relative prices in each country. These prices represent the opportunity cost of consuming an extra unit of one good in terms of a country's other goods. Specifically, the presence of a *lower opportunity cost* for a commodity in one country is equivalent to a *comparative advantage* for that country in the production of the commodity.

For example, in Table 22.1, because resources are finite, if Americans decide to consume an extra ton of rice, it is equivalent to giving up one-third of an automobile. In Japan, one ton of rice is equivalent to one-quarter of an automobile. Without trade, Americans face a higher opportunity cost when they decide to consume an extra ton of rice than the Japanese. The Japanese therefore have a comparative advantage in rice production. However, in automobiles, the opposite is true. The opportunity cost of consuming an auto in the U.S. is three tons of rice, while in Japan it is four. Because the opportunity cost of consuming autos is less in the U.S., the U.S. has a comparative advantage in auto production.

**Specialization and Comparative Advantage.** Opportunity-cost differentials based on relative productivity differences between countries provide the basis for trade. Goods with higher domestic opportunity costs compared with foreign opportunity costs will be imported; goods with higher opportunity costs produced abroad will be exported. Therefore, international trade will induce expansion in domestic industries with lower relative opportunity costs and contractions in domestic industries with higher relative opportunity costs. This specialization can increase the total output produced by trading partners.

From the data in Table 22.1, total output of automobiles and rice can be increased through specialization, even though Japan has an absolute advantage in producing both commodities. Consider a 120-hour transfer of labor from rice production to automobile production in the U.S. This will lead to the production of 2 extra automobiles at the cost of 6 tons of rice. If 80 hours of labor time are transferred from automobile production to rice production in Japan, rice output will rise by 8 tons, and automobile production will fall by 2. As a result of these resource transfers within countries, net-world automobile production remains the same, but net-world rice production rises by 2 tons. International trade must ensure that the gains from specialization are reallocated in an appropriate manner between producing and consuming countries.

## The Terms of Trade

Once trade opens between countries, the opportunity cost of acquiring goods changes from the domestic opportunity cost to the opportunity cost established as a result of trade. The opportunity cost of domestic goods in terms of foreign goods is represented by the *terms of trade*. The terms of trade are the rates at which domestically produced goods trade for foreign goods on the world market.

### THE RANGE OF TERMS-OF-TRADE VALUES

The pretrade relative prices that prevail in each country determine which country has a comparative advantage in producing particular commodities. The terms of trade determine the relationship between commodity prices in the world market. Again consider the example of Japanese and American automobile and rice production shown in Table 22.1. In the U.S., before trade begins, 1 automobile is equivalent to 3 tons of rice. Any terms of trade that allow Americans to obtain more than 3 tons of rice for an automobile will induce Americans to engage in trade. In Japan, before trade begins, 1 auto is equivalent to 4 tons of rice. Foreign trade will be worthwhile for the Japanese as long as an automobile can be purchased for less than 4 tons of rice. The range of values between the price ratios in each country before trade sets bounds upon the terms of trade that will prevail after trade begins. For the U.S. and Japan, the terms of trade must lie between 3 and 4 tons of rice per auto.

## Resource Transfers

In the above example, the fact that comparative advantage provides a basis for international trade does not negate the fact that the Japanese are more efficient in producing both automobiles and rice. Thus, while differences in opportunity costs between the U.S. and Japan suggest that Japan should export rice and the U.S. should export autos, increased production of both autos and rice might be achieved by moving Japanese production techniques to the U.S. or by moving American workers to Japan.

Unfortunately, there are some fundamental problems with this approach. First, production techniques may not be transferable. Climate and endowments of natural resources might play an important role in explaining higher output per labor hour in certain countries. Proximity to input markets due to different levels of urbanization lead to differences in efficiency. While population shifts are possible between countries, they also create crowding problems because land is in fixed supply. Individuals in countries may not wish to open their borders to individuals from other countries; those moving to different countries must adjust to a different culture. Individuals may derive utility from living where they are in spite of the fact that their real incomes might be increased by moving someplace else.

Aside from these considerations, productivity differences can result from different work ethics. Hence, moving laborers from one country to another will serve only to lower efficiency in the more productive country. The fact that resources and other factors of production are not freely mobile explains why all countries cannot adopt the most efficient means of production and why differences in comparative advantage can persist.

# JOINT PRODUCTION, PRODUCTION POSSIBILITIES, AND GAINS FROM TRADE

Comparative advantage is reflected in differences between the relative prices of goods in different countries. When such differences are present, the basis for trade is established. Through specialization, each country increases production of the good produced relatively more efficiently; this leads to greater consumption possibilities for trading partners. In other words, production and consumption decisions made before trade is established are inefficient. This is true in a global-resource-allocation sense compared with the consumption possibilities available to countries through establishment of international trade.

*Pre-Trade Production Possibilities*

The efficiency gains of specialization can be observed by forming a joint-production-possibilities curve for trading partners. This curve is based upon the production-possibilities curves for individual countries. Again considering automobile and rice production in the U.S. and Japan, recall from Table 22.1 that one Japanese auto requires 40 hours of labor; one ton of Japanese rice, 10 hours; one U.S. auto, 60 hours; and one ton of U.S. rice, 20 hours. For simplicity, assume that both Japan and the U.S. are endowed with 120 hours of labor. In this situation, maximum Japanese rice production equals 12 tons and maximum Japanese auto production equals 3 autos. In the U.S., six tons of rice can be produced with 120 hours, or the U.S. could produce 2 autos. For both the U.S. and Japan, Figure 22.1 presents the production-possiblilities curves given these technological possibilities.

## PRODUCTION POSSIBILITIES AND OPPORTUNITY COST

It is assumed that rice production can be transformed into auto production only in fixed proportions. Therefore, both countries face straight-line production-possibilities curves. For Japan, as seen in the slope of its production- possibilities curve, four tons of rice must be given up to free the resources necessary to produce one auto. The slope of the U.S. production-possibilities curve is minus three. This means that U.S. technology requires that three tons of rice be forgone to produce one auto. These slopes are also reflective of the pretrade opportunity costs in each country in their rice and automobile

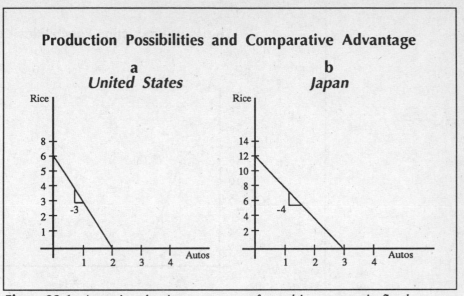

**Production Possibilities and Comparative Advantage**

Figure 22.1 contains two graphs labeled **a United States** and **b Japan**.

**Figure 22.1** *Assuming that inputs are transformed into output in fixed proportions, the United States and Japan are seen to face straight-line production-possibilities curves. Each country is endowed with 120 hours of labor; because the Japanese can produce both more rice and more autos, they are more efficient producers. In the United States, production of one auto requires that three tons of rice be given up. In Japan, four tons of rice must be sacrificed per auto. The United States therefore has a comparative advantage in auto production.*

production. Finally, the slopes of the production-possibilities curves represent the range of values within which the terms of trade between the U.S. and Japan must lie.

**The Joint-Production-Possibilities Curve**

By systematically considering specific output levels from each country's individual production-possibilities curve, the combined production-possibilities curve for the U.S. and Japan is derived. Suppose Japan and the U.S. both specialize totally in rice production. Using the production-possibilities curves shown in Figure 22.1, the joint output of both countries will equal 18 tons of rice with no automobile production. This is one point on the Japanese-American production-possibilities curve shown in Figure 22.2. Twelve of the 18 tons of rice are provided by Japan; the remaining 6 tons are provided by the U.S.

With Japan continuing to specialize in rice, the U.S. can increase its auto output by 2 units. However, in accordance with its technological possibilities, it must give up 6 tons of rice (3 tons per auto). Thus, another point on the joint production possibilities curve is found where 2 autos are produced along with 12 tons of rice. Because rice was substituted for autos in accordance with U.S.

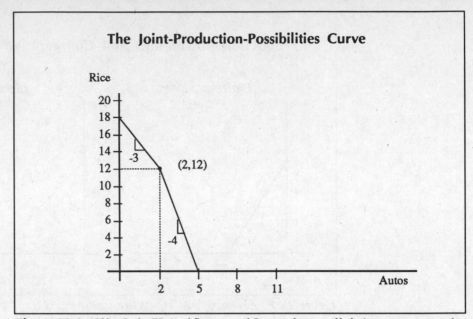

**The Joint-Production-Possibilities Curve**

*Figure 22.2   If both the United States and Japan devote all their resources to rice production, 18 tons are produced. Similarly, five autos can be produced with complete specialization in autos. With Japan fully specialized in rice, in accordance with United States production possibilities, 6 tons of rice must be sacrificed to produce two autos. If additional autos are to be produced, 4 tons of rice per auto are lost, consistent with Japanese production possibilities.*

technological possibilities, the slope of the production-possibilities curve between zero and 2 autos is minus 3.

With the U.S. totally specialized in auto production, additional world auto output can occur only when Japan reduces rice production. If Japan reduces rice production from 12 tons to zero, it can produce 3 autos (4 tons per auto). Total auto production when both countries specialize in auto production therefore equals 5. In moving from 12 tons of rice and 2 autos to no rice and 5 autos, production takes place in accordance with Japanese substitution possibilities. Thus, over the range of auto production between 2 and 5, the slope of the joint-production-possibilities curve equals minus 4. Consistent with the differing opportunity costs between countries, the joint-production-possibilities curve is kinked at the point where U.S. substitution of rice for autos gives way to Japanese substitution of rice for autos.

## COMPARATIVE ADVANTAGE AND JOINT SPECIALIZATION

In the U.S., 3 tons of rice must be sacrificed to free a quantity of labor sufficient to produce 1 auto. In Japan, production of 1 auto requires a 4-ton rice sacrifice. Based on these opportunity-cost differences, the theory of comparative advantage suggests that the U.S. should specialize in auto production and

Japan in rice production. With complete specialization production will take place at the kink in the joint-production-possibilities curve. The U.S. will produce 2 autos and no rice; Japan will produce 12 tons of rice and no autos.

At the point of complete specialization, the combined output of both countries reaches a level that could not be attained without specialization. For example, if the U.S. and Japan both produce 1 auto, as seen in their individual production-possibilities curves in Figure 22.1, joint production of rice would equal only 11 tons, 3 by the U.S. and 8 by Japan. Similarly, aside from the point of complete specialization, 12 tons of rice can be produced by both countries only if auto production falls below 2 units. From its production-possibilities curve, as its contribution to the 12 tons of rice, Japan can manufacture 1 auto and grow 8 tons of rice. If the U.S. produces the remaining 4 tons of rice, it will use 80 labor hours. This leaves only 40 labor hours for auto production, 20 less than the 60 required in the U.S. to produce one auto.

## THE TERMS OF TRADE AND TRADE POSSIBILITIES

Through complete specialization, both countries enjoy greater production possibilities. However, trade can take place only if the terms of trade fall within the pretrade opportunity costs. For the U.S. and Japan in the example, the pretrade opportunity costs are, respectively, minus 3 and minus 4 tons of rice per auto. After trade begins, the actual terms of trade and degree of specialization are determined by the underlying supply and demand conditions that exist in each country for autos and rice.

Assume that an appropriate balance is achieved in the international market when 3.5 tons of rice exchange for one automobile. Given these terms of trade, the U.S. might export 1 auto to Japan in exchange for 3.5 tons of rice. With complete specialization, the U.S. produces 2 autos. Total U.S. consumption after trade consists of one auto and 3.5 tons of rice. Observing the pretrade production possibilities curve for the U.S. in Figure 22.1, if 1 auto is to be consumed, only 3 tons of rice would be available for consumption. Thus, through trade, the U.S. is able to consume at a level beyond its original production-possibilities curve; it consumes an extra half ton of rice. Similarly, along Japan's pretrade production-possibilities curve, the consumption of 1 auto is possible along with the consumption of 8 tons of rice. Through complete specialization, 12 tons of rice are produced; 3.5 tons are traded to the U.S. for an automobile, and 8.5 tons are available for consumption. As with the U.S., after trade, the consumption bundle available to Japan lies outside Japan's pretrade production-possibilities curve.

## CONCAVE PRODUCTION POSSIBILITIES

The fixed-opportunity-cost model presented here can be extended to cover the more standard case of production-possibilities curves that are concave and bend outward from from the origin. Such production possibilities arise when inputs cannot be transferred from the production of one output to another without experiencing an efficiency loss. In other words, the transfer of given quantities of input from production of one output to production of another leads to smaller and smaller increases in output. Such transfers affect the opportunity cost of producing output and can have an effect on the degree of specialization found after countries establish trade.

# BARRIERS TO FREE TRADE

Given the benefits of specialization and international trade discussed in the previous section, it may seem difficult to understand the calls for protection from foreign competition heard frequently in the news. Generally, foreign competition is labeled unfair; its injurious effects on U.S. workers are often highlighted. On the other hand, many economists believe that establishing trade barriers to protect every industry or group of workers adversely affected by foreign competition is equivalent to legislating inefficiency and waste as worthwhile business objectives. According to this perspective, only through free trade can the advantages of international trade be realized and the benefits of competition enjoyed.

## Arguments Against Free Trade

While economists are quick to point out the advantages of trade, the fact is that increased specialization does displace workers in industries where the U.S. does not have a comparative advantage. For society as a whole, the long-run advantages of trade may outweigh any short-run disadvantages. But for factory owners faced with the prospect of bankruptcy and workers faced with the prospect of unemployment, retraining, or moving to a new location in search of work, the gains from trade offer little consolation. To the extent that taxes must be raised to help displaced workers, all members of society pay more and in a sense pay a subsidy to other Americans consuming foreign goods. Aside from the employment effects of trade, other arguments against free trade focus on developing and maintaining domestic industries for defense and other purposes that are seen as important for the nation's self interest. Calls for imposing trade barriers in response to barriers established by trading partners are often heard. A summary of the arguments against free trade is presented in the following sections.

### EMPLOYMENT EFFECTS

Foreign competition is often criticized because it displaces U.S. workers. The fact that trade opens up job opportunities in the U.S. is generally ignored. Criticism is most notable when the U.S. runs a large trade deficit—when the volume of U.S. imports exceeds the volume of U.S. exports, especially during a recession. It is argued that if U.S. consumers would only purchase more

American goods, the trade deficit would be reduced, employment in the U.S. would increase, and the recession would end. Though analytically sound, this argument overlooks the factors underlying American demand for foreign goods. Americans would purchase American goods if they thought their value per dollar exceeded the value per dollar of foreign goods. Thus, when there is a call to "buy American," American consumers are asked to create employment opportunities for American workers in exchange for goods yielding less satisfaction per dollar of expenditure. Otherwise, Americans would already be buying American.

Nevertheless, many individuals believe that increasing employment opportunities for Americans is a goal worth sacrificing for. This is considered especially true when Americans have lost out to foreign competition because of unfair trade practices. Where U.S. industry has failed to keep pace with world competition because of poor management or inefficient workers, this argument is less persuasive. By supporting less efficient American production, the ability of the U.S. to compete successfully in the world market is reduced, and potential gains from trade are lost.

## FOREIGN DUMPING

In the 1980s many Americans became concerned about foreigners "dumping" their products on the U.S. market. *Dumping* refers to imports sold at prices below the cost of production. Although selling below cost should result in bankruptcy, foreign industries engaging in such practices are able to stay in business because they are paid subsidies by their governments. Because of this, even American producers making use of the most up-to-date technology could be driven from business, leaving the door open for monopoly control of certain products by foreign industries. The argument calling for trade protection in this circumstance is similar to the call for legislation against monopoly in domestic industries. The problem is determining whether lower foreign prices reflect production costs associated with superior technology or are set at levels designed to reduce American competition.

## CHEAP FOREIGN LABOR

Wage rates in the United States are among the highest in the world. All else being equal, this would make American workers less desirable employment prospects for firms able to locate in other countries. However, all else is not equal. American workers tend to be among the most highly educated and the most productive in the world. Through the theory of comparative advantage and the gains associated with specialization and trade, the availability of low-cost labor in other countries suggests that those countries should engage in labor-intensive activities. The U.S. should move toward economic activities that take advantage of the highly skilled nature of its work force. This is true even though the process of transition to less labor-intensive activities may be difficult for displaced American workers.

## THE INFANT INDUSTRY ARGUMENT

The infant industry argument is based on the idea that certain newly established industries need protection from foreign competition until firms become competitive enough to stay in business without protection. For example, a country desiring to establish and develop its own automobile industry would face problems organizing production and training a suitable work force. Establishing a market for its product would also be difficult because consumers would not be familiar with the new automobile's characteristics. To give such an industry a chance, limitations on the availability of foreign substitutes are imposed through quotas or tariffs. Subsidies are also provided to keep the protected product's price low. This helps it compete in the world market. Weaning infant industries from their sources of protection is the major problem. If the product cannot eventually compete on its own, government may wind up financing a perpetual money-loser.

## SELF-SUFFICIENCY AND DEFENSE CONCERNS

Specialization and exhanging goods through international trade is fine as long as no disruptions to trade are experienced. During times of peace such disruptions represent a short term inconvenience. For example, during the various energy shocks of the past 20 years, consumers experienced several episodes of long waiting lines and highly unstable prices in return for cheap foreign oil. There is little doubt that achieving self-sufficiency in fuel production would reduce living standards for Americans not involved in fuel-producing industries.

During times of war, dependence on foreign sources of supply might impede a country's ability to defend itself. Thus, in spite of the gains from trade, maintaining international order might be impossible. Threats might have to be dealt with through undesirable concessions. To prevent this, industries essential to the nation's defense might be protected from foreign competition. Problems arise in determining which industries are critical to a nation's defense. Virtually every sector can make an argument that its output is essential. Problems also arise over the long run; as it attempts to maintain inefficient industries for defense purposes, a country's productivity declines and weakens its defense posture.

## TRADE BARRIERS ESTABLISHED ELSEWHERE

It is often argued that the U.S. should counteract trade barriers in other countries by establishing trade barriers of its own. However, other countries may respond by raising more barriers to trade. As each additional barrier to trade is established, the potential gains from trade are further reduced.

## Methods of Controlling Trade

Once arguments against free trade are accepted, there are a number of methods by which imports can be curtailed—mainly tariffs and quotas. The ultimate effects of either restriction are higher prices for domestic consumers and potential retaliation by trading partners.

### TARIFFS

Tariffs act like a tax on foreign goods. As foreign goods become relatively more expensive in the U.S., demand for substitute American made goods increases. However, because of the outward demand shift for American goods and the tariff on foreign goods, American consumers wind up paying more.

### QUOTAS

Quotas limit the quantity of foreign goods that can be sold in the U.S. Quotas also have the effect of raising prices for American consumers. In the market for the foreign good, the limited supply drives up its price. Substitute American goods will therefore experience an increase in demand, driving up their prices. The American consumer pays more.

### OTHER NON-TARIFF BARRIERS

In addition to quotas, governments can impose quality standards designed to protect domestic industry and impede free trade. One example is European restrictions on beef from the U.S. that has been fed growth hormones.

*In this chapter, international trade and the importance of comparative advantage and specialization have been examined. Different opportunity costs in the production of commodities are sufficient to bring about trade between nations. As nations begin to expand the output of goods produced with a comparative advantage and decrease the output of goods produced with a comparative disadvantage, increased specialization will lead to increases in the consumption possibilities of all trading partners.*

*Engaging in international trade will impose costs on owners and employees of industries adversely affected by foreign competition. Businesses may close and workers may become unemployed. This fact often leads to calls for protectionism, tariffs and quotas. Such restrictions of free trade are paid for by consumers who suffer price increases equal to differentials between competitive world prices and more highly priced domestic products.*

# 23

# *Input Markets: Land and Capital*

*In analyzing optimal input use and input supply, land, labor, and capital each possess special qualities. As seen in Chapter 20, labor's unique characteristics are especially important in understanding the shape of the labor-supply curve, the effects of unions, and the effects of discrimination. In this chapter relevant characteristics of land and capital markets are examined. For land, special problems arise because its supply tends to be fixed. For capital, because its services can extend beyond the period when it is purchased, future as well as current conditions must be accounted for in determining the optimal quantity.*

## LAND

As an input, *land* is generally considered as the geographic area where productive activities take place. As a generic term, *land* represents finite natural resources used as inputs into the productive process. When considered as a geographic area or as a finite resource, the most interesting feature of land as an input is that it is fixed in quantity. In other words, land's supply curve is vertical; the supply of land is totally inelastic.

**Rent: The Price of Land**

Because its supply is totally inelastic, rent, the price of land use, will be determined by the location of the demand curve for land. The quantity of land available remains fixed whether it is used or not. As with the demand for any input, the demand for land is based on its marginal-revenue product. Derivation of labor's demand curve and the role of marginal productivity are discussed in Chapter 20. The derivation presented there can be generalized to any input, including land. Demand and supply curves are used to determine land's rent; however, there are some complications because the land can be used only by a single producer.

### DETERMINING EQUILIBRIUM RENT

In Figure 23.1, demand curves for two firms are shown. These are assumed to be representative of the demands by many firms for use of one fixed land parcel. For example, a grocery store, gas station, dry cleaner, and numerous other businesses may be interested in a street corner. Because it is associated with the highest marginal-revenue product, the highest demand curve must determine the price of the land. The higher demand curve allows the firm possessing it to outbid other firms for the land's use.

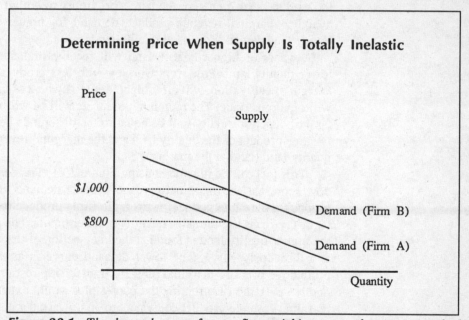

**Figure 23.1** *The demand curves for two firms wishing to use the same parcel of land are shown. Because its demand curve is higher, Firm B can outbid Firm A for use of the land. The price of land is determined at the intersection of the highest demand curve and the totally inelastic supply curve.*

Since the higher demand curve is relevant for this piece of land, rent will equal $1,000. A rent above this level could not last; the marginal revenue product of land (the extra revenue the firm earns by using the last piece of land) would be below the rent paid for use of the land. Marginal costs would exceed marginal benefits.

If rent fell below $1,000, no increase in the land's use could be achieved. As seen along its demand curve, the firm would like to use more land at a lower rent. However, the quantity of land is fixed. Because the top curve is assumed to represent demand by the firm with the highest marginal-revenue product, the land's rent would ultimately be bid back up to the equilibrium level of $1,000.

## DIFFERENTIAL RENT AND LAND AT THE MARGIN

Consider the production of some output, such as corn, on different parcels of land. Differences in the quality of land imply that inputs can be used more efficiently on some parcels than others. Using the same quantities of other inputs on different pieces of land will lead to production of different levels of output; higher-quality land will lead to higher output levels than lower-quality land. *Quality* refers to such aspects as the fertility of the soil, the proximity of the land to other inputs, or the land's proximity to output markets. Because of a higher marginal-revenue product, demand for higher-quality land will be higher than demand for lower quality land.

Owners of higher-quality land will receive higher rent than owners of lower-quality land. Producers working with less productive land, land at the *margin* of cultivation, will offer higher rent to owners of high-quality land; this will bid up its price. The premium producers will be willing to pay to work on land of superior quality will be equal to the difference between the marginal-revenue product of the quality land and the marginal-revenue product of lower quality land (land at the margin).

This fact can be illustrated using Figure 23.1. The demand curves for land now represent the marginal-revenue–product-demand curves for two firms producing the same good. However, the firms produce on different parcels of land. The firms use the same quantity of other inputs. The price commanded by the higher-quality land is found at the intersection of the higher demand curve and the supply curve. The lower demand curve is associated with the less productive or more marginal plot. By transferring resources to the more productive plot, the firm renting the poorer plot would experience an increase in marginal-revenue product equivalent to an upward demand shift.

The maximum amount that the firm renting the less productive land would be willing to pay for the more productive land is given by the distance along the vertical supply curve between the two demand curves. This amount is $200. The owner of the more productive land (versus the firm renting it) captures the entire rent due to its increased productivity.

## ECONOMIC RENT

Because land's supply is fixed, even a zero price for land is sufficient to call it into production. Land such as a vacant city lot is a potential productive factor and is available for use regardless of its price. Thus, rent, the price of land, always represents a premium above the amount necessary to induce land to be part of some production process. Economists have extended this concept to other inputs. They define *economic rent* as a payment to any factor of production above the amount necessary to call forth its services in some line of production.

In Figure 23.2, a typical supply curve for some input is shown along with a demand curve. The equilibrium price of the input is found at the intersection of supply and demand. Moving along the supply curve, to induce higher quantities of the input into the market requires a higher input price. Once the equilibrium price is determined, all input quantities below the intersection of supply and demand are paid an amount higher than that necessary to elicit their services. For example, for the fourth unit of input, a price of $4 is sufficient to call forth its services, yet it is paid $5. The triangular area below the $5 price and above the supply curve up to the point of equilibrium represents the total economic rent paid to owners of this input. Given the market price of $5, the fourth unit earns a rent of $1.

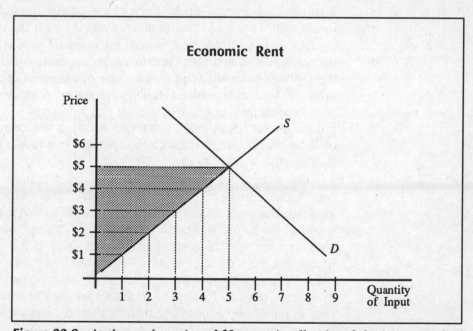

**Figure 23.2** *At the market price of $5 per unit, all units of the input supplied except the last are paid a price in excess of that necessary to bring them forth for sale. A price of $4 is necessary to bring forth the fourth unit. Because the market price is $5, economic rent on the fourth unit is $1. Total economic rent is the triangular area below $5 and above the supply curve to the point of equilibrium.*

Rent will be zero if the supply curve is horizontal, or perfectly elastic. In this case, a minimum factor payment is required to elicit any quantity of the input. Conversely, the entire payment to the factor is rent when supply is vertical, or perfectly inelastic, as in the case of land.

# THE FIRM'S CAPITAL STOCK AND INVESTMENT

Unlike labor services, which are used in the production process at the same time they are purchased, capital goods such as machinery or structures have a lifetime that extends well beyond their date of purchase. Unlike land, which also has a lifetime that extends into the future, capital eventually depreciates and becomes worthless. Therefore, the decision by a firm to purchase capital involves consideration of the price of the capital, capital's contributions to revenue throughout its lifetime, and the rate at which capital depreciates.

The fact that future time periods are involved adds another dimension to the problem of ascertaining the firm's optimal quantity of capital. To determine the additions to revenue that the purchase of a piece of capital equipment will bring, the firm must predict its future sales and the price at which its output will sell. Account must be taken of the fact that a dollar of revenue received in the present is worth more than a dollar of revenue to be received in the future. All of these considerations must be incorporated in a model that determines the firm's optimal capital stock.

There are at least three ways economists determine the optimal use of capital and/or the level of investment. Each of these techniques implicitly or explicitly makes use of the market interest rate. First, an approach based on the marginal productivity of capital can be used. This approach is similar to that used to determine the optimal quantity of labor and other inputs. Second, investment projects can be evaluated in terms of their rates of return. Given the rate of interest, this involves estimation of the opportunity costs of different investment choices. Finally, implicit comparisons between interest rates and rates of return can be made by calculating *net present value* or by examining a measure known as the *internal rate of return*.

## The Rental Rate of Capital and Optimal Capital Use

One way of getting around the problem of time in determining the optimal quantity of capital is to assume there is a rental market for capital goods. The firm is thought to rent the capital from someone else. In this way, the firm need not consider the fact that the capital it rents lasts for many periods. It will pay a daily, weekly, monthly, or yearly rate for the use of capital, just as it does for the labor it hires.

The demand for capital is derived in the standard way. Assuming that the firm operates in a perfectly competitive industry, the capital-demand curve is equivalent to the firm's value of the marginal-product-of-capital curve. This curve shows the addition to the firm's revenues obtained throught the sale of the output produced by hiring an extra unit of the input.

The value of the marginal product is capital's marginal product multiplied by the price of output. Through the law of diminishing returns, as the firm hires additional units of the capital, capital's marginal productivity declines. As shown in Figure 23.3, the value of the marginal-product curve is downward-sloping; additions to revenue decline as more units of capital are rented.

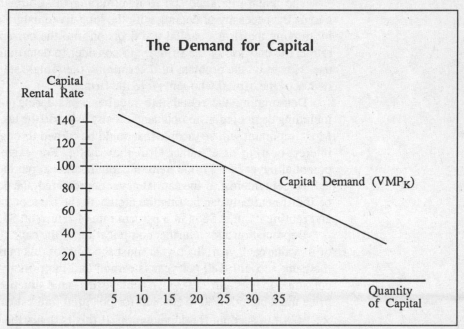

**Figure 23.3** *The capital-demand curve is the firm's value of the marginal product curve for capital (VMP$_K$). As long as the value received from the sale of output produced by using an extra unit of capital exceeds the rental price that must be paid, it makes economic sense to rent that unit. With the rental rate given as $100, 25 units of capital are optimally used.*

The *rental rate of capital* is the amount the firm must pay for using a unit of capital. Optimality requires that the firm hire additional units of capital until the rental rate equals the value of the marginal product of capital. If the value of the marginal product for a unit of capital is greater than its rental rate, the additions to the firm's revenues from employing that unit exceed costs. The addition to profit is positive, and the firm should rent more capital.

Because the value of the marginal-product curve determines how much capital should be hired given the rental rate, it is equivalent to the firm's demand curve for capital. As seen in Figure 23.3, at a rental rate of $100 per unit of capital, 25 units of capital are used. Beyond 25 units, the value of the marginal product of capital is less than the rental rate; additions to profit are negative, and the firm loses money. Under 25 units, revenues from the sale of the output produced by additional units of capital exceed the costs of additional capital, so more units of capital should be hired.

## THE RENTAL RATE OF CAPITAL

The rental-rate approach to determining the optimal quantity of capital avoids the necessity of dealing with the long-lived nature of capital. It does so by moving the firm's capital-use decision into the current period. The rental rate is the only factor the firm has to consider to determine its optimal capital use. However, the problem of determining the rental rate still remains for the owner of the capital who rents it to the firm.

Determining the rental rate requires considering a number of factors, including depreciation, maintenance costs, risk, and the tax treatment of capital. Most important will be income that could be earned through the purchase of an interest-bearing asset rather than the capital. For example, suppose that a potential buyer of a $1,000 item of capital can also put the $1,000 in the bank at 8 percent interest. If the capital never depreciated, the potential buyer would be indifferent between putting the money in the bank or purchasing the capital and renting it out at $80 (an 8 percent rate of return on $1,000) per year.

Depreciation adds a further complication. If the capital item loses 5 percent of its value each year, the owner must account for this in the rental price. With the bank account, $80 per year is earned and the principal, or initial deposit, continues to be worth $1,000. To achieve this same situation, the capital's rental price must include $80 to account for potential interest earnings plus $50 (.05 × $1,000) to account for depreciation. If this is done, the owner of the capital will first have the $80 that could be earned in a bank as interest. At the end of the year, the capital originally worth $1,000 is worth $950 because of depreciation. However, because a $50 charge for depreciation was included in the rental rate, the owner is just as well off as if the initial $1,000 were placed in a bank.

Risk, taxes, and other factors must also be accounted for in determining the rental rate. For example, investment tax credits can make capital purchases more attractive than financial investments. The risk that capital equipment will become obsolete before a full return has been made must also be included in the rental rate.

## Optimal Investment and the Rate of Return

Another means of determining the optimal level of investment is based on the firm's ranking of investment projects by their expected *rates of return*. The rate of return is the net income resulting from an investment, divided by the cost of the investment. For example, if a firm pays $1,000 for a machine and earns $1,100 at the end of the year from the sale of the output produced by the machine, the rate of return is ($1,100 − $1,000)/$1,000, or 10 percent. As an alternative to undertaking investment projects, the market rate of interest represents the next best return that could be earned by the firm. To determine which investment projects should be undertaken, the firm compares the rate of return of each project with the market rate of interest. Optimality requires that a firm continue to undertake investment projects as long as the rate of return exceeds the rate of interest.

Suppose the market rate of interest is 10 percent and the firm has the possibility to undertake a project that yields a return of 20 percent. Even if the firm had to borrow money at 10 percent, it would still be better off undertaking this project. Instead of earning nothing, it will earn the difference between the rate of return and the interest cost. If the firm can finance the project without borrowing, it should; it will earn ten percent more than it would by purchasing an interest-bearing asset that pays 10 percent. All projects that yield a return greater than or equal to 10 percent should be undertaken. (Although a return of 10 percent is exactly equal to the rate of interest, the project earning this return does not earn a rate less than the rate of interest.)

## Discounting and the Internal Rate of Return

Through the process of ranking investment opportunities by their rates of return, a means of determining optimal investment levels is found. However, the problem of estimating the rate of return for an input that lasts many years remains. *Discounting* is a means by which dollars to be received or spent in the future can be valued in terms of *today's* dollars. By understanding the discounting procedure, the basis for comparing future costs and revenues and estimating rates of return is established.

### PRESENT VALUE

Even under the assumption that there is no inflation, a dollar received today is worth more than a dollar to be received at other times in the future. A dollar received today can be placed in a bank and will earn interest. Thus, if the rate of interest is 5 percent, at the end of one year the dollar received today is worth $1.05. Seen in a different light, with a 5 percent rate of interest, 95 cents put into the bank today will be worth approximately $1 in one year. Thus, the value today of $1 to be received in a year is about 95 cents today. The *present value* of $1 in one year is about 95 cents.

404    *Introduction to Economics*

## DISCOUNTING, OR FINDING THE PRESENT VALUE

Underlying the fact that future values are worth less than present values is some fairly simple mathematics. It can be best understood by first considering how present values are transformed into future values and then working in reverse. The present value of $1 today is naturally $1. The transformation of $1 held in the present into its future value in one year involves accounting for the fact that the future value of the dollar equals the original dollar plus the interest that can be earned on the dollar. Thus, with $r$ representing the rate of interest and Present Value denoting the amount of the initial deposit,

$$Future\ Value\ in\ One\ Year = \$1.00 + 0.05(\$1.00)$$

or

$$Future\ Value\ in\ One\ Year = (1.05) \times (\$1.00)$$

or

$$Future\ Value\ in\ One\ Year = (1 + r) \times Present\ Value$$

After one year, the future value of some initial sum earning the prevailing rate of interest is always $(1+r)$ times the present value. Therefore, by rearranging terms, the present value can be solved for in terms of the future value and the rate of interest:

$$Present\ Value = \frac{Future\ Value\ in\ One\ Year}{(1 + r)}$$

Suppose now that the future value of an amount deposited for two years is to be determined. After one year, the interest on the initial deposit and the initial deposit will equal

$$[(1 + r) \times Present\ Value]$$

Left in the bank for a second year, this amount would still be available, plus it would earn interest. The future value after two years will equal

$$Future\ Value_2 = (1 + r)[(1 + r) \times Present\ Value]$$

or

$$Future\ Value_2 = (1 + r)^2 (Present\ Value)$$

Solving for the present value, it is seen that

$$Present\ Value = \frac{Future\ Value_2}{(1+r)^2}$$

This analysis can be extended in time to consider the present value of a sum of money to be received in $n$ years, where $n$ is any number of years. The formula will appear as

$$Present\ Value = \frac{Future\ Value_n}{(1+r)^n}$$

**Discounting: An Example.** Suppose a firm estimates that the revenues it will receive in 5 years from the sale of its output will equal $200,000. If the interest rate is 7 percent, the present value of this sale will equal

$$\frac{\$200,000}{(1+0.07)^5} = \frac{\$200,000}{1.40255} = \$142,597.24$$

If the $200,000 is to be received in 10 years, its present value is

$$\frac{\$200,000}{(1+0.07)^{10}} = \frac{\$200,000}{1.96715} = \$101,669.86$$

Finally, if the $200,000 is to be received in 50 years, its present value will equal

$$\frac{\$200,000}{(1+0.07)^{50}} = \frac{\$200,000}{29.457} = \$6,789.55$$

The further in time the $200,000 is to be received, the *less* it is worth in the present. Should the interest rate increase, the present value would decrease. For example, if the interest rate is 10 percent, the present value of $200,000 to be received in 50 years drops to

$$\frac{\$200,000}{(1+0.1)^{50}} = \frac{\$200,000}{117.391} = \$1703.71$$

## NET PRESENT VALUE

By calculating an investment project's *net present value*, a firm can decide whether the project should be undertaken or whether the funds to be used for the investment should instead be used to purchase a financial asset that earns the market rate of interest. Calculation of the net present value involves discounting all the future revenues received and all the future costs incurred from some investment project. Because the discounting procedure transforms future revenues and costs into present dollars, an immediate comparision of the net gain or loss from undertaking the project is possible. If the net present value is positive, undertaking the project is conceptually equivalent to earning an immediate return on the investment. It follows that the project should be undertaken.

Net present value is expressed as follows: Let $R_t$ represent the revenue received from the investment in future period $t$ ($t$ might be next year or 10 years from now). Let $C_t$ represent the costs incurred in purchasing or maintaining the investment in period $t$. For simplicity, assume that the project exists for only 3 periods. The net present value of the investment is then defined as

$$Net\ Present\ Value = \frac{R_1}{(1+r)} + \frac{R_2}{(1+r)^2} + \frac{R_3}{(1+r)^3} - \frac{C_1}{(1+r)} - \frac{C_2}{(1+r)^2} - \frac{C_3}{(1+r)^3}$$

In other words, net present value is equal to discounted future revenues minus discounted future costs. Because both revenues and costs are transformed into their present value (their worth right now), a positive value indicates the presence of an immediate rate of return from undertaking the project. An immediate rate of return on a project is clearly superior to purchasing an interest-bearing asset; interest is earned only with the passage of time.

**Optimal Investment and Net Present Value.** All projects with a net present value greater than zero should be undertaken. A zero net present value means that the rate of return from the project is exactly equal to the rate of interest. This leaves the investor indifferent between purchasing the investment good and purchasing a financial asset that earns the market rate of interest. If net present value is less than zero, the investment should not be undertaken; a greater return can be earned by purchasing an interest-bearing asset.

**The Net-Present-Value Formula.** Combining revenues and costs from each period, it is possible to define net present value as the discounted net revenue (revenue minus cost) from each period.

$$Net\ Present\ Value = \frac{R_1 - C_1}{(1+r)} + \frac{R_2 - C_2}{(1+r)^2} + \frac{R_3 - C_3}{(1+r)^3}$$

Using summation notation to form an equivalent expression,

$$Net\ Present\ Value = \sum_{t=1}^{3} \frac{R_t - C_t}{(1+r)^t}$$

Because the index in the summation can run for any length of time, the general formula for net present value is found by replacing the number 3 with the number of periods considered.

## THE INTERNAL RATE OF RETURN

The *internal rate of return* represents the discount rate at which the net present value becomes zero. It thus represents the lowest market rate of return consistent with undertaking an investment project. For simplicity, all the costs of an investment project that yield returns for *n* periods are incurred in the initial period. The net present value is defined as

$$R - C = \sum_{t=1}^{n} \frac{R_t}{(1+r)^t} - C$$

For now, *r* is interpreted as a variable discount factor rather than the fixed market rate of interest. As *r* rises, future returns are discounted at a higher and higher level. This causes the ratio $\dfrac{R_t}{(1+r)^t}$ to become smaller and smaller. Ultimately, if the discount factor, *r*, gets big enough, the sum of all future discounted returns will equal and then be exceeded by costs.

The discount rate that makes net present value zero is the internal rate of return. It makes the potential investor indifferent between putting money in an interest-bearing account at a rate of interest equal to *r* or pursuing the investment project. The question is whether the rate of interest available in the market is greater or less than the internal rate of return. If the market rate of interest exceeds the internal rate of return, the potential investor is better off forgoing the investment and earning the market rate of interest. In this case, use of the market rate of interest in the net-present-value formula will lead to a negative net present value. Conversely, if the internal rate of return is greater than the market rate of interest, use of the market rate of interest in the net-present-value formula would lead to a positive value.

**The Internal Rate of Return: An Example.** Assume that an investment project involves a cost of $1,000 this period and yields $1,200 next period. The problem is to find the rate of return that causes the net present value to equal zero. Given these assumptions, because costs incurred this period do not have to be discounted, the equation for calculating the internal rate of return is

$$R - C = \frac{\$1,200}{(1+r)} - \$1,000 = 0$$

Rewriting this equation yields

$$\$1,200 = (1 + r)\$1,000$$

or

$$\frac{\$1,200 - 1,000}{\$1,000} = 0.2 = r$$

Hence, the internal rate of return is 0.2 (20 percent). As long as the market rate of interest is less than 0.2, the investment project should be undertaken.

If the market rate of interest is 0.25, the net present value will equal

$$\frac{\$1,200}{(1 + 0.25)} - \$1,000 = \$960 - \$1,000 < 0$$

Discounted future returns ($960) fall short of costs ($1,000). Interest rates above 0.2 will always lead to a negative net present value, implying that the investment should not be undertaken. Interest rates below 0.2 will lead to positive net present values and imply a rate of return from the investment in excess of the market rate of interest.

*I*mportant aspects of land and capital markets have been explored in this chapter. Because land is present in fixed quantities regardless of its market price, the rent land earns is a premium above the amount necessary to call its services into production. The notion of economic rent extends this concept to other factors of production.

*Problems associated with the long-lived nature of capital have been addressed in three ways. Through use of the rental rate on capital, the optimal level of capital use is found by making use of a marginal-productivity-based demand curve for capital. At the theoretical level, this method of finding the desired quantity of capital corresponds to finding the optimal quantity of labor and other inputs. The relationship between rates of return and market rates of interest provides another means of determining optimal investment levels. An investment should be undertaken as long as its expected rate of return exceeds the market rate of interest. Use of the net present value and the internal rate of return provides a means of estimating rates of return for projects and determining if they are worthwhile.*

*The real-world complications associated with determining optimal use of land, labor, and capital presented in this and previous chapters go far beyond those presented here. Nevertheless, the fundamental concepts and techniques explored here underlie most advanced treatments of such problems.*

# 24

# *An Analytical Approach to Consumer Choice*

*T*he model of consumer behavior presented earlier can be re-expressed using graphs and equations to provide clearer insight into the nature of the consumer-choice problem. In terms of analytical difficulty, such analysis represents the high point of introductory microeconomics courses and the starting point at the intermediate level. Use of the techniques presented here ties together the entire model of consumer choice, including the role of optimization, the derivation of the demand curve, and income and substitution effects. Aside from further illustrating the nature of the consumer-choice problem, the graphic and analytical methodology corresponds quite closely to that used to portray the cost-minimization problem faced by firms.

As with most forms of economic analysis that make use of graphic techniques, the key to understanding lies in transforming visual images into meaningful representations of real-world economic activity. Complete understanding will be achieved only with a thorough knowledge of the basic economic concepts behind the graphs. In developing the analytical model presented in this chapter, the focus is therefore on definitions, graphical representation of important relationships, the meaning inherent in these relationships, and the predictions concerning consumer behavior obtainable by manipulating the graphs.

# THE MODEL OF CONSUMER CHOICE

From an economic perspective, consumers face the problem of maximizing their utility subject to a budget constraint. The budget constraint is a representation of the consumer's scarce resources, here assumed to be a fixed level of income. Market prices are assumed to be given for the consumer; that is, the consumer is not able to alter the prices that prevail in the market. No matter how much of any particular commodity he or she decides to purchase, it is insignificant compared with the commodity's total output.

Consumer preferences must also be represented. Distinctions are made between higher and lower levels of utility or satisfaction as well as the way utility changes in response to the substitution of one good for another. Maximization of utility occurs in conjunction with the consumer's budget constraint; therefore, the solution to the consumer's maximization problem involves the simultaneous interaction between utility and the budget that allows attainment of utility. For simplicity, the model of consumer choice is developed in a two-goods economy. The results emerging from this analysis are readily extended to the case of many goods.

# THE BUDGET CONSTRAINT

The graphic representation of a consumer's budget constraint involves accounting for the consumer's income, the quantities of goods purchased, and the prices that must be paid for these goods. These factors are examined by developing the equation showing the relationship between income and expenditure when all income is spent on available commodities. Through manipulation of this formula, an equation for the budget constraint can be derived, and the consumer's budget constraint can be graphed.

## The Balance of Income and Expenditure

Suppose a consumer has an income of $Y$ dollars and desires to purchase some combination of two goods. The quantities purchased of the two goods are denoted $Q_1$ and $Q_2$, and the corresponding prices of these goods are denoted $P_1$ and $P_2$. Assuming that the consumer spends all of his or her income on good 1, good 2, or some combination of these goods, the following equation describes the relationship between income and expenditure:

$$Y = P_1 Q_1 + P_2 Q_2$$

Total income is equal to total expenditure on good 1 plus total expenditure on good 2. To see this, first note that income, $Y$, is measured in dollars. For example, in a given year, income might equal $25,000. The equality sign between the right and left sides of the equation signifies that the units of both sides of the equation are exactly the same. The quantities $Q_1$ and $Q_2$ have units consistent with the product represented. Thus, if $Q_1$ represents the quantity of books purchased, the units will be the number of books. Quantities are multiplied by their respective prices. Prices are measured in dollars per unit of good. Again assuming that $Q_1$ represents the quantity of books purchased, $P_1$ has units equal to dollars per book. It follows that the product $P_1Q_1$ represents the total dollars spent on books (the book units cancel). Similar reasoning implies that the product $P_2Q_2$ will also be in dollars; this product represents the consumer's total expenditure on good 2.

## THE CONSUMER'S BUDGET: AN EXAMPLE

Suppose that the consumer has an income of $100 that can be spent on movies and hamburgers. To attend a movie, a price of $5 must be paid; each hamburger consumed costs $2.50. With $100, choices for this consumer include attending 20 movies and eating no hamburgers or eating 40 hamburgers and attending no movies. Other combinations are possible. For example, consuming 30 hamburgers and attending 5 movies results in complete expenditure of the $100 budget. In fact, assuming that fractions of goods can be purchased, there are an infinite number of consumption combinations that exactly use up the consumer's income. The problem is to find the one combination that provides the consumer with the highest level of utility.

## The Budget Constraint Equation

With two goods, a fixed income, and fixed product prices, the consumer's budget equation balances income and expenditure:

$$Y = P_1Q_1 + P_2Q_2$$

To portray all the choices open to the consumer, this equation is solved for either $Q_1$ or $Q_2$. Arbitrarily selecting $Q_1$, the balance equation is transformed by subtracting the product $P_2Q_2$ from each side and dividing by $P_1$. The solution for $Q_1$ then appears as

$$Q_1 = \frac{Y}{P_1} - \left(\frac{P_2}{P_1}\right)Q_2 \tag{24.1}$$

When graphed with $Q_1$ on the vertical axis and $Q_2$ on the horizontal axis, this result is recognizable as the equation for a straight line. As seen in Figure 24.1, its intercept is $\dfrac{Y}{P_1}$ and its slope is $-\left(\dfrac{P_2}{P_1}\right)$. Consistent with the balance between income and expenditure, points to the right of the budget constraint are not affordable; points to the left of the budget constraint are affordable but leave some income unspent; points on the budget constraint are both affordable and exactly exhaust all income.

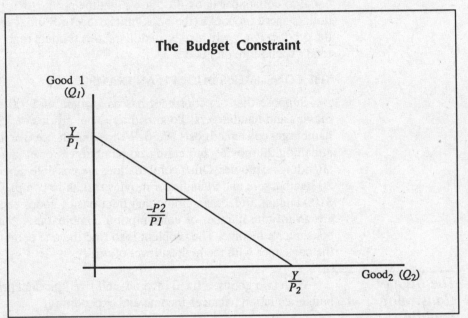

**The Budget Constraint**

**Figure 24.1**  *The budget constraint shows all the combinations of two goods that a household can afford given a fixed income. If all income (Y) is spent on good 1, $\dfrac{Y}{P_1}$ units can be purchased, while $\dfrac{Y}{P_2}$ units of good 2 can be purchased if all income is spent on good 2. The ratio of these values, the rise and run of the budget line, therefore equals $\dfrac{-P_2}{P_1}$.*

## THE INTERCEPT OF THE BUDGET LINE

Both the intercept and slope of the budget constraint have economic interpretations. If income is $100 and the price of good 1 is $5 per unit, the intercept value will equal 20. This means that if all income is spent on good 1 and no income is spent on good 2, it is possible to purchase 20 units of good 1. The $Q_1$ intercept therefore represents the quantity of good 1 that can be purchased if all income is spent on good 1. It can be shown that the $Q_2$ intercept is $\dfrac{Y}{P_2}$, the amount of good 2 that can be purchased when all income is spent on good 2.

## THE EFFECTS OF CHANGING INCOME

The vertical intercept of the budget constraint is $\dfrac{Y}{P_1}$; its horizontal intercept is $\dfrac{Y}{P_2}$ while its slope is $-\left(\dfrac{P_2}{P_1}\right)$. Therefore, an increase in income, $Y$, will cause the budget line to shift out, parallel to itself; its slope is not affected by income. A rise in income enables the purchase of more of both goods. Because the intercepts represent the quantities of each good that can be purchased if all income is spent on one or the other, a rise in income naturally leads to increased intercept quantities.

The effects on the budget constraint of a rise in income are shown in Figure 24.2. The consumer's initial income is $100. Prices of $5 per movie and $2.50 per hamburger enable the purchase of 20 movies if all income is used to purchase movies and 40 hamburgers if all income is used to purchase hamburg-

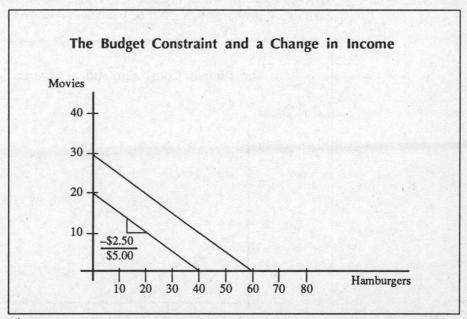

**The Budget Constraint and a Change in Income**

*Figure 24.2  A rise in income enables the consumer to purchase more movies, more hamburgers, or more of both goods. On the vertical axis, when income rises from $100 to $150, the number of movies it is possible to purchase at $5 per movie rises from 20 to 30. If all income is spent on hamburgers, the number that can be purchased at $2.50 each rises from 40 to 60. Because prices are constant, the slope of the budget constraint does not change.*

ers. These values, respectively, represent the vertical and horizontal intercepts of the original budget line. With prices unchanged, a rise in income to $150 enables the consumer to purchase either 30 movies or 60 hamburgers. The rise in income leads to the new budget line with these quantities as its intercepts. Because prices haven't changed, it is parallel to the original budget line.

## THE EFFECTS OF CHANGING PRICES

The effects of price changes on the budget line can be understood by considering what happens to the intercepts with a change in one price. If all income is spent on good 2 and the price of good 2 falls, more units of good 2 can now be purchased; its intercept will move outward. With good 2 graphed on the horizontal axis, the budget constraint becomes more horizontal. Because the price of good 1 has not changed, its intercept will not change; if all income is used to purchase good 1, after a decrease in the price of good 2, there will be no change in the quantity of good 1 the consumer can purchase. If the price of good 2 increases, similar reasoning implies that the horizontal axis will move inward. Changes in the price of good 1 will lead its intercept to move out or in depending, respectively, on whether its price falls or rises.

The situation associated with a decline in the price of hamburgers from $2.50 to $2 is shown in Figure 24.3. With $100 of income, the maximum quantity of hamburgers that can be purchased rises from 40 to 50; hence, the

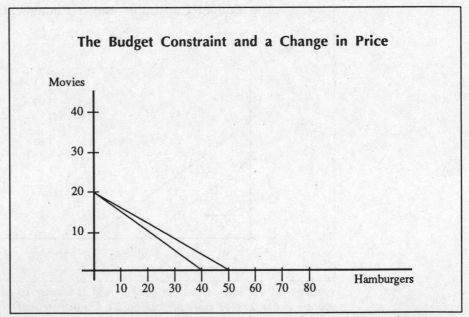

**The Budget Constraint and a Change in Price**

*Figure 24.3* *When the price of hamburgers declines form $2.50 to $2 each, the maximum quantity that can be purchased rises from 40 to 50. Because the price of movies is unchanged, its intercept is not affected. The budget constraint has become more horizontal.*

hamburger intercept is shifted out. Because the price of movies is unchanged, there is no change in the movie intercept.

### INTERPRETING THE SLOPE OF THE BUDGET LINE

From Equation 24.1, the slope of the budget line is $-\left(\dfrac{P_2}{P_1}\right)$. It has important implications for fully understanding the model of consumer choice. To understand the economic information present, it is necessary to determine the units that emerge from the ratio of prices. The price of good 2 has units of dollars per unit of good 2; the price of good 1 has units of dollars per unit of good 1. Because the dollar units cancel, the ratio of the price of good 2 to the price of good 1 will be in *units of good 1 per unit of good 2*. This ratio shows the rate at which good 1 can be transformed into good 2 given prevailing market prices. It therefore represents the opportunity cost to the consumer of transferring consumption from good 2 to good 1.

**Slope Units: An Example.** Assume that good 1 is movie tickets with a price of $5 per ticket and good 2 is hamburgers with a price of $2.50 per hamburger. The ratio of prices will then equal

$$-\left(\frac{P_2}{P_1}\right) = -\left(\frac{\$2.50/hamburger}{\$5.00/movie}\right) = -0.5\ movies/hamburger$$

In other words, assuming that it is possible and desirable to consume fractions of a product, every time the decision is made to consume an additional hamburger, the opportunity to see one-half of a movie is lost. Consume two hamburgers and miss an entire movie. The minus sign reflects the fact that to obtain more of one good, some of the other good must be given up.

**The Budget Line's Slope and Opportunity Cost.** The interpretation of the budget line's slope as the amount of one good that must be given up to acquire an additional unit of another good corresponds exactly to the definition of the opportunity cost between two goods. Opportunity cost was previously seen in the slope of the economy's production-possibilities curve. The concave shape of this curve (bending away from the origin) illustrates the fact that society cannot transfer inputs perfectly from the production of one output to another. However, an individual's desire to consumer more or fewer units of a good does not alter society's resource use sufficiently to affect the rate at which one output can be transformed into another. The constant slope of the budget line reflects this fact. This is also inherent in the assumption that the commodity prices paid by the consumer are constant. Regardless of how much of either good the consumer purchases, it is insignificant compared with total commodity output.

# *MODELING CONSUMER PREFERENCES*

The budget line represents the constraint faced by the consumer. Relative prices determine the slope of the budget line, while income determines its location. The second major component required for the model of consumer choice is a representation of the consumer's tastes and preferences. While every consumer in society has different preferences, it is possible to model a number of attributes likely to be consistent with the behavior of a typical consumer. These attributes are reflected graphically in the shape of lines known as *indifference curves*. By using indifference curves to represent the consumer's choice patterns over the range of potential commodity combinations, the unique mix of products that maximizes the consumer's utility will be found.

## Indifference Curves

An *indifference curve* shows all of the consumption combinations of two goods that provide the consumer with a constant level of satisfaction or utility. In other words, given any two bundles (market baskets) of goods on the same indifference curve, the consumer will be just as happy to have one bundle as the other. For example, a consumer might be just as happy with a small sailboat and a Cadillac as with a larger sailboat and a Chevrolet.

### DERIVING AN INDIFFERENCE CURVE

The shape of a typical indifference curve can be found by considering the bundles of possible commodities that are likely to leave a consumer with the same level of utility. In Figure 24.4, suppose the consumer derives a certain level of utility from consuming 10 movies and 20 hamburgers. This bundle of goods is labeled *A* and is assumed to be one point on an indifference curve. The objective is to locate other combinations of movies and hamburgers that leave the consumer equally satisfied—that is, to find other points on the consumer's indifference curve.

**The Downward Slope of the Indifference Curve.** For most goods, it is reasonable to assume that consuming more units leads to higher levels of utility than fewer units. Therefore, reductions in the quantity of movies with the number of hamburgers fixed, reductions in the number of hamburgers with the number of movies fixed, or reductions in both the number of hamburgers and movies will lead to reduced utility. In Figure 24.4, the range of values that lead to a reduction in utility is enclosed within the solid lines intersecting point *A* below 10 on the vertical axis and below 20 on the horizontal axis.

Alternatively, consumption of greater quantities leads to greater utility. Therefore, increases in the number of movies, holding constant the number of available hamburgers; increases in the number of hamburgers, holding constant the number of movies; or increases in both the number of hamburgers and movies will lead to increased utility. This range of values is contained within

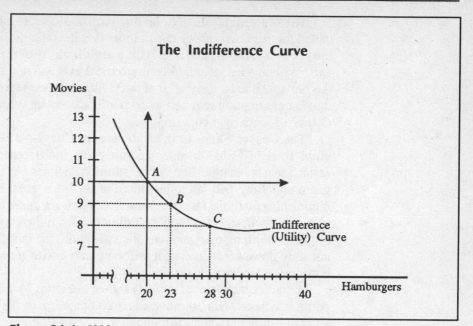

**Figure 24.4** *If 10 movies and 20 hamburgers are consumed, utility will be reduced if either the number of movies or the the number of hamburgers is diminished. Utility will rise if the number of movies or hamburgers increases. To maintain the same level of utility, sacrifices of hamburgers must be compensated with extra movies and vice versa. Hence, the indifference curve is downward- sloping. Diminishing marginal utility implies that utility will be constant along a convex utility curve, as shown.*

the solid lines intersecting point *A* above 10 on the vertical axis and above 20 on the horizontal axis.

By excluding combinations of goods that either increase or decrease utility, determining the shape of the indifference curve has become more manageable: The indifference curve cannot lie in either of the excluded regions. Given the remaining area, points on the indifference curve must be such that any *decrease* in the quantity of one good is met with a sufficient *increase* in the quantity of the other good so that the level of utility is unaffected. The utility lost due to a decline in the consumption of one good must be exactly offset by the utility gained from an increased consumption of the other.

While the particular degree of substitution required to fulfull this condition will vary from consumer to consumer, the indifference curve must be downward-sloping. This is observed in Figure 24.4. The indifference curve must pass through the point associated with 10 movies and 20 hamburgers. It cannot pass through either of the regions that would lead to an upward slope.

**The Convex Shape of the Indifference Curve.** Assuming that the law of diminishing marginal utility is in effect, more can be said about the shape of the indifference curve. When the law of diminishing marginal utility holds, as

**The Marginal Rate of Substitution.** The slope of an indifference curve is called the *marginal rate of substitution*. It is the ratio of the marginal utility of the good on the horizontal axis to the marginal utility of the good on the vertical axis. With movies measured on the vertical axis and hamburgers measured on the horizontal axis, the marginal rate of substitution represents the change in movie consumption required to keep utility constant when there is a one unit change in hamburger consumption.

**The Convex Shape of the Indifference Curve—The Diminishing Marginal Rate of Substitution.** Along a given indifference curve, economists assume that the marginal rate of substitution declines. As units of one good are given up, utility will fall unless more of the other good is consumed. With a diminishing marginal rate of substitution, more and more units of the good that is gained are needed to offset the utility lost from the good given up. Because of the diminishing marginal rate of substitution, the indifference curve will be not only downward-sloping; it will be convex with respect to the origin—it bows inward toward the origin.

A convex indifference curve is shown in Figure 24.4. It passes through the point associated with 10 movies and 20 hamburgers. To maintain a constant level of utility in moving from point *A* to point *B*, giving up 1 movie requires that 3 additional hamburgers be consumed instead. To maintain the same level of satisfaction, in moving from point *B* to point *C* the sacrifice of another move requires that 5 hamburger be consumed in its place.

## THE INDIFFERENCE-CURVE MAPPING

Consumers derive the same or varying levels of utility, depending upon the bundle of goods they consume. While some combinations of goods can keep utility constant, others will lead to increases or decreases in the level of utility. In fact, as represented by the nonintersecting curves in Figure 24.5, the commodity combinations of two goods are associated with an infinite number of indifference curves. Points on indifference curves are associated with consumption bundles yielding the same level of utility. Curves closer to the origin represent lower levels of utility. Some amounts of the two goods along the curve are smaller than the amounts for indifference curves farther from the origin. Because they correspond to a higher level of utility, consumers prefer to be on higher indifference curves.

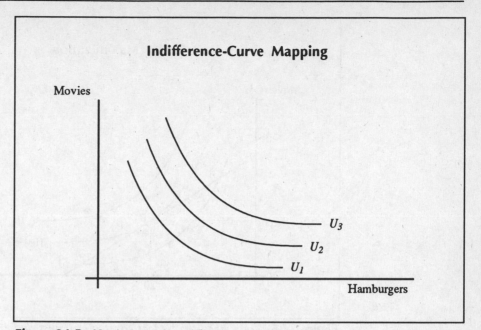

**Indifference-Curve Mapping**

Movies

$U_3$

$U_2$

$U_1$

Hamburgers

**Figure 24.5** *Nonintersecting utility curves are assumed to fill the entire graph, showing the consumer's preferences for movies and hamburgers. Higher levels of consumption are associated with higher indifference curves and therefore higher levels of overall satisfaction.*

# CONSUMER CHOICE AND MAXIMIZING UTILITY

To achieve the greatest level of satisfaction given income and relative prices, the consumer must reach the highest indifference curve consistent with the budget constraint. Figure 24.6 presents the consumer's budget constraint and three representative indifference curves. Consumption bundles outside the budget constraint are not affordable. Purchasing any combination of goods to the right of the constraint at prevailing prices would lead to a level of expenditure in excess of the consumer's income. It follows that the utility associated with indifference curve III cannot be attained.

Portions of indifference curve I do lie within the budget constraint and thus are affordable. However, indifference curve II, which is tangent to the budget constraint, is also affordable and lies above indifference curve I. Because indifference curves are not allowed to cross one another, no other indifference curve besides curve II can provide more utility and still be affordable. Therefore, the consumer will choose to consume at point *B* where the budget line just

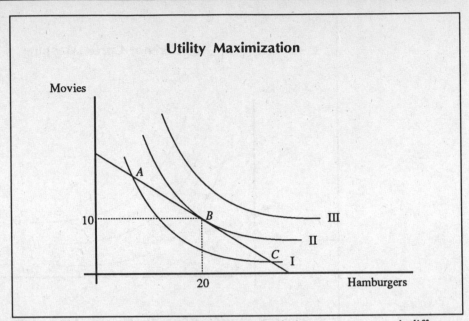

**Figure 24.6**  *Only when the budget constraint is just tangent to an indifference curve is utility maximized. Indifference curves higher than the curve tangent to the budget line are not affordable. Curves below this level are affordable, but utility can be increased by consuming at the point of tangency.*

touches the indifference curve II. Ten movies and 20 hamburgers lead to the highest level of satisfaction for this consumer.

**Interpretation of the Utility-Maximizing Condition**

The slope of the budget line is equal to the marginal rate of substitution. With movies graphed on the vertical axis and hamburgers graphed on the horizontal axis, the marginal rate of substitution equals the negative of the ratio of the marginal utility of hamburgers to movies: $-\dfrac{MU_H}{MU_M}$. The slope of the budget constraint will equal the negative of the ratio of the price of good hamburgers to movies: $-\dfrac{P_H}{P_M}$. At the point that maximizes utility, the indifference curve is tangent to the budget constraint. Their slopes are equal at this point. When the consumer maximizes utility, the minus signs will cancel, and the following condition will hold:

$$\frac{MU_H}{MU_M} = \frac{P_H}{P_M}$$

Rearranging terms,

$$\frac{MU_H}{P_M} = \frac{MU_H}{P_M}$$

This is exactly the optimality condition for the consumer that was presented in our initial discussion of consumer behavior. The marginal utility per dollar of expenditure must be equal for both commodities.

### RATIONALITY AND MAXIMIZING UTILITY

With the budget line–indifference curve representation shown in Figure 24.6, consider the situation that prevails at other points on the budget constraint when the consumer is not consuming at point $B$. For example, if the consumer chose to consume at point $A$, because the indifference curve is steeper than the budget constraint, the following condition would hold:

$$\frac{MU_H}{MU_M} > \frac{P_H}{P_M}$$

Rearranging terms,

$$\frac{MU_H}{P_H} > \frac{MU_M}{P_M}$$

The ratio $\frac{MU_H}{P_H}$ represents the marginal or extra utility derived from the last dollar spent on hamburgers. Similarly, $\frac{MU_M}{P_M}$ represents the marginal utility derived from the last dollar spent on movies. Because the utility derived from an extra dollar spent on hamburgers exceeds the utility derived from from an extra dollar spent on movies, it is rational for the consumer to reduce spending on movies and increase spending on hamburgers. As the consumer does so, he or she will move along the budget constraint toward its point of tangency with indifference curve II. At this point, because of the declining marginal utility for hamburgers and increasing marginal utility for movies, the marginal utility per dollar of expenditure is equal for both goods.

Should the consumer move beyond point $B$, the extra utility per dollar spent on movies will exceed the extra utility per dollar spent on hamburgers. The rational consumer will increase spending on movies and decrease spending on hamburgers, thereby moving back toward the optimum point of tangency.

# THE EFFECT OF INCOME AND PRICE CHANGES

With the consumer's preferences assumed constant, changes in the level of income or in the price paid for either of the two goods will lead to changes in the location of the budget constraint. In turn, this will lead to a new point of tangency with an indifference curve and alterations in the level of utility. Understanding how the consumer is likely to respond to such changes provides important information regarding the demand for products purchased by consumers.

*Changes in Income*

A rise in income causes the budget constraint to shift out, parallel to itself, because an increase in income will enable the consumer to purchase proportionately more of both goods and the slope of the budget line equals the ratio of commodity prices. It is not a function of the level of income. In Figure 24.7, the consumer is initially faced with the lower budget constraint and maximizes utility at point *A*. When the budget constraint shifts out, the consumer is able to purchase more of both goods. The point of tangency between the new budget constraint and the new indifference curve occurs at point *B*, which lies above

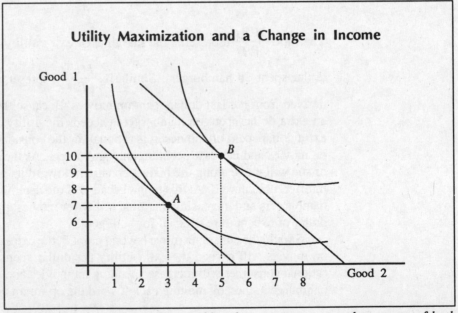

**Figure 24.7** *A rise in income enables the consumer to purchase more of both goods. The optimal point of tangency moves from point A to point B. Optimal consumption of good 1 rises from 7 to 10 units, while optimal consumption of good 2 rises from 3 to 5 units.*

and to the right of the original point of tangency. Therefore, the consumer's level of utility is increased with the increase in income.

## A Change in Price

A decline in the price of one good, holding income and the price of the other good constant, enables the consumer to purchase more of the good whose price has fallen if all income is spent on this good. If all income is spent on the good whose price has not fallen, it is not possible to purchase any more of it. Hence, the intercept of the budget constraint for the good whose price has fallen will move outward, and the intercept for the good whose price has not changed remains the same. Assuming that the price of good 2 declines, this effect is shown in Figure 24.8. The consumer originally maximized utility at point *A* but is now able to achieve a higher level of utility at point *C*.

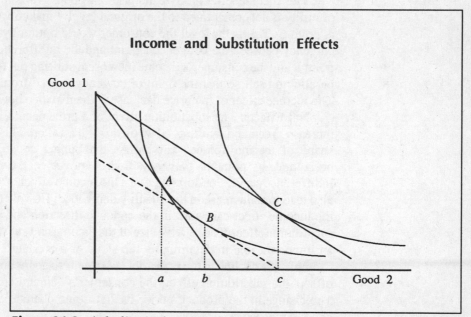

**Income and Substitution Effects**

**Figure 24.8** *A decline in the price of good 2 moves the consumer from point A to point C, a movement that includes an income and a substitution effect. The substitution effect from a to b is defined as the increase in good 2 that comes about due to its price decrease, assuming that the consumer must remain on the original indifference curve. The income effect, the movement from b to c, is the increase in consumption of good 2 that would occur at the new relative prices, given a rise in income.*

## THE INCOME AND SUBSTITUTION EFFECTS

The decrease in the price of good 2 increases the quantity purchased from *a* units to *c* units. It is possible to divide the total increase in the amount of good 2 purchased into that part caused by the decline in the relative price of good 2 (the *substitution effect*), and that part due to the fact that the decline in the price of good 2 enables the consumer to purchase more of both commodities (the *income effect*).

**The Substitution Effect.** To measure the substitution effect, imagine that the relative price of good 2 falls but that the consumer is forced to remain on the initial indifference curve. The budget line will become more horizontal, but it pivots along the original indifference curve. At the new relative price, the point of tangency between the original indifference curve and the hypothetical budget constraint (the one consistent with the lower price of good 2) occurs at point *B*. Note that the hypothetical budget constraint is parallel to the consumer's new budget constraint. The amount of good 2 consumed would increase from *a* to *b* solely because its relative price has fallen. This is the substitution effect.

**The Income Effect.** After the price of good 2 falls, the consumer's level of utility is not constrained to the original level. Final consumption takes place at point *C*. This is the level the consumer would optimally choose if the initial tangency between the budget constraint and the indifference curve occurred at point *B* and the consumer's income increased, shifting out the budget constraint parallel to itself so that the point of tangency moved from point *B* to point *C*. The income effect of the price decrease is the distance between points *b* and *c*.

**Net Effects.** The substitution effect of a price decrease always leads to an increase in demand for the good whose price has fallen. This is due to the convex shape of the indifference curves. As the budget constraint becomes more horizontal, its point of tangency always moves to the right along a given indifference curve. For normal goods, the income effect of a price decrease will also lead to an increase in the quantity demanded. However, for *inferior* goods, the income effect can work in the opposite direction and may even offset the substitution effect. The relative size of the income and substitution effects plays an important role in determining the slope of a product's demand curve. For example, if a decline in the price of a good leads to an income effect that exactly offsets the substitution effect, the consumer's demand curve will be vertical. The change in the product's price has led to no change in the quantity of the good demanded.

## Utility Analysis and the Consumer's Demand Curve

The analysis of price changes on the utility-maximizing quantity of a good provides the basis for deriving the consumer's demand curve. The top graph in Figure 24.9 shows a situation in which declines in the price of good 2 cause the consumer's budget constraint to pivot outward. Holding constant the price of good 1, the price of good 2 decreases from $5 per unit to $3 per unit to $2.50 per unit. Points of tangency with the highest indifference curve move from point *A*, to point *B*, to point *C*. The optimal quantity of good 2 rises from 10 to 14 to 20 units. Graphing the relationship between price and quantity demanded in the bottom part of Figure 24.9 yields the familiar downward-sloping demand curve.

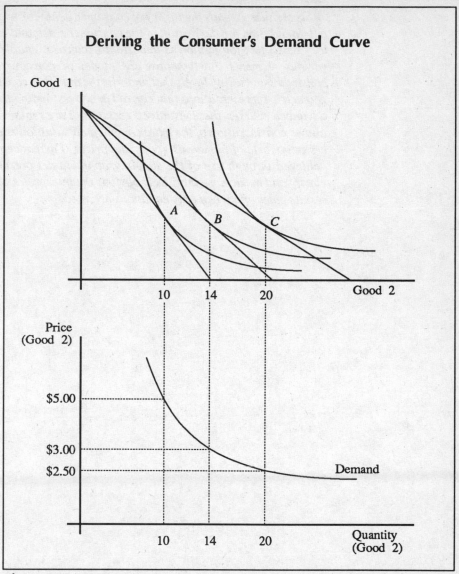

**Figure 24.9** *Declines in the price of good 2 lead to higher optimal level of its consumption. The relationship between optimal consumption of good 2 and its price is the consumer's demand curve.*

In deriving this demand curve, it is assumed that the consumer's income and tastes are fixed along with the price of the other good. If this exercise had been carried out assuming a higher level of income for the consumer, a lower price for good 1, or stronger tastes for good 2, the resulting demand curve would be located further to the right. This is consistent with the demand shift factors discussed earlier.

*T*his chapter extends the theory of consumer behavior by providing the analytical foundation for derivation of the consumer's demand curve. At the introductory level, this foundation is important because it enables visualization of the various elements that compose the model of consumer choice. The budget constraint and utility levels that underlie the model of consumer choice are given geometric representations that can aid in understanding these concepts. In more advanced courses, these visual representations are replaced with equations. This allows consideration of the more complicated situation encountered by consumers in a world of numerous goods and prices. The concepts and understanding achieved through use of the simple graphic model presented here can help to clarify and make more intuitively obvious the interpretations of purely algebraic results emerging when only equations are used.

# 25

## *Cost Minimization and Input Demand: An Analytical Approach*

*A*s *with the model of consumer behavior, the analysis of output and costs for firms can be restated using graphs and equations. This restatement provides additional insight into the technological and cost relationships faced by the typical firm and the factors it must consider to make optimal decisions. The techniques and framework presented here form the basis of many types of analysis in microeconomic theory. They serve as the foundation for deriving input-demand equations and analyzing changes in input demand over time. Input-demand equations are used in developing the cost functions discussed in detail earlier and understanding how costs change as input use changes.*

*There is a very close correspondence between the analytical techniques used to study the actions of consumers and the techniques used to study the behavior of firms. Both consumers and firms are assumed to engage in optimizing behavior. Consumers maximize utility subject to a budget constraint. Firms maximize output subject to a cost constraint. Alternatively, firms may try to minimize costs subject to producing a given level of output. As in the analytical chapter on consumer behavior, the focus of this chapter is on basic definitions, graphic representation of important relationships, the meaning inherent in these relationships, and the inferences that can be drawn by manipulating graphs.*

# OPTIMAL INPUT USE

Suppose that a firm seeks to maximize the output it produces. To do so the firm can purchase any combination of inputs it desires, but it must not exceed some predetermined acceptable level of total cost. The *cost constraint* represents the firm's choices regarding the combinations of inputs it can hire without exceeding the acceptable overall cost. The prices for inputs are assumed to be taken as given and fixed; because the firm's use of inputs is very small in relation to the overall size of input markets, increases or decreases in the amounts of inputs used by the firm are assumed not to affect input prices.

In addition to the cost constraint, to complete the model of optimal input choice, the technology with which the firm transforms inputs into output must be represented. The nature of the firm's production function must be captured geometrically. This representation must account for the fact that greater use of all inputs will lead to the production of more output. In addition, the assumption that substitution can take place between inputs in producing the same level of output must be incorporated.

The complete model involves simultaneous consideration of the cost contraint faced by the firm and its technological possiblities. Therefore, optimization involves a unique interrelationship between costs faced by the firm in hiring inputs and the firm's ability to transform those inputs into output. For the sake of simplicity, the model is developed for a firm that makes use of only capital and labor. The optimality conditions emerging from this analysis are easily extended to the case of many inputs.

# THE FIRM'S COST CONSTRAINT

The graphical representation of a firm's cost constraint involves accounting for the predetermined level of costs the firm is willing to incur, the quantities of labor and capital to be hired, and the prices that must be paid for labor and capital. The quantities of labor and capital purchased are denoted $L$ and $K$ respectively, and the corresponding prices of these inputs are denoted $w$ and $r$. If the firm wishes to spend exactly $C$ dollars on the inputs it hires, the following equation will describe the relationship between total cost and total expenditure on labor and capital:

$$C = wL + rK$$

The total cost incurred by the firm is equal to the total amount spent on labor plus the total amount spent on capital. The product of the quantity of labor and the wage rate represents the total dollar expenditure by the firm on labor. Similarly, multiplication of the quantity of capital by its price yields the firm's total expenditure on capital.

## The Balance between Cost and Expenditure

Suppose that to achieve a production goal the firm is willing to incur a cost of $2,000. Labor commands a wage of $20 per worker and the amount paid to owners of capital equals $100 per unit. If the firm hires only labor, 100 workers can be hired ($20 × 100 = $2,000). If the firm desires to use only capital, it can use 20 units ($100 × 20 = $2,000). Assuming that fractions of labor and capital quantities can be purchased, there are infinitely many input combinations consistent with the firm's set level of total cost and the factor prices it must pay. For example, hiring 20 workers and 16 units of capital is also consistent with $2,000 of expenditure on inputs. The problem is to find the one combination of inputs that provides the firm with the highest level of output, given the cost it wishes to incur.

### THE EQUATION FOR THE COST CONSTRAINT

With two inputs, a set level of total cost, and fixed input prices, the cost balance equation is

$$C = wL + rK$$

Solving for the quantity of labor,

$$L = \frac{C}{w} - \left(\frac{r}{w}\right)K$$

When graphed with $L$ on the vertical axis and $K$ on the horizontal axis, this is recognized as the equation for a straight line. As seen in Figure 25.1, its intercept is $\frac{C}{w}$ and its slope is $-\frac{r}{w}$. Both the intercept and slope of the cost constraint have economic interpretations.

**The Intercepts of the Cost Constraint.** If total cost is $2,000 and the wage rate paid to labor is $20 per unit, the vertical intercept value will equal 100. This means that if labor is the only input hired, it is possible to purchase 100 laborers. The vertical intercept therefore represents the quantity of labor that can be hired when all input costs consist of expenditure on labor. The horizontal intercept is $\frac{C}{r}$; this is the amount of capital that can be employed when all costs are composed of expenditure on capital.

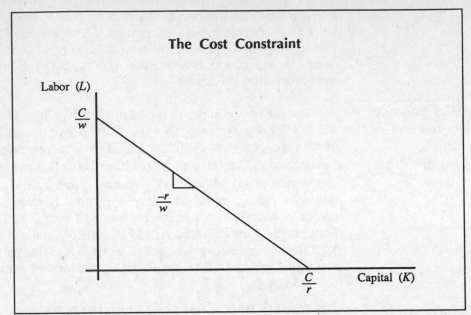

**Figure 25.1** *If the firm uses its entire cost allocation (C) to purchase labor,* $\frac{C}{w}$ *units can be purchased. If only capital is used,* $\frac{C}{r}$ *units will be used. Points along the cost constraint are consistent with exactly C dollars worth of expenditure. Given a rise of* $\frac{C}{w}$ *and a run of* $\frac{C}{r}$, *the slope of the curve is* $-\frac{r}{w}$.

**The Effects of Changing Total Cost.** The vertical intercept of the cost constraint is $\frac{C}{w}$, its horizontal intercept is $\frac{C}{r}$, and its slope is $-\frac{r}{w}$. An increase in the firm's acceptable level of total cost, $C$, will therefore cause the budget line to shift out, parallel to itself; the slope is not affected by total cost. When total cost increases, the firm can purchase more of both inputs. Because the intercepts represent the quantities of each input that can be purchased if all costs are composed of expenditure on one or the other input and because input prices are fixed, a rise in total cost leads to proportionately increased intercept quantities.

The effects of a rise in total cost are shown in Figure 25.2. At the prevailing wage of $20 per laborer and rental rate of $100 per unit of capital, the firm's initial cost of $2,000 enables it to purchase either 100 laborers or 20 units of capital. These input levels, respectively, represent the vertical and horizontal intercepts of the original cost constraint. The firm can also purchase any input combination of capital and labor along this cost constraint.

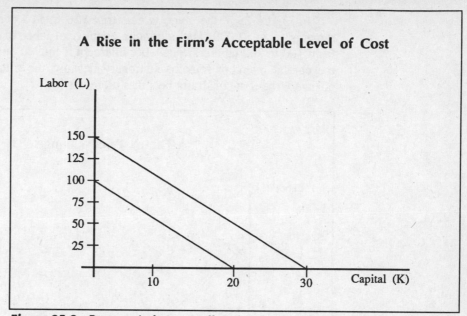

**Figure 25.2** *Because it does not affect the price of labor or capital, a rise in the firm's acceptable level of cost leads to a parallel outward shift in the cost constraint. Here, total cost rises from $2,000 to $3,000 given a capital price of $100 per unit and a wage of $20 per laborer.*

Holding input prices constant, a rise in total cost to $3,000 enables the firm to hire either 150 laborers or 30 units of capital when all costs are allocated to either labor or capital. The rise in total cost therefore leads to a new cost constraint with these input quantities as its intercepts. Because the wage ($w$) and capital's price ($r$) have not changed, the slope of the cost constraint is unaffected by the rise in cost; the new cost constraint is parallel to the original cost constraint.

**The Effects of Changing Prices.** The slope of the cost constraint is $-\dfrac{r}{w}$.
A decrease in the wage causes the ratio of the price of capital to the wage to increase. Hence, the cost constraint will become more vertical when wages fall. This will also occur if the value in the numerator rises, which happens when the price of capital increases.

In terms of the intercepts, a decline in the wage enables the firm to purchase more labor. Therefore, if all costs are incurred in hiring labor, a greater quantity can be employed; the labor intercept will move out. If the price of capital is unchanged, the cost constraint pivots outward from the stationary capital intercept. Similarly, if the price of capital falls but the wage remains the same, the cost constraint will pivot outward from its point of intersection with the labor axis. It will intersect the capital axis at a higher level.

In Figure 25.3, the wage is cut from $20 to $10 per laborer; total cost remains set at $2,000. The maximum quantity of labor that can be hired rises from 100 to 200 laborers. The labor intercept is moved out to reflect this fact; the capital intercept remains stationary because the price of capital is unchanged; the cost constraint becomes more vertical.

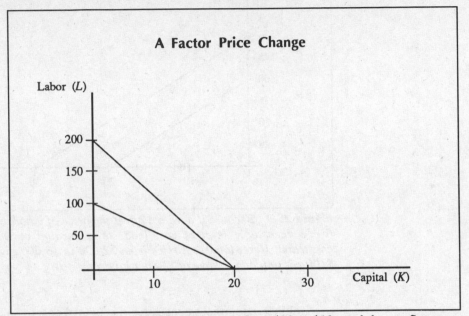

**Figure 25.3** *With a decline in the wage from $20 to $10 per laborer, firms can employ 100 extra workers if only labor is hired. The maximum quantity of capital that can be hired remains unchanged because the capital price has not changed.*

## INTERPRETING THE SLOPE OF THE COST CONSTRAINT

The slope of the cost constraint reveals the relative costs involved in substituting units of labor for units of capital. This can be observed through analysis of the units of the slope. The wage paid to labor has units equal to dollars per laborer. The capital price has units of dollars per unit of capital. When written as $-\left(\dfrac{r}{w}\right)$, the dollar units cancel, the labor units rise to the numerator, and the expression represents the number of laborers that can be hired for the price of one unit of capital. This ratio represents the rate at which labor can be substituted for capital at existing input prices. The minus sign reflects the fact that when additional units of labor are employed, fewer units of capital can be used if total cost is to remain unchanged.

**Interpreting the Slope: An Example**. Suppose that the wage is $20 per laborer and the price of capital is $100 per unit. The ratio of the price of capital to the wage equals 5. This implies that the firm can hire 5 laborers for the price of 1 unit of capital equipment.

$$-\frac{r}{w} = -\left(\frac{\$100/unit\,of\,capital}{\$20/laborer}\right) = -5\ laborers\ per\ unit\ of\ capital$$

Because the price of capital and the wage are assumed fixed, the slope of the cost constraint represents the constant rate at which the firm is able to transform labor into capital and not increase its total cost. It can also be thought of as the firm's opportunity cost of capital in terms of labor.

# TECHNOLOGY, SUBSTITUTION, AND THE PRODUCTION FUNCTION

Aside from the cost constraint, finding the optimal quantity of inputs requires a representation of the technological possibilities faced by the firm in transforming inputs into outputs. These possibilities are represented in the form of a production function—a table, graph, or mathematical formula that shows the maximum output that can be produced with various input combinations. One means of representing the production function is a series of lines known as *isoquants*.

## Isoquants

An *isoquant* shows all the combinations of capital and labor that lead to production of the same level of output. The isoquant therefore shows how capital and labor can be substituted without affecting the quantity of output. It is assumed that isoquants are downward-sloping and convex (bending inward) with respect to the origin. Isoquants located further from the capital-labor origin represent higher levels of output because they are associated with use of more capital, labor, or both inputs. Isoquants are also known as *production-indifference curves*.

### DERIVING AN ISOQUANT

The shape of a typical isoquant is found by considering the range of input combinations that will lead to production of the same quantity of output. In Figure 25.4, suppose the firm uses 10 laborers and 5 units of capital to produce 100 units of output. This input combination is assumed to lie on a particular isoquant. The objective is to locate all other combinations of labor and capital that lead to the production of 100 units of output.

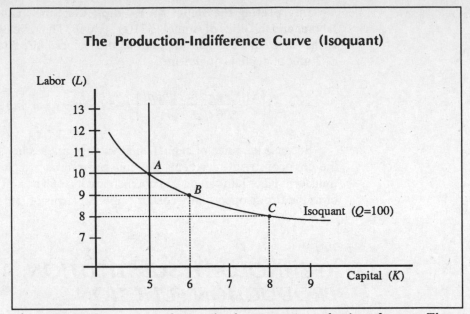

**Figure 25.4** *Greater use of inputs leads to greater production of output. There-fore, when one input is increased or decreased with the other input held constant, output will rise or fall. To maintain the same level of output, an increase in the use of one input must be offset by decreased use of the other. Therefore, the isoquant is down-sloping. Because of the law of diminishing marginal productivity, the isoquant is convex with respect to the origin.*

**The Isoquant's Downward Slope.** Holding the level of the capital constant, greater quantities of labor lead to greater quantities of output. Similarly, holding the level of the labor constant, greater quantities of capital lead to greater quantities of output. Finally, if both capital and labor are increased, output will increase. Therefore, two regions can immediately be ignored in determining the position of the isoquant. In Figure 25.4, these regions are found by drawing a horizontal and vertical line through point *A*, the point associated with 5 units of capital and 10 units of labor. Points within the region above and to right of point *A* involve use of more capital and the same labor, more labor and the same capital, or more of both capital and labor. Hence, input combinations in this region are associated with output levels greater than 100 units. In the region below and to the left of point *A*, less labor is used with the same capital, less capital is used with the same labor, or less of both labor and capital are used. Hence, the level of output associated with points in this region must lead to the production of less than 100 units of output.

By excluding input combinations that either increase or decrease output, the isoquant must be downward-sloping. Otherwise, it could not pass through point *A* and remain clear of the excluded regions. Points on the isoquant must be such that any decrease in the quantity of one input is met with a sufficient increase in the quantity of the other, so that the level of output is therefore unaffected.

**The Marginal Rate of Technical Substitution and the Isoquant's Convex Shape.** The slope at any point on an isoquant is known as the *marginal rate of technical substitution*. As we move along an isoquant, economists assume that the marginal rate of technical substitution declines. As less use is made of one input, more of the other must be used or else output will decline. With a diminishing marginal rate of technical substitution, more and more units of the input whose use is increasing are required to offset the output lost with each unit reduction in the other input. Because of this relationship, the isoquant must be convex; it bends inward toward the origin.

A typical convex isoquant is shown in Figure 25.4. It passes through the point associated with 10 laborers and 5 units of capital. In moving from point *A* to point *B*, using 1 less unit of labor requires using 1 more unit of capital to keep output constant. However, because of the diminishing marginal rate of technical substitution, in moving from point *B* to point *C*, 2 extra units of capital must be used to compensate for a 1 unit reduction in the number of laborers employed.

**Marginal Productivity and the Marginal Rate of Technical Substitution.** The marginal rate of technical substitution is equal to the ratio of the marginal product of the input on the horizontal axis to the marginal product of the input on the vertical axis. By definition, the marginal productivity of an input refers to the change in output that occurs with a one unit increase in the quantity of that input. Using the symbol $\Delta$ to denote a change in the variable considered, the respective marginal productivities of capital and labor are denoted $MP_L = \dfrac{\Delta Q}{\Delta L}$ and $MP_K = \dfrac{\Delta Q}{\Delta K}$. The marginal rate of technical substitution (MRTS), then appears as

$$\text{MRTS} = \frac{MP_K}{MP_L} = \frac{\dfrac{\Delta Q}{\Delta K}}{\dfrac{\Delta Q}{\Delta L}} = \frac{\Delta L}{\Delta K}$$

The slope of the isoquant is the change in labor input required to keep output constant given a one unit change in the quantity of capital employed. This slope is represented by $\dfrac{\Delta L}{\Delta K}$ and is equivalent to the margainal rate of technical substitution.

**The Isoquant Mapping.** Working through the firm's production function, input combinations that lead to the same level of output are represented by an isoquant. When inputs are used at greater levels, higher levels of output are produced. These higher levels can also be represented by isoquants. The entire range of input combinations is filled with nonintersecting isoquants. These represent the various levels of output associated with various input combinations. Isoquants closer to the origin represent lower levels of output. Some combinations of the two inputs used to produce output are less than the combinations for isoquants farther from the origin.

## OPTIMAL INPUT USE

The cost constraint shows an infinite number of combinations of labor and capital that lead to the same cost. Along any isoquant, the infinite number of input combinations that lead to production of the same level of output is shown. The firm's problem is to find the one input combination that is optimal. This ideal amount of capital and labor must be consistent with the firm's objectives. The firm may wish to maximize output without exceeding a certain predetermined level of cost, or it may wish to minimize cost subject to producing a predetermined quantity of output.

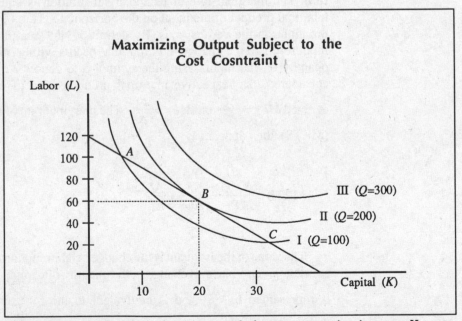

*Figure 25.5*  *At the point of tangency with the cost constraint, isoquant II represents the highest level of output consistent with desired cost. Achieving output level III entails too great a cost. Output level I is within the cost constraint. However, this output level is not optimal; more output can be produced along the cost constraint at its point of tangency with isoquant II.*

## Maximizing Output Subject to a Cost Constraint

To produce the highest level of output possible given the total cost it wishes to incur and the input prices it faces, the firm must reach the highest isoquant consistent with the cost constraint. Figure 25.5 presents the firm's cost constraint and three isoquants. Curve I represents all input combinations that enable production of exactly 100 units of output. Input combinations allowing production of 200 units are represented by curve II. Along curve III, capital and labor are combined so that 300 units of output can be produced.

Points beyond the cost constraint represent input combinations whose costs are in excess of the firm's desired expenditure. Therefore, the output level associated with isoquant III cannot be attained. Portions of isoquant I do lie within the cost constraint, and thus can be produced. However, isoquant II, which is tangent at point *B* to the cost constraint, is also consistent with the desired total cost, and it lies above isoquant I. Any isoquant above curve II will be outside the cost constraint; therefore, the firm will maximize its output at point *B* on isoquant II. The firm will produce 200 units of output; it will employ 60 laborers and 20 units of capital.

## Minimizing Cost Subject to an Output Constraint

Suppose the firm desires to produce 200 units of output at the minimum cost. Compared with the previous case, the level of output is now given, and the problem is to find the least cost means of producing it. With input prices given, the slope of the cost constraint is predetermined. Figure 25.6 shows three cost constraints consistent with prevailing input prices but different overall levels of cost. Cost curve I represents the lowest overall level of cost. However, it lies below the isoquant associated with 200 units of output; therefore, it does not allow hiring a sufficient quantity of inputs to produce the output required. Cost curve III allows production of 200 units of output using the input combinations found at its two intersections with the isoquant. However, 200 units of output can be produced at lower cost. This is seen at the point of tangency between cost curve II and the isoquant at point *A*. This tangency condition, here based on the assumption that firms minimize cost subject to producing a desired output, is equivalent to the optimality condition that results when firms maximize output subject to a cost constraint.

### INTERPRETATION OF THE OPTIMALITY CONDITION

At the point of tangency between the isoquant and the cost constraint, the slope of the constraint is equal to the slope of the isoquant. The slope of the isoquant is the marginal rate of technical substitution. It equals the negative of the ratio of the marginal product of capital to labor. The slope of the cost constraint equals the negative of the ratio of the price of capital to the price of labor. At the optimum point, whether the firm maximizes output subject to a cost constraint or minimizes cost subject to an output constraint, the minus signs will cancel, and the following condition will hold:

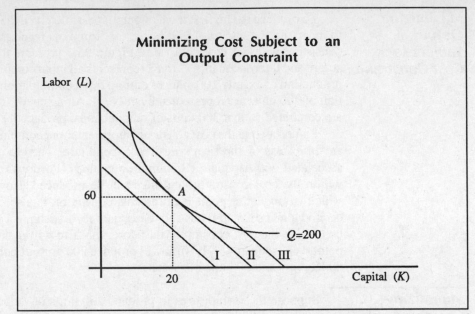

**Figure 25.6**  *If output is constrained instead of cost, the optimal level of labor and capital are again found at the point of tangency between the isoquant and the cost constraint. Cost constraint I does not allow production of the desired 200 units of output. Constraint III enables production of 200 units, but it can be done at lowest cost along constraint II.*

$$\frac{MP_K}{MP_L} = \frac{r}{w}$$

Rearranging terms, note that

$$\frac{MP_K}{r} = \frac{MP_L}{w}$$

At the optimum point, the extra output gained from a dollar spent on capital is exactly equal to the extra output gained from a dollar spent on labor.

The reason this situation is optimal can easily be seen by considering the case in Figure 25.5 when the firm is not producing at point *B*. If the firm decides to produce at point *A*, aside from the fact that the same cost is now incurred in producing less output, it is also true that the isoquant is steeper than the cost constraint. Therefore, the marginal rate of technical substitution is greater than the ratio of the price of capital to the wage:

$$\frac{MP_K}{MP_L} > \frac{r}{w}$$

Rearranging terms, it follows that,

$$\frac{MP_K}{r} > \frac{MP_L}{w}$$

The ratio $\frac{MP_K}{r}$ represents the output produced from the last dollar spent on capital. Similarly, $\frac{MP_L}{w}$ represents the ouput produced from the last dollar spent on labor. Because the output produced from spending an extra dollar on capital exceeds the output produced from an extra dollar spent on labor, it is in the firm's interest to reduce spending on labor and increase spending on capital. As the firm does so, it moves down along the cost constraint toward the point of tangency between isoquant II and the cost constraint. In the process, the law of diminishing returns is at work. Because more of it is used, the marginal product of capital decreases. Because its use is diminished, the marginal product of labor increases. Ultimately, at the point of tangency, the marginal productivity per dollar of expenditure is equal for both inputs.

Should the firm move beyond point $B$, the output produced per dollar spent on labor exceeds the extra output produced per dollar spent on capital. Therefore, the firm will increase spending on labor and decrease spending on capital. It moves back along the cost constraint toward the optimum point of tangency.

*Optimality and Changes in Input Prices or Total Cost*

Through use of isoquants, the cost constraint, and the optimal tangency condition, the amounts of capital and labor required to produce a given output at minimum cost is determined. Use of these relationships can be extended to examine the effects of changes in input prices and changes in the firm's desired total cost. Analysis of such changes provides information on the degree to which inputs can be substituted for one another, given changes in relative input prices. It also shows how input proportions change at different output levels when relative input prices remain the same. For firms, such information is important for planning. For economists, it is important for determining the effects of such changes on the quantity of capital and labor employed in various industries.

### THE EFFECTS OF CHANGING COSTS: THE EXPANSION PATH

With input prices constant, a ray connecting all points of tangency between an outward-shifting cost constraint and the firm's isoquants is known as the *expansion path*. The shape of the expansion path provides information on how input use changes when total cost changes. When input prices remain unchanged, a rise in the cost the firm wishes to incur will cause the cost constraint to shift out, parallel to itself.

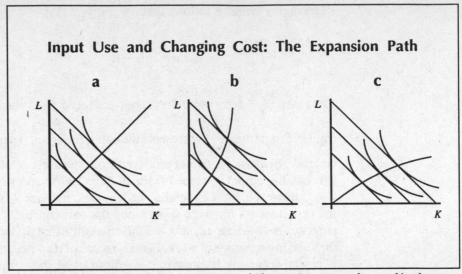

**Figure 25.7**  *As the firm's cost constraint shifts out, inputs can be used in the same proportions, as shown in the left panel, or different proportions, as shown in the middle and right panel. In the middle panel the labor-to-capital ratios rises as more output is produced. In the right panel it falls. The relationship between changes in input use and changes in output is known as the firm's expansion path.*

Figure 25.7 shows three effects on relative input use given changes in cost. In the first panel, as the cost constraint is shifted out, inputs are used in the same proportion at each tangency point; a straight line passes through each of these points and through the origin. The slope of a straight line is constant. In addition, at any point on a straight line emanating from the origin, the slope is equal to the ratio of the vertical distance from the origin to the horizontal distance from the origin. This is the ratio of the rise of the line to its run. Therefore, the ratio of capital use to labor use at all points of tangency is equal.

In the second panel, points of tangency between cost constraints and higher isoquants are associated with the use of relatively more labor and relatively less capital. The opposite situation is shown in the third panel where relatively more capital is used as output increases.

## THE EFFECTS OF CHANGING INPUT PRICES

When the price of an input falls, the firm is able to hire additional units of that input and still hold costs at a predetermined level. In addition, by holding constant the use of an input whose price has declined, the firm can hire additional units of the other input by using the surplus funds made available by the other input's price decrease. When an input's price changes, the cost constraint adjusts its position and leads to a point of tangency with a new isoquant. The degree to which the firm hires additional units of the cheaper input or employs greater quantities of other inputs can be analyzed by observing how the point of optimality changes.

In Figure 25.8, it is assumed that the price of labor has fallen. This is illustrated by the cost constraint's upward pivot. If all costs were incurred in employing labor, additional units could be hired. The capital intercept remains the same because the price of capital has not changed. When the cost constraint pivots, the point of tangency changes from point *A* along the lower isoquant to point *B* along the higher isoquant. Consistent with the decrease in the price of labor, the firm increases its use of labor from 60 to 70 laborers, but it also increases its use of capital from 10 to 20 units. As shown here, the decrease in the wage led to an increase in both the quantity of labor and the quantity of capital. In addition, the amount of output the firm is able to produce has increased, even though total cost remains the same.

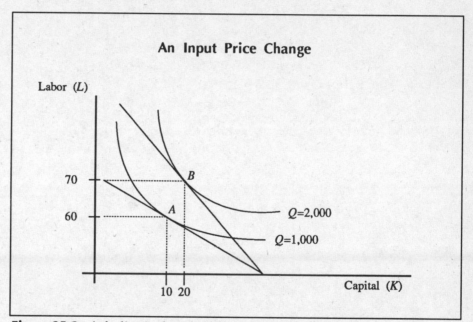

**An Input Price Change**

**Figure 25.8** *A decline in the price of labor leads the firm to increase labor input from 60 to 70 workers. Capital use also rises from 10 to 20 units. Because tangency occurs along a higher isoquant, more output can be produced.*

*P*ortrayed graphically, the production and cost characteristics of typical firms reveal the nature of the problems involved in finding optimal levels of input use. Tangency conditions between isoquants and cost constraints are entirely consistent with what common sense would dictate in determining how to spend additional dollars on inputs. Given a choice between spending a dollar on one of two inputs, the firm should hire the input that leads to the greatest addition to output.

The production function and cost constraint can be manipulated to draw other conclusions concerning the relationship between inputs, output, and costs. The basic model is used to develop the family of cost curves discussed in previous chapters and to understand their theoretical characteristics. It is also used for development of input-demand equations for capital and labor and forming measures of subsitution between inputs. These uses are covered in more advanced courses in microeconomics. In these courses, the simple relationships illustrated represent the foundation for visualizing and understanding the complete nature of the constrained optimization problem faced by firms.

# 26

# *The Economist's Tool Box*

*Economists use a variety of theoretical concepts and analytical techniques. Understanding these concepts and techniques provides a means of quickly gaining insight into the nature of a wide range of real-world problems without necessarily being experts in all aspects of these problems. In this chapter, the most important concepts and techniques used by economists are presented and explained. The chapter does not pretend to cover fully all the analytical techniques, underlying principles, and subtleties encountered in conducting economic analysis. It is hoped that students new to the study of economics can improve their intuitive grasp of these much-used and often-mentioned tools of economic analysis.*

## *THE CLASSIFICATION OF UNDERLYING PRINCIPLES*

Economic methodology rests upon basic definitions, laws, and conventions regarding the behavior of economic agents and the nature of technology. With an understanding of these essential elements, dealing with specific real-world economic problems involves decomposing the characteristics of any given situation into appropriate categories. The boundaries of analysis are set through use of simplifying assumptions. These assumptions establish the variables whose values are to be determined within the model and those whose values will be taken as given. Assumptions are also made concerning optimizing behavior on the part of economic agents; firms may be assumed to maximize profits; consumers seek to maximize utility. Assumptions are combined with accounting identities that describe budget or cost constraints. Assumptions regarding the nature of production (diminishing returns) and/or consumption (diminishing marginal utility) are also used. These considerations lead to explanations and predictions concerning how the variables of concern in the model will respond to changes in the level of other variables, inside and outside the model. Finally, the predictions of the model are compared with real-world-data. The data used for this part of the analysis must correspond to the variables described in the economic theory. A good model will yield predictions that correspond closely to actual observations.

## Economic Laws and Conventions

The wide array of assumptions and conventions concerning the behavior of consumers, firms, and technology generally lead to establishment of equilibrium for the individual, firm, or market under consideration. Through the use of assumptions, those variables whose values are determined in the model are specified along with the time frame for analysis. Familiarity with these assumptions makes understanding economic models much easier and is often essential for complete comprehension of the analysis.

### ENDOGENOUS VERSUS EXOGENOUS VARIABLES

*Endogenous* variables are those whose values are determined within a model. In the basic model of supply and demand, the endogenous variables are price and quantity. Equilibrium values are found at the point where the supply and demand curves cross. Changes in endogenous variables lead to movements *along* a curve. Thus, when price increases in the supply-demand model, the quantity demanded will decline along the demand curve and the quantity supplied will increase along the supply curve.

*Exogenous* variables are determined by factors lying outside those considered in the model. In the supply-demand model, exogenous variables include such factors as tastes, income, and technology. Changes in exogenous variables lead to *shifts* in the curves used to model particular activities. Thus a change in tastes toward a particular product will cause its demand curve to shift out. More of the good will be demanded at each price.

### THE SHORT RUN AND THE LONG RUN

By convention, the short run refers to a time horizon in which at least one input to a production process is held fixed. In the long run, all inputs are free to vary to optimal levels. In microeconomics, short-run analysis underlies the various models used to describe the behavior of firms in perfectly and imperfectly competitive markets. Thus, in the short run, the firm faces one average-total-cost curve from which marginal cost is determined. In the long run, an *envelope*, or connection of points on optimal short-run average-cost curves forms the long-run average-cost curve.

In macroeconomics, the short run represents a period of time in which prices are not able to adjust freely or completely. In the long run, when all such adjustments have been made, the economy will operate at the potential level of GNP. With regard to the actual time it takes for the macro economy to reach long-run equilibrium, Keynes noted that "in the long run we are all dead."

## OPPORTUNITY COST

The opportunity cost of a given action represents the value of all the alternative goods and services forgone by pursuing that action. For example, the opportunity cost of attending college includes not only the goods and services that could be purchased with money used for tuition and books but also the income that could have been earned by working instead of attending school. Along the production-possibilities curve, opportunity cost represents the goods given up or lost in moving from one point on the curve to another. As another example, the opportunity cost of holding money is the interest that could be earned if the money was placed in an interest bearing account.

## THE LAW OF DEMAND

According to the law of demand, as the price of a good increases consumers will desire to purchase fewer units of the good. Lying behind this law is utility-maximizing behavior by consumers.

## THE LAW OF SUPPLY

According to the law of supply, as the price of a good increases, firms will desire to increase the quantity of the good they offer for sale. Lying behind this law is profit-maximizing or cost-minimizing behavior by firms.

## THE LAW OF DIMINISHING MARGINAL UTILITY

An individual's utility function shows how goods consumed are transformed into utility or satisfaction. Greater consumption leads to increased satisfaction. Assume that the consumer is allowed to consume only one good. According to the law of diminishing marginal utility, as consumption of this good increases, utility will also increase, but at a decreasing rate. As an example, with the consumption of all other commodities held constant, the addition to total utility derived from consuming an individual's first hamburger will exceed the addition to total utility derived from consuming a second hamburger. The extra utility from the second exceeds the extra utility from the third, and so on.

## THE LAW OF DIMINISHING RETURNS

A firm's production function shows how it is able to transform inputs into output. In the short run, assuming that capital and labor are the only inputs, only one input is allowed to vary. According to the law of diminishing returns, as the amount of this variable input increases, output will also increase, but at a decreasing rate. The law of diminishing returns is also known as the law of diminishing marginal productivity. As an example of the law of diminishing returns, with all other inputs held constant, the extra output produced by the tenth unit of labor hired will exceed the extra output produced by the eleventh unit of labor hired.

## RETURNS TO SCALE

Returns to scale involve the relationship between changes in a firm's output and proportional changes in all of a firm's inputs. If all inputs are doubled and output doubles, returns to scale are said to be constant. If all inputs are doubled and output more than doubles, the firm has increasing returns to scale. If all inputs are doubled and output less than doubles, the firm has decreasing returns to scale. Because all inputs are free to vary, returns to scale involve a long-run situation. It should not be confused with the law of diminishing returns which is based on the assumption that at least one input is held constant.

## EQUILIBRIUM

In its most general form, equilibrium refers to a situation in which there are no endogenous forces present that will cause change. In the supply-demand model, equilibrium occurs when the quantity demanded equals the quantity supplied at a single price. Deviations from this price will lead to excess demand or excess supply, which in turn place upward or downward pressure on prices. Because such pressure represents a force that will cause change (if unimpeded by price controls), excess demand and supply situations are not equilibrium states.

In the macro economy, equilibrium occurs when aggregate expenditure equals GNP. In other words, the value of goods purchased equals the value of goods produced. Disequilibrium occurs when expenditure exceeds or falls short of production. Unplanned inventory shortfalls or buildups will result. These cause adjustments in output that restore equilibrium.

## PARETO OPTIMALITY

Pareto optimality refers to a situation in which no individual can be made better off without making someone else worse off. This means that production, consumption, and exchange are so efficiently organized that no reorganiztion of these activities will result in a gain to one person without harming others.

## ALLOCATIVE EFFICIENCY

Allocative efficiency occurs when the price charged for a product is exactly equal to its marginal cost of production. In this circumstance, the value placed on the good by consumers, reflected in the price paid, will equal the value of the resources used to produce the good sold, seen in its marginal cost. A price in excess of marginal cost implies that consumers value the product more highly than the value of the resources used to produce it. When marginal cost exceeds price, the value consumers place on the product falls short of the value of the resources used in production.

## Totals, Marginals, and Averages

Output, costs, revenue, utility, and profit are among the most important variables in economic models. In analysis it is often useful to examine these variables and their values from a variety of perspectives. The total, marginal, and average values of variables constitute three basic ways of viewing them.

### TOTALS

The most common way of measuring a variable is its total value. For example, total output or product is composed of the physical quantity of goods produced by the firm. Total cost is the total amount spent by a firm in hiring the inputs necessary to produce total output. Total revenue represents the dollars received by the firm from the sale of its total output. Total utility is the overall level of satisfaction an individual receives from consumption of a bundle or combination of goods.

### TOTALS AND MARGINALS

Marginals represent changes in totals. The change in the total is caused by a change in another variable related to the total. A rise in the level of a firm's output leads to a change in its cost; more inputs must be hired to produce the output. Marginal cost refers to the change in total cost given a one unit change in output.

The definition of any marginal value in economics will always contain the word *change* or *extra* twice. (Other synonyms for *change* will also work.) For example, consider Marginal revenue: The change in total revenue given a one-unit change in output sold; Marginal utility: The change in total utility given a one-unit change in the quantity consumed of some good; Marginal product: The change in total product (output) that occurs given a one-unit change in the use of some input; Marginal profit: The change in total profit that comes with the sale of an additional unit of output. By definition, marginal profit is the difference between marginal revenue and marginal cost. The marginal-revenue product is defined as the extra revenue earned by a firm from the sale of the output produced when the firm hires an extra unit of some input.

The basic relationship between totals and marginals extends to macroeconomics as well. For example, the marginal propensity to consume represents the change in total consumption expenditure given a one-dollar change in disposable income.

### AVERAGES AND TOTALS

In economic theory, averages are formed when one variable that is related to another variable is divided by that variable. For example, average cost is defined as total cost divided by the level of output produced. Average revenue represents total revenue divided by the quantity of output sold. The average product of labor is equal to total output divided by the quantity of labor used to produce the output. From macroeconomics, average consumption is defined as total consumption divided by the level of disposable income; this measure is also known as the average propensity to consume.

## MARGINALS AND AVERAGES

Averages, unlike marginals, represent ratios of *levels* of variables rather than ratios of *changes* in the levels of variables. In addition, when the average is rising, the marginal is above the average, and when the average is falling, the marginal is below the average. If the average is neither rising nor falling, the marginal and average are equal.

This relationship between marginals and averages is best understood through use of an example. The average rainfall in a region is calculated by adding the number of inches of rain falling in previous years and dividing by the number of years considered. This year's rainfall represents an addition to the total rain that has fallen in the region; it represents the region's marginal rainfall. In revising the average to account for this year's rainfall, the average will increase if this year's rainfall exceeds the average of past years. The average will fall if this year's rainfall is less than the average of past years. Finally, if the rain that falls this year exactly equals the average from past years, the overall average will remain unchanged. Similarly, if the marginal cost of producing a unit of output exceeds the average cost of producing previous units, average cost will rise. When marginal cost is less than average cost, average cost will fall. When marginal cost equals average cost, average cost is constant.

At the maximum or minimum point of the average (where it neither rises nor falls), the marginal and average are equal. This means that a marginal curve always crosses the corresponding average curve at its minimum and maximum points.

## Marginal Relationships and Optimality Conditions

Microeconomic analysis makes use of a wide variety of marginal conditions between variables of interest. These conditions result from the fact that firms and individuals are assumed to engage in optimizing behavior. Depending on the underlying assumptions, optimal quantities of variables such as output, profit, utility, or input use are determined. The relationships between variables are generally classified in terms of the marginal benefit or marginal cost they bring to the optimizing agent.

### MAXIMIZING PROFIT

The most notable of all marginal conditions involves the equality between marginal cost and marginal revenue. This condition is required if a firm is to maximize its profits. As output increases, marginal cost is assumed to increase because of the law of diminishing returns. Marginal revenue is assumed either to stay constant, as in the case of pure competition, or decrease, as seen in the case of imperfect competition where to sell more output, the firm must lower its price.

The firm should produce those levels of output where marginal revenue is above marginal cost. The truth of this statement stems from the definitions of marginal cost and marginal revenue. As long as the revenue received from the sale of a unit of output exceeds the cost of its production, there will be a net addition to profit (marginal profit is greater than zero). As output expands, marginal cost rises, while marginal revenue falls or stays the same. The difference between marginal cost and marginal revenue will shrink, and the additions to profit become less and less. Finally, the output level at which marginal cost exactly equals marginal revenue will be reached. Beyond this point, marginal cost will be in excess of marginal revenue; additions to profit will be negative. Production of more output will cause total profit to fall.

## SHORT-RUN OPTIMAL INPUT USE

*Firms should continue to hire additional units of a factor of production as long as the marginal revenue product exceeds marginal-factor cost.*

Using labor as the factor of production, the marginal-revenue product is the extra revenue the firm receives from the sale of output produced by hiring an extra unit of labor. However, the output produced by additional workers declines because of the law of diminishing returns. Therefore, the marginal revenue product will decline. The decline in revenue will be less severe if the firm is a price-taker in a perfectly competitive market; it declines more quickly if the firm faces a downward-sloping demand curve for its product and must lower its price to sell additional units of output.

Marginal labor cost represents the amount that must be paid for the services of an extra unit of labor. This amount will be constant if laborers are wage takers. It will increase if hiring additional quantities of labor implies moving up the labor-supply curve.

If the marginal-revenue product is greater than the marginal-labor cost, with the employment of an extra unit of labor the firm experiences an increase in revenue in excees of its increase in cost. It therefore profits by hiring that unit of labor. For low levels of labor input, it is assumed that the marginal-revenue-product curve lies above the marginal-factor-cost curve. As more labor is hired, the marginal-revenue product declines, while marginal-labor cost remains the same or increases. The excess of revenue over cost therefore declines as input use expands. Finally, the point of equality between the marginal-revenue product and marginal-factor cost is reached. Hiring additional units of labor results in additions to cost that exceed additions to revenue. No further amounts of labor should be hired.

## LONG-RUN OPTIMAL INPUT USE

*In maximizing output subject to a cost constraint or minimizing cost subject to an output constraint, firms should hire inputs to the point at which the ratio of the marginal product per dollar spent on each input is equal.*

Marginal product is defined as the extra output produced through the use of an extra unit of input. The price of an input is its cost per unit. The ratio of an input's marginal product and price therefore represents the output that is produced by spending an extra dollar on that input. In terms of capital and labor, if the output produced by spending an extra dollar on labor exceeds the output produced by spending an extra dollar on capital, extra labor should be employed. Because of the law of diminishing returns, as additional units of labor are hired, labor's marginal productivity declines. Thus, the marginal product per dollar spent on labor will decrease; ultimately it will move to equality with the marginal productivity of capital.

## MAXIMIZING UTILITY

*For consumers, utility is maximized at the point where the marginal utility per dollar spent on all goods is equal.*

Marginal utility refers to the extra utility a consumer receives from the consumption of an extra unit of some good. The price of this good has units equal to dollars per unit of the good. Therefore, the ratio of the marginal utility of a good to its price represents the utility the consumer receives by consuming an extra dollar's worth of the good. If the utility a consumer receives by spending a dollar on one good exceeds the utility derived from spending a dollar on another, rationality dictates that the good providing more utility for a dollar's expenditure be purchased.

Under the law of diminishing marginal utility, as extra units of a good are consumed, the extra utility derived from its consumption decreases. Therefore, in terms of marginal utility per dollar of expenditure, a point of equality will ultimately be reached between the good initially possessing higher utility per dollar and the other goods consumed by the individual.

## OPTIMAL INVESTMENT

*Investment projects should be pursued as long as the marginal efficiency of investment is greater than the market rate of interest. Along the investment demand schedule, the optimal level of investment is determined by the interest rate.*

The marginal efficiency of investment represents the rate of return on an investment project. When all investment projects are ordered by their rates of return, the marginal-efficiency-of-investment schedule, or investment-demand schedule, is derived. The market rate of interest represents the return that can be earned by putting money in the bank or purchasing a financial asset. If the return from the investment exceeds the return from the market rate of interest, the investment project should be undertaken because it yields the greater return.

Thus, firms should undertake all investment projects along the investment-demand schedule whose rates of return exceed the rate of interest. Ultimately, a project just paying the market rate of interest will be reached. All subsequent projects result in rates of return that fall short of the rate of interest. These projects should not be undertaken.

## Percentage Rates of Change and Elasticity Measures

Because of their use in so many areas of economic analysis, elasticity measures rank in importance with such concepts as the law of diminishing returns and the law of diminishing marginal utility. In order to understand what is measured by an elasticity, it is important to be familiar with the definition of a *percentage rate of change*. Aside from their use in elasticity formulas, percentage rates of change are important in describing the growth of economic variables, such as the price level and GNP.

### THE PERCENTAGE RATE OF CHANGE

The *percentage rate of change* in some variables represents the change in the variable divided by the average value of the variable from before and after the change. Symbolically, the percentage rate of change in the price of some good is written $\frac{\Delta P}{P}$. Thus, if the price of a good rises from \$12 per unit to \$16 per unit, the change in price equals \$4; the average of the prices before and after the change equals \$14 [(\$12 + \$16)/2]. The percentage rate of change, the ratio of \$4 to \$14 equals 0.286 and represents the relative magnitude of the price increase. In other words, the price increase from \$12 to \$16 amounts to 28.6 percent of the average price. Because the numerator and denominator of the percentage change formula are measured in the same units, the units will cancel. This makes the percentage rate of change a unit-free measure.

To see the importance of the percent change calculation, consider a \$4 price increase for another good whose price rises from \$100 to \$104. In this case the percentage change is 0.039, or 3.9 percent. Even though both prices increase by \$4, the percentage change is far less for the more expensive good. Making use of percentage rates of change therefore allows relative comparisons for changes in variables that are greatly different in their initial magnitude.

**The Inflation Rate.** Inflation refers to a sustained increase in the price level. The inflation rate is the growth rate or percentage rate of change in the price index between two adjacent periods. By convention, in calculating the inflation rate, the base-period price level is used in the denominator, rather than the average price level. For example, if the price index in 1989 stands at 253 and the price index in 1990 equals 300, the rate of inflation between 1989 and 1990 is (300 − 253)/253 = 0.186, or 18.6 percent. The price level in 1990 stands 18.6 percent above the price level in 1989.

### ELASTICITIES

An elasticity is the ratio of percentage changes for two related variables. The percentage change of the variable in the numerator must be caused by the percentage change in the variable in the denominator. Because the percentage changes in the numerator and denominator are unit-free, the elasticity measure is also unit-free. Therefore, elasticity values for quantities measured in different units, such as dollars, tons, miles, or hours, can be consistently compared.

**The Elasticity of Demand.** The elasticity of demand is the ratio of the percentage change in quantity demanded to the percentage change in price that causes the change in quantity. This ratio provides information on the relative size of the quantity change due to the change in price.

Under the law of demand, the percentage change in quantity that occurs given an increase in price will always be less than or equal to zero. If the ratio of the percentage change in quantity demanded to the percentage change in price has an absolute value greater than 1, the proportionate decline in quantity demanded was greater than the proportionate increase in price. Quantity demanded is highly responsive or *elastic*, with respect to price changes. If the percentage change in quantity demanded is less than the percentage change in price, the elasticity value will be less than 1 in absolute value. In this case, quantity demanded is relatively unresponsive, or *inelastic*, with respect to changes in price.

# DISCOUNTING AND COST-BENEFIT ANALYSIS

One of the most interesting aspects of an investment decision is that the return from the investment comes in the future while the costs of the investment are usually incurred in the present. Two problems emerge in such a situation. First, while present costs can be known with precision, it is unclear in an uncertain world how future revenues earned from an investment can be determined. Second, a problem arises in comparing revenues received in the present with future revenues. Future revenues are not worth as much as present revenues of the same magnitude. In other words, a dollar received today is worth more than a dollar received next year.

Economists have little to say about the future returns investors expect to receive on their individual investments. However, through the process of discounting—converting future revenue flows into their worth at the present—economists are able to account for differences in the time revenues are received or costs incurred.

*Present Value and the Rate of Interest*

When asked why a dollar today is worth more than a dollar next year, most students respond that the dollar received in the future is worth less because of inflation. While this may be true, even in a world without inflation, the dollar next year would still be worth less than a dollar today. The reason involves interest. If, for example, the market rate of interest is 5 percent, to have a dollar next year requires that only about 95 cents be placed in the bank today. In other words, given the rate of interest that can be earned, there is no difference between the 95 cents today and $1 in one year. It follows that a dollar to be received in two years is worth even less than 95 cents.

## FINDING THE FUTURE VALUE

Suppose you deposit a sum of money in the bank and leave it there for a number of years earning interest. After $n$ years, the initial amount deposited will have a value given by the formula

$$Future\ Value = (1 + r)^n\ Present\ Value$$

The present value is the initial amount deposited. The rate of interest is denoted $r$. If $500 is placed in an account at an interest rate of 9 percent, its future value in 50 years will equal $37,178.76.

## FINDING THE PRESENT VALUE

The present value of a sum to be received $n$ years in the future is determined by the formula

$$Present\ Value = \frac{1}{(1 + r)^n} \times Future\ Value$$

At a 9 percent rate of interest, how much is $37,178.76 to be received in 50 years worth today? Using the present value formula, the answer is $500. What is the present value of $1,000,000 to be received in 100 years if the rate of interest is 12 percent? The answer is approximately $11.97!

## DISCOUNTING AND CHANGING THE RATE OF INTEREST

Discounting (the present-value calculation) is used to determine the present value of future costs and benefits. When used for this purpose, the interest rate chosen makes a great difference in the final result. Based on the present-value formula, because it appears in the denominator, an increase in the rate of interest will *decrease* the present value of any future sum of money to be received. For example, at a 3 percent rate of interest, the present value of $1,000,000 in 100 years is equal to $52,032.84, compared with $11.97 at 12 percent.

*Cost-Benefit*
*Analysis*

Cost-benefit analysis involves calculation of the present-value dollar costs and benefits of activities such as building a dam, highway, or chemical-waste facility. Comparison is then made to determine whether the potential benefits exceed costs by a sufficient amount to warrant undertaking the project. This information is also used for ranking projects. The project with the greatest benefits compared to costs can be determined.

Investors or the government might be willing to undertake certain projects when future costs are heavily discounted using a high rate of interest. Thus a project that involved $1,000,000 in costs exactly 100 years from now would require only $11.97 in revenues today in order to break even at an interest rate of 12 percent. It would require $52,032.84 in revenues to break even at a 3 percent interest rate. When revenues occur far into the future and costs are incurred in the present, the opposite situation holds. One million dollars in revenues to be received in 100 years justifies a project that costs $11.97 when the interest rate is 12 percent. If the interest rate is 3 percent, a cost of $52,032.84 can be incurred for a project generating a million dollars in 100 years.

### ENVIRONMENTAL COSTS AND THE INTEREST RATE

The rate of interest used in cost-benefit calculations is very important in assessing the future environmental damages associated with present economic activity. For projects involving billions of dollars in future environmental costs, use of a sufficiently high rate of interest in discounting can make even such high costs seem small. This can lead communities to undertake activities that place a large burden on future generations. Unless careful attention is paid to the interest rate and other details involved in comparing future costs and benefits, the actual impact of the project can be different from what people are led to believe.

As an example, consider the comparison of benefits and potential costs involved in generating electricity using nuclear power. Because nuclear waste is radioactive for such long periods, a disaster sometime in the distant future can easily be discounted to almost zero today through the choice of an appropriately high rate of interest. Should an accident occur, those who ultimately experience these costs cannot discount them. They will have to bear the full brunt. Use of a lower interest rate would make the future costs higher in the present. This is why many economists and environmentalists recommend using low or zero rates of interest to discount the costs of activities that may cause irreversible environmental damage.

# REAL VERSUS NOMINAL VALUES

In economic analysis it is important to distinguish between changes in physical quantities of output and changes in the dollar value of output. By definition, a value always represents the product of a price and a physical quantity. Therefore, when a value increases, it is not obvious whether the increase is due to increases in price, increases in physical quantity, or a combination of both. Nominal values incorporate both price and physical-quantity effects. Real values measure only physical-output changes. Separating physical quantity changes and price changes is equivalent to transforming nominal values into real values.

## Converting Nominal Values into Real Values

*To transform a nominal value into a real value, divide by an appropriate price index.*

A real value represents physical output valued at the prices that prevailed in some selected previous period, known as the base period. Therefore, when nominal values for various years are transformed into real values, the real values can be compared. The physical quantities are all weighted by the same prices.

For example, nominal GNP in 1990 can be written as $P_{90}Q_{90}$, the product of the price level that prevailed in 1990 and the physical output produced in 1990. Through use of a price index, the prices used in this nominal quantity are transformed into the price level that prevailed in some base year. If 1987 is the base year, the appropriate price index will appear as $P_{90}/P_{87}$. Dividing nominal GNP in 1990 by this price index yields $P_{87}Q_{90}$. The physical output in 1990 is now weighted by the price level that prevailed in 1987. Nominal outputs for other years can also be transformed into 1987 prices, enabling the comparison of actual physical outputs between years.

### PRICE INDICES

A price index is a number representing the ratio of prices in a given year to the prices that prevailed in some base year. When divided into a nominal value from some given year, the price index reweights the nominal value in terms of the prices that prevailed in the base year. The *Laspeyres price index* is a price index that weights prices using base-year quantities. As an example of how the Laspeyres index is calculated, assume that there are three goods produced in the economy. The prices and quantities produced in 1990 are shown in Table 26.1 along with the prices and quantities that prevailed in 1987, the base year.

## Prices and Quantities for the Laspeyres Index

| | 1987 | | 1990 | |
| --- | --- | --- | --- | --- |
| | Price | Quantity | Price | Quantity |
| Good 1 | $10 | 35 | $12 | 30 |
| Good 2 | 5 | 120 | 7 | 140 |
| Good 3 | 22 | 60 | 25 | 70 |

*Table 26.1*

The value of output in the 1987 base year is the sum of the value of each product produced: ($10 × 35) + ($5 × 120) + ($22 × 60) = $2,270. When the prices prevailing in 1990 are weighted in terms of 1987 quantities, the value of 1987's output becomes ($12 × 35) + ($7 × 120) + ($25 × 60) = $2,760. This amount represents how much output in 1987 would cost if valued at 1990 prices. The ratio of this value to the actual value of output in 1987 represents the amount by which the value of output changes due solely to price changes between 1987 and 1990. This ratio is $2,760/$2,270 = 1.22. Expressed as a percentage, the price index is 122. Prices in 1990 are about 22 percent higher than in 1987.

In summation notation, the value for the Laspeyres index is

$$\sum \frac{P_t Q_0}{P_0 Q_0}$$

where $P_t$ represents the prices from the current year and $P_0$ and $Q_0$, respectively, represent prices and quantities from the base year. In the formula, summation takes place over all goods considered.

**Using the Price Index.** The real value of the 1990 output is found by dividing by the nominal value by the price index. The nominal value of output for 1990 equals ($12 × 30) + ($7 × 140) + ($25 × 70) = $3,090. Thus, ($3,090/122) × 100 = $2,532.

Comparing the nominal value of 1990's output with 1987's output might initially lead one to believe that output increased by

($3,090 − $2,270)/$2,270 = 0.36, or 36%

This overstates the amount by which actual output grew because price effects have not been removed. In real terms, output growth between 1987 and 1990 equals ($2,532 − $2,270)/$2,270 = 0.12 or only about 12 percent.

*Real versus Nominal Interest Rates*

The *real rate of interest* is defined as the nominal rate of interest *minus* the rate of inflation. The nominal rate of interest is the percentage quoted by banks and other financial institutions as a return on bank deposits or financial assets. Therefore, the real rate of interest represents the actual rate of interest after the effects of inflation have been accounted for. For example, a sum of money placed in the bank for a year might earn 5 percent nominal interest. However, if the rate of inflation is 3 percent, the actual growth in the purchasing power of the bank deposit is only 2 percent, the real rate of interest.

*This chapter provides a quick reference to many of the most important definitions, conventions, and analytical basics used in economic analysis. Familiarity with these concepts is essential in understanding the models used by economists to describe, explain, and predict real-world events. These models rest upon an analytical foundation composed of combinations and extensions of the ideas presented here.*

# Index

Total revenue (*cont'd*)
   and demand-elasticity, 230–234
   finding, 286–287, 308
   and straight-line demand, 303
Total utility, 250–251
Total variable cost, 268
Trade. *See* International trade
Transactions costs, 54
Transactions demand for money, 116–117
Tying contracts, 341

## U

Uncertainty, 54
Unemployment, 53–56
   categories of, 55–56
   costs of, 56
   cyclical, 55–56
   frictional, 55
   measuring, 55–56
   and potential GNP, 135
   structural, 55
Unemployment benefits and price rigidities, 139
Unemployment rate, 55
Unionization, effects of, on monopsony, 361–362
Unions, role of, 357–362
Usury laws, 32
Utility
   cardinal, 250
   concept of, 250
   and consumer choice, 250–252
   marginal, 250–251
   ordinal, 250
   total, 250–251
Utility analysis, and the consumer's demand curve, 424–425
Utility maximization, 450
   and consumer choice, 249–259, 298, 419–421

Utility maximization (*cont'd*)
   interpretation of, 420–421

## V

Value added approach to GNP, 43
Variable(s)
   dependent, 10
   endogenous, 24–25, 444
   exogenous, 25, 444
   independent, 10
Variable cost
   average, 268, 272
   marginal, 269
Velocity of circulation, 165
Vertical aggregate supply, and classical economics, 140–141
Vertical demand, and tax incidence, 245
Vertical supply
   and potential GNP growth, 140–141
   and tax incidence, 246
Vertical supply curve, and economic rent, 245–246

## W

Wage increase
   income effect of a, 356
   substitutions effect of, 356
Wage setting, impact of unions on, 359–360
War costs, 52
Wealth effects, 65, 128, 149
Wealth transfers, 54
Wheeler-Lea Act (1938), 342
Worker safety, 342–343

## Y

Y intercept, 15

# OTHER BOOKS IN THE HARPERCOLLINS COLLEGE OUTLINE SERIES

## ART
History of Art 0-06-467131-3
Introduction to Art 0-06-467122-4

## BUSINESS
Business Calculus 0-06-467136-4
Business Communications 0-06-467155-0
Introduction to Business 0-06-467104-6
Introduction to Management 0-06-467127-5
Introduction to Marketing 0-06-467130-5

## CHEMISTRY
College Chemistry 0-06-467120-8
Organic Chemistry 0-06-467126-7

## COMPUTERS
Computers and Information Processing 0-06-467176-3
Introduction to Computer Science and Programming
    0-06-467145-3
Understanding Computers 0-06-467163-1

## ECONOMICS
Introduction to Economics 0-06-467113-5
Managerial Economics 0-06-467172-0

## ENGLISH LANGUAGE AND LITERATURE
English Grammar 0-06-467109-7
English Literature From 1785 0-06-467150-X
English Literature To 1785 0-06-467114-3
Persuasive Writing 0-06-467175-5

## FOREIGN LANGUAGE
French Grammar 0-06-467128-3
German Grammar 0-06-467159-3
Spanish Grammar 0-06-467129-1
Wheelock's Latin Grammar 0-06-467177-1
Workbook for Wheelock's Latin Grammar
    0-06-467171-2

## HISTORY
Ancient History 0-06-467119-4
British History 0-06-467110-0
Modern European History 0-06-467112-7
Russian History 0-06-467117-8
20th Century United States History 0-06-467132-1
United States History From 1865 0-06-467100-3
United States History to 1877 0-06-467111-9
Western Civilization From 1500 0-06-467102-X

Western Civilization To 1500 0-06-467101-1
World History From 1500 0-06-467138-0
World History to 1648 0-06-467123-2

## MATHEMATICS
Advanced Calculus 0-06-467139-9
Advanced Math for Engineers and Scientists
    0-06-467151-8
Applied Complex Variables 0-06-467152-6
Basic Mathematics 0-06-467143-7
Calculus with Analytic Geometry 0-06-467161-5
College Algebra 0-06-467140-2
Elementary Algebra 0-06-467118-6
Finite Mathematics with Calculus 0-06-467164-X
Intermediate Algebra 0-06-467137-2
Introduction to Calculus 0-06-467125-9
Introduction to Statistics 0-06-467134-8
Ordinary Differential Equations 0-06-467133-X
Precalculus Mathematics: Functions & Graphs
    0-06-467165-8
Survey of Mathematics 0-06-467135-6

## MUSIC
Harmony and Voice Leading 0-06-467148-8
History of Western Music 0-06-467107-7
Introduction to Music 0-06-467108-9
Music Theory 0-06-467168-2

## PHILOSOPHY
Ethics 0-06-467166-6
History of Philosophy 0-06-467142-9
Introduction to Philosophy 0-06-467124-0

## POLITICAL SCIENCE
The Constitution of the United States 0-06-467105-4
Introduction to Government 0-06-467156-9

## PSYCHOLOGY
Abnormal Psychology 0-06-467121-6
Child Development 0-06-467149-6
Introduction to Psychology 0-06-467103-8
Personality: Theories and Processes 0-06-467115-1
Social Psychology 0-06-467157-7

## SOCIOLOGY
Introduction to Sociology 0-06-467106-2
Marriage and the Family 0-06-467147-X

Available at your local bookstore or directly from HarperCollins at 1-800-331-3761.